Dreaming

The Advanced Seminar Series
is published with generous support
from the Brown Foundation.

School of American Research
Advanced Seminar Series

DOUGLAS W. SCHWARTZ, GENERAL EDITOR

Dreaming

Contributors

Ellen B. Basso
Department of Anthropology
University of Arizona

Michael F. Brown
Department of Anthropology
and Sociology
Williams College

Gilbert Herdt
Department of Behavioral Sciences
University of Chicago

John Homiak
Department of Anthropology
Smithsonian Institution

Benjamin Kilborne
California Institute of the Arts

Waud Kracke
Department of Anthropology
University of Illinois at Chicago

Bruce Mannheim
Department of Anthropology
University of Michigan

William Merrill
Department of Anthropology
Smithsonian Institution

Douglass Price-Williams
Socio-Behavioral Group
University of California
at Los Angeles

Barbara Tedlock
Department of Anthropology
State University of New York
at Buffalo

DREAMING

Anthropological and Psychological Interpretations

Edited by
BARBARA TEDLOCK

SCHOOL OF AMERICAN RESEARCH PRESS
SANTA FE, NEW MEXICO

School of American Research Press
Post Office Box 2188
Santa Fe, New Mexico 87504-2188

Distributed by the University of Washington Press

Library of Congress Cataloging-in-Publication Data:

Dreaming : anthropological and psychological interpretations / edited by Barbara Tedlock.
p. cm.
Originally published: Cambridge ; New York : Cambridge University Press, 1987.
Includes bibliographical references and index.
ISBN 0-933452-81-0 (pbk. : alk. paper) : $15.95
1. Dreams. 2. Dreams—Cross-cultural studies. I. Tedlock, Barbara.
BF1078.D72 1992
154.6'3—dc20 92-8250
CIP

 Library of Congress Catalog Card Number 92-8250. International Standard Book Number 0-933452-81-0. First paperback edition, 1992.

Contents

Preface

We all dream several times a night, even if we cannot remember doing so, and recent laboratory research has demonstrated that dreaming is not limited to any one state of sleep, nor even, surprisingly, to sleep itself. Universal though dreaming may be, when I convened a week-long advanced seminar on the subject at the School of American Research in Santa Fe in 1982, leading to the publication of this book, it had become so marginalized within anthropology that it took an extended effort to find ten appropriate participants. The research of our predecessors, which had reduced one of the most remarkable areas of human creativity into a psychological tool and quantifiable object for testing cross-cultural hypotheses, led to a situation in which very few ethnographers were interested in discussing dreams.

Not only is dreaming a human universal (and apparently present in many animals as well), but dream *interpretation* is a cultural universal. While few anthropologists who went into the field during the 1970s set out to collect dreams, a number of us found ourselves listening to individuals recounting and interpreting their dreams. Although dreams were of but slight social significance within American culture at the time, our anthropological subculture, which values holistic, long-term fieldwork that brings intimate interaction with individuals, encouraged us to document whatever our subjects found important.

While the earliest ethnographic studies of dreams were in a distinctly Freudian idiom, phrased as tests of his key concepts concerning dream symbolism among non-Western subjects, by mid-century dream ethnography had become part of a new subfield known as Culture and Personality, in which the manifest content of dreams was analyzed, counted, and tabulated in various ways. By the mid-1970s a major refiguration of social theory and practice had begun, turning attention to the description of alternative meaning and knowledge systems in their own terms. In this new intellectual environment, ethnographers stopped treating dreams as though they were museum objects that might be arranged, manipulated, and quantified like items of material culture, and began to focus their attention on studying dream interpretation systems as complex communicative processes. It was this change, from objectifying the dreams of the ethnographic Other to participating within dream-telling contexts, that reopened dreaming as a significant research topic within anthropology.

Before our seminar in Santa Fe, there had been but a single prior conference centering on dreams that involved significant anthropological participation. That was "Le Rêve et les sociétés humaines," sponsored by the Near Eastern Center of the University of California at Los Angeles and held in France in 1962, which included four prominent anthropologists among the participants: George Devereux, Dorothy Eggan, A. I. Hallowell, and Weston La Barre. The papers, edited by G. E. von Grunebaum and Roger Caillois, were published four years later in the volume *The Dream and Human Societies* (1966). In planning for a second dream colloquium, to take place twenty years later, I felt that it was crucial to include a wide range of current anthropological approaches, social as well as psychological and cultural. More specifically, I sought individuals who could talk both within and across recent theoretical orientations, including semiotics, hermeneutics, sociolinguistics, and structuralism, as well as cognitive, performative, and symbolic analysis. Then, in order to ensure profitable discussions that might open the possibility of new directions in dream research, I looked for participants who had strong psychoanalytic backgrounds but who had nonetheless conducted traditional ethnographic fieldwork, with careful attention to native languages and concepts. I also searched for linguistic anthropologists who were interested in discussing important psychodynamic issues. By the time I convened the seminar on November 15, 1982, I had found a serious working group of scholars who, while they were happy to present their own research and theoretical orientations, were also willing to listen to other participants who represented other, even antithetical, positions. Each of the chapters in this book has been modified by our attempts to talk across various subfields and theoretical bents in order to place dream research in a more central position.

Our endeavor was successful in that our seminar discussions in Santa Fe, together with the set of papers published here, have resulted in a dramatic increase in the number of articles, Ph.D. dissertations, and books in which anthropologists treat the process of dreaming as a major subject. In fact, there has been more research published by anthropologists about dreams in the past ten years than in the sixty-year period immediately following Charles Seligman's (1923) request for records of native dreams, so that he might test Freud's hypotheses about dream construction and his method of deciphering dream symbolism. Even now the study of dream sharing, representation, and interpretation as interactive processes is in its incipient stage, but if I were to convene another dream seminar the problem would be how to select participants from among the numerous researchers who have made the ethnography of dreaming one of their primary research subjects.

Several of the concepts and topic areas discussed and critiqued here have already been addressed and expanded upon by our colleagues. For example, ethnographers have accepted our suggestion that the narrow psychoanalytic concept of the "manifest content" of a dream should be expanded to include not only the dream report but also dream theories and cultural dream interpretation codes. And they have followed up on our critique of the unreflexive use of the term "soul," with its strong Christian overtones and its suggestion of an entity existing independently of a human body, as a translation for various native concepts referring to emergent entities that engage with the human mind during the dreaming process. Michele Stephen, for example, in a volume she recently edited with Gilbert Herdt, *The Religious Imagination in New Guinea* (Rutgers University Press, 1989), notes that the Melanesian concept generally glossed as "soul" does not relate primarily to concern with survival after death, but to the influence on conscious experience of emotions and desires belonging to another self hidden from ordinary awareness. As such it more closely resembles our concept of the "unconscious" than a supernatural entity.

Not only have anthropologists engaged with several key ideas presented in this volume, but psychologists have also done so. They have even suggested that by studying the psychologies of non-Western cultures that have given a great deal of attention to the phenomenology of dreaming, we might expand our own understanding of the phenomena. The cognitive psychologist Harry Hunt, in *The Multiplicity of Dreams: Memory, Imagination, and Consciousness* (Yale University Press, 1989), suggests that while "tribal people" have described several distinct types of dreaming, each with its own line of development, there has been an unfortunate narrowing of dreaming within the West to a single paradigmatic type. He traces this development to Freud, who fixed on dreams based on the reorganizations of previous interpersonal and emotional experiences, and notes that this approach seems to fit Freud's own dreams. As for Jung, his interest in cohesive dream-visions, full of geometric and mandalalike patterns, and in encounters with mythological beings, monsters, and strange animals, fits his particular dreams. Hunt suggests that the non-Western multiplicity of dreams, including several distinctive nightmare types, should be taken into account in modern psychological studies rather than continuing the common practice of reducing the complexity of the dreaming experience to a single type of dream.

During the twenty-year period between the first dream colloquium and our own, the majority of anthropological papers on the topic of dreaming were contributed by researchers working in relative isolation from one another. Following the publication of our seminar volume, however, cultural anthropologists began convening symposia and publishing their results together. For example, in 1988, at the International Congress of Americanists in Amsterdam, a session entitled "Forms and Uses of Dreams in Amerindian Societies" was organized by the French anthropologist Michel Perrin. Topics presented there included the importance of dreams to self-identity among the Dene-Tha of Canada, myths and dreams among the Guajiro of Venezuela and Colombia, nightmares and night terrors among the Mapuche of Chile, and the convert as dream warrior in seventeenth-century Peru. A conference volume was scheduled to be published in Quito, Ecuador, in 1992.

During the 1991 American Anthropological Association meetings in Chicago, Laura Graham and Greg Urban organized an invited session entitled "Re-presentation of Dreams," which was devoted to the question of how dreams are socialized and artistically shared in the form of public reenactment within diverse communities. Themes presented included social dreams and shared songs among the Temiar of Malaysia, dreams given to an ethnographer by a Pakistani Sufi saint, Quiché Mayan dream presentation and re-presentation, the social circulation of dream narratives among the Shokleng, songs and dialogic dreams among the Xavante, and Kagwahiv dream-narrative markers. An international colloquium on the epistemological and cultural aspects of dream socialization was organized by Sylvie Poirier, of the Université Laval, as a special session of the Canadian Anthropological Society Meetings held in Montreal in May of 1992.

Dream ethnographers have also begun to participate within primarily psychological contexts. Several ethnographers, including myself, attended the first world conference on dreaming held in Moscow during August of 1991. The other participants included psychologists, psychiatrists, Jungian analysts, and philosophers from Canada, the United States, Mexico, Panama, Holland, Greece, Indonesia, Australia, Japan, China, Russia, Siberia, Lithuania, and Armenia. The unconscious, as manifested in dreams, is a new area of inquiry in what was, at the time of the conference, the Soviet Union. While there had been an interest in the topic during the teens and early twenties, and several of Freud's works were translated into Russian, in 1926 Lenin banned all discussion of the unconscious as unscientific and lacking in class consciousness, and ordered all books dealing with the topic removed from the shelves of libraries and bookstores. Later there was a brief period in the mid-1950s when Khrushchev allowed a public exchange of ideas concerning the unconscious, but this ended abruptly during the 1962 Cuban missile crisis. With perestroika, in the 1980s, came international exchanges on all topics, including dreams and the unconscious. During the 1991 conference, which took place during the attempted coup to depose President Gorbachev, there were presentations on the use of dreams among the survivors of the Chernobyl nuclear power-plant disaster, dreams in Dostoevski's fiction, Armenian folk dream interpretation systems, the role of dreams in Mayan cultural revitalization, and the current ambivalence towards dream interpretation in Chinese society.

This conference, which was co-sponsored by the Russian Center for the Study of Non-Traditional Medicine and the American Association for the Study of Dreams (ASD), together with the annual meetings of the ASD, provided a much-needed forum for dream ethnographers to meet their psychological colleagues. *Dreaming*, a new, international, peer-reviewed journal in which anthropologists can publish articles that will be read by psychologists, was founded by the ASD in 1991. In all the various forums reviewed here, the majority of anthropological participants have been recent Ph.D.s who have made the study of dreaming one of their primary areas of research.

Because field research on dreaming and the unconscious re-emerged primarily among ethnographers with interests in linguistics and psychology, the creative production and imaginative aspects of the language and public enactment of dreaming have emerged as central topics. Ethnographers who actively participate within native contexts and learn the local cultural uses of dream experiences have meanwhile started paying attention to their own dreams. This latter practice has made us aware of our own unconscious responses to the peoples and cultures we are attempting to understand and describe.

As the organizer of the School of American Research seminar, whose results are presented here, I am pleased that our group effort has generated a renewed interest in dreaming as a significant subject for anthropological research. For the success of the seminar itself, I would like to join all the participants in thanking the Board of Managers of the School of American Research and Douglas W. Schwartz, SAR president. We are also grateful to the seminar house staff for making our stay there so comfortable, and to Jane Kepp, director of publications, for her editorial help and encouragement in the original preparation of this book, as well as her continued support in bringing out this new paperback edition.

Barbara Tedlock

Dreaming

1 Dreaming and dream research

BARBARA TEDLOCK

> The dream is halfway between the poem and the paramecium. Like the paramecium it is a product of nature, not created by man's will. But like the poem, it is a product of art, dependent upon man's imagination.
>
> JAMES HILLMAN

DREAMING AND WAKING REALITIES

Dreaming is a universal experience, one that individuals may attempt to induce or avoid, remember or forget. From the earliest times dreams and their classification, narration, and interpretation have been of considerable interest to humankind. But just what sort of experiences are dreams? Today, in Western culture, we recognize dreaming as self-related but we do not accord this experience the same status as waking reality and thus we do not fully integrate dream experiences with our other memories. However, since reality itself is an indeterminate concept influenced by imaginative and symbolic processes, there are cultures other than our own in which waking, dreaming, and various in-between experiences, though they may be distinguished, may well not be sorted out according to the simple oppositional dichotomy of real versus unreal, or reality versus fantasy.

One early anthropologist who did not recognize the possibility that reality itself might be culturally defined made ethnocentric generalizations of this type: 'The entire life of primitives was nothing but a long dream' (Tylor 1870:137), or 'the savage or barbarian has never learned to make the rigid distinction between imagination and reality, to enforce which is one of the main results of scientific education' (Tylor 1871:445). On the basis of similar judgments, Lucien Lévy-Bruhl (1923, 1926, 1928) described so-called primitive man as having a different type of reasoning from educated man. As Irving Hallowell (1966) noted, such notions are downright absurd, given that humans could not have evolved without making some sort of distinction between dream experiences and those of the waking physical world.

A sharp dichotomy between dreaming or internal subjective reality and waking or external objective reality, together with a devaluation of dreaming, can be traced back to the scholastic inheritance from the ancient Greeks, most especially to Aristotle. He dismissed dreams as nothing but mental pictures which, like reflections in water, are not like the real object (Hett 1935). But, as Carl O'Nell (1976) observed, while dreaming was already depressed in value within the West by the time of the emergence of naturalistic or scientific thought, it was not until the development of Cartesian mechanistic dualism in the seventeenth century that dreams were finally placed totally within the realm of fantasy or irrational experience. It must be remembered, however, that the Cartesian irreducible dualism of 'spirit' and 'matter,' which denies the common principle from which the terms of this duality proceeded by a process of polarization, was an historical development within Western philosophy. A majority of the world's peoples have not focussed their thinking around oppositional dualism, and thus have not isolated dreaming within the unreal realm of 'spirit.' Rather, it is a rationalist proposition that dreaming is somehow a lesser or, in Wendy O'Flaherty's (1984) terms, a 'softer,' more subjective, false, private, illusory, or transient reality than the 'harder,' more objective, true, public, real, permanent reality of waking life.

The question of the nature of reality is a central philosophical issue that affects the way in which dreaming is valued in a particular culture. For example, the authors of the thirteen ancient Indian spiritual doctrines known as the Upanishads (written in their current forms between 1000 B.C. and 800 B.C.), which focus on the nature of ultimate reality, value dreaming above waking reality. The *Prásna Upanishad* teaches that there are four levels or states of consciousness – waking, dreaming, dreamless sleeping, and transcendence – progressing along in the direction of the 'most real.' A discussion of the precise degree and nature of reality in dreaming is found in the *Brihadāramyaka Upanishad*, which treats dreams as emissions, projections, or creations that take place during the 'twilight juncture' between this world and the world beyond:

> There are no chariots there, no harnessings, no roads; but he [the dreamer] emits chariots, harnessings, and roads. There are no joys, happinesses, or delights there; but he emits joys, happiness, and delights. There are no ponds, lotus-pools, or flowing streams there; but he emits ponds, lotus-pools, and flowing streams. For he is the maker. (O'Flaherty 1982:56)

Here dreaming is a liminal state in which the dreamer realizes the relationship between two worlds, neither of which is fully real or unreal.

In later yogic and mystical traditions, especially within Mahāyāna Buddhism, there evolved a more extreme philosophical position in which waking and dreaming realities are both described as illusions (Evans-Wentz 1958:144–5). Each of these illusions has nineteen mouths; five senses (hearing, sight, touch, smell, taste); five organs of action (speech, handling, locomotion, generation, excretion); five vital breaths; and the sensorium, intellect, egoism, and thinking (Coxhead and Hiller 1976:13). What makes dreams illusions is that their seeming immateriality is itself an illusion. Yogis have developed a system for the control of dreaming illusions; as they describe it, their bodies enter the sleep state while their minds remain conscious, experiencing dream images as 'thought-forms' (Evans-Wentz 1958).

A middle position, formulated by medieval Muslim philosophers and elaborated by Sufis, described an order of reality existing between physical and spiritual reality (Corbin 1966, 1972; Rahman 1966). This realm, which Corbin (1966:406) called the 'imaginal world' (*mundus imaginalis*), is 'a *third world* halfway between the world of sensible perception and the world of intelligibility.' The imaginal is not a form of unreality but rather a perfectly real world of autonomous forms and images, and 'the existence of this world presupposes that it is possible to leave the sensible state without leaving physical extension' (ibid.: 407). Thus the imaginal, or world of images, is not 'imaginary'; rather, if one approaches it through the faculty of imaginative consciousness or active imagination, the figures and images have an existence of their own (Corbin 1966, 1972; Kracke and Price-Williams, this volume).

Enthusiasm for the imaginal, although it has never perhaps reached the most extreme level of 'softness' found in Mahāyāna Buddhism or Taoism, surfaces again and again in Western culture within literary and artistic circles. The Renaissance concentration on imagination (Muratorio 1745) was revived during the Romantic period as a reaction to the rationalism of the eighteenth century. Later revivals included the symbolists and decadents in the 1890s, the dadaists in 1916 through the early 1920s, and the surrealists from the 1920s until the mid 1940s. As critics and cultural historians have noted, the embrace of dreaming, spiritualism, and mysticism by participants in these various artistic movements was motivated by a desire to flee from an increasingly materialistic society (Jullian 1971). Today this consciously blurred reality permeates the mass media, in comic books, television, and film (Kinder 1980).

Because most ethnographers are members of Western cultures in which dreaming is either greatly undervalued or else, in artistic inversion, greatly overvalued, the problem of the attitude towards and type or degree of reality accorded to the experience of dreaming by various indigenous peoples is a highly problematical issue in the ethnography of dreaming, and one which we have not as yet properly addressed. Since what is and what is not 'reality' is itself a cultural and social projection (Turner 1976, Price-Williams, this volume), what do we mean by *real* experiences anyway? As members of Western society, we are living at a time when our own concepts about reality have undergone tremendous changes, resulting in a polarization between two complementary paradigms of institution and impulse (Turner 1976). Within the institutional paradigm true reality is revealed only when we are in total control of our faculties, while within the impulsive paradigm reality is revealed during dreaming and other alternative forms of consciousness. As a result it is rather difficult for ethnographers to decide what individuals from radically different cultures mean by reality. Are these individuals to be understood as impulsives who consider dreaming the only true reality? Are they institutionals who consider dreams non-reality? Or maybe, like so many of ourselves, they are in between and find dreaming a form of potential or emergent reality. Further, whom have we been talking with when we arrive at this type of generalization, a man or woman, child or adult, layman or shaman? Is there perhaps more than one notion about reality simultaneously present within different segments of a society, or even within the mind of a single individual? These are very difficult questions.

In this volume Michael Brown argues that for the Aguaruna of Peru, while dreams figure prominently in day-to-day decision-making, they have no monopolistic hold on reality. Rather, dreams are experiences that reveal emergent possibilities, or events that are developing, rather than accomplished facts. Only when dreams or visions are intentionally induced by psychotropic plants do they have an instrumental effect on practical activities. George Devereux (1956) made a similar observation about the Mohave, for whom common 'omen dreams' do not necessarily reflect what will actually happen, but what could happen, whereas the rarer 'power dreams' of shamans and warriors are instrumental.

Phenomenologically oriented ethnographers have observed that in many non-Western societies dreaming and waking reality are not fully segmented or compartmentalized worlds but are rather overlapped experiences. Thus, for example, in fieldwork with both urban and rural Guajiro in Venezuela, the Watsons found that dreaming is described as reality in all senses, not only depicting or foretelling actual events that will occur in the future, but commenting on the dreamer's present physical and spiritual status (Watson and Watson-Franke 1977; Watson 1981). The Ojibwa of Manitoba, who dream profusely and have a culturally instituted dream fast (Hallowell 1966), are like the Guajiro in describing the dream experience as an *actual* experience of the self. Further, they do not conceptualize separate or parallel dreaming and waking realities, but rather have a unified spatio-temporal frame of reference for all self-related experience. Thus, a man who dreamed that a rock opened and he pulled his canoe inside it said that later when he was *awake* out hunting he recognized the exact rock he had visited in his dream. However, this should not be interpreted as indicating that this man, or the Ojibwa, live in a world of dreams. Dream experiences are never confused with waking experiences since the kinds of persons in dreams (which could include a rock) are not the same kinds of persons with whom the individual is most concerned in ordinary waking life.

But what exactly *did* this Ojibwa see in his dream? Was the dream image identical to a sense image, or was it an imaginal, or metaphoric, or symbolic image? What are we to make of the reported situation of the Pokomam Mayans of Guatemala (Reina 1966:186), who interpret the events in dreams as real actions carried out by the soul of the dreamer after it leaves the body at night, but who relate these actions to waking life by reversing their meaning? How is something simultaneously literally true but interpreted in reverse? Do dreams lie? Apparently so, at least among the Lacandón Mayas, who say that dreams are 'a kind of lie' foretelling the future 'but not at face value' (Bruce 1975:19–20). Not surprisingly, Lacandón dream interpretation depends upon the unlocking of constellations of symbolic associations and metaphors (Bruce 1979).

The problem of the degree of literal or (in semiotic terms) 'indexical' truth, versus figurative, metaphoric, or 'iconic' truth encoded in dreams is discussed in this volume in the chapters by Bruce Mannheim, Waud Kracke, and Gilbert Herdt. Using his own recent ethnographic data from a Quechua-speaking community in southern Peru, together with ethnohistoric documents, Mannheim discovered that these people treat dreams figuratively at the narrative level but literally with respect to their lexicon of dream signs. The Kagwahiv of Brazil, according to Kracke, use a single linguistic form in narrating dreams, whether they are referring to dream images or representations, which are interpreted metaphorically, or to the human soul, which is given a literal existence. For the Sambia of Papua New Guinea, Herdt found that the phenomenology of the dream world parallels the secular world, but that in dreams it is the 'soul' (a Sambia metaphor for the unconscious) that directly experiences, while 'thought,' consisting of norms that filter ideas and feelings, relays the images of the dream world and interprets them metaphorically.

For the Kalapalo of Brazil, as discussed in this volume by Ellen Basso, the experience of dreaming is that of the dreamer's 'self' rather than the dreamer directly, and is thus an experience of a hidden personal reality that is only inchoately perceived in waking life; thus dreaming is interpretable metaphorically. When describing their canonical dream imagery and its meanings, the Kalapalo close the distance between dreaming and waking realities by treating dream actions as causes of future effects in waking life. This causal connection is strong enough that under certain circumstances, such as an upcoming wrestling competition with visitors from other villages, they avoid sleeping lest they dream of a bad action that would then cause that action in waking life. A similar problem arises at Zuni (Tedlock, this volume), where men, women, and children stay up all night while masked dancers impersonate the dead, lest they dream of joining the dancers in the land of the dead. The Kalapalo, also like the Zuni, reason post hoc, insisting that a sudden turn of events during waking life must have been preceded by a dream, even when no such dream can be remembered. Thus for both the Kalapalo and the Zuni the dreaming experience itself is 'performative,' in the sense that it is already part of the *doing* of something, and not merely a *description of the doing* of something.

In the Zuni case, although dreams produce certain effects simply by having occurred, the linguistically coded perception of the experience of dreaming leaves the dreamers unable to act while their future state of being is revealed. Upon awakening a dreamer then acts out the events, turning the intransitivity of dreaming into the transitivity of the acting out of dreaming. This is accomplished, in the case of dreams that are classified as 'good,' by keeping them inside the heart and silently, but nevertheless verbally, dreaming them along in the waking world. Dreams that are classified as 'bad,' which usually concern illness or death, are reported to family members, who may arrange to have the dreamer publicly whipped by a masked deity in order to reverse or break the chain of causality. Thus, Zunis do not confuse dreaming with waking reality but rather take an active interest in deciding which elements of their dreaming reality they will allow to invade their waking reality.

Among Plains Indians, according to George Devereux (1969) and Arthur Amiotte (1982), dreams are considered as extrapsychic events, occurring simultaneously on various planes of reality in both sacred and linear time as well as in sacred and physical geography. In these cultures there are formal vision quests, known as 'crying for a dream,' in which individuals at certain life-stages actively seek communication with supernaturals through a combination of waking and sleeping dreams. Through these dream rituals comes 'that "stuff" of ethnicity that causes the Lakota to persist as tribal people in a twentieth century society' (Amiotte 1982:32). Devereux noted, and Roy D'Andrade (1961) has emphasized, that in societies in which dreams are considered to integrate with, or participate in 'objective reality,' dreams are more egosyntonic, or ego strengthening, for the individual. Further, since dream events tend to be rather similar to waking events in these same societies, they are interpreted literally rather than metaphorically.

It is not only in societies with institutionalized vision quests or dream fasts that dream events are described as real events taking place in the objective, external world and thus interpreted literally. The Rarámuri of Mexico described incredible personal experiences, including flying and remarkable transformations, to William Merrill (this volume), but made no mention of the fact that the events had taken place in dreams until he directly asked them. However, he notes that a man would not beat his wife for being unfaithful if the only evidence of infidelity was a dream, because action in a dream is that of a soul rather than a person, and thus the transgressor in the dream was his spouse's soul rather than her person. In the future, however, the dreamer would be more attentive, looking for additional indications of his wife's adultery during waking life. Thus, although Rarámuri dreamers clearly link dreaming and waking realities, to state that they do not distinguish between them would be incorrect, even though these two realities co-exist and interact within the same pluralistic universe rather than being segmented into parallel realities.

The Arapesh of New Guinea (Tuzin 1975) also believe that dreams are literal experiences of a dreamer's wandering soul, interpreting them in terms of the immediate waking social situation. For example, a woman's erotic dream about a man other than her husband was interpreted as caused by this man's magical ability 'to enjoy sport' with her spirit, the husband was regarded as cuckolded, and the woman's dream lover agreed to desist from his evil magic. Donald Tuzin argues that Arapesh dream interpretation is a fantasy construct which is external to the dreamer and thus shields repressed material, just as much as our own tendency to deny dreams any significance whatsoever shields us from our own psychodynamic processes.

The dream problem in North American society

Individuals in American society who experience vivid dreams may allow them a certain reality during sleep, but upon awakening dispel or try to forget them (Collins 1977). However, although most Americans publicly profess the cultural belief, or stereotype, that dreams are meaningless fantasies or confused mental imaginings with no true or lasting reality dimensions, a dream occasionally carries such a strong emotional impact that it is remembered and returns later to consciousness. When this happens, cultural belief wavers slightly, causing the dreamer to wonder if dreams, or at least this one dream, might mean something after all. But if the dreamer tries to tell this dream it may prove difficult. The first problems concern the choice of audience and discourse frame. Since dream telling is not an ordinary public communication in American society, the potential dream sharer faces a difficulty in finding the proper context for the speech event. For example, should it be told at the university to a group of colleagues over lunch? Or is this too public a discourse frame?

There is a special formal but private frame in which the narration and elaboration of a dream while lying flat on one's back on a couch might fill up a good portion of a forty-five-minute psychoanalytic hour. However, as a dreamer soon learns, dreamsharing is far from unproblematic in traditional psychoanalysis, where the surface or manifest content of a dream is insufficient and must be amplified by free association. Our dreamer also learns that the dream as narrated is not meaningful as such but rather that the 'true' message of the dream begins with the translation of the manifest dream into a latent, or underlying, discourse which is removed from the original dream experience. This is necessary because of the Freudian hypothesis of the origin of manifest dream content within the four primary dream-work processes – condensation, displacement, symbolism, and secondary revision (Freud 1900:277–508).

There are maverick psychoanalysts, however, like Masud Khan, who treat the analytic exchange quite differently; instead of using analytic space as 'work space,' he uses it as a 'play space' (Curtis and Sachs 1976:354). Through what he calls a 'mutuality of playing dialogue' between himself and his patients he helps them to tell dreams in a way that does not kill the dreaming experience by reducing it to anecdotal narrative (Khan 1976). Other clinical approaches to dreaming are found in analytical psychology (see Hall 1977, 1983; Hillman 1979; Berry 1982; McGuire 1984). Perhaps the best known of these is the technique of active imagination, in which one starts with dream images, hallucinations, affects, moods, or emotions, and in a waking state allows them spontaneously to unfold without conscious criticism, thus enriching the original experience (Jung 1916). Jung also suggested the use of auxiliary artistic techniques such as drawing and automatic writing, which have subsequently undergone considerable elaboration within various media, including clay modeling, painting, and sandplay (Berensohn 1968; Tucci 1969; Kalff 1980). Another popular technique is Gestalt therapy, in which the dreamer is encouraged to think of his or herself as a microcosm and to act out all of the images in the dream as though they were parts of his or her own self (Downing and Marmorstein 1973). Various other techniques, united under the banner of psychosynthesis (Assagioli 1965), include oneirotherapy (Frétigny and Virel 1968); guided imagination (Leuner 1969; Hannah 1981; Herdt, this volume); reverie (Bachelard 1971); the directed daydream (Desoille 1966); and waking dreams (Watkins 1981; Price-Williams, this volume).

For those in our society who are interested in dreams but do not wish to share their dreamlife within the context of a therapeutic setting, there now exist various non-clinical or lay alternatives including dream appreciation groups, associations, newsletters, and journals such as *The Dream Network Bulletin*, *Gates*, *Sundance*, and *Dreamworks*. There are also dream interpretation books specifically for the layman, dream workshops held irregularly at several locations mainly on the east and west coasts, and informal dream communities in several places – including New York City, Sausalito, and Virginia Beach – where dreams can and should be told, acted, danced, written, or painted (see McLeester 1977).

Let us suppose that our American dreamer, although not a member of any dream appreciation group or therapeutic community, is nevertheless so impressed by a particular dream experience that he or she decides to tell it. Now there is the problem of translating the evanescent visual dream images into a connected verbal narrative that is an interesting and acceptable dream text or story (Khan 1976:327–8; Kracke, this volume). Nevertheless, however haltingly, the dreamer narrates the wonderful dream to his colleagues. If there is a philosopher in the group, the next difficulty may take the form of a question such as, 'Well, that's an interesting story, but how do I *know* that you had such a dream experience?'

All unknowingly our poor dreamer has stumbled upon an area of hot debate in both philosophy and psychology. Some of the key questions are: Does sleep mentation exist? How do we know that it does? Is a dream report a valid indicator of sleep experience? These questions became important ones when Malcolm (1956, 1959) challenged the 'received view' of dreaming in the West as conscious, though illusory, experiences that occur during sleep to an unconscious dreamer who then recalls them upon awakening. Malcolm's argument follows Wittgenstein's (1953:184) in saying that an inner process such as dreaming needs to have an outward criterion to establish its ontological reality. If sleepers are *un*conscious during sleep and thus without images, thoughts, impressions, feelings, presentations, sensations, and judgment, then dreams cannot be considered 'experiences' in the same sense that conscious mental phenomena are experiences. Since a person who dreams of climbing a hill is not *really* doing so, the dream is not a valid experience. Appeals to especially vivid or lucid dreams and the supposed continuity of dreaming with waking life are simply misguided, since if dreaming and waking experiences were really the same, then the person could not have been truly asleep.

This strong attack on the received or commonsense view of dreaming as a form of conscious mental experience created a controversy in dream research, with both experimental psychologists and philosophers responding. A few of them noted that the demand for an inner private process like dreaming to have an outward public criterion for verification had been met in the case of somniloquy, at least, since they had dozens of accurate records of both what the dreamer said during sleep and his or her waking dream report (Ayer 1960; Arkin 1981). The philosophers, who have long been deeply concerned with the issue of consciousness and dreaming, responded to Malcolm's salvo on many other fronts as well, with a flurry of critical essays (see Dunlop 1977).

One interesting response was provoked by Malcolm's conclusion that contemporary scientific dream research 'was conceptually confused, misguided, ultimately simply *irrelevant* to dreaming' (Dennett 1977:228). Dennett, after briefly reviewing highlights of the scientific literature on dreaming, posits three dream processes: neural events taking place in the dreamer's brain during sleep, memory-loading, and composition, or the combining of what is presented and recorded. He follows this with an anecdote from his own dreamlife in which he had been searching for a neighbor's goat. When he found her she bleated baa-a-a – and he awoke, to find her bleat merging with the buzz sound of an electric alarm clock. Then, after dismissing the received view that the suspect concept of 'precognition' is needed to explain his dream, he proposes a cassette-theory as an alternative to both Malcolm and the received view. Simply stated, this theory posits a 'library,' in the brain, of undreamed dreams, with various indexed endings; in the case of Dennett's own dream, the alarm clock buzz had the effect of retrieving an appropriate dream and inserting it into the memory mechanism. Thus precognitive dreams, and perhaps even all dreams, are never dreamed at all but just recalled upon waking, and (as in the case of *déjà vu* experiences) we just think we had them. The physicalistic theory of consciousness which lies behind these intriguing arguments is based on neurophysiological research which is rapidly upsetting commonsense notions about the dreaming process, philosophical theories of mind, psychological theories of consciousness, psychoanalytic theories of regression, and anthropological notions of cultural relativity.

DREAMING IN THE LABORATORY

The important discovery of the change of electrical activity in the brain at the moment of sleep onset (Berger 1930) led to a further discovery, in the early 1950s, of the correlation of periods of rapid eye movements (REMs) with dreaming (Aserinsky and Kleitman 1953) and the identification (with the aid of the electroencephalogram, or EEG) of four distinct stages of sleep. Investigators found an association between REM periods and EEG Stage I, which occurs first as one goes 'down into sleep' and which includes an increase in neuronal activity in the visual cortex, increase and variation in respiratory rate, reduced blood pressure, speeding up and variation of heart rate, penile erections, and the loss of muscle tone (Rechtschaffen 1973). Since most of these REM correlates suggest arousal but the loss of muscle tone suggests the opposite, REM sleep came to be called 'paradoxical sleep.'

All healthy adults experience four to five REM sleep periods, or dreams, of between 10 and 40 minutes' duration each 90 to 100 minutes during seven hours of sleep. The importance of REM sleep to the individual was noticed by researchers when subjects deprived of REM time for several consecutive nights made up for lost REM on following nights by an average increase of 40% in REM sleep over their normal levels (Dement 1960; Foulkes 1966:202–7). Researchers who have studied people claiming nearly total inability to recall dreams have found that these 'non-dreamers' have REM periods marked by more eye movements plus more alpha EEG activity than 'dreamers,' indicating that they are more aroused during sleep than dreamers are; ironically, one might assume that they should better remember their dreams (Foulkes 1966:56). Since, however, they claim that they do not, this is a prime area for a combination of psychological and cultural research and explanation. To date, it has been suggested that people differ in remembering dreams for various reasons, including personality, salience, motivation, and conscious development of visual imagery (Hiscock and Cohen 1973; Cohen 1974; Bro 1979; Fishbein 1981; La Berge 1985). Given the dominant visual character of REM mentation, some investigators consider dreaming as constructed from visual memory stored in the right hemisphere rather than from the verbal memory of the left hemisphere (Galin 1974; Antrobus and Ehrlichman 1981; Kracke, this volume).

More than thirty years of laboratory research on dreaming conducted on hundreds of professed dreamers and non-dreamers alike has totally upset the commonsensical notion that not everyone dreams and certainly not every night, as well as the early anthropological notion that the amount of dreaming in a given culture could be variable. Today, we can re-evaluate those strange, putatively factual ethnographic reports that there are seasonal variations in dream occurrence in Central Africa (Hodgson 1926:67), or that 'the ordinary run of natives dream less than we do, if only because they live less hectically' (Williams 1936:30), or that the Trobriand Islanders 'dream little' (Malinowski 1927:89). Such reports can all be written off to ignorance, to the reporting of negative evidence, or else to a failure to separate the experience of dreaming from dream recall and/or dream sharing in a given society.

After laboratory dream researchers had noted that there were correlations between eye movement direction and dream content, they eventually formulated the 'scanning hypothesis,' according to which REMs indicated the dreamer's surveillance of a visual field. Thus, a person whose REMs were mostly horizontal should report horizontal imagery upon awakening, whereas one whose REMs were mostly vertical should report vertical imagery. Further, since there was no rapid eye movement during slow-wave non-REM (NREM), and since the few dreams reported from these periods were more thoughtlike and lacked the hallucinatory quality of REM dreams, it was hypothesized that dreams reported during NREM periods were not actually 'dreams' but only memories of preceding dreams (Dement and Kleitman 1957). However, this strict REM/NREM dichotomy was later modified by other researchers, who noted that although NREM dream reports seem to be primarily conceptual and cognitive, they are somewhat dreamlike and are not solely explicable in terms of the recall of previous REM-sleep dreaming (Kamiya 1961; Foulkes 1966:103–20). More recently the scanning hypothesis has been radically revised, since REM sleep is now known to occur in fetuses, neonates, the congenitally blind, and decorticate cats, in whom the scanning of a visual field is highly unlikely (Rechtschaffen 1973:178–80). The nature of scanning has also been re-examined and shown to contain contortional and oblique movements never seen during the waking state, which suggests that something different from normal waking visual perception is occurring (Jouvet 1975:511–12; Hobson 1980:17).

Further, because of the large amount of neuronal activity present in the brain during REM time some researchers view the REM period of sleep as a conscious form of mentation (see Hartmann 1967; Rechtschaffen 1967). Other theorists carry this one step further, stating that dream symbols constitute a form of inner communication, the elements of which are a decipherable code consisting of orderly transformations of an individual's cognitive responses acquired during conscious waking life (Klinger 1971; Antrobus 1978; Foulkes 1978; Cohen 1979). Recently there have been reports from dream laboratories indicating that dreaming is a necessary part of the nightly process whereby recent waking experiences are consolidated as memories (Fishbein 1981).

Another important recent discovery in neurophysiology is the finding that during sleep the pontine brainstem cells, which during the waking state receive impulses from the balance organ, are activated by the same groups of cells that normally trigger eye movement, resulting in the same kinesthetic effect for the dreamer as if the balance organ were stimulated (Hobson 1980; McCarley 1981; McCarley and Hoffman 1981). As a result, dreamers alternately perceive themselves, or others, as moving in space. Thus the Kagwahiv perception and description of the sensation of dreaming in kinesthetic terms (Kracke, this volume) turns out to be founded in a reality that includes a physiological dimension, as do hundreds of other dream reports, from all types of societies, in which dreaming is described as travelling in space, and/or as things – people, animals, ancestors, ghosts, or gods – coming at the dreamers from outside their bodies (see Basso, Brown, Merrill, Tedlock, this volume). Long ago, Raymond Firth (1934) noted among the Tikopia a dual dream causation theory in which dreams may occur either when a non-human spirit comes and sits on the dreamer's chest or else when the dreamer's own spirit or life principle leaves his body and wanders around outside in the external world.

DREAMING AND COGNITION

Psychological research indicates that the supposed unity in human cognitive functioning is rather precarious at best, with much shifting between hierarchically arranged substructures (Hilgard 1973, 1977). Although this neodissociationist theory arose in the area of hypnosis, it now seems to be capable of a wider application (Arkin 1981:285–8; Kihlstrom 1984; Price-Williams, this volume). In a parallel development psychoanalysts have conceptualized the human mind as constructed of interactive conscious and unconscious components, with various degrees of independence and interdependence within shifting hierarchies in which a given segment may have subordinate or supraordinate relations at various times (Kernberg 1976; Kohut 1977). Neurophysiologists indicate that both sleep and wakefulness are actually 'mixed' states in which several neural systems participate in a multitiered organization at different brainstem levels (Morgane and Stern 1974). Thus, as Hofstadter has humorously pointed out, although there is now much scientific evidence that people consist of many subpersons who are each less complex than the overall person, this 'hierarchical organization of personality is something that does not much please our sense of dignity' (Hofstadter and Dennett 1981:342).

It is precisely this Western 'sense of dignity,' with its underlying Christian monism, that has made complex non-Western theories of mind, with their many separate segments or 'souls,' seem either foolish or threatening to members of Western society. Meanwhile, the threat from recent neurophysiological findings has provoked a search for a single, highly unified, rational 'self' to replace the many 'selves.' Crick and Mitchison (1983) have proposed that the function of REM time is a synapse-weakening, damping-out, or reverse learning process in which certain parasitic modes of neocortical activity are eliminated. So, thanks to REM processes the sleeper's hallucinatory dreams (parasitic modes of mentation generated by the primitive brainstem) will fail to reach consciousness. We dream in order to forget our unconscious dreams, and not only are dreams meaningless, but remembering dreams could be harmful to rational mentation. This new theory not only fits the American stereotype of the meaninglessness of dreams but gives us a rationale for not remembering our dreams and not encouraging others to tell theirs. The scientific community, however, is reportedly unenthusiastic about the possibility of confirming the hypothesis (Melnechuk 1983:34).

Instead, as laboratory researchers in Canada have recently reported, the major function of dreaming is to be noticed, and once noticed, dreams can sustain any interpretation whatever concerning their function, including that of modern science and scientific cultures where dreams are assigned the function of having no consentually determined function (Moffit *et al.* 1985). They also point out that during this century, when scientific philosophy and cognitive psychology have discouraged the notion that dreams have any function beyond the personal, the consequences of this cultural belief are vast. Thus, although it has been argued that dreaming, like waking perception, is a cognitive event consisting of the reorganization of memories in a narratized imaginal form, cognitive psychologists with rare exception (e.g., Neisser 1967; Shweder and LeVine 1975; Haskell 1984) have so far ignored dreaming. This is a sorry state of affairs since, as David Foulkes expresses it, 'dreaming . . . comprises a surprisingly large part of what we do with our minds, and the potential to narratize dreams is as surely wired into the human brain as is the potential to speak language' (1982:276).

Laboratory researcher Rosalind Cartwright (1981) has recently proposed a twenty-four-hour model of human cognitive behavior in which waking thought, unlike sleeping thought, is described as having foreground and background dimensions, both of which have access to external and internal information plus memory. She notes that when we are awake, we easily shift from full control over our attention, or foreground, and slide into our background thoughts, but that when we do so we continue to monitor the external world. Further, when there is a major shift in cognitive control from outside information to inner information, the thought style changes to one that is either more regressed verbally or more imagistic; these changes correspond to characteristic dream reports from NREM and REM sleep awakenings, respectively. Laboratory research indicates that there is a natural rhythmicity in which fuzzy background thoughts and images occupy the foreground of attention at intervals of about ninety minutes, not only at night but throughout the day (Globus 1972). Cartwright suggests that the mental activity of sleep might be described as a second cognitive system whose purpose is to process the self-evaluative and affective component of waking information and integrate it into a storage system that contains our ideas about ourselves.

The link between self-evaluation, affect, and dreams has also been discussed at some length by David Foulkes (1982), who found that preschoolers aged three to five report very few dreams on REM awakenings and that the few dreams reported have an absence of affect, are populated primarily by animals, are exceedingly brief (a sentence or two), and have imagery that is highly susceptible to influence from body states such as fatigue, hunger, or thirst. Also, the scenes and situations lack social interactions and have a static and nonnarrative quality, with a lack of motoric self-involvement and self-representation. On the basis of comparative data from higher age groups, he has suggested that there is a slow developmental progression that is discretely related to the course of children's waking cognitive growth. In waking research with preschoolers it has been observed that they are not adept at creating kinematic imagery (Piaget and Inhelder 1971). The animal predominance in their dreams fits with findings that the earliest verbal symbolizations refer to animals, and that the stories children tell contain many more animal than human characters (Applebee 1978). The hypothesis is that waking and dreaming imaging develop in tandem with the acquisition of language skills (Piaget 1962; Foulkes 1978, 1982).

Cognitive developmental approaches to dreaming should, however, be modified by the inclusion of cultural variables. For example, in research on Hausa children, Shweder and LeVine (1975) disputed the validity of the 'doctrine of invariant sequence' in dream experience, whereby children learn to distinguish dreams as a separate, nonreal category of experience in a predetermined, noncultural fashion. Instead, their investigations revealed that many Hausa children did not first relinquish their conviction that dreams are real, but rather abandoned the last concept, that dreams are external experiences, first. Their explanation is that the crowded sleeping conditions in Hausa society produce a situation in which a sibling who fails to observe dream events may shatter a child's belief that the dream happens outside the body. Thus the developmental process is more flexible than hypothesized and more susceptible to cultural influence.

Soft cognition or ASC

In addition to REM sleep, millions of ordinary, healthy people all over the world experience many other alternative or altered states of consciousness (ASC), during both waking and sleeping (Tart 1972; Holden 1973). Erika Bourguignon (1972:422–9) has argued for a common frame of reference, or continuum, with REM sleep (including both ordinary and ritualized dreams) representing one pole, possession trance (with impersonations) the other pole, and trance (with hallucinations) as the mid-point between them. She suggests various intermediary steps, beginning at the possession end of the spectrum with glossolalia and dialogue with spirits; near the trance mid-point fall shamanic ecstasy and various fugue and drug states; near the REM sleep pole are to be found daydreams and hypnagogic imagery.

Although there is an extensive literature on most of these states of consciousness, to date there has been little anthropological or psychological attention paid to the end of the continuum nearest REM sleep, which includes the area of daydreaming, waking dreams, lucid dreaming, and the hypnagogic state. Psychological research in these borderland phenomena has been aided by biofeedback and hypnotic techniques. In the case of lucid dreaming a subject is taught to maintain consciousness during the transition from waking to sleeping (Tholey 1983; La Berge 1985); otherwise, subjects are taught to become more relaxed and immersed within their own internal worlds by shifting away from decision-oriented thinking into more passive and fleeting visual imagery (Stoyva 1973; Price-Williams, this volume). Laboratory sleep research has demonstrated the everyday occurrence of fleeting images in the hypnagogic or sleep-onset period. During this twilight zone between waking and sleeping many people experience unusual bodily sensations, including the inability to perform voluntary movements, known as sleep paralysis (SP), and visual, auditory, and kinesthetic imagery of various sorts known as hypnagogic hallucinations (HH) (Vogel, Foulkes, and Trosman 1966; Foulkes 1966:121–37). Laboratory researchers have noted that imagery reported by subjects awakened during this early sleep stage, designated as W for 'waking,' is different from imagery reported later during the REM sleep stage. At this early stage the images are briefer, have less affect, and are more like a succession of slides than like a movie (Vogel, Foulkes, and Trosman 1966:77).

Persons who suffer from the sleep disorder known as narcolepsy, which is characterized by an uncontrollable urge for daytime sleep, temporary waking paralysis, and disturbed nocturnal sleep, experience unpleasant, vivid, and emotionally charged hypnagogic hallucinations and sleep paralysis (Vogel 1960; Guilleminault, Dement, and Passouant 1976; Ribstein 1976; Soldatos, Kales, and Cadieux 1978; Tedlock, this volume). Researchers have suggested that sleep-onset REM periods (instead of the normal NREM periods) characterize the early nocturnal sleep of narcoleptics (Billiard 1976:77). It has also been shown that vivid hypnagogic hallucinations (HH) and sleep paralysis (SP) occur in normal subjects whenever REM-state phenomena intrude into sleep onset or awakening (Hishikawa 1976). These brief (one to two minutes) episodes, sometimes accompanied or just preceded by terrifying nightmares (HH) characterized by the inability of the dreamer to perform voluntary movements (SP), have been delineated and separated from night terrors (NTs), which occur later in sleep, often in EEG Stage IV. These latter experiences are typically signalled by intense screams from the dreamer and are accompanied by autonomic arousal, including heavy perspiration, doubling and even tripling of the heart rate, and overt fight–flight behavior (Fisher *et al.* 1975; Arkin 1981:365–72).

The value of separating reports of intense nightmare experiences with HH and SP from other types of nightmare experiences has been discussed by Waud Kracke (1979a) for the Kagwahiv of Brazil and by David Hufford (1982) for Newfoundland. Through a combination of fieldwork and knowledge of modern laboratory dream research they were able to show that the particular kind of dream that combines hallucinating semi-arousal (HH) during sleep onset or waking with sleep paralysis (SP) is a phenomenologically real category at both the folk and scientific levels. For the Kagwahiv these terrifying dreams are caused by ghosts of the dead who approach and then touch or even throttle the dreamer (Kracke 1979a:132–4). In Newfoundland the experience of 'being hagged' involves a supernatural attack in which 'the Old Hag' comes into the room, approaches the bed, and then presses on the chest of or attempts to strangle the dreamer, who can neither move nor cry out (Hufford 1982:1–11). Similar types of nightmare experience have particular salience among Zulu men, who regard nightmares of the suffocation type with horror and often are hospitalized as the result of ensuing anxiety symptoms (Lee 1958:268).

The recognition of this type of nightmare experience with anxiety-producing SP and HH may be widespread. Fijians, Zunis, and Quichés all separate dreams with sleep paralysis from ordinary nightmares both phenomenologically and linguistically (Herr 1981:337; Tedlock, this volume). At Zuni, there is a subcategory of 'bad dreams' glossed as 'violent dreams,' including the seeing or sensing during semi-wakefulness of a nearby ominous presence, often a dead person, which engenders in the dreamer an inability either to move or cry out. Within the Quiché category of 'bad dreams' there is a special type glossed as 'to have something suddenly appear,' in which a ghost rapidly approaches a dreamer who can neither move nor cry out.

For the Eskimo, Joseph Bloom and Richard Gelardin (1976) report dreams in which a ghost or spirit suddenly appears to a dreamer upon going to sleep or waking up, and there are specific native terms in both Inupik and Yupik for this type of dreaming experience. However, since they were unaware of the widespread linkage of HH with sleep onset or waking, they lumped Eskimo sleep paralysis with arctic hysteria, labelling both as experiences in the 'non-empirical world' (Bloom and Gelardin 1976:24), by which they apparently meant that they were experiences of an illusory world rather than that they were not based on observation. From a phenomenological point of view, the Eskimo data might be better understood as an example of an *empirical* attitude toward the dreaming experience.

Here we must pause to remember that some cultures are much more interested in and sophisticated about alternative or altered states of consciousness (ASC) than our own. As Price-Williams (1975, 1978) has noted, contemporary Western analysis of altered states would seem primitive to peoples who have been living with and actively developing these types of consciousness for centuries. When such sophisticated knowledge develops in small-scale, unstratified societies, Brown (this volume) argues, the cause may be that leaders in these societies use dreams as bridges between self and others rather than leaving them in the private realm, amplifying their personal power by extending their abilities into the realm of ASC. As more anthropologists and folklorists become aware of both laboratory and field findings in dream research, they may discover further recognized and named categories of dream and nightmare experience, which may turn out to match up experientially, or phenomenologically, across cultures.

THE ANTHROPOLOGY OF DREAMING

The earliest important anthropological interest in dreaming was directly stimulated by Freud's famous book *The Interpretation of Dreams* (1900). Thus in England, for example, Seligman (1921, 1923) asked colonial officials and missionaries to send him records of native dreams or parts of dreams so that he might test Freud's concept of 'type dreams,' in which the same manifest content was supposed to have the same latent meanings across cultures. He argued that if key type dreams were present in data collected in this way, 'then we shall have to admit that the unconscious of the most diverse races is qualitatively so alike that it actually constitutes a proved common store on which fantasy may draw' (Seligman 1924:41). His 'store' metaphor points to the objectifying notion of dream symbolism as a trait that might be measured or weighed by officials who called in natives and wrote down their dream reports, or even just parts of dream reports. He ignored the importance of communicative context, both within these cultures and in the continuing negotiation of reality between colonial administrators and indigenous peoples.

This lack of sensitivity to the context and the way in which one's research is conducted may seem surprising to us today, but Lincoln (1935) also ignored the influence of social setting on his own collection of Navajo dreams, a transaction that took place in the Black Mountain Trading Post, near Chinle, Arizona. These dream reports, together with others that he culled mostly from North American Indian ethnographies, were then separated into unsought or spontaneous dreams occurring in sleep, which he called 'individual dreams,' and sought or induced and tribally important 'culture pattern dreams' (ibid.:22). These analytical categories, however, did not correspond with the classificatory schemes of the societies he examined; he failed to address the important issue of indigenous dream classification and dream theories. He also failed to distinguish between the dream as an experience in sleep and its narration.

Beginning during the 1940s, much of the anthropological work on dreaming had as its main goal the creation of a corpus of manifest dream contents that were then analyzed, counted, and tabulated in various ways for numerous reasons (Sears 1948; Eggan 1952; Dittmann and Moore 1957; Griffith, Miyagi, and Tago 1958; O'Nell 1965; Gregor 1981). Meanwhile, in psychology, Calvin Hall (1951) together with Robert Van de Castle (Hall and Van de Castle 1966) and Vernon Nordby (Hall and Nordby 1972) developed a comprehensive scoring system that allowed researchers to categorize elements from the manifest content of dreams, including settings, actors, objects, interactions, and emotions. They, together with sociological and anthropological colleagues who added a non-Western dimension to their data base, have apparently felt satisfied that they have demonstrated meaningful cross-cultural similarities and differences in dream content relating to gender, developmental, and personality differences.

It may well be, as Vincent Crapanzano (1981) has argued, that the comparativist focus on the dream report and its extractable contents is an expression of Western culture and is thus culture-bound. In turning his anthropological gaze on Western thought, as revealed in Freud's *The Interpretation of Dreams*, he noted that the encounter between psychoanalyst and client is limited by a particular epistemological configuration, or *episteme*, in which priority is given to the referential or indexical function of language and to the dream text as an objectification of, or reduction to, that function. In the spirit of Jacques Derrida (1976), he notes that this *episteme* is rooted in the culture of alphabetic literacy, and he warns anthropologists who study dreams to be wary of its limitations.

Waud Kracke speaks to this problem in the present volume when he criticizes Ricoeur (1970) for describing the dream as a 'text' to be interpreted, noting that what this view neglects is that the dreamer has direct access to the spatial-sensory dream experience. He is quick to point out, though, that by the time a dream is narratized this imagery has been filtered through a complex, language-centered thought process which imposes a disjunctive temporal sequencing on to the continuity of dream space. But there are cultural contexts in which the dream is not so much filtered as quickly left behind in favor of well-established forms of discourse that have little place for its particularities. For dreamers in the Jamaa movement in Zaire (Fabian 1966) and among the Atjeh of Sumatra (Siegel 1978), the actual event or experience of dreaming with its visual content is of surprisingly little interest to the dreamers; what is of interest is that certain genres of dream legitimate the dreamer's use of a set of signs as a means of communication. Under the influence of such findings, Fabian (1966:560) has asserted that 'psychology is concerned with dreams as internal *experiences*, reflections of the subconscious,' whereas 'dreams as intentional *messages*, i.e. culturally defined means of communication, are the domain of anthropology.' The importance of dreams as messages is well taken, but the trouble with dividing up the territory of psychology and anthropology so neatly is that it would leave psychologists free to ignore the fact that their study of the dreaming experience is partially dependent on their subjects' communication of such experiences by culturally determined means, and it would leave anthropologists free to ignore the fact that dream communication in other cultures is partially dependent on native theories about the dream experience.

As Gilbert Herdt indicated during our discussions, as well as in his paper published here, it is not enough to know what people dream about; we must also know how and what parts of their dreaming experiences they communicate to others. Studying dream sharing and the transmission of dream theories in their full contexts as communicative events, including the dialogical interactions that take place within such events, is not just a method for the extraction of data that are already there. When fieldwork is conducted along these lines, it is no longer possible to ignore the fact that both the researcher and those who are researched are engaged in the creation of a social reality that implicates both of them (Fabian 1974; D. Tedlock 1979; Homiak, this volume). But even though we anthropologists have long subscribed to the method of participant observation, it still comes as a shock to us when we discover how important our participation is in helping to create what we are studying.

John Homiak, in his chapter in the present volume, discusses how he suddenly realized one day, after months of active participation in the Rastafarian communicative event of 'reasoning,' that his mentor and consultant, Mobutu, was actually training him as a follower rather than just letting him watch and behave appropriately. And it was with this discovery that he realized that Rasta elders tell their visions within this particular social context not only to fuse waking and dreaming realities, and thus help to create a religiously based counter-cultural reality, but that they wanted very much to stimulate and train followers, like himself, who could carry the Rastafarian message abroad. Herdt was also surprised, but in a different way, when he realized the therapeutic dimension of his role as sympathetic dream listener to Nilutwo, and when he realized that Nilutwo was sharing forbidden dreams with him that he never shared with anyone else.

These are unsettling but exciting developments in fieldwork that other anthropologists have also found themselves in the midst of (see S. LeVine 1981; Kracke 1981; Tedlock 1981). For many of us at the seminar, dreaming had not been the main focus of our research but instead had intruded upon us as a topic. Dreams might be a frequent topic of conversation for the ethnographic 'Other,' but certainly had not been in our own society – nor had they been a major topic in the recent anthropological literature. Most of us were in the field during the 1970s, when 'the dream-work movement,' which encourages public dream telling, became a social movement in our society (see Ullman and Zimmerman 1979; Hillman 1983, 1985). Thus, during our research, instead of immediately accepting dream sharing as normal communication, we taped or wrote down whatever dream narratives were shared with us, together with native interpretations, and then filed them away as curious data.

When we returned home from the field, most of us focussed our attention on such normative anthropological topics of the time as myth and ritual. The study of dreaming, along with many other rather interesting topics concerning individuals, had long since become marginalized in anthropology as a result of the collapse of the Culture and Personality school of the 1950s (Bock 1980:131–8). In my own case it was not until after I had written my dissertation on Quiché Maya divination ritual that I turned to the topic of dreaming. Then, after struggling with my materials alone I decided to organize a seminar at the School of American Research to which a combination of ethnographically, linguistically, psychologically, and psychoanalytically oriented anthropologists were invited. At the time I felt that it would be important not to let one subfield or theoretical orientation dominate the others, and I hoped that by working closely together for a week we might be able to develop some novel approaches to the study of dreaming.

But before we could generate any new methodologies or approaches to dreaming we found ourselves evaluating those of the past. We had a long discussion concerning the pros and cons of using Hall's (1951) content analysis on our dream materials. This method is based on the assumption that there are neutral 'dream reports' out there, and that these reports are not only collectible in large numbers but are somehow free from the effects of cultural categorization, interpretation, and intercultural interaction. Our field experiences led us to question all of these assumptions. For example, as Herdt pointed out, in societies that have various forms of discourse to be used in different social situations, many dream experiences are never shared and others are shared only in a specific culturally determined context. Thus, if a researcher who was unfamiliar with these communicative issues visited New Guinea, where Herdt worked, he could not gather a sample of dream reports that would be suitable for comparative purposes.

In my own research among Zunis in New Mexico I found that it was very difficult to gather dream reports that are categorized as 'good' in this Pueblo society since telling a good dream would diminish its positive effect on the dreamer. Thus, a sample of the manifest content of reported dreams would be nonrepresentative of the dream corpus. Further, since Hopis are also reluctant, for the same reason, to share 'good' dreams, Dorothy Eggan's (1952) finding that the famous Sun Chief Don Talayesva had a high ratio of 'bad' to 'good' dreams fails to confirm her hypothesis of unease in his personality. Rather, it could simply indicate that however aberrant Talayesva may have been in other ways, he shared or withheld dreams according to Hopi categories. Among the Rarámuri, on the other hand, there is a low ratio of threatening to non-threatening dream reports; Merrill (this volume) argues that this does not reveal Rarámuri personality structure but rather tells us about their world view.

In light of these and other critiques we agreed that the concept of manifest content should be expanded to include more than the dream report. Ideally it should include dream theory or theories and ways of sharing, including the relevant discourse frames, and the cultural code for dream interpretation. We also discussed the problem of internal contradictions that exist within cultural systems such as dream theory or interpretation, as well as the possibilities of finding heterogeneous systems coexisting at the same temporal horizon. Thus, a negative stereotype of the experience of dreaming can be combined with the empowerment of women through dreaming, as among the Atjeh of Sumatra (Siegel 1978), or with reports of many pleasant dream experiences, as among the Rarámuri. And even the existence of five rather different Kagwahiv theories about the dreaming process (Kracke 1979a) need not indicate confusion on the part of native consultants or anthropologists, or the presence of serious acculturation or deculturation. From the co-existence of two rather different etiologies of the dreaming experience recorded in Mesopotamian cuneiform tablets that date from the second century B.C. (see Kilborne, this volume), it would seem that heterogeneity is nothing new.

We also discussed at length the general problem of reductionism and of the inappropriate imposition of oppositional dualism in many areas of anthropology, including theory formation, data gathering, and the presentation of findings. Thus Herdt critiqued Freud's reduction of the unconscious to a series of mechanistic drives and suggested that what is needed now is a multidimensional model of conscious, preconscious, and unconscious awareness. Herdt, Kracke, and Brown all rejected Freud's irreducible oppositional dualism between latent and manifest content, as correlated with primary and secondary thought processes, since this distinction ignores cultural effects on the symbolism of dreams. Kracke noted that it denigrates primary-process, or sensory-imagistic thinking, as inferior, more primitive, or developmentally earlier than secondary-process thinking. He called our attention to recent psychological research indicating that primary-process thought is as capable of development as secondary, and that they are in constant interaction with one another. Brown observed that recent experimental evidence indicates that primary-process thinking appears to be converted into secondary-process the instant the dream is recalled, which means that cultural forces enter at a very early stage. Brown also rejected the instrumental/expressive dichotomy of symbolic anthropology, arguing that instrumental acts themselves contain expressive aspects – for example, tools are elements of a meaningful labor practice – and that we must analyze the dialectic between expressive and instrumental components of all acts and utterances. Kilborne and Homiak rejected the sacred/profane, rational/non-rational, and insider/outsider dichotomies, noting that such categorization by researchers obscures the ways in which classificatory schema are *used* by members of a society.

In the context of discussing Ellen Basso's paper we agreed that serious translation problems are posed by indigenous terms indicating a segment of the self that becomes most aware in dreaming, alternately described as remaining inside or travelling outside the body of a dreamer. Basso advocated not translating the indigenous term while I followed Scandinavian ethnologists in using a 'free-soul' and 'breath-soul' distinction. Kracke suggested that compound terms such as 'interactive self,' 'dreaming self,' 'free-soul,' 'life-soul,' 'breath-soul,' or 'body-soul' would be useful in indicating to our readers that we do not mean 'soul' in the ordinary way we think about it in English, which has been influenced by Christian monism. Basso agreed and accepted 'interactive self' as a good translation for the Kalapalo concept *akũa*. However, since we failed to reach a general group consensus on a global solution to this important translation issue, we have made individual translation decisions in our papers that we hope will give the reader a feel for the various indigenous meanings.

We did, however, reach a general consensus on two useful modifications of the psychoanalytic interpretation of dreams. First, we all came to agree with Kracke, Herdt, and Price-Williams that the very nature of dream sharing, which brings a multiplicity of desires to light (Lacan 1968; Ricoeur 1970), requires a revised view of the 'self.' Such a revision might parallel Freud's notion of 'component egos' (1913b:41); or the multiple me's and I's in Bettelheim's (1983) attempt at retranslation of key Freudian concepts; or Hillman's (1979) splitting up of the abstract self, body-ego, and dream-ego or imaginal-ego. Secondly, we were in agreement with Kracke that the distinction between primary process (unconscious and preconscious dream thoughts) and secondary process (conscious dream reports) is much too rigid and not nearly fluid enough to accommodate subtle interchanges of dream and reality that occur in the so-called 'dream cultures' in which so many of us have worked.

The question of the similarities and differences between dreams and myths engaged us at several points during our discussions, as when we critiqued Adam Kuper's (1979) structuralist treatment of a series of dream reports as mythic texts. He ordered the dream texts, which were collected by George Devereux (1969) from a Plains Indian, as modes of argument in which a problem is resolved through a series of rule-governed transformations of the initial dream situation. Although we felt that he succeeded in indicating underlying linguistically coded analytical rules, the question remained whether such rules actually lie behind the creation and narration of this individual's dreams. Since most of what we can know of others' dreams is through verbal reports of them, it seems reasonable to treat dream accounts as linguistic texts. But are dream accounts the same sorts of narrative texts as myths?

On the contrary, as Kracke argued both in discussion and in his paper published here, although there are parallels in narrative style between myth telling and dream telling in many cultures, dream narratives everywhere move from sensory imagery to verbal form, while myths move from language to sensory imagery. Thus he rejects the psychoanalytic tendency to interpret myths as though they were dreams. Likewise, Mannheim argued that in attempting to explain dream signs in terms of other cultural media in a reductive fashion, one trivializes the question of the relationship between dreams and other expressive media. As an alternative he advocates studying the precise nature of the linkage between dreams and myths by treating dreaming as a 'cultural system,' or organized conventional set of signs, which is articulated with but structurally autonomous with respect to other systems, such as narrative.

In taking a semiotic approach to his Quechua field data Mannheim found that contemporary interpretations of dream signs represent a near total reversal and replacement of the interpretations recorded in a seventeenth-century priest's manual from the same community. He points out that Quechua dream interpretations encode only the semantic dimension of language and thus have meaning only in terms of the immediate relationship between signifier and interpretant, while myths encode both the semantic and syntactic dimensions. Thus the transience of dream signs over the past four hundred years is due to the fact that they are tied to isolated individual words, whereas Quechua myths, which have greater staying power, are tied not only to vocabulary but also to grammar. The relationship of dreams to omens is quite different. Since their meanings are determined by strictly semantic criteria, unlike myths and rituals, dreams and omens fit together in a single 'premonitory' cluster within a single interpretive system that focusses on isolated signs.

In discussing Mannheim's paper, Kilborne noted that it is mistaken to treat dream reports as forms of 'private' symbolism which might then be contrasted or compared with the 'public' symbolism of myths. Instead, dream reports and dream interpretations are inseparable from the social and political situations in which they occur, thus functioning as forms of communication in their own right (see Friedrich 1985). Herdt warned that since dream reports are among the most complex forms of human communication, it is all the easier to distort both the motivations and meanings of speakers. Dream reporting is constrained by social roles and situations, dream theories, modes of narrative discourse, and ideas of self and personhood. Only by carefully noting the discourse frames that organize behavior, as well as personal scripts that organize motivations and fantasy, can one compare dreaming in one culture or society with dreaming in another.

Through a controlled comparison of Zuni and Quiché Maya dreaming and dream interpretation as distinctive culturally constituted communication systems, I demonstrated how lower-level symbolic systems are nested within higher-level ontological and psychological systems. Differences in Zuni and Quiché dream reporting and interpretation then are predictable, in part, from differences in their respective theories about the constitution of the self and about what parts of the self participate in dreaming. Both Basso and I, in our papers, stressed the importance of separating the mere descriptions or reports of dream experiences from what Austin (1962) called 'performative' utterances, which involve the *doing* of something rather than just the *saying* of something. However, since Zuni dream sharing involves actions other than speaking, I had to go beyond Austin's performative to include various alternative physical and mental actions by which Zunis carry dream actions forward, continuing them in the waking world. Just how widespread the Zuni and Kalapalo active or performative attitude towards dreaming may be is hard to say at this time. Basso suggested in discussion that Sambia restrictions on the telling of certain kinds of dreams in certain contexts may indicate the presence of a similar attitude in Sambia culture. Herdt agreed with her, and it should also be mentioned that Meggitt (1962) reported that among another New Guinea people, the Mae Enga, a dream is regarded as a context of action.

Rather unexpectedly, we found ourselves repeatedly discussing both waking and dreaming omens during our seminar. The stimulus for this discussion was Price-Williams's paper, which was intended to alert us to the interface between waking and dreaming consciousness. He accomplished this by introducing two psychological concepts, 'waking dream' and 'mythopoetic function.' The idea of a 'waking dream' was first used by the psychologist Léon Daudet for the conscious experience of images. The idea of a 'mythopoetic function' was first used by the classicist Frederick Myers, for whom it covered the weaving of fantasies during trance or reverie. Later the psychiatrist Gustave Flournoy extended the concept to include a region of the unconscious that is continually engaged in producing myths and fictions that manifest in both night and day dreams. Since our seminar in Santa Fe many of us have found both of these concepts very helpful in our own work.

Douglass Price-Williams, both in his paper and during our discussions in Santa Fe, suggested that what anthropologists have been coding variously as dreams, visions, or omens might better be described as parts of a larger category or continuum between the dream in sleep and the dream in waking consciousness, and he suggested that emphasis be given to the activity of dreaming rather than to dreams as objects. We were all very taken by this shift from object to activity and have adjusted our thinking accordingly. Homiak found both mythopoetic function and waking dreams to be very useful ways to think about the Jamaican public communicative event known as 'reasoning,' in which elders in the Rastafarian movement, while in a state of reverie, weave together mystic and prophetic imagery of racial protest. The Andean crossover in the interpretation of dream signs and omens that Mannheim discussed, along with my own Zuni and Quiché data, clearly indicates that what ethnographers have categorized as 'omens' in the past might better be labelled 'waking dreams.'

As might be expected from the genesis of the seminar, our discussions during the seminar, as well as our individual chapters published here, various languages from neighboring fields – including semiotics, sociolinguistics, psychoanalysis, hermeneutics, and natural-language philosophy – are used in order to help us to analyze this alien and difficult topic. Thus, for example, in the context of discussing Kilborne's paper, Mannheim suggested that dream interpretations are communicative events that might usefully be described with the aid of Roman Jakobson's (1960) formulation of the speech act. By stating that dream interpretation is a communicative event, one presupposes a 'sender' (dream teller) and a 'receiver' (dream listener), as well as a 'referent' or narrative event (dream experience), the actual narration of which is the 'message' (dream story). What is said in the interpretive system is the 'code' (dream explanation) structuring the relationship between the narrative event and the message. Finally, the physical 'channel' and psychological connection (psychodynamics) between the sender and receiver enable them to enter and stay in communication.

Thinking about dreaming as a psychodynamic communicative process – instead of examining a single dream or group of dreams as reified objects or written texts to be analyzed solely according to Freud's notion of the dream-work, Hall's content analysis, or Lévi-Strauss's structural analysis – entails a major shift in perspective. We feel that such a shift should have important implications for future dream research, whether in the laboratory, the philosopher's study, the clinician's office, or the field. The present book differs from previous anthropological contributions to the study of dreaming in being the product of a convergence between anthropologically informed psychoanalytic and psychodynamic approaches to dreaming on the one hand with natural-language, sociolinguistic, semiotic, and interpretive approaches to the study of meaning on the other. To understand why such a convergence occurred at this time, at the boundaries of linguistic, psychological, and interpretive anthropology, one need only reflect that the analysis of meaning in general (see Basso and Selby 1976), including how and what is signified, has only recently come to occupy a prominent place within anthropology.

2

Myths in dreams, thought in images:

an Amazonian contribution to the psychoanalytic theory of primary process

WAUD KRACKE

We tend to see dreams and myths as belonging to opposed categories of experience. Dreams are personal, unsharable, highly fluid private experiences of a predominantly sensory nature. Myths are public, fixed linguistic forms, a kind of literature. Yet there are indications that in many cultures, besides the famous Australian aboriginal ones (Stanner 1972), dreams and myths are regarded as closely related. Their association is marked, for example, by parallels in narrative style between myth telling and dream telling. In Cuzco Quechua, the tense suffix *-sqa* is used alike in recounting dreams and myths; it refers to events not experienced directly by the speaker in a normal state of mind but known either through hearing from others or under an altered state of consciousness (Mannheim, this volume; cf. Cusihuamán 1976:170–2). Certain Quiché Maya dream narratives are punctuated with the quotative *cacha*', 'he/she/it says,' which is also used in other narratives that do not deal with personal experiences, including myths (Tedlock, this volume). Some revitalization cults, like the Rastafarians (Homiak, this volume), do not draw a sharp distinction between dream and myth – a circumstance that led Kenelm Burridge (1960) to coin the term 'myth-dream.'

Why are these two apparently disparate modes of human expression so often classed together or treated similarly? The proposition that dreams and myths are related is, of course, nothing new, but I will propose a somewhat different reason for the linkage between them. Drawing on examples of myths and dream accounts from the Parintintin, or Kagwahiv, Indians of Brazil,[1] I will argue that myth in its dramaturgic (not merely narrative) form and in its construction as a series of vivid images depends on inner visualization for its communication and impact; thus, myths are constituted in a spatial-sensory modality like that of dreams. This leads me to Freud's psychoanalytic theory of 'primary process,' and some revisions recently proposed in its formulation, and finally back to an observation that was my own starting point for this paper: the frequency with which images and themes from myths are incorporated into Kagwahiv dreams.

DREAMING IN KAGWAHIV PARINTINTIN LIFE

The Parintintin are a Tupi-speaking people now numbering about 150, living in small settlements in the tropical forest along the Madeira River, a tributary of the Amazon in Brazil. They are one of several closely related groups who call themselves 'Kagwahiv.' Until pacification in 1923 they were headhunters, living at war with most of their neighbors. Although they have now been integrated into the larger society of the Brazilian interior as gatherers of cash crops, they still maintain many aspects of traditional culture. Prominent among these are the animated narration of myths and folktales, and the almost daily recounting of dreams.

Dreams like myths, in Kagwahiv culture, are to be told. Waking at daybreak, or in the middle of the night at 2 or 3 a.m., one may often hear someone narrating a dream to a few others as they warm themselves by the fire. During the day over work, a person may interrupt gossip about current events to entertain work companions with a dream. Myths are also told in similar circumstances, by the fire during a wakeful period at night, or for entertainment while working on a common task. When someone comes to visit after a long absence, the host may announce that he has dreamt of the guest's arrival. Not long thereafter, if the visit is a somewhat formal one, or if it has been some time since the previous one, the host and guest may exchange myths before turning to more topical conversation.

Both dreams and myths are marked in their narration by distinct grammatical forms. When a dream is being narrated, the particle *ra'ú* occurs in the tense-marker slot of nearly every sentence (Kracke 1979a).[2] Myth is marked in a less specific stylistic manner, but also involving tense-markers. Myths are punctuated with reiterated particles for long past events, *ymỹa* and *raka'é*, often conjoined with the marker *po* indicating indirect transmission, something of which the speaker does not have firsthand observational knowledge.

The sharing of dreams is governed by certain prescriptions deriving from their prophetic nature. A dream that is inauspicious in its augury for the future is told quickly by the fire, to cancel out its prediction (as among the Zuni – see Tedlock, this volume); while an auspicious one, if shared at all, is told well away from the fire, to insure that its favorable prediction is not cancelled. I have seen a headman sit in the middle of the settlement, well away from the cooking fires, and tell a dream (in one instance, an erotic dream that would hold a favorable forecast for hunting) to everyone within hearing.

Dreams are not only told on a regular basis in Kagwahiv society, but are earnestly discussed to ascertain what they 'mean'; what event or development they augur, or what state of the spiritual surround they reflect (see Kracke 1979a). Dreams foretell the future, either literally or by way of an extensive list of metaphorically or metonymically based formulae. Souls of relatives may announce their departure from the world in a dream, and nightmares are direct perceptions of the presence of an *añáng* ('ghost' or 'demon'). Dreams, like myths, are sources of significant information about the nature of the world and the spiritual beings in it, and, like myths, they are to be shared, puzzled out, and understood.

Further associations between myths and dreams are embedded in Kagwahiv beliefs about dreams, and in their patterns of experience while dreaming. Some of the links between oneiromantic portents and their referents, the events they predict, are by way of myth. A sexual dream, for example, predicts the killing of a tapir because the tapir, in a well-known myth, was the adulterous lover of Kagwahivahẽ. More important, perhaps, dreams provide an avenue of communication with superhuman beings otherwise known primarily in myth. In dreams, some older Kagwahiv, especially ones with shamanistic aspirations, commune with spirits of the sky and other mystical beings. In this they are like the shamanic healers of old who, in trance during the curing ceremony, would visit various healing spirits on earth and in the sky, following the mythic footsteps of Pindova'umi'ga, chief of the Sky People (see Kracke 1982). These shamans (*ipají*, 'possessed of power') exercised some of their power through dreams, and it is often said that 'anyone who dreams has a little *ipají*.' Similarly, in explanation of their special skills and powers, most of the protagonists of myths are said to have had 'a lot of *ipají*,' to have been very powerful shamans. Thus, although Kagwahiv do not explicitly put it this way, dreams provide individual knowledge of spiritual reality to match the communal knowledge which myths provide of the nature of spiritual reality.

SOME PRELIMINARY OBSERVATIONS ON DREAMS AND MYTHS

Dreams are paradoxical. They are a form of *thinking* while asleep which, in the vividness of their sensory imagery, more closely resemble waking perception than the faint sensory experience accompanying daytime thoughts. Both sides of their paradoxical nature are reflected in Kagwahiv beliefs. That dreams are a form of thinking is recognized in explanations for the particular things one dreams about: 'I was thinking about such-and-such as I went to sleep,' the dreamer would explain; 'I carried it into sleep with me and brought it with me into my dream.'[3] This is a perfect description of 'day residues' as they participate in the formation of a dream. Or a person may attribute his or her dream to a desire for the event dreamt of. At the same time, dreams are held to be a special kind of perception, but of a different reality from that perceived by the waking senses. Through his dreams, the dreamer senses the presence of *añáng*, or receives messages from the dying souls of relatives, or is able to detect signs of the future.

The Kagwahiv noun *ra'úv*,[4] which is used to refer to the appearance of a person or thing in a dream (and from which is evidently derived the tense particle *ra'ú* used to mark a dream narrative) reflects this paradox in the apparent ambiguity (from our point of view) of its intention, or *designatum*. In one sense, it simply means an image which represents or stands for something else. Thus, children at play roasting a leaf 'tapir' over a stone 'fire' are using the leaf as a *tapi'íra ra'úva*, and the rock as a *tatá ra'úva* or 'play representation' – Piaget's (1951:94) 'ludic symbol' – of a tapir and a fire, respectively. A picture of a canoe is *yhára ra'úva*. Generally, when one says 'his *ra'úva* said . . .,' one simply means that a person's image appeared in one's dream and spoke. But in certain instances the *ra'úv* may be the actual soul – in Tedlock's term (this volume), a 'free-soul,' one that leaves the body. When a dying person's *ra'úv* appears in a dream to a relative to announce the death, it is clearly the soul itself that appears in the dream, not just a thought-image. Thus the extension of this concept *ra'ú* includes a range of *denotata* from an 'image' or 'representation' of something or someone to a person's 'soul' appearing as an image to someone else.[5]

This thought/perception process of dreaming has other special characteristics. In contrast to waking experience, the images and spaces in dreams tend to be in flux, with fluid transitions from one space or image to another. In addition, dreams pursue their plots in relative freedom from the physical, logical, and moral constraints of diurnal cognition. Also, when one awakens to daytime reality, they are difficult to recall. These last two characteristics are the ones that Freud (1900) capitalized on most fully in developing his theory of dreams. He added to these the observations that dreams often have an uncanny access to memories from early childhood, and that they regularly express, disguised and in visual metaphor, wishes related to the core of our selves to which our waking thought is scarcely privy (if at all). Freud later added (1923b, 1925a), and more recent analysts reiterate (French and Fromm 1964), that dreams also express the emotional conflicts to which these wishes give rise. But the characteristic of dreaming that I would like to dwell on is the predominantly sensory-spatial, especially visual, nature of the dream experience, and the relationship of this to verbal 'texts,' both within the dream and when the dream is recounted.

It is a commonplace that we know others' dreams only through verbal narratives of them. What psychoanalysts analyze, it is said, is not a dream but the 'text' of one, the spoken or written narrative by the dreamer of his dream experience (Pontalis 1981). 'It is not the dream as dreamed that can be interpreted,' writes Ricoeur (1970:5), 'but rather the text of the dream account.'[6] Hence psychoanalysis is cast by Ricoeur (1970), Habermas (1971), and others as a hermeneutic discipline, and it has become fashionable to speak of the dream as a text to be exegetically interpreted, and to regard all psychoanalytic interpretation as an exercise in exegesis (Breger 1980). What this view neglects is the simple fact that the dreamer himself, with his or her more direct access to the spatial-sensory experience of the dream, plays a critical part in its psychoanalytic interpretation (even when the analyst is not the same as the dreamer). The visual and sensory images of the dream may play as important a part in the interpretation, through the dreamer's associations to visual elements, for example, as the text of the dream account.

Yet, even our own dreams may often be remembered by their narrative texts. In the most literal sense, I can often not recall what I have dreamt in the middle of the night unless I have written it down or told it to someone. Frequently, I find, the act of writing down or the telling is itself sufficient to fix the dream in my memory. Once thus fixed in my mind, I have available for retrieval a memory of the imagery of the dream. But even the imagery remembered is frozen, and highly filtered; it has lost the fluid, evanescent quality of constantly being in transition from one image to another that characterizes the dream as it is dreamt and the vivid concreteness of the 'dream experience' (Khan 1976). 'It seems to me I am trying to tell you a dream,' says Marlow in the *Heart of Darkness*, 'making a vain attempt, because no relation of a dream can convey the dream-sensation, that commingling of absurdity, surprise, and bewilderment in a tremor of struggling revolt, that notion of being captured by the incredible which is of the very essence of dreams' (Conrad 1910:94–5).

In remembering a dream consciously, we filter it through our language-centered thought processes; and as Georges Longrée (1978) demonstrates, in a semiotic discussion of verbal interpretation of drawings, any verbal translation of a visual image is greatly impoverished and distorted. Disjunctive verbal categories belie the continuity of visual space, and a verbal description imposes on the elements of the visual gestalt a temporal sequence which is indeterminate in the visual presentation. The eye may traverse the visual field of the drawing in an infinite variety of sequences or paths, but the verbal account must choose only one. The dream images that remain in memory, then, while they do retain something of the visual experience of the dream, are not identical with the dream as dreamt. They are selected and shaped by the act of cognition that made them conscious, and by the narrative secondary elaboration in which the dream is retold to oneself to remember it.

A dream recounted ends as a narrative; a myth begins as one. But the verbal narrative is only part of a myth, perhaps the least important part. A myth, as I mean the term here, is a sacred story that is told and enacted in the telling, fixed in its story line but not in its exact narrative form. Each telling is different, even by the same teller, according to the audience and the teller's mood or message. Good Kagwahiv storytellers tell myths in action accompanied by narrative, and the narrative text itself is replete with vivid onomatopoeic elements.

The telling is a multimedia production. Both by its form of presentation and by the imagery in the myth itself, the telling arouses sensory imagery in the listener, often charged imagery that is close to the level of repressed emotional conflicts. Like poetry, myths communicate their message by depicting (albeit verbally) vivid visual, acoustic, and even tactile images. The fact that the sensory imagery is presented in a principally verbal medium, as Bettelheim (1977:59–60 and passim) stresses for fairy tales, itself increases the vividness with which the images can be constructed in the mind of the listener. As poetry confirms, the image evoked in the mind of the listener is more powerful and personal than any offered ready-made.

The dream, especially if told, moves from sensory imagery to verbal form, while the myth moves from language to sensory imagery. Yet even this account is incomplete, for, as the Kagwahiv observation on dream formation suggests, dreams may have their origin in verbal daytime thought, or 'day residues.' Conversely, the myth remains in the myth-teller's mind in the form of imagery as well as in words; perhaps especially in images, for the words may vary greatly from telling to telling. An old storyteller volunteered to draw pictures for me illustrating all the most important myths, which were by far the most interesting and complex drawings that were done for me. And one more proof of the central place of imagery in myths is in the readiness with which a myth is translated into images in the storyteller's dreams – which I will come to after a short digression into theory.

PRIMARY-PROCESS THINKING: A REFORMULATION

Such is the similarity between dreams and myths that psychoanalysts have been tempted to interpret myths as if they were dreams. Abraham (1909) called myths the dreams of a culture. Freud, noting the transparency with which childhood fantasy themes are represented in many myths, wrongly concluded that the 'primitive mentality' is childlike and lacks repressions; a myth which continues to exert strong influence in psychoanalytic social theory today. But these psychoanalytic studies of myth, though they neglected the cultural dimensions of mythology,[7] did contain a valid and important observation. Many of the images in myth embody, sometimes in cultural metaphors, but often quite openly and directly stated, themes of emotionally charged fantasy such as frequently appear in our culture in disguised form in dreams. In day-to-day thought such fantasies – oral conception, male fantasies of giving birth, and so on – remain on an unconscious level, but in myth they are often quite explicit.

Freud (1900) formulated the kind of thought process that goes on in dreams as the 'primary process,' a highly condensed, visual, or sensory, metaphorical form of thinking. The materials with which dreams work are 'day residues,' and the kind of logic which Freud called primary process, or 'dream-work,' is a way of using these sensory materials in metaphorical ways to express complex configurations of thought and feeling, and to resolve contradictions between incompatible desires; or between desires, aspirations, and self-image (French and Fromm 1964). A major problem of the dream-work is what Freud called the 'means of representation in dreams,' or how to express complex ideas using just the sensory materials at hand in the day residues.

Lévi-Strauss (1966), although he sees myths as addressing contradictions in cosmic concepts and social principles rather than in personal wishes and aspirations, finds in myths a pattern of thought very similar to this aspect of the dream-work. He encapsulates this in the concept of *bricolage* (ibid.:17). Myths take bits and pieces of reality that come to hand from nature or from social processes – contrasting species of plants or animals, economic processes from daily life, or whatever – and use them selectively as sources of imagery for expressing and resolving basic problems and contradictions inherent in social life, or in the particular social patterns and cosmology of a culture. The dream, in psychoanalytic conception, is a form of *bricolage* much like a myth: it selects images from among the day residues ready to hand, and uses them to express metaphorically an emotional conflict, and to work out (or work toward) some resolution of it (French and Fromm 1964).

Further, the elements that go into a myth – or the relations between those elements, for what Lévi-Strauss treats is always structures of relations among elements – are subjected to certain transformations, both within a myth and between different myths which are related culturally or thematically. And the kinds of transformations these relations are subjected to, within a myth or going from one myth to another, are not altogether dissimilar from the kinds of operations Freud postulated in primary-process thought. Prominent among such transformations is that of reversal, also used frequently in dream construction. Although the motive of reversals is different – disguise of an unacceptable thought in a dream for Freud,[8] a kind of logical play or an assertion of difference for Lévi-Strauss – the structure is the same. Similarly, displacement, or the interchangeability of corresponding elements in like relations, plays a significant part in Lévi-Strauss's myth analyses. Condensation, or multivocality, is undeniably a characteristic of the elements of a myth viewed as symbols, as has been stressed for ritual symbols by Victor Turner (1967, 1978).

There is one strong difference between Freud's formulation of dream-work, or dream thinking, and Lévi-Strauss's ideas on the logic of myth, and this difference leads to the heart of some recent challenges to existing psychoanalytic theory. Freud saw primary process as a primitive form of thought, an underdeveloped form of the lineal, rational, reality-oriented, linguistic thinking that he called 'secondary process.' This is in stark contrast with Lévi-Strauss's view of mythic thought, which finds in the mythic *bricolage* a complex, profound, and sophisticated form of thought directed toward fundamental philosophical and ethical problems of social life.[9]

Recent thinkers in psychoanalysis have challenged Freud on this. Pinchas Noy (1969) was, I think, the first to suggest that primary process is not simply a rudimentary form of secondary-process thought, but a separate type of thinking equally capable of refinement on its own terms. According to him, the advanced, more developed level of primary-process thought is the metaphorical form of thinking with images used in the visual arts and in poetry. Dreams themselves may be complex and 'artistic.' The function of primary-process thinking, Noy argues – whether the rudimentary sort found in children's dreams or the elaborated and sophisticated kind found in artistic thought – is to integrate experiences related to the self, as opposed to secondary-process thinking, which is oriented to the mastery of external reality.

A more recent contribution of David Galin (1974) advances the argument further. Galin showed that Freud's primary-/secondary-process distinction, and the associated opposition between unconscious mental processes and conscious ones, parallels the difference between right- and left-brain thought processes mapped out by Roger Sperry (1968) and his associates. Conscious, secondary-process thought, like the thought processes of the left hemisphere, is centered on language and is linguistically communicable, linked up with what Freud calls 'word-presentations'; whereas unconscious primary-process thought, like the thinking that takes place in the right hemisphere of the brain, has no access to verbal communication but is linked only with sensory 'thing-presentations' (Freud 1915:201–15; 1923a:10–11, 20–1). Galin's suggestion for neurological correlates of conscious and unconscious thought, or primary and secondary processes, gives strong support, as McLaughlin (1978) points out, to Noy's argument. Primary-process thought (right hemisphere thinking) is a qualitatively different kind of thought from secondary-process (left hemisphere, language-connected thinking) and is just as much subject to maturation and refinement as the latter. The question is not, as Freud posed it, How does one develop into the other? but rather, How are the two coordinated and interrelated through life?

Remembered dreams and performed myths are both forms of production that bridge the verbal, logical characteristic of conscious thought with the sensory-spatial-imagistic form of thought that reaches its most elaborated level of integration in art. The recall, and even more the recounting, of a dream brings the sensory-proprioceptive imagery of the dream to consciousness and thus begins a process of integrating it with logical-linguistic thought. Myth, on the other hand, is a mode of eliciting sensory-proprioceptive imagery in the listener's mind, in a context of culturally provided, linguistically coded forms. If primary process is a mode of thought that integrates new emotional experiences into the self-experience, then myths may provide a kind of culturally shared model for integrating particular kinds of new experiences: a store of fantasy themes on which individuals may draw for help as they encounter new experiences and new emotional problems of the type anticipated by the myth to use in weaving their fantasies and dreams.

MYTHS IN DREAMS

What do we mean by myth as a form of thought? Lévi-Strauss offers general hypotheses about what mythic thought accomplishes. But if myth is thought, who is doing the thinking?

The most direct answer might be the person who first made up the myth, or the sequence of storytellers who developed and refined its form. But the creators of the myth are no longer available, except insofar as the myth is improvisational and recreated by each teller. The more important aspect of myth as thought is how the myth is apprehended by each person who 'knows' the myth – listener and teller alike, for they cannot be sharply distinguished – and the part that the myth plays in their understanding of the world and in their thought. For evidence about how the myth is embedded in the thought processes of individuals, what is better than to examine the instances where a myth, or part of one, is woven into the texture of a dream (see Eggan 1955, 1966)?

In dreams that were recounted to me during depth interviews which I conducted during my fieldwork with the Kagwahiv in 1968 and 1973, mythic elements appeared relatively frequently, either explicitly in the manifest content of the dreams, or in the latent content as made clear through free associations to the dream. In many instances the expression of the dream's latent meaning in the manifest content hinges on a myth; and in a few cases I was told dreams that recapitulated a myth verbatim, with the dreamer or some person close to the dreamer in the place of the protagonist.

Such dreams which incorporate myths wholesale are interesting for several reasons. For one thing, unlike a myth, a dream is a personal creation of the dreamer, and its emotional meaning to the dreamer can be understood through the dreamer's free associations to it. Psychoanalytic interpretations of myths have no such means of validation, for a myth is a communal product, and its emotional meaning, the common emotional chord it strikes, cannot be understood through anything comparable to free associations. But when an individual appropriates a myth by dreaming it, the emotional meaning of the myth *to him* can be understood by eliciting his free associations to it, and by noting what part the dreamt myth plays in the flow of themes and fantasies in the interview in which he brings it up. More important for our purposes, however, such instances give us the most direct possible example of congruence between the structure of dreams and myths. By examining such cases, we may note where the two forms of expression converge, and also, where the mythic form is altered in incorporation into a dream, where they diverge. In this way we can learn something about the structure of both dreams and myths.

Let me give an example of such a dream. The dreamer, Mohã'gí, is a warm, nurturant, lively old man who loves to tell folktales and myths. He tells them vividly and merrily, and the more salacious the stories, the better. His interviews up to this point have been full of recollections of youthful loves and liaisons. Dreams discussed in the previous interview, and earlier, expressed his desire to possess the healing power of shamans of old, the power of knowledge that was lost with the death of the last shaman some years before.

Mohã'gí has been married all his adult life to Lucira, a woman who speaks her mind freely and often contentiously but whose underlying warmth and concern make her widely beloved. They had an arranged marriage when both were young, so their union has been lifelong: not without its moments of friction, but basically loving and strong. They had but one daughter, of whom Mohã'gí was so fond that when she married he went to live with her, subordinating himself to her husband, a reversal of the traditional pattern of father-in-law authority. Lucira had such a difficult pregnancy with this daughter that, with Mohã'gí's concerned concurrence, she took a medicine to make her sterile thereafter; a decision that I sense he, and perhaps she as well, now somewhat regrets.

In the sixth interview I had with him, Mohã'gí told me three dreams, at least one of which incorporates a myth. By comparing the way in which the three dreams express the same fairly evident meaning we can compare myth and dream as modes of expression.

(1) José Bahut [a rather shiftless fellow], just now this morning I dreamt of him. He ate a great deal indeed. I went and said to him: 'You are eating a lot of yams.' His belly was out to here, in my dream. José stole them, in my dream. I said to him: 'Where did you find the yams?' 'In the garden.'

(2) Yesterday I dreamt of a *tapy'yntín* [Brazilian]. Joaquim's his name, no, José Nascimento ['Birth' in Portuguese]. He said to me: 'Don't you want merchandise?' 'No, very expensive.' 'No, I'll give it to you!' I dreamt of *cauĩtĩ* [*cachaça*, 'cane liquor']. 'Don't you want *cachaça*, compadre?' Nascimento had a lot of merchandise. 'I'll give you sugar, coffee three kilos, soap two bars, cartridges.' 'You'll get me some cartridges?' 'O.K. I'd like some manioc flour' [said Nascimento] 'O.K. I'll go toast it.' I toasted five *arqueiros*. I dreamt of this happening there at Pereira's. A long time ago the other, his brother Manuel, used to work here.

(3) I dreamt Homero distributed lots of fish. 'Puta! Where did you catch so many fish?' 'There at Japec.' He caught a lot of fish. He caught a lot: *acará*, *tucunaré*, *jaraquí*, *traíra*. He caught them with a net, I dreamt.

Elaborating on the first dream, Mohã'gí remarked that José Bahut was so fat he looked pregnant. This led into a conversation between us about pregnant women. Homero's daughter, he commented, 'is just beginning to be pregnant, I just noticed it. Only after another month, another month [i.e. many months] she will give birth. I don't know if it will be a little girl or boy.' In the course of the conversation, I asked about childhood memories of pregnancies. He at first responded that he did not remember when he first saw a woman pregnant, then added: 'Ah! First saw it in the water. At first there were no little boys. The *tapy'yntín* [Brazilians] also didn't have any. Only, at first, Mbahíra' – and he launched into the story of how Mbahíra acquired a daughter:

Mbahíra said to his wife: 'Ah. I'm going fishing.' He cut a piece of bark off a tree, and then made a fish-image lure. An *aracú* came [He shot it and threw it behind him; however, Mohã'gí omits describing this scene, which is well known to his listeners, and goes straight on to the phrase Mbahíra hears from behind him.] 'Papa, turn around this way!' He turned around, and the *aracú* fell. Later on, the *acará* came. [Again, he heard the voice from behind him:] 'Papa, turn around this way!' He turned around, and it fell. He turned around this way. Later on, the *jandiá* [catfish] came. The catfish. 'Turn around . . .!' He turned around. 'You're my daughter!' White, beautiful . . .

Here, his account of the myth was interrupted, but it would normally go on to tell how Mbahíra brings his daughter home and shows her off to his wife and his companion, each of whom asks in turn, 'Where did you get such a beautiful daughter?' She roasts corn for him, and prepares the first corn beer [*cauĩ*] which delights him.

Instead, the conversation went off to illicit sexual relationships he was either witness to or had heard about in his childhood (which he recounts with delight), and marriage arrangements and exchanges. He mentions that he has no son to exchange and that he married his daughter off when she was quite small because: 'I didn't want my daughter pregnant the way O. [an unmarried teenager] got pregnant. Pregnant at random . . . I don't want her pregnant like that. It's bad. Now if it has a father, that's good.'

It is not immediately self-evident that any of these dreams are based on a myth. Only in the course of his associations does the dreamer reveal that the third dream, in fact, turns on one. As this myth makes clear, *male parturition* is the theme of the third dream. In the first dream too, as the associations confirm, the man is presented as pregnant.

Each of the three dreams offers a different metaphorical image for the common topic of male pregnancy. The first dream represents it as something stolen. Since harvesting potatoes from a garden is woman's work and garden produce is a woman's, it is something stolen *from a woman*. The image in which it is presented is also one of *oral conception*, a frequent childhood fantasy about conception. (This image also occurs in the origin myth of crops, in which an old woman swallows a snake egg and conceives a snake in her belly.) José Bahut is appropriate for the dream image because, aside from being noted as a glutton and a thief, he is also talked about for accompanying his wife into the fields when she gave birth and acting as her midwife, something no self-respecting Kagwahiv man would do.

The food image in this dream could also be an allusion to the Kagwahiv belief about gestation, according to which it is the husband's, or consort's, *feeding* of the baby with his semen in repeated intercourse that is responsible for the baby growing. A single act of intercourse is not enough; the man's continued feeding is essential.

The second dream is less clear, but here too the process of cooking manioc flour[10] could also be an allusion to the gestation process. Mohã'gí explained to me on another occasion that the cooking of crushed manioc tubers (poisonous in their raw state) into the staple coarse meal called 'manioc flour' is a mysterious transformation brought about by tiny hovering insects with shamanic power that make it swell up. Preparing manioc flour is also a woman's task, although men do, upon occasion, perform it. Here, Mohã'gí does the 'gestating' in exchange for food provided by another man.

The third dream is the one that takes the idiom of a myth to express the same idea: the fantasy of being able to perform the female creative act of bringing forth a child. The myth alluded to in this dream is, of course, the story of Mbahíra's creation of a daughter, which Mohã'gí went on to recount. The notion of male pregnancy is expressed even more openly in another Kagwahiv myth, which was told to me by an old woman, the wife of my principal source of myths; her husband was reluctant to tell it. Originally it was men who had the children, so the story goes, but owing to certain anatomical problems with this arrangement of men giving birth, Mbahíra decided to transfer this privilege (if privilege it be) to women.

A man's fantasy of being able to give birth is not an infrequent one in our own culture, though one that is noted in the psychoanalytic literature only in the last twenty-five years or so (Jaffe 1968). Its roots are in the period around the fourth or fifth year of life when a child is struggling with understanding gender roles and the differences between the sexes, and with mapping out the possibilities of what he or she is or will eventually be capable of. Freud's 'Little Hans' (1909) is a prime example of such a fantasy, although Freud himself did not fully recognize it. Some of Hans's anxieties over his wish to have a baby stemmed from just the anatomical difficulties that the Kagwahiv myth cites in justification for Mbahíra's establishment of the current situation.

What is of primary interest to us here, however, is not the *content* of the dream and its meaning to the dreamer, but rather the *form* in which that meaning is expressed. These three dreams offer respectively three different visual-kinesthetic metaphors of the processes of conception, gestation, and birth. Each metaphor draws on an image from daily economic life: horticulture and eating, exchange and cooking, and fishing. Each also contains a strong proprioceptive or kinesthetic image: swallowing, stirring the manioc flour in the oven, and pulling fish from the water in a net. Furthermore, the myth on which the third dream is modeled contains a strong proprioceptive image which is stressed in Mohã'gí's telling: the image of turning around to look behind could be taken as a metaphorical statement of the reversal implicit in the idea of male procreation.

There is also a progressive development through the three dreams of a hierarchy of modes of transaction in relations between the sexes. In the first dream, it is stealing food from a woman's garden; in the second, the barter of foodstuffs; in the third, the reciprocity of the male and female economic roles, implicit in the myth's theme (only alluded to in the dream) of Mbahíra fishing while his daughter prepares agricultural foods.[11]

The myth itself draws on the metaphor of the economic roles of men and women in order to convey a *social* message. Juxtaposing images drawn from the respective economic contributions of men and women to the family, the myth poses a social dilemma and offers a resolution to it. In Kagwahiv society, whose political structure is built on bride service and uxorilocal residence (Kracke 1978), the father-daughter bond is a foundation of the social order. Yet daughters are born of mothers and spend their days together in cooperative economic activities. The resolution to this threat to the social order: assert, mythologically, that daughters are born of their fathers only.

The metaphors in the three dreams, and in the myth on which one of them is based, are constructed from daily life experiences, but present highly charged fantasy themes: oral conception and male pregnancy. The dreams, just as much as the myth they incorporate, engage in ingenious *bricolage*. Conversely, the myth which provides one dream with its central image draws on a number of devices and modes of presentation which, while typical of myth, also recall features common to dreams. First, one may note how the myth creates a vivid sense of space and spatial relationships: *down into* the water, *up out* of it, the fish *falling down*, Mbahíra's daughter *getting up* to go home with him, and the mysterious transformations taking place *around behind* the protagonist. This last expresses in spatial-kinesthetic form the reversal implicit in the main theme of the myth, a man 'delivering' his daughter. The myth also moves from an everyday domestic scene to extraordinary events taking place on the margin of the river, and then back to the domestic scene.

In the myth, as it is usually told, Mbahíra repeatedly hears from behind him a voice saying: 'Toroky'vú apĩ! Toroky'vú apĩ!' ('let's groom [pick lice], Papa! Let's groom, Papa!'). In the context of the story, this everyday phrase – an affectionate utterance that might be heard any day in family life, bespeaking domestic tranquility – takes on a formulaic character. Like a spoken phrase from the day that recurs decontextualized in a dream, it is doubly out of context in the myth when uttered by a dying fish on the wild and magical river bank. Here, it anticipates and announces the ultimate outcome, the daughter's affectionate relationship with her father. Note too, here again, that this phrase in itself evokes, by synecdoche, the vivid image of a daughter sitting behind her father on the hearth, or on the doorstep, affectionately plucking lice from his hair, a *visual* image of domestic tranquility.

The myth, finally, consists of a series of discrete scenes, each pictured in relatively vivid concreteness (though leaving details open for the listener's imagination): Mbahíra takes leave of his wife; he fishes by the river; he returns home to present his daughter to an astonished wife; and so on. This series of images with minimal connecting tissue, blurring one into the other, is a feature of many myths which is quite like dreams. And here, it was one of these images that Mohã'gí appropriated from the myth for his dream.

For a second example of myth in dreams, let me turn to what is probably the most widely told and popular of Kagwahiv stories, 'Kagwahivahẽ Makes Love with the Tapir.' This myth, which I have already alluded to as the source of the oneiromantic symbolism whereby a dream of genitals predicts the killing of a tapir, occurs in more than one dream. Kagwahivahẽ makes manioc cakes (*cauiapo'á beijus*) in secret to take to her lover, the tapir. She tells her husband she is going bathing, takes her young son with her, and goes to the beach of the river. There she leaves her son (who in one version says 'You go defecate, Mama!'), crosses the river, and calls *'cauĩapo'á reré'* (*reré* is a word 'in the tapir language'). The tapir comes and eats the manioc cakes and they make love.

Her husband gets suspicious (in some versions, his brother sees what is going on and tells him) and follows her one day and finds out about it. Vowing vengeance, he sends her off to visit relatives. He has their teenaged daughter prepare manioc cakes and call the tapir in imitation of her mother. When the tapir comes, thinking she is Kagwahivahẽ, the husband and his companions kill him with bow and arrow, and make a stew of the meat and eat it on the spot. (In one version they fed it to Kagwahivahẽ on her return.) When she comes back, she makes manioc cakes and calls the tapir. He doesn't come. Only his ghost answers. She finds the spot covered with blood and the butchered remains where he had been killed. Angry and grief-stricken she takes her children to the beach and dives in with all of them. They turn into porpoises and her husband shoots an arrow which strikes her in the head. And that is why porpoises, who are to this day called Kagwahivahẽ, have a hole in the back of their heads.

Like the story of Mbahíra's acquisition of a daughter, this myth embodies themes which correspond to highly charged fantasies. In this case, the themes involve sexual rivalry and jealousy, and violent retaliation. In bringing these themes into conjunction with an emphasis on mother-son and father-daughter relationships one can see this as a slightly displaced version of an Oedipal myth. The tapir, who appears on the other side of the river as the five-year-old boy, and is left on the bank by his mother, could be interpreted as a kind of fantasy alter ego of the boy himself. Correspondingly, the teenaged girl, in identification with her mother's sexuality, allies herself with her father in defeating her mother and destroying her mother's sexual capabilities. Certainly a child of appropriate age listening could identify with the children in the myth in this fashion, especially if helped along by being told that the child in the story was of his or her age.

I would like to comment here on two instances in which this myth occurs in dreams. In one, as in the previous case, it appears in the latent content, the dream reference to the myth being confirmed by a spontaneous recounting of the myth in association with the dream; in a second case, the myth is the manifest content of the dream.

The dream which alludes to the myth of Kagwahivahẽ in the latent content occurred in my fifth interview with Jovenil, a young headman and father of nine about whom I have written extensively (Kracke 1978, 1979b, 1980). The interview was one that Jovenil had been reluctant to begin and was full of long silences, as if he was struggling with some thoughts and feelings he was not yet ready to talk about. I sensed that he was particularly reluctant to talk about his dreams, and later on in the interview I asked him if he was concerned that because of telling me these dreams their predictions of good hunting would not come true (Kracke 1979a:141–2).

He did, however, tell me two dreams at the beginning of the interview. In one, Jacó Aguarajuv, whom in the previous interview Jovenil had disparaged for his stinginess in distributing game, came down from his settlement way upriver and distributed a roast tapir he had killed, giving Jovenil a piece. At the same time, a widely liked Brazilian woman who had been married to a deceased Kagwahiv arrived at the settlement from downriver with her half-Kagwahiv son. In association to this dream, Jovenil talked about the long-standing friction between himself and Jacó, and described an altercation with him at a recent fiesta which had come to blows, and his own efforts to patch it up. Later in the interview, a question about his talking back to his father brought him back to the theme of fighting: Brazilians say that one should not fight with one's father; yet 'when Brazilians fight, it's to kill a relative . . .' Although his father admonished him not to fight, he used to wrestle with his brother in fun, but then, 'We don't fight the way Brazilians do.' It was at this point that he asked: 'Has Mohã'gí told you the story "Kagwahivahẽ Had Repeated Intercourse"? ' He then launched into a full rendition of the story. Perhaps significantly, he omitted the little boy going down to the bank with his mother, and played down the bloody details of the tapir's death.

The dream excerpts and highlights one scene of the myth: the men roasting and sharing the slain tapir's meat. But selecting this convivial scene negates the fundamentally violent theme of the story, a theme which is in tune with the aggressive thoughts Jovenil went on to voice, but concurrently deny, after telling the dream. This more violent theme is absent from the dream but, as the associations confirm, implicit in it.

The tapir is alluded to in another dream context in the same interview. While talking about symbolic predictions in dreams, Jovenil recalled a dream he had had some time ago. While out hunting once with a companion, José Bahut, he had dreamed of José's big penis. That dream, he told me, would have meant that he would bag a tapir, but he told it by the fire. He saw a tapir, but as a result of his indiscretion, he missed it.

A dream in the next interview, two days later, picked up this image of José Bahut's penis (which turned out to have had an important part in Jovenil's childhood sexual explorations), and reiterated the theme of sexual rivalry and castrative retaliation of the Kagwahivahẽ story. I will not go into this dream, which I have discussed elsewhere (Kracke 1979a: 143–5; 1980:256–8), except to remark that Jovenil's dreaming of sexual rivalry and castration just after telling me the myth confirms that these themes were on his mind when he told the myth. Hence the myth embodies such concerns for Jovenil. At least he thinks of it in that context and borrows symbols from the myth to express such feeling.

Our interest is not primarily in what the myth, and the dream constructed with imagery from the myth, express in emotive terms, but in *how* they express it. Both the myth and the dream, as in the first example, are composed of everyday events: baking manioc cakes, going swimming and hunting, roasting and sharing meat. These are woven together in oppositions which metaphorically evoke important personal or cosmological issues. The dream, in addition, is composed of events the dreamer heard or thought about the previous day, as Jovenil enumerated. These are facets of the *bricolage* that characterizes both of them. Both the myth and the dream also contain vivid imagery stressing spatial relationships; *across* the river and *into* it are key movements signaling important shifts in the myth, while *upriver* and *downriver* movements are stressed in the dream and may well have metaphorical importance given oppositions between Jacó, a quarrelsome and stingy Kagwahiv, and the warm and generous Brazilian woman who is paradoxically sympathetic to Kagwahiv culture and values. This myth, like the Mbahíra story, also contains a repeated formulaic phrase.

This myth introduces a further feature which many of the most often-told Kagwahiv myths share: a clear invitation for the listener to take a point of view. The myth's characters are identified, sometimes explicitly, with listeners of corresponding ages. In another story, the myth of how the chief of the Sky People abandoned earth and left us here below, the narrator uses pronouns to place himself and his listeners clearly with those so abandoned. These devices encourage listeners to identify with appropriate characters in the myth.

In one instance a woman whom I interviewed, Aluza, reported dreaming the Kagwahivahẽ myth practically verbatim, with herself in at least one role. Kagwahivahẽ's husband in the dream was her own husband, Jovenil, and in a first-person reference to 'coming home to my house,' she implicitly took the part herself of Kagwahivahẽ in the dream. But she also elaborated the role of Kagwahivahẽ's daughter as if, on one level, she experienced herself in that role as well, though she assigned it in the dream to her husband's sister, not, interestingly, to her own nine-year-old daughter.

Aluza's dreamt version of Kagwahivahẽ demonstrates the intense personal involvement she has in the story, as well as showing how different individuals may experience the same story with a quite different emphasis and point of view. But the very fact that she reproduces the myth in her dream testifies to the major point I am making here: the congruity between dreams and myths in the kinds of thought processes involved in them, which makes it possible, literally in this case, to put one in the place of the other.

CONCLUSIONS

Myths are highly condensed formulations of basic human issues, including emotional conflicts at an intimate level as well as philosophical problems posed by society and the relationship of society to nature. In this they are like dreams, and like dreams, they are highly elaborated metaphorical constructs with multiple levels. While they are structured by language, both in the medium of their presentation and in their content, they draw heavily on spaces and spatial configurations, and on visual, sensory, and kinesthetic imagery. An important part of the experiences of such verbal literature is the personal imagery it evokes in the listener, imagery that is unique to each person participating in the myth-telling event. Such personal imagery is easily woven into dreams as well, and so both the form of the myth and the nature of its content (the issues it addresses) facilitate its use in the dreams of those for whom a particular myth is meaningful.

This congruity between dreams and myths extends to the kinds of thought processes embodied in both, the imagistic, metaphor-rich form of thinking that Freud labeled 'primary process.' This does not mean, however, as Freud's term implies and classical analysts were accustomed to infer, that mythic thinking is a 'primitive,' developmentally earlier, inferior form of thought. As the complexity and subtlety of mythic thought, and the dreams of creative people attest (see Rothenberg 1979), 'primary-process' thought is as capable of refinement and development as is 'secondary-process.' And both forms of thought are enriched in development by interplay with each other. This interplay is one contribution of dreams to our mental life that can best be tapped by cultures and individuals that take dreams seriously, giving waking thought to them. Just the same can be said of myths, and of other forms of artistic expression as well, all of which elaborate and elevate this sensory-imagistic form of thought to higher levels of complexity and subtlety, and link it in interplay with the logical-verbal thought so characteristic of secondary processes.

Dreams also play an important part, as is increasingly recognized, in mastering new affective experiences and assimilating them with past experiences and into one's self-schemata (Cartwright 1977:131–3; Jones 1970:167–89; Palombo 1978). Myths, too, provide a kind of template for mastery and assimilation of new emotional experiences. With their highly condensed imagery which, like ritual symbolism, links conceptual problems of the social order with frequently occurring personal fantasies, all expressed metaphorically in culturally meaningful images, myths offer a store of culturally framed condensations of fantasies which can stimulate the personal fantasy process for integrating difficult new experiences. And the frequent occasions when a myth, or myth fragment, appears in a dream and mediates the dream's meaning can be understood as instances of this use of myth as a ready-provided form for the experience-integrating process.

Myths are like dreams in having a 'story line' which is more directly expressive of an inner emotional-aesthetic structure than is conventional narrative. They proceed with an inner emotional logic which overrides external constraints of causal sequence, motivation of protagonists or the possibilities of everyday physical and social reality that constrain the more prosaic and factual narratives of day-to-day life. Myths are like dreams, too, in the kinds of operations they perform on their material in developing their arguments, as can be seen by comparing the kinds of transformations Lévi-Strauss points out in mythic logic with the mechanisms Freud uncovers in dream-work. And as Freud pointed out in *The Interpretation of Dreams* (1900, chapter

6D), these operations are especially appropriate for the expression of complex ideas in the visual or sensory medium of thought that dreaming constitutes. An example of such an operator in myth is the 'around behind' motion in the Bahíra myth that expresses the reversal of the powers of the sexes that is central to the myth's social meaning. The very prominence of spacial relations in myth – above and below, crossings and recrossings of rivers – as well as the vivid sensory images and comparisons one often finds in mythic scenes makes the analogy of myth with dream thought obvious. And finally, the frequent occurrence in both myths and dreams of the kinds of highly charged images and themes that are characteristic of children's ponderings and fantasies about the body and its functions, birth and death, and sexual relationships and feelings is a common element which pychoanalysts have often stressed.

What is the significance of the comparison? Why belabor it? Simply this: myths are obviously a highly developed art form, an 'oral literature' (to use a paradoxical and misleading characterization) which can attain great subtlety and complexity of structure and thought. If dreams and myths partake of the same fundamental kind of image-based thinking, then the type of thought process characteristic of dreams is capable of high development, and of the expression and elaboration of complex and subtle ideas. Dream thinking, or primary process, is not merely a degenerate, regressive form of adult logical thought, but is rather a distinct form of thinking. At the seminar, when we chose to call this thought process 'imaginal thought' we meant to suggest that it was as valid as logical, categorical thought, but appropriate for different kinds of problems.

NOTES

1. My fieldwork in 1967–8 was supported by an NIMH fellowship and an NSF grant and carried out with the kind permission of the Serviço de Proteção aos Índios (now FUNAI).
2. In transcribing terms in the Kagwahiv language, I have used a slightly modified version of the alphabet devised by Helen Pease and La Vera Betts. An apostrophe (') indicates a glottal stop; v is a bilabial fricative (as in Spanish) but in final position is pronounced as a bilabial stop, p; j is pronounced dzh; ch is tsh as in English; and y represents a high back unrounded vowel, a 'guttural u' sound; a is pronounced as in f*a*ther; e as in p*e*t; i as in pet*i*te; o as in *ou*ght; u as in fr*u*it. A tilde (~)

over a vowel indicates that it is nasalized. Stress is indicated by acute accents (′) on emphasized syllables.

3. *Arokí hehe, arohayhú.* The concomitant causative verb prefix *-ro-* used in both these verbs (with *-ki*, 'sleep,' and *-hayhú*, 'dream') indicates that the subject participates in the event caused by him (see Kracke 1979a).
4. *Ra'úv* can refer equally to the image of an inanimate object occurring in a dream or to a person's image. It thus refers to the image itself, not to the idea that the image appearing in the dream is an emanation of the person's 'soul' (since an inanimate object is not referred to as having a soul). In this the *ra'úv* differs from the Kalapalo *akũa* (Basso, this volume) which only appears in the dream as a human image. Otherwise, however, it is interesting to note that there is a parallel range of meanings in the extensions of the two terms, since *akũa* can refer to a reflected image or shadow as well as to the objectified self of the dreamer or of a person appearing in the dream.
5. There was some discussion at the seminar over whether such terms can truly be considered polysemic, or whether apparent variations in meaning are merely variant expressions of a single underlying meaning. My position is that, while there is undoubtedly a core concept which links the various senses of a term like *ra'úv*, one can and must distinguish between different senses. When we say that food has 'soul,' we do not mean that it is sentient or that it will go to heaven or hell after death.
6. Ricoeur conceives the dream primarily as the dream of *another*: 'The dream is a spectacle unknown to us; it is accessible only through the account of the waking hours' (1970:15). And, 'the dreamer, in his private dream, is closed to all; he begins to instruct us only when he recounts his dream' (ibid.:16). The problem is a different one when the dreamer confronts the memory, however imperfect, of his own dream spectacle.
7. Freudian interpreters of myth, such as Rank (1909) and Róheim (1945, 1952), have tended to neglect and even deny the social level of meaning of myths. Anthropologists tend to deny the presence of unconscious, emotion-laden fantasy themes (see Spiro 1979). Yet both levels must be attended to. Given the highly condensed multivocal nature of mythic symbolism, the multiple levels of metaphor in myth allow of a level of emotional fantasy, speaking to personal unconscious conflicts, condensed into the same images that provide a commentary on social ideology. These levels are parallel to the 'orectic' and the 'ideological' poles of meaning in a ritual symbol (see Turner 1967:28–9, 54).
8. Reversal in a dream can have varied significance, such as the contrast between reality and how one would like things to be.

9. To be sure, Lévi-Strauss also contrasts *bricolage* with scientific thought, but they are contrasted as two distinct types of thinking, not as an 'undeveloped' kind versus a 'developed' one. This contrast (of *bricolage* with science) is perfectly in keeping with the argument of this paper.
10. Manioc preparation could be an allusion to the last part of the myth in which Mbahíra's daughter prepares various kinds of processed corn products for him.
11. Note that these themes could all very well refer to the intimate relationship that he was developing with me, a *civilizado* with trade goods and curative powers, in the form of medicines, to offer. 'What kind of relationship will I offer him?' might be one question posed by the dream triad. This observation draws attention to another feature of the primary process expressed in dreams and myths, namely its 'pointing' or *indexicality*. As a vehicle of transference, primary-process thought is immediate and pragmatic; it *points* to the current situation, the current relationship (see also Crapanzano 1981).

3
Selfhood and discourse in Sambia dream sharing

GILBERT HERDT

Dreams are among the most complex of all human communications. Any serious student of dreams knows this and the knowledge should give us pause, as Freud and many others have said. As long as we choose only to make normative dream interpretations our object of analysis, we are in less danger of distorting the motivations or meanings of speakers. This task poses difficulties, however, when there are different speech contexts and types of discourse through which dreams are told. When we interpret actual dream reports, we are on even shakier ground. Even the manifest meaning of such reports is questionable when we are not told about the speaker's intentions or the context of the dream reports. So when we turn to the task of elucidating the whole range of conscious, subliminal, and unconscious awareness of a particular person's dream report, our difficulties multiply. In many Melanesian societies we face a double problem. On the one hand, there are culturally based life-cycle stages (childhood, initiate life, adulthood) that inherently conflict with one another, bringing experiential discontinuities and thus repression, which factor into dream sharing; while on the other, three modes of discourse – public, secret, and private – delicately negotiate between these developmental phases of contrary experience.

The general aim of this chapter is to explore dream sharing among the Sambia of Papua New Guinea, utilizing the case of one Sambia man, Nilutwo, whom I studied between 1974 and 1979, as the foreground.[1] After sketching the setting, I will then describe the social structural and symbolic parameters of dream sharing. My primary objective is to demonstrate the differences between various dream communications. I subsequently distinguish between the part of Nilutwo's awareness of all dream experience he knew but often hid, and the part which he shared with others. For heuristic purposes we may label these parts 'self' and 'person' (Geertz 1966). This slippery jargon must not be allowed to obscure the fundamental phenomenology of Sambia: What I call a dream was an event my soul experienced in another, parallel world, which my thought recalls and I – my self – share. I examine dream reports to interpret how dreams helped Nilutwo bridge, through pragmatic and other means, his experience of himself, and I conclude by considering some theoretical implications of my account.

THE SETTING

Sambia, who number over 2,000, are a hunting and horticultural people living in small hamlets (50–150) in river valleys within the rugged rainforests of the Eastern Highlands Province. Intra-tribal warfare, which was constant and destructive until pacification in 1964–5, was the key factor in the formation of local groups and the politics of intergroup relationships (Herdt 1982b). And while it has been gone these many years, violence is still common enough to cause continuing concern. The persons with whom I work grew up when warfare was still a reality; therefore, in that timeless realm of the unconscious, for them, war still reigns. Violence in the past could become war, and I believe that conflictual events are still perceived as having that potential, and are thereby represented, in daydreams and nightdreams. Dreams bore upon ritual through explicit instructions that initiates should watch their own dreams for omens of impending attack. Elders hammered into boys (learning is too soft a word to describe the process) this dire order from initiation onwards. Moreover, and a higher-order dynamic sum of the above: masculine character structure developed in this environment to produce prowess and the aggressiveness needed for battle, plus the watchfulness and suspiciousness necessary to anticipate attacks and battles. This suspiciousness invaded many aspects of social relationships, defined everyone as friends or enemies, and soured marriages by virtue of men's social paranoia regarding the potentially deadly sorcery powers of their wives from enemy hamlets.

Nowadays, even though various social conflicts or disputes occurring in the valley seem thematically to have replaced warfare, suspiciousness still inhibits and thereby frames some kinds of dream sharing and dream experience in conscious, subliminal, and unconscious ways. As a result of this social paranoia, guided imagery was difficult to use as a research technique among Sambia.[2] To take Nilutwo as an illustration, by virtue of his warrior socialization warfare is and will always be 'one of the communications to which he has pledged himself' (Freud 1933:9); thus his dream reports were full of conflict.

SELFHOOD AND DREAMS

Personhood is different from selfhood; these notions influence dream experience, sharing, and interpretation directly, through desires and perceptions, and indirectly, through types of dream narratives. The Sambia folk concept of a person is a configuration of elements including a body, names and name-songs, and a social history. As a person, this individual fills one or more social roles with corresponding social/ritual statuses at different life-cycle stages. Everyone has a soul, which is an attribute of personhood, before and after death. One's soul emerges in the mother's womb, the result of maternal (blood) and paternal (semen) sources. Souls are vaguely sex-linked, so that men believe their souls are more strongly influenced by their fathers, indicating animation or consciousness attributed to the soul. Thought (*koontu*) is distinct from one's soul (*koogu*).[3] Thought indicates intention, will, and active volition. Infants, for example, have souls from fetal life on, but they have little or no thought until around age two, when they can respond to their names and carry out a request. But not until initiation do boys have much thought that counts; that is, they are irresponsible because they are not accountable to ritual and moral norms. Finally, spirit familiars (*numelyu*) are acquired later through various initiation ceremonies (Herdt 1977). These familiars – animals, plants, beings – are counterparts of one's soul; they aid the soul in various ways, can be seen in dreams, and generally support good health and longevity. The soul, thought, and familiars are basic constituents of personhood for Sambia. After death, the soul remains as one or another kind of spirit or ghost;

familiars are released, eventually to go to other agnates; whereas the person's thought merely 'dies.' What remains of known persons are their accomplishments in the physical world and people's memories of the deceased.

What is selfhood? Here we face a tricky epistemological contrast with personhood that I can only outline. On the level of public discourse, the image of personhood is expressed by the concept of thought. Thought, as a concept, is subtly indexed to thinkable social expectations, norms, beliefs, and so on that are expressed in public speech. In this sense, a person refers to *koontu* in the constructions 'I think' (*mi koontu-tuv* . . .), as a verb, or 'my thought' (*koontu-tungankuno*), as a noun. This usage, however, denotes only one part of thought. What about the personal pronouns in these conventional constructions? In private discourse the public stress on thought fades to become background for the idiosyncratic self, and 'me': private communications about one's subjective experience, including beliefs, feelings, and impulses. This sense of selfhood we may label the private self, whereas thought corresponds to the norms of personhood. Together, these elements comprise one's total self-experience (which is not the same as consciousness). These distinctions are not emically recognized, but my analysis is supported by cultural and linguistic usage in relation to dreams.

Dreams (*wunju*) are experiences and events that occur to someone while asleep. When one sleeps the soul leaves the body and roams in different places, near or far, familiar or unfamiliar, as if it could glide on the wind. The soul takes one's thought with it, leaving the body empty. If someone says, 'I dream (*nyoo kwunyen-nu wunju*) such and such,' he is saying, 'my soul visits places my thought sees' (in sleep); and when he relates these image-experiences, that is a dream report. All that happens in a dream is thus *wunju-wulu*, 'dream-things,' which this concept expresses as real events. This point is important for it explains why dreams are not viewed as memories of dreams (in our sense) but narratives of events. The cultural ideology is that the dream world parallels the secular one, which the soul directly experiences and thought relays the waking images of. One's soul and thought thus gaze on the same events, which a person or private self relates.

Because all dream events occur not to the person but to the soul, all dream figures and images are supernatural. So events can be fantastic – for example: flying through the air; leaping rivers; copulating with forbidden persons; men entering evil places like caves or menstrual huts;

snakes that turn into airplanes; having superhuman strength or being paralyzed with unreal terror. Such events can strike one's soul because they are dream-things. All human figures in dreams are interpreted as spirits. Big men, either living or deceased, are seen as forest spirits (*ikeiaru*); prominent or strange women are hamlet spirits (*aatmwogwambu*). All other persons, the dead and living too, are interpreted as ghosts (*kumaamdu*), whose intentions in dreams are always bad. Worse yet are the bogs (*boongu*) seen in dreams, for their nature spirits are evil and try to engulf men. Shamans and cassowary hunters, who often report dreams, are believed to have more frequent contacts with spirits in dreams by virtue of their spirit familiars: humanlike beings for shamans and *aatmwogwambu* spirits – called 'the mother of cassowary' – for hunters. In general, Sambia dread their spirits, which are vindictive, capricious, and evil; chronic dreamers are thus in touch with a great power. From our perspective, it is not surprising that such dreamers show forms of deviance in their personalities.

At this point I should pause to underline the fact that most of the features of my account thus far are consciously espoused by Sambia and accord with their folk model. But questions remain. Is the soul perhaps a symbol of – or 'cultural screen' (Eggan 1961:565) for – unconscious parts of an individual's awareness? Do conflictual memories or social conflicts from the past remain in thought and get expressed privately, or have Sambia succeeded in relegating them to the soul's sleeping experience? These questions pertain to my general theme of desires expressed through speech. I will examine each of them, but first we need now to study the place of dreams in natural discourse.

DISCOURSE FRAMES

It can be argued that in general Sambia persons operate and behave in three types of social situations: public, secret, and private. Social action in these situations corresponds to three different types of discourse: public talk (*iyungacheru yungalu*, literally 'free talk'), secret talk (*iooluyungalu*, literally 'hidden talk'), and private talk (no marked category). These discourses are, in turn, structured by cultural rules, premises, expectations – frames that organize behavior. These narrative frames have, in turn, counterparts in 'personal scripts' that organize self-experience, motivations, fantasies. Taken together, these social situations, discourse frames, and scripts constitute what I have elsewhere (Herdt 1982b) called identity contexts.

Public discourse is the most common narrative mode. It is associated with secular and domestic situations in women's houses, gatherings in the plaza of hamlets, gardening parties, and public meetings. Mixed audiences of men, women, and children define the frame, public business.

Secret discourse is less common and is sexually segregated. Talk concerning ritual secrets forbidden to the uninitiated frames this mode. It can occur in three main situations: the clubhouse (but even there it is whispered and more common at night); the forest, when men are alone; and in cult-houses, on the rare occasions of initiation when ritual teaching occurs formally. Both men and women have their own separate secret discourses, which neither is supposed to know the contents of (Herdt 1982a). Secret ritual knowledge is stratified, furthermore, by age and ritual grade. Fragments of secret discourse may emerge anywhere, wedged in between public and private talk, which is why the ethnographer can spend years decoding euphemisms, circumlocutions, metaphors, and double entendres that hide their meanings (*kablu*) or secret ritual narrative meanings (*pweiyu kablu*).

Private discourse concerns oneself's innermost thoughts and desires, some of which may be forbidden. No public social situations correspond to private talk. Magical knowledge passed from parent to child about gardening, hunting, sorcery, and so on belongs to this domain. More significant – because more frequent and intimate – all sexual experience, impulses, and fantasies are private talk. Sambia are a prudish people who value virginity and have strong feelings of shame regarding coitus. Children hide their sex play, adults hide coition. Homosexual intercourse is both secret and private. Adultery is so strongly condemned that when rumors turn into scandalous public accusations, one or both parties may attempt suicide (cf. Hogbin 1947). People thus hide certain thoughts and monitor their speech, and the concept of hidden-thought (*ioolu-koontu*) is not one that Sambia like to discuss. Like secrecy itself, silence is the general principle in public and private discourse regarding idiosyncratic secrets of the self.

Each of these three modes of talking is culturally supported by implicit and explicit rules, taboos, and expectations that 'carry,' as it were, the information corresponding to each domain of verbal and nonverbal experience and action. The systemic interlinkages between them are subtle and complex. One might argue that in Western culture there is only public and private discourse. With the Sambia, secret societies add a third domain that screens both ritual secrets and the individual unconscious. But secrecy cannot be reduced either to unconscious conflict or to the social tactics for power over women. Secrecy is produced by an internal systemic contradiction in Sambia culture of which it is *the* symbolic solution. When opposing social groups must exchange women who become de facto group members, and who must, as opposed sexes, rear boys – whose primary allegiance to father opposes their sentimental attachments to mother – social and intrapsychic conflicts undermine basic principles of group cohesion. The general interpretive risks of institutionalized secrecy are particularly germane to the analysis of dream talk.

Dreams are mentioned in public, secret, and private situations. This is so in spite of the barriers and controversies between the narrative modes of discourse outlined above. However, not all dreams are shared across all situations, as we should expect. Context is clearly the key factor here in constraining dream talk. Recall, though, Sambia dream theory: dreams are events that happen not to the person of the speaker, but to his or her soul. Sambia believe that the dreamer is not responsible for what the soul does. The person is responsible for what he says, or rather, more accurately, for the thought deriving from dreams he communicates. It seems it is self that mediates between soul and thought and decides what to say. But now we face another problem. Why are some dreams never shared with anyone? The answer lies in how one's private self perceives desires to be expressed in dreams. This subtle point is related to a different problem in understanding the standardized dream interpretation system of Sambia. Since dream reports are context-specific and some dreams never reach the light of social day, can all dream interpretations be based on a unified semiotic code (Sperber 1976)? If not, why have Sambia fooled themselves into believing that different persons have the same dreams?

DREAM SHARING

What structures dream sharing? For expository purposes this subject can be broken down into several components.

Dream time

There is a general notion of dream time (*wuju-tunga-kuno*, present infinitive) that is used in a dual sense. First, and rather rare, is the period of the ancestors, unknown and faceless, who shaped present-day customs. I would note here the semipublic statements that rituals were literally 'dreamed-up' by ancestors out of their dreams. In this sense, too, dream time merges with myths, the stories handed down from ancestors. Less rare, the dream time is used as an idiom to cover the reporter's experience in dreams. In this respect, the communicator's retrospective feeling of being in dreams is timeless and boundless. Both notions are diffuse; they appear to link in social imagination the past and the present through dreams and, in a vague way, to displace responsibility for present-day custom and behavior on to dreams (cf. Stanner 1972).

Dream reporting

Two concepts pertain to dream reporting: dream talk (*wunjuyungalu*) means people's speech when actually sharing dreams, and dream story (*wunju-koongundu*), the stylized tradition of telling stories of different kinds.[4] Dream talk is the more spontaneous, as when relating a dream immediately on waking. Dream stories may be old dreams that are especially vivid, memorable, or salient to the speaker or the context in which a dream is retold. Dream talk is harder for me to follow than dream stories, which seem edited, more coherent and rational. But both modes of dream sharing may be unframed in speech, for example, reports begin without saying, 'Now I am going to share a dream.' I have heard dream stories go on for five to ten minutes before it was clear they were dreams rather than secular events. Indeed, Sambia themselves sometimes, usually toward the end of a narrative, ask the speaker if such-and-such was a dream; and privately, several people have told me they get confused hearing dreams plugged into public discourse when the speaker never clarifies what is a secular or a dream event.

Contexts of disclosure

What are the main situations in which dreams are shared? First, there is the residence wherein one sleeps (women's or men's house). People may share dreams there any time they awaken from sleep. Second are healing ceremonies in which shamans perform publicly, or secretly, in rituals. Dreams may be shared by shamans or others when dreams are deemed relevant omens to the healing situation. Third are initiation rituals: here, dreams may be shared by elders and shamans when their significance bears upon ritual events. Dream interpretations for ritual secrets are also taught here. In general, dreams used in healing ceremonies are seen as public discourse, whereas dreams used in ritual are secret discourse. Fourth are either public or secret storytelling sessions done primarily by adult men and elders, who may incorporate dream tales. As with sleeping-quarter dreams, though, private dreams may be shared with one's intimate cronies. Fifth is gossip. Dreams pertaining to public, secret, and private discourse may be disclosed to others (usually of the same sex) in gossip and rumors. Sixth are hunting, trading, and gardening trips that serve as occasions for sharing dreams which reveal omens about the trip's success, or events that are going on back home while away. Nowadays, trips to the distant patrol post and longer periods of living away on the coast for plantation work are acculturated settings for dream sharing.

Aside from these situational constraints, social status factors such as sex, age, and ritual status also influence dream sharing. Men generally report dreams more frequently than women, a social fact correlated with the lower status of women. Older people share more dreams than do younger. Children occasionally share dreams, but such are often dismissed as trivial or of false (*koonanu*) significance. However, the children of shamans perceived as likely to be called as shamans and to inherit their parents' familiars are encouraged to share dreams, and all children's nightmares are perceived as dangerous enough to be shared (see Herdt 1977). Initiates rarely disclose dreams for fear of being scoffed at and thus shamed. Nonetheless, they are ritually instructed to share dreams that portend fights or other disasters, and hunting catches. Here we can see that they are placed in a double-bind that only age resolves. After marriage, youths are believed to have more thought, and to know more of what is important; therefore, they more freely relate dreams believed to be of true (*naimbaltnu*) significance. Sexual dreams are not shared till adulthood, and only then in secret or private contexts.

Dream interpreting

In a society in which dream reporting is so situation-specific and contingent upon the speaker's social status, we should expect all interpreting to involve transformations in reported dreams: in terms of subjective changes in the reporter's dream images, words, or feelings after waking and remembering, and/or by intersubjective changes introduced by the act of interpreting when sharing the dream with others.[5] In the latter case, transformations in the dream are dependent upon the type of discourse in which the interpretation occurs, that is, public, secret, or private. Since it is axiomatic that all dreams occur not to the speaker but to his or her soul, it would seem obvious, as Wagner (1972:69) has argued, that New Guinea peoples 'interpret their dreams metaphorically.' Because Sambia can, however, refer their dreams to different modes of discourse as metaframes for interpretation, I shall argue that the act of dream disclosure in one context or another is a pragmatic act, entailing pragmatic significance for interpreting, whereas the dream content is symbolically interpreted. My remaining points about dream sharing concern aspects of this distinction between metaphoric and pragmatic framing.

Dreams as omens

Let us return to rather basic matters: Why do Sambia share dreams? and, Why do they invest time in interpreting them? These two problems are separate but related. Sambia share dreams because they are part of their basic experience, from childhood on. They provide pleasure, introject doubt, or cause anxiety, as the case may be. As a dream watcher in the village, I would add three observations. First, most people forget most of their dreams after awakening. Only exceptionally significant dreams are remembered and retold later. Secondly, the dreams people share are usually troubling and produce anxiety after waking. Like other troubling feelings, Sambia say such dreams are 'heavy on the stomach' and 'weigh the liver down.'[6] Sharing such dreams seems to help remove the heaviness or relieve the weight. Thirdly, the more dreams are shared, the more stylized they become. Thus, dream stories in public discourse are edited and stereotyped to the extent that they may pass into the corpus of public cultural knowledge (see Meggitt 1962).

Dreams are interpreted primarily because Sambia believe they reveal bad omens about future events such as warfare, hunting, birth, death, gardening, sickness, and travels. Shamans frequently share dreams and later express post hoc reinterpretations of their dreams that make it seem they had foretold correctly what happened. These dream interpretation principles seem widely shared in Melanesia, and they imply an animistic premise sometimes ignored: the soul, by traversing the spiritual world, contacts beings or powers through dreams that reveal the fate designed for living persons. Dream interpretations thus warrant the time and energy invested in them, especially by shamans, to tap into the future and thereby try to modify fate.

Typical dreams

There is a set of characteristic or typical dreams many Sambia have had.[7] What is typical about these dreams is that they refer to the same images or themes, and they are typically shared in public, less often in secret. Examples include: climbing pandanus trees to fetch mature nuts or fruit that turn out to be rotten or immature, then feeling cheated or disgusted; crossing a river that floods, sweeps away a bridge, and threatens to drown the dreamer, who awakes with a fright; crossing a bog that rises up, trying to engulf the dreamer, who may get caught or fly up a tree; being chased by malevolent people who attempt to overcome and kill the dreamer; or seeing a raging fire or a fog sweep through an area, the dreamer awakening just as a hamlet is consumed. Such dreams are commonly reported and characteristically interpreted in public, depending on the context of disclosure (e.g., healing situation), the speaker's status, the thematic dream scenario (e.g., rotten pandanus fruit usually means someone's hunting will be fruitless), and the interpreter's status (e.g., shamans versus elders). I have never done a random sample of typical dream interpretations but Nilutwo counted some thirty typical dreams of this sort.

Typical secret dreams are few. I recorded only standardized interpretations for five ritual images, and two related images, secretly taught to initiates. These dreams are referred only to secret or private discourse.

It would seem that all typical dreams would be referred to public or secret discourse, but this is not so.[8] A few troubling dreams are never reported except in private. Wet dreams belong to this category; though men believe their peers all have wet dreams on occasion, they are only privately reported. So do virtually all sexual intercourse dreams, except those in which no ejaculation is reported. Several pragmatic dream experience factors here come into play: whether the dream concerned heterosexual or homosexual contacts; whether or not one 'knows' the sexual contact; whether it is by seduction, force, or mutual assent; as well as the other interpretive features noted above (for example, speaker and so on). Sexual dreams are not the only sensitive subjects. Dreams in which one kills and/or eats meat are dangerous, sometimes being interpreted as acts of witchcraft and/or cannibalism.

Acts of interpretation

Dream interpretations can be done in any context. To reiterate: there is no specific situation centered on dream interpreting, but healing ceremonies have dream sharing and ad hoc interpretations made in relation to the patient. The narrative constraints on dream sharing and disclosure noted above apply also to acts of interpretation. What needs to be added is: why individuals seek others' interpretations of their own dreams; what persons are perceived as dream interpretation experts; and how these experts acquire their interpretive expertise.

Sambia seek dream interpretations mainly for two reasons. First are the troubling dreams that 'weigh heavy' on them. My impressions about this heaviness are that people relate dreams to public or secret discourse when the dreams do not violate norms and/or they bear on conflictual social relationships that are already a focus of public discourse, for example, property disputes between villagers. Second, people seek interpretations when they are beginning new or risky ventures and omens would shed light on their success, for example, long hunting trips and large communal gardening forays. In either case, individual and/or collective catharsis is a potential outcome of the dream interpretation in public. In the latter case, too, risky ventures may generate anxiety that the dream interpretation, like a magical rite, can resolve.[9] But of course it may not work out that way: the choice of asking for an interpretation in public can result in catharsis from dream sharing, though the interpreter can raise new anxieties for the dreamer by his or her interpretation. In any case, it seems that the desire to comply with public social norms (or secret ritual norms) entails a pragmatic risk for the person that 'going public' with such a dream experience is safer than keeping it private.

Shamans and certain elders are viewed as dream interpretation specialists. Shamans not only dream and share dreams frequently, but are mediators between the secular and spiritual worlds. They hold trance power to influence spirits and retrieve souls, giving them direct access to 'dream-things.' Since prominent shamans are often war leaders, elders, and cassowary hunters, they bring to the act of dream interpretation wide cultural knowledge and understanding of vested interests in the village. Their motivations vary, but frequent dream sharing and interpretation in public do enhance their roles and social esteem (Herdt 1977). They are committed as authorities to the maintenance of the social order, to keeping thought in line with social norms. Perhaps in this sense key shamans are augurs of Sambia society. Individuals seek interpretations from those shamans or elders closest to them (agnates and affines) who are most trusted. Not only are they usually nearby and available, but they 'know' more about the persons involved and can be trusted to provide interpretations of benefit to the individual and collective good.

Elders and shamans acquire their interpretive knowledge from having heard others transform dreams. Most of these people grow up in households wherein one or both parents often tell and interpret dreams.[10] We may view this collective knowledge as pragmatic to dream interpretation in the sense that it is cultivated and more heavily worked through compared to persons unwilling or unable to commit their thought and selfhood to public review.

NILUTWO'S DREAM SHARING

Nilutwo was a troubled, gifted, and often difficult married man in his thirties. He had been a prolific dreamer since his teens and his success at cassowary hunting was unmatched by anyone. Yet many saw him as a misfit: he was not a shaman and had no other special skills or status; women regarded him as a 'rubbish man'; he had had several bouts of 'crazy' episodes in his adolescence; he finally had to abduct a woman for his wife; and he was constantly getting into trouble over adultery attempts and squabbles with clan brothers.

Let me interject here a note about my relationship to Nilutwo, for otherwise his dream reports are less useful and psychologically unfocussed regarding me, our talking, and the communications I made that led him to trust in and talk to me. In 1974 I arrived in the village as if a freak intruder from another world. I was white, young, rich (for instance, had tennis shoes), and took up residence where no European ever had. He could never understand why I was so different from the white plantation owners or government officers who wanted only his labor or taxes. I paid him little attention at first; he seemed ingratiating and a little too intent on impressing me that he was whiteman-sophisticated and wealthy (for example, in having a radio). He was friendly, though, and sometimes helped me as a translator, in which job he proved to be miserable. Even Tali, my ritual expert and his friend, finally insisted we find someone else. But then, as Nilutwo was feeling dejected, I began to notice that he often talked about his dreams, and I discovered why: his cassowary hunting. So I asked him to teach me about hunting, and in a few hours he was sharing dreams. Thereafter, I invited him to sit with me alone, gave him some tobacco and tea, and he would just talk and talk dreams.

That is how it went for nearly two years. He would enter my house and, in private, relate his dreams. He was never so comfortable with me alone as when sharing his dreams. I would ask him an open-ended question or two and he would be off into his dream world. I gave him some trade goods and money on a regular basis: I think he was amazed at first that anyone would 'pay' him to do what thrilled him.[11] We need not doubt that this procedure influenced his dream sharing and reinforced him to do better what he had been doing for years. Nonetheless, he continued hunting and sharing dreams with others. Between 1974 and 1976, I spent some 200 hours working with Nilutwo in private on his dreams. I also saw him interacting in public in many social situations over the years. In 1979 we spent another fifty hours over the course of a few months. Later in 1979, following a tragic accident in which he fell from a tree while gardening, Nilutwo died.

Nilutwo was sensitive, tempestuous, often angry, demanding, greedy, jealous of how I shared myself with others, and suspicious. More than with others I tried to be supportive, available, and caring. This posture was not merely altruistic; for months I feared offending him, causing him to storm out never to return. This subjectivity should be seen as my subliminal awareness that Nilutwo was fragile and not as able as others to cope with my more normally demanding posture. Nilutwo needed me, for he was a loner: he often looked out at me from small, dark eyes that showed uncertainty and loneliness; he referred to himself as *wampus* – Pidgin for 'loner' and 'only child'; he feared he would go crazy; feared his wife would run away or be 'stolen' by another man; feared others did not like or respect him; and feared I would abandon him. My own concern that he would leave was in part a response to his anxieties, but I saw him until the end. When at times I had to do something else and did not 'pay' him, he would still tell me his dreams; and over the years Nilutwo showed a need to share his dreams and related feelings with me, alone, because he *was* 'alone,' that is, there was no one else with whom he could directly discuss certain conflicts.[12]

What is the developmental basis of Nilutwo's dream sharing? Nilutwo had extraordinarily vivid and rich memories of his childhood, including dreams recalled from thirty years before (cf. Kracke 1980:257). His mother shared dreams with him and encouraged him to go cassowary hunting, which included her providing interpretations of some of his childhood dreams pursuant to cassowary lore.[13] His biological father frequently reported dreams, and his shaman stepfather was a prominent dream reporter and interpreter. For some years after initiation until puberty he had few dreams save the vague nightmares many initiates report of evil dark figures who chase and try to kill them. After third-stage initiation, Nilutwo fought in several important battles and had scars to prove it; he began hunting cassowary concurrently with having heterosexual wet dreams. In short, the re-emergence of his dreaming came at entry into adult manhood.

Let me now skip a few years to the period when I knew him as a husband and father. Nilutwo was a prolific dreamer, by which I mean that he had one or more dreams virtually every night; if he napped during the day he would often dream; his dream reports were often long and complex, and his associations afterwards were frequently as lengthy as his dream report. Sometimes, he would drift in his dream reports by referring to experiences that came to him as he shared a dream. When I asked him to associate ('What did you feel then?', 'What do you think about that?', 'Has that ever really happened?', 'What does that mean?') he would say additional things omitted the first time round. His dream talk had, for me, a familiar contour that seemed plausible and coherent, even when the images or sensations were fantastic. Nilutwo was a chain-smoker and he often smoked when we talked. When he shared dreams, I felt he was transfixed into another realm, wherein he allowed himself to re-experience things that had happened to him in sleep the night before; I was merely present with him in the daylight, hearing his voice and seeing his face and body express what he was reliving. He did not merely report these experiences as intellectualized memories, for his voice would spontaneously speed up or quiet down, he would shudder, grimace, contort, reveal fear or disgust (mechanical spitting would follow), smile – whatever; nor was he 'putting on a show,' for I have seen him do emotive performances in public, and those theatrics almost never crept into his private dream reporting. His dream sharing was, in a word, unself-conscious; he permitted me access to his private self, not just his personhood. After a time, I felt that Nilutwo was often 'slipping frames' between his dream experiences and the feelings they generated while sharing them, without realizing it, and the longer we talked, the more I felt myself become part of his total dream experience.

Nilutwo had typical dreams. He also had idiosyncratic dreams that no one I knew ever shared with me.[14] But, as time passed, his dream sharing behavior changed in this regard. He then no longer stressed the typicality of his dreams. For example, he had no reluctance in sharing shame-filled wet dreams and, in 1975 and 1976, these were frequent.[15] We also discussed his life story. Later (especially in 1979) he began sharing erotic daydreams, personal scripts that got him into trouble.[16] Meanwhile I was studying other people's dreams. The cumulative effect of all this work was my growing awareness that Nilutwo's dreams were peculiar to himself in certain ways and – while he never explained it to me this way – I realized he was having dreams he never shared with anyone but me. Let us explore this point.

Here is a short typical dream from Nilutwo in mid 1975:[17]

I climb up a pandanus tree – I think it has food [nuts]. There is a bog below. I cut the nuts and they fall to the water. The bog rises . . . I am scared . . . then I look at my hands and they turn into bird wings. I fly into the air and land atop a tree. I see the bog and it subsides to its place. I awake with a start. I think to myself, 'Why did I have a bad dream?'

Nilutwo had no associations. This dream could be shared with others in public. Most of his dreams are much longer and more complex, and I have described two of them – one private, one public – elsewhere (Herdt 1981:342–7). I will draw on some other abridged examples:

(1) Dreams and day residue

I am in the nearby bush. I make a square hut [untraditional]. It was raining and a bog started to form. The water turned red. G.'s younger wife is there.[18] She won't help me dig a trench to get rid of the water . . . 'I have a baby: I can't help you,' she says. I was furious, hit her, broke her nose; blood poured out. Then I saw Imano's [younger clan brother] wife. She says, 'I have no children: I'll help you.' We dug the trench. The red water spilled out. I said to the first woman: 'You're no good; I hope the water carries you away.' She cried. The other woman was okay; she had big full breasts. I woke up.

Associations N.: 'Why did I dream about those women? Why did I hit my sister-in-law? I feel sorry . . . Last night I was near G.'s hut. His older wife [not the one above] screamed at G.: "You've used all our firewood! When I was young you used to screw me all the time. Now I'm older and you're not interested, you let me do all the work." I told G. he was a bad husband: "Now she's old and you don't care for her." That dream was bad. I feel sorry for the older woman. Why did I hit the other one? Well . . . they're both stingy, those women. They don't share food.'

Comments What Nilutwo does not say is that he has tried to butter-up both of his elder brother's wives, but they have rejected his adulterous advances, and that he fights constantly with G. Here we can see Nilutwo moving in and out of the dream experience in relation to the real fight the night before. He seems to have displaced anger towards G. onto G.'s younger wife, whom Nilutwo desired. He could have made this dream public, but I do not think he did.

(2) *Dreams as omens*

I see Y [another clan brother]. He is setting an eel trap in the river. The river is flooded. We see a tidal wave coming but there is no bridge. G. comes. He says, 'Since you angered me – I dammed the water and released it to mess up your trap.' We argue. Me and Y. want to fight him. We try to push him off the bridge but miss. We run off to another place and see T.[19] We tell her what G. did. She says, 'Why did you fight with your brother?' We told her he almost killed us. I woke up.

Associations N.: 'Yesterday, G. and Y. were arguing over a taro garden patch. Two other men kept them from fighting. When you argue like that, taro won't grow . . . I think G. is trying to get my wife. He keeps saying his old wife is used up and no longer exciting. Wait, tomorrow I'll really scold him. Is he the only one with a penis? [Nilutwo then refers to a ritual law forbidding adultery.] He's not going to get my wife.'

Comment Nilutwo told this dream to several of his cronies. The next day, Nilutwo did confront G., but he did not mention this dream.

(3) *Complex interpretations*

I am at a small hut. I say to Y., 'Let's go check my [cassowary] traps.' We go and find a trapped tree kangaroo. Its tail is red-furred; its face is multicolored, the nose yellow. Kwam and Kwol [stepbrother and his father, Nilutwo's classificatory father] come and tell us they've caught another possum. We compare their coloration . . . Then I see boys trapping birds near a tree in bloom. They cut a nearby pandanus; its leaves are all yellow: 'It wants to bear offspring [nuts],' I thought. We see a bog nearby . . . so we set traps. Then they take a bull-roarer and twirl it but it doesn't cry! I say, 'You're just boys – let me, it'll really sing.' I was awakened by my dog.

Comments G.H.: 'What does it mean?' N.: 'When pandanus is yellow like that it means a woman will die. That's like women's things. The red-tailed kangaroo predicted that Y. and Kwol would fight this morning, as they did. [The two men squabbled that morning. In the period of this dream they often argued because Y. wanted to marry a woman betrothed to Kwol's son, who was then away on the coast.] If we'd cooked the possum, Y. would have beaten Kwol, but we didn't. The [yellow] markings on the other [possum face] mean that if a man goes up a tree, he could fall down. Or some child may die.'

(4) *Dreams edited for the public*

In the following examples we have dreams that can be referred to public discourse and interpreted contextually and intratextually (see Tedlock 1981). Here is a typical 'cassowary' dream. Nilutwo set a trap and that night he had this dream:

I am in our village. A Wantukiu [neighboring tribe] woman comes. She didn't have a real grass skirt, only an apron made of tree skin. Her thighs were completely exposed. She says, 'Look at me.' She smiled and buttered me up. 'Let's do it, there's no one around.' Her vagina was hot, I put my penis inside and instantly ejaculated. I woke up.

Associations N.: 'I hid the sperm, I didn't want my wife to see it or I'd have been shamed. Why do I spend my water like that? My wife doesn't know I have wet dreams. You [Nilutwo] won't tell women . . . I'm going to check my traps: I may have a big one [cassowary].'

Comments Later that day, Nilutwo shared this dream in public, but he omitted that he copulated with the woman or ejaculated. Why? N. told me: 'You [Nilutwo] can't tell this to others, it's shameful. Then men would know I'm thinking about screwing and stealing their women' (see Herdt 1981, ch. 5).

(5) *Forbidden dreams*

I see a woman from Kwoli hamlet. She had on nice decorations . . . she was at the menstrual hut. She went inside. I started to follow but another man said, 'You can't go in there!' 'I'm no child. I'm a man,' I said. I went in, sat down and tickled her back. She asked me, 'What do you want?' 'I want some tobacco' . . . we laughed and smoked. We played around, my cock was tight. But just as we were going to screw, a boy [uninitiated] came by. 'What are you two doing?' 'We are playing,' I said. But I felt shame and woke up.

Associations N.: 'I was angry that I didn't screw her. If I had made a cassowary trap, I'd go and check it – I'm sure I'd have one.'

Comments Nilutwo did not tell this dream to anyone else. He felt uneasy telling me. He has had similar dreams before, many of them involving much older, even aged, women. This dream concerns a forbidden idea: men can never approach menstrual huts, let alone enter them. He had no other associations or interpretations. Some time later, I asked two other men if they had ever had dreams about menstrual huts. Both said no; that it was taboo to go near menstruating women or menstrual huts. They dismissed the idea of such dreams as preposterous. They said they had never had such dreams and they denied that other men would ever see such dream-things.

May we say, in this last example, that Nilutwo's forbidden desires could never be expressed anywhere, to anyone, except in the nihilism of a strange ethnographer's private quarters? Yes, and other examples could be adduced to make the same point. Nilutwo shows us through his dream sharing that he 'knows'[20] there are great differences between public, secret, and private dreams; and some dream experiences are so private (forbidden) that they cannot be shared with anyone. Except me. The psychodynamics and symbolism of these few dreams are complex and I shall not attempt to tackle them here, for that would digress from my main concern with dream sharing. Instead, I wish to understand and interpret the relation between Nilutwo's personhood and self in these secret dreams, so I will now return to my initial problems.

THE SELF IN NILUTWO'S DREAM SHARING

Nilutwo was born into a society in which the conflictual effects of war were all around: death, illness, and sexual polarity were no strangers to him. There were good things in his life too. Yet what come through in his dreams are conflict, trauma, danger, and death. His life experience reflected this divisiveness in myriad ways, which we see reflected and disguised in his dream reports. Nilutwo could not choose not to dream; he had to adjust to constant dreaming. But he could choose what dream-things to report, to whom, where and when. And he *had* awareness that he was making choices. More precisely: sociocultural constraints broadly set the 'room for maneuver' he had in sharing dreams, but his desires predetermined how and why he maneuvered between the dreams and reality of his life.

In Nilutwo's case we see vividly the subtle and transparent links between his desires and the alternative discourses for expressing them. Dream theory dictated that his soul experienced the dream world. He publicly reported dreams that seemed indexed to typical dreams, or related to interpretations he knew or could foresee that 'placed' his dream experience safely in the domain of normative thought. He was not responsible for those dream-things, only accountable for reporting them, as we see in dreams (4) and (5) above. His personhood was vouchsafed by that dream sharing, which also consoled him, the 'him' being here what he actually did and said in public dream sharing.

Nilutwo's private dreams are another matter. They reveal the discrepancies between atypical wishes and social norms. Those dreams he kept to himself. He hid dreams in three ways. First, by acting on his dream interpretation in real relationships without letting other persons know the dream stimulus of his social action; second, by telling only part and hiding the other part of dreams; and third, by not acting upon or telling a dream at all, except to me. All these dreams were still interjected into his awareness; it's just that, by keeping them private (or secretly confined to me), he kept them removed from the center of his social life. Nilutwo was troublesome and he and everyone else knew it.

Dream (4) illustrates this. Sometimes his impulses got the better of him and he acted them out (for example, through his adultery attempts). But he was no fool and, indeed, his keen intellect had brought him through many disasters and perhaps thwarted many more. He knew he had dangerous desires. His dream sharing reveals that. Was he merely being selfish by not reporting all? No, I think the situation is more complex than that. Some of his wishes and daydreams were expressed in his nightdreams. Remembering that experience on waking was an initial danger, he saw something forbidden inside. Once the dream occurred, however, his desire had already been acted out in the dream world; and that extra feeling of realness was enough to further motivate him and bridge into reality his reluctance to go against norms. To put that dream experience into words moves it a step closer to being acted on in reality. In other words, if you do something in dreams you *can* really do it; and if you then share it, it is very close to being done. Hiding dreams – as in dream (5) – is a form of impulse control and impression management, at least in Nilutwo.

This outsider view calls into question Sambia dream theory in several ways. Thought is indexed to social norms as expressed by persons in public life. The soul's experiences of dream-things can oppose thought, removed from the shackles of normative personhood and social action. Thus, thought is the *rapporter* for the soul, but it does not report all. But thought seems closer to soul in Nilutwo's experience, and I would note that he had a different notion from others about thought and soul. Nilutwo told me in 1975 that thought was just another kind of 'spirit,' albeit different from the soul. At the time I thought this idea was confused, and I ignored it as his confusion. In 1979 I saw differently; for himself, he was of course right on the mark. Nilutwo's soul experienced in dreams what most men in waking life cannot accept, think, and act upon; what is more, he remembered these experiences. For Nilutwo, then, there was less distance between his public thought and his soul. The soul is here represented, in our terms, as a metaphor for the unconscious. It so happens, for whatever reasons, that conscious and unconscious were more fully available to Nilutwo all the time, awake and dreaming. So his self hid other dreams that did not conform to the thought of his personhood. By providing a situation in which Nilutwo could talk about forbidden things, I created a special kind of private discourse previously unavailable to him and others. I allowed him to say the unsayable. He never really moved to the next point of understanding; seeing dream theory as a very sophisticated defense against parts of his reality and forbidden desires enabling him to discover his mistrust of himself. It was just as well, for I was not prepared to protect him against that insight.[21]

It now seems clear that Nilutwo's constant dreaming was both a social sign that he was a misfit and a personal symptom of his more than normal intrapsychic and social conflict. People saw his chronic dreaming as both amazing and odd. They valued it because they believed it brought them cassowaries, and they were right. Nilutwo used to get angry with his private self and soul about dreaming because he could not get a night's peace. 'Why won't my soul rest sometimes?' He was not a misfit because he had dreams. Rather, his aberrance was reflected in constant dreams, which caused him to have to choose whether to make them public or not. That turmoil created other problems. Nonetheless, he could not surrender the desires that brought him pleasure, and so much unhappiness.

CONCLUSIONS

Dream studies like this one suggest that to understand the culture and experience of dreams we need to know not just what people dream about, but how and what parts of their dreams they share. And we need to know better not just people's interpretations or dream codes, but the modes of discourse through which dreams are interpreted and why. Accepting this view plunges us into the fundamental problems of psychoanalysis, hermeneutics, and other disciplines that study meaning in humans.

Let me summarize my findings. Sambia dream and often share their dreams. Their dream theory interprets dreams as events that happen to the soul in sleep. They can share these experiences in either public, secret, or private situations, each of which has a characteristic narrative pertaining to it. They express dream events through their 'thought,' the person's norms that filter conscious memories, feelings, and ideas experienced in dreams. Dream reporting is thus constrained by many factors including personhood, social roles and situations, dream theory, types of talking, and, of course, self-experience. I have argued that thought, which relays dreams in public and secret talk, is indexed to social norms and typical dream interpretations. Private dream sharing is less restricted by these social norms, and it may communicate idiosyncratic, asocial, or even antisocial dream events and associations. But since cultural dream theory purports that one is not responsible for one's soul's experience, an interpretive puzzle emerges: Why are some dreams kept private and others never shared?

My solution depends on the general principle that Sambia tacitly perceive all speech acts as expressing desires. Thought is essentially treated as a metaphor for personhood, with its jural and moral trappings. Therefore, the expression or confession of bad dreams pertaining to real social conflict does not violate this pattern, since Sambia tacitly recognize that by making them public one is still operating in the status quo system that attempts to remedy societal conflicts. Herein lies the pragmatic significance of the difference between responsibility and accountability. The person is not responsible for his soul's experiences but is accountable for everything he says. Referring a dream to private discourse means that Sambia cannot or will not be publicly accountable for sharing that experience elsewhere. It means, in other words, that private or hidden dreams may contain desires that are dangerous, forbidden, selfish, or antisocial (see Foster 1973). If we split up someone's experience, we may say that thought has two parts – public and private self – that are signified by their desires expressed in speech.

It seems 'self-evident'[22] that Sambia use their concept 'soul' in the way we use 'unconscious.' Their constructions make this view persuasive and parsimonious. As metaphors, thought is to normative consciousness as soul is to idiosyncratic unconsciousness in Sambia discourse. Ambivalent attributions about the development and sex of the soul speak to this issue.[23] The soul is an available concept of personhood – an individual and collective representation – on to which are projected asocial dream thoughts, words, and acts, in public, secret, or private. The self, the 'I/me' in private dream sharing, is closer to soul, and knows it. When Nilutwo said to me, 'I went inside the menstrual hut,' he knew (somewhere inside himself) that his soul had done what he, his private self, desired. That is why he kept the dream secret. Still, it is not that the soul does in dreams whatever the self bids, or vice versa; that is too simple. (What about nightmares?) Rather, what is problematic for Sambia is that dreams *are* so available to them; dreams reveal unconscious desires and fears; and while persons desire to relieve their private 'heaviness' on the one hand, they must not see or let others see what these dream-things disguise, on the other hand. This dilemma poses a delicate problem.

We might say more properly that it is a dilemma entangled in the social divisions and polarized discourse of Sambia society. These divisions were noted above: war, sexual antagonism, familial conflict, and discontinuities in the psychocultural development of personhood and selfhood. The institutionalization of disparate discourses enwraps and maintains these divisions, which constrain dream sharing by providing boundaries for normative and aberrant parts of experience. Yet, the dilemma of what to do with forbidden desires in dreams remains. As Marie Reay (1962:460) put it, when 'tension is so pervasive a quality' of social relationships, 'an extroverted people who are aware of an unresolved ambivalence in their relationships have some expectation, no matter how naively they formulate it, that such inner tensions abound.' By providing a standard dream theory and interpretational system, Sambia have attempted symbolically to handle their developmental and societal conflict registered in dreams. By institutionalizing alternate narrative contexts and disparate discourses, society provides metaframes for pragmatically compartmentalizing inner tensions. The polarity between personhood and private self has thus made 'necessary the production of symbolic solutions' (Paul 1980:289) via the ideology of dreams and the soul, and the forms dream sharing takes. Taken together, then, all forms of dream sharing provide Sambia with a special system of internal discourse for commenting on selfhood and society which we Westerners lack.

With this perspective we may return to the final two questions raised above: Do Sambia really have the same dreams? Do they have one or several codes for interpreting their dreams? Sambia genuinely believe that others have had some of the same dreams. Sharing this belief is an important sign of their sense of community. It is a metacommunication that they have shared many life experiences, persons, and places. Sharing a dream theory and typical interpretations of public dreams supports their view. Moreover, they do not test each other's dream experience to verify whether the images, sensations, and ideas felt in each other's dreams are the same. Instead, Sambia assume that when someone shares a dream in which such-and-such images and actions seem to occur, that dream equates to ones they have had. Their interpretive system thus unites people's dreams on the levels of iconic imagination (bogs, trees, fires, women) and metaphoric meaning (women are hamlet spirits; you'll catch a cassowary). Because these narrative equivalences seem to link thought and soul, conscious and unconscious, listeners assume an isomorphism between all levels of experience. Ultimately, though, these assumptions depend upon the cultural principle of dream sharing that moves inside experience outside, and language, which converts self-experience into verbal, conventionalized representations.

And what of private and hidden dreams? Here the Sambia have not so much fooled themselves as ignored what they do not want to know. My guess is that most Sambia have had some forbidden dreams, though perhaps they are soon repressed. True, Nilutwo was deviant, yet in his disturbances we see a striking form of what is perhaps widespread but more quiet in others: hidden thought and forbidden desires revealed through dreams. Up to a point, shamans or others like Nilutwo are rewarded for novelty and creative images including omens, new songs, names, cassowary catches, ritual innovations, and material gains thought to derive from dreams. Yet because dreams bridge past and present, there are from one's past certain things that have no place in adult life and, indeed, threaten to undermine it. Thus, in allowing this special channel of communication from the unconscious (however much screened), private and secret narratives developed to keep threatening, asocial dreams from public life, for they would, ultimately, disrupt the social order. They remain hidden; and so, Sambia can rightly believe others have the same typical dreams since the untypical ones rarely reach the public. Normative thought keeps them hidden.

Is there a unified code of interpretation? This question speaks to the same issues above, but at different levels. We have seen that there are situational determinants of dream sharing. These affect dream interpreting. It is not just that dreams are interpreted contextually, that is, the performative stylizations applied to healing ceremonies are different than those relevant to secret rituals. For what is the goal of a particular dream talk? In general, aside from its other functions, dream sharing can be done for entertainment, the texts of which provide amusement and relief from daily tensions (Freud 1908); thus, the catharsis of dream sharing. But catharsis can only be accepted when it has positive consequences for the group. In other words, the standardized dream theory and interpretations provide a 'cognitive binding of tension rather than its immediate release in acting out' (LeVine 1982:141), keeping self in line with personhood.

Next are the divergent modes of discourse that permit pragmatic choices for disclosure. Since there are secret typical dream interpretations, one could argue that the secret versus public modes are divergent dream codes. Typical secret dreams are rare; more common are ritual images that are mixed in with non-ritual images in men's dream sharing. Here, we must distinguish between the private interpretations of a dream reporter and the public messages sent to his audience. Because of public metaphors for secret ritual symbols, it is easy for men to make communications that disguise their 'true' meanings vis-à-vis women and the uninitiated. In this sense, then, shared euphemisms and double entendres are public signs for a secret code of dream messages in public discourse (Barth 1975; Schwimmer 1980). Finally, there is language. Perhaps at the syntactical and semantic levels one can argue that in spite of cross-situational differences, a secret ritual code, and personal intentionality, language still provides for a unified meta-code of interpretation among all Sambia. If a woman stands as a symbol of a female hamlet spirit, and spirits are both signified and verbalized, belief in the female spirit becomes the spoken spirit that becomes the dreamed woman (Ricoeur 1970:500–1). This signification can be inferred among men in waking life: a trapped cassowary is referred to as a 'woman who has hanged herself'; and women, cassowaries, and hamlet spirits are interchangeable signs in men's ritual discourse. Whether these interlinkages apply also to women and children remains to be seen. This semiotic system would come full circle if it could be shown that when men refer to hamlet spirits in dream reports they are imagining women.

I have suggested that in order to understand Sambia dream sharing in its full range of discourse we need a multidimensional model of awareness: conscious, preconscious, unconscious. But Freud's classic theory is inadequate for the task. To argue that the Sambia notion of soul is used as a sign of unconscious motives or their behavioral outcomes in speech is not to argue that this is *The* Unconscious which Freud reduced to mechanic drives expressed in the dream-work.[24] For the culture and experience of Freud and his patients lack the reality dimensions of Sambia dream sharing. Dreams are normal communications for Sambia; the significata of dreams are more homogeneous; and their dream theory provides Sambia with a fantastic stage – the supernatural dream world – on which to play out and project their conscious and unconscious desires in public and private. This symbolic reality thus allows Sambia to talk about unconscious motives all the time while defended by a sophisticated theory that keeps them from realizing it. Misfits like Nilutwo remind us of the dilemmas such a world creates, for people can still not share all private experience. But the point is that the Sambia unconscious is more public and natural than Freud's; I cannot imagine that symbolic reality does not shape their experience when they are alone in their dreams.

Had Freud known of such alternative dream systems he might have constructed his own dream theory differently. As in many other areas of behavior, symbolic and pragmatic, Freud (1916–17:132) saw that dream discourse revealed 'a far-reaching distortion and for that reason cannot be judged at first glance.' One had to distinguish between latent and manifest content correlated with primary- and secondary-thought processes. It is no accident that the exceptions to this principle, children's dreams, poetry, and certain folktales, reveal the latent and manifest meanings to coincide without distortion.[25] In the case of children's dreams, Freud believed that children were naive, had less to hide, and made no division between 'play' and 'reality.' Distortion in adults was necessary to screen out painful memories, impulses, or wishes that opposed the reality of adult social norms. Here, we see that Freud's view parallels that of Sambia public dream sharing. Unfortunately, Freud never understood that the symbolic basis of dream-work lay in culture, transformed into language for dream reports (Ricoeur 1970:500–51). And in this context we can add that shared dreams, like myths and religious practices, are expressed through shared symbolic structures, not merely private fantasies (Herdt 1981:267ff.; Kracke 1979c), a general principle that Freud, like Róheim, never fully grasped.

I do not think that anthropological studies of complex mental phenomena like dreams can do without a concept of the unconscious. Or without models of mind. Such theory-building is still at an early stage. In dream research, moreover, it seems that we should avoid too much reliance on neat logical/linear models of experience, seek both normative and aberrant forms of dream experience and interpretation, and encourage studies of cross-cultural comparison (Shweder and LeVine 1975). I am particularly leery of studies that heavily depend on the Freudian distinction manifest/latent content – which generally ignore the symbolic reality of culture and its effects on dream-work; which see dreams as inappropriate special communications; which assume the interrogator's role in getting confessions through dream discourse (Foucault 1980); and which uncritically postulate an opposition between 'work' and 'play.' For, at the very least, manifest content must include dream sharing, dream reports, dream interpretations, the cultural code for interpreting, and the relationship between all the frames of discourse at all levels of awareness. What then is *not* manifest content? The latent patterns of unconscious desires, as judged by the psychoanalyst. But as Rycroft (1977) has shown, this latent content is so diffuse that it, too, is ultimately drawn from culture. Better that we return to describing what people actually do, say, and think in relation to their dreams, and interpret in context what seems public, hidden, or unconscious (Tuzin 1975).

Perhaps we need to look again seriously at these seemingly 'childish' dream theories of tribal peoples. They present their own alternative metapsychologies of human existence. Many use dream sharing of sorts that are subtle and deceptively transparent at the same time; they are challenging to study from the native's point of view. But, until we do that, we will not take seriously the propositions that culture may actually change experience inside of dreams, or that the productions of dreaming do actually become absorbed and transformed into culture.

NOTES

1. I gratefully acknowledge support from the following institutions for fieldwork among Sambia (1974–6, 1979, 1981): the Australian National University; the Australian-American Education Foundation; the National Institute of Mental Health; the Department of Psychiatry at U.C.L.A.; the Wenner-Gren Foundation; and the Stanford Center for Youth Development. I also wish to thank the Anne P. Lederer Research Institute for funds that supported the writing of this chapter. Many thanks to Barbara Tedlock for her incisive comments and editing, and to Renato Rosaldo for his valuable insights on an earlier draft of the chapter.
2. In 1979 I clinically used with several persons the technique of active imagination learnt at U.C.L.A.'s Neuropsychiatric Institute. My aim with Sambia was to supplement nightdream reports with other fantasy materials in areas in which persons had conscious blocks. However, I never used this technique with Nilutwo.
3. *Koontu* and *koogu* are different words constructed from the same root prefix morpheme, *koo*, which generally marks male gender. Their linguistic closeness probably attests to the closeness of their significata.

4. *Aambelu-koongundu*, 'stories about women,' *pweiyu koongundu*, 'ritual teachings'; myths are closest to dreams as narrative traditions (Herdt 1981:267–9).
5. Both these phases involve secondary revision in Freud's (1900:526–46) sense, though the 'shreds and patches' (ibid.: 528) that fill in the gaps of a dream report are more appropriately indexed to the discourse of a report in the intersubjective sense.
6. These traditional idioms refer to physical sensations and images: the liver (*kalu*), not the heart, is felt to be the center of the body, wherein powerful emotions are felt in dreams; ghosts or spirits are seen to eat animal flesh, which is metaphorically interpreted as human flesh – namely, someone's liver – so divination reveals that a sick person's soul has been stolen or liver speared or eaten by spirits. Attacks on persons (souls) result in liver ailments, since the soul and liver are implictly linked (M. Strathern 1968).
7. In Freud's (1900:274–310, and passim) sense. See Schieffelin 1977; Stephen 1982; Wagner 1967, for Melanesian examples.
8. It seems that we have not fully described the range of stereotypical or cultural standardization of dream sharing in this respect (DuBois 1944:192; and see Eggan's 1961:565–6 discussion). Some dreams are more 'manifest' than others, and some dream sharing has been subjected to such reinterpretation that only stylized, not idiosyncratic elements, remain. A strong case could be made that certain Sambia folktales are typical dreams that have become crystallized into cultural narratives.
9. This is in line with Malinowski's functionalist view of magical rites (see Homans's 1941 review). This view of dream interpretation has not been particularly stressed in the literature, but it seems to accord with the Melanesian ethnography.
10. Because shamans can easily induce mild trance states in themselves by smoking, children of shamans will frequently have seen their parents in trance states, in both healing ceremonies and in domestic life. Thus, dream interpretation is for them bound up with altered states of consciousness. Shamans use hallucinogens in ritual initiation ceremonies only, wherein dream interpretations are also made.
11. My circumstances in the field made it desirable and necessary to remunerate informants for time they would have spent doing other things. In Nilutwo's case this payment (especially money) was very important in our relationship in many ways. However, I am convinced that he did not make up stories or invent dreams merely for payment; that he was not merely a confessor nor I his indelible interrogator (Foucault 1980); and in the end

I don't think the money mattered very much (see Herdt and Stoller n.d. for a fuller discussion).

12. Nilutwo's transference to me – the aspects of the process whereby he displaced feelings and ideas from previous figures in his life on to me, or projected on to me previous object-representations and significance from caretakers – should be described here, especially in relation to his dreams, but I fear that a partial explication would be more harmful than none. So, I shall leave it that he did transfer to me; I think our talking helped him; and by 1979 he had grown more comfortable with me because he had expressed some conflicts through our talking.
13. Who knows (certainly not Nilutwo) from what sources those interpretations were drawn? But we see here the difficulty and foolishness of rigidly distinguishing between public/secret/private discourse in that most intimate of all Sambia relationships, the tie to one's mother.
14. Though I collected dreams from several other men and women over a long period of time, and casually collected dreams from many others, I would not claim that no other Sambian has had such dreams, only that I think these in Nilutwo are rare.
15. Men commonly have wet dreams like this during post-partum periods of sexual taboo with wives. During this period, Nilutwo's wife was nursing their baby and they could not have sex.
16. Nilutwo had florid daydreams about copulating with several women, some of which he acted out in pseudorape/adultery attempts that failed. These outrages led to fights, litigation, and so much pressure that eventually he was alienated from virtually all of his own clansmen. Many women despised him. But, curiously, his wife (who is an honorable person) stuck with him until the end.
17. These dream reports are extremely abridged from the original.
18. G. is Nilutwo's elder clan brother and closest friend.
19. T. is G.'s aged mother and a maternal substitute for Nilutwo.
20. A complex knowing, not fully conscious or subliminal, metaphorical or unconscious; more a knowing by what he says and doesn't say, and doesn't dare reflect upon.
21. I see now that Nilutwo's transference flowered under the influence of a naive listener-interrogator-researcher, unwitting quasi-therapist in ways that created anxiety in me and with which I did not consciously deal. My asking Nilutwo to do culturally standardized interpretations of his dreams – indexed to the question 'What does that mean?' – was a definite defense for both Nilutwo and me; see Herdt and Stoller (1983).
22. 'To be "self-evident," a proposition or premise must be out of

reach and unexaminable: it must have defenses or roots at unconscious levels. Similarly, to be "self-evident," a proposition or premise must be either self-validating or so general as to be but rarely contradicted by experience' (Bateson 1980:58). The term 'unconscious' as used here is not The Unconscious of Freudian theory.

23. In public discourse men allow that the soul originates in the womb; in ritual discourse they stress the 'masculine' character of their souls, indexed to certain ritual practices like drinking tree sap; and in private talk the soul seems sexless and genderless. I think these views hedge on the tacit feeling that the soul is sentimentally bonded to the mother: the child's heart (in our Western sense of emotional investment) first belongs to its mother, whence came its 'soul.'
24. In the early Freud, such a model would see the Sambian concept of soul as id, thought as ego, and standardized dream interpretation (like spirits) as super-ego.
25. On children's dreams: 'Here the manifest and the latent dream coincide. *Thus dream-distortion is not part of the essential nature of dreams*' (Freud 1916–17:128). On poets: 'The writer softens the egoistical character of the daydream by changes and disguises, and he bribes us by the offer of a purely formal, that is, aesthetic pleasure in the presentation of his phantasies' (Freud 1908:43). In Freud's (1913b) view, adults made favored fairy-tales into screen memories. But in Bettelheim's (1977:7) treatment of children's experience, fairy-tales allow the direct expression of daydreams and fantasizing 'in response to unconscious pressures.'

4
The implications of a progressive theory of dreaming

ELLEN B. BASSO

In a strikingly large and disparate group of societies the experience of dreaming is held to have a close, even determinant, connection with the future life of the dreamer. In marked contrast to Western psychoanalysis, but very much in keeping with pre-rationalist dream theories, dreaming is interpreted by using the contemporary experiences of the dreamer to construct a vision of some aspect of the dreamer's future life. These theories of dreaming hold in common with psychoanalysis the notion that dreaming is an experience which cannot be understood literally, that dreams contain disguised meanings requiring interpretation.

Freud (1900) described the process of dream construction as 'regressive,' involving a return to the sensory images of the unconscious. His psychoanalytic theory suggests that dream symbols should be interpreted by looking to the dreamer's past. Jung (1948) followed Freud in interpreting the symbols of a dream through what is known of the dreamer's past, but he held the dream to be a 'spontaneous self-portrayal, in symbolic form, of the actual situation in the unconscious' (ibid.:263). Thus, there are many ideas about dreaming that are perhaps closer to Jung's notion concerning the prospective function or purpose, which is to teach the dreamer to understand certain aspects of the self so as to find the right solution to a mental problem. For Jung, the prospective function of dreams 'is an anticipation in the unconscious of future conscious achievements, something like a preliminary exercise or sketch, or a plan roughed out in advance. Its symbolic content sometimes outlines the solution of a conflict' (ibid.:255).

In addition, the attitudes towards dreams in these societies and the processes of interpretation by means of which their 'hidden meanings' are revealed to the dreamer certainly support Jung's suggestion that dreams have the ability to alter or influence the conscious mental life of the dreamer, and thus have a 'continuity forwards.' Hence, while the regressive theory of dreaming adopted by psychoanalysis emphasizes adaptation to past experiences, a progressive view of dreaming, such as that of analytic psychology, suggests the salience of anxiety about the future for determining dream imagery.

Anthropological and psychoanalytic discussions of dreaming seem inevitably to come to rest on the problems of how self-identity is constructed, the nature of biologically conditioned universals of human existence, and the very meaning – to the dreamer and within a social context – of life and death. It is therefore all too easy to rely upon the ready vocabulary of psychoanalysis and of theology for a translation, or interpretation, of a people's dreaming theory. Yet the result of this common anthropological practice is that the contrasts between the dream theories of most Western analysts and the progressive theories of non-Western peoples have been obscured simply by virtue of how native terms are glossed. What is missed is information concerning just how a dreamer's experience and a dreamer's future are connected in such native theories, and it is consequently difficult to understand from many putatively ethnographic accounts just what the ontological implications of such theories might be. Yet, the idea that dreaming involves future (not past, not current) experiences of the dreamer (though the images may have connections with the dreamer's distant or recent past experiences) is of considerable interest to us. This is not just because it is common outside the Western rationalist tradition, but for what it can suggest to us about some fundamental problems concerning culture and the individual: How is the human developmental process imagined? Why and under what circumstances is anxiety about the future created? What are the connections between these matters and reflection upon the self as it occurs in particular settings? How is consciousness itself understood? These questions, of course, can be best addressed by placing them in a particular cultural context. While it is impossible to clarify fully the problems they raise in such a short chapter, they serve me here as a framework for examining the implications of a particular Amazonian theory of dreaming.

KALAPALO DREAMING

The Kalapalo Indians of central Brazil, a Carib-speaking community of fewer than 200 people, are a people whose dreaming is interpreted quite clearly with reference to the future of the dreamer. They serve admirably as an example for pursuing the implications of such a theory.[1]

As with all of us, dreaming for the Kalapalo is an experience of life that releases the imagination and memory. Thus, the interpretation of dreaming requires special linguistic resources and frames of reference other than those appropriate for speaking about the ordinary waking life of either the individual or the community at large.

Dreaming is understood as a process, described by means of intransitive verb forms (*-ïŋï*, 'to sleep'; *-eni-*, 'to dream'; *-ïi-*, 'to remember'; *-fesu-*, 'to wander')[2] rather than (as in English) a series of discrete incidents or events given nominative labels. In other words, there is no Kalapalo word for 'dream,' but several ways of speaking about the experience of 'dreaming.' Thus, it would be a distortion of their understanding of the matter to reify 'the dreams' of Kalapalo as if they were objects with specific contours of significance interpretable solely by means of their content.

The wandering of the self

Dreaming is said to occur when, during sleeping, a person's *akũa*[3] or imagined 'interactive self' awakens or 'arises' (the word *tikaĩdyu* is used to express this idea) and 'wanders' until an experience is achieved. Such an experience of the self (*akũa*), in contrast to the essentially passive intransitive state of the dreamer, is typically active and transitive. The notion of purposeless 'wandering' suggests that this is an accidental *engagement*, for the dreaming begins when the *akũa* in fact ceases to wander and starts to participate in some event in an active fashion. Following are three comments on this process that explain the relation between sleeping, dreaming, and the wandering of the *akũa*:

A progressive theory of dreaming

When we are asleep, we are sound asleep, and our *akũa* wake up and begin to roam around. Then we dream.

When we dream, our *akũa* wander around and so we see where it goes.

Two friends went traveling. At night, while they were both lying down – it was very dark – one of them saw his friend get up from himself. 'What's the matter with my friend?' This other person got up and walked away, but his friend's body was still lying down. But when in the morning the man woke up, he was all right.

The Kalapalo also recognize that some images experienced during dreaming are caused by the process of remembering; dreaming can be explicitly associated with the memory of recent events, and sometimes dreaming is described as if it were a way of remembering:

When people were talking about the things you had brought us, that's what I dreamed about.

If you're thinking about someone, your mother perhaps, then when you're sleeping soundly, your mother's *akũa* will visit your *akũa*.

Powerful beings and dreaming

Dreaming is said to occur as well when a sleeper is visited by a powerful being. These entities have two dominant characteristics. The first is their transformative power (*itseketu*), or the ability to create effects or achieve goals by means of song spells (*kefege*). The second is their wildness or unpredictable violence (*aŋiko*). Powerful beings are typically given the names of natural life forms, celestial or material objects in the world of Kalapalo waking experience. These labels suggest their physical appearance and characteristic behavior or, more correctly, the nature of the song spells they possess, for powerful beings are thus creative, transformative beings by virtue of their musical abilities. Although the activities of powerful beings are described in mythology as if they were activities performed by human agents, the Kalapalo understand these events differently. They say that performed song spells created these events, which are desired effects, expressed in chanted texts that are blown at certain objects or patients.

Powerful beings are drawn to an interactive self when it detaches itself from a person's physical body and begins to wander about. When this happens the powerful being appears in human form rather than, as Ugaki (a woman of about sixty years of age) put it, 'the appearance they take in their own settlements.' But powerful beings can also appear in waking life, and when they do they are recognized by their uncanny appearance: human, yet with eyes that are pupil-less beams of light.

However, a powerful being never appears in a direct or obvious way – standing squarely in the person's path, for example – but always makes its presence known in an oblique manner. When encountered in waking life, Kalapalo only see it after their attention has been gradually drawn away from whatever they are engaged in at the time. First comes a sense that the environment is altered: a man persists in hearing footsteps behind him on the path, a stick or bit of earth is suddenly tossed in another man's direction so that he turns around, and yet another begins to hear mysterious music. Outside the settlement it is only after such occurrences that Kalapalo come to realize they are being observed by a powerful being. At home, powerful beings are more commonly experienced during a weakened or diminished state of consciousness, as when people are struck by a very high fever, or after a shaman has induced narcosis by inhaling powerful smoke from his pair of foot-long cigars. But loss of objective awareness is also a consequence of an encounter with a powerful being; a person is struck dumb and immobile, or falls into convulsions.

The appearance of powerful beings in dreaming, or when a person is awake – at which time they are called *afitsatu* ('dangerous apparitions') – affords Kalapalo the opportunity for directly acquiring knowledge about them, detailed and often esoteric information about the specific properties of such beings which a person can subsequently use in the event that the vision is not fatal. Successful contact with a powerful being is of great importance to the person involved and a man who frequently has such experiences may, after a period of apprenticeship, become a shaman. The word for shaman is *fuati*, 'one who is inherently characterized by knowledge,' this knowledge having been directly acquired from powerful beings:

> I dreamed an *itseke fuati* gave me some tobacco to smoke.
> After I smoked the *itseke* gave me something but I couldn't see clearly what this was.
> The *itseke* told me to swallow this *ŋuto* [an object contained in the shaman's body that helps to attract harmful missiles sent by powerful beings or witches so as to help the shaman withdraw them].

First I was dreaming of all kinds of *itseke*. I almost died.
Then my relative here said to me, 'Go find the arrows of that *itseke*.'
I was dreaming they were on top of a tall tree.
The others blew tobacco at me,
  while I smoked until I became unconscious.
Then I went to get the arrows.
That's all.

I almost died when I went fishing on the Culiseu River.
After two days my stomach began to hurt.
I had eaten a little salt.
I began to vomit.
Then I was really sick.
I was vomiting.
I had diarrhea, like water.

I didn't know where I was;
  it seemed as if I was back at the settlement.
M. wanted to bring me back home, but I said,
  'Wait, I want to see what will happen to me.'
The others went fishing but I didn't go with them.
I wasn't eating any fish,
  I wasn't drinking any cold manioc soup,
    nothing.
I asked the others, 'Where am I?'
They said, 'By the Culuene River.'
I told them, 'I thought I was back at the settlement.'
That night someone came to me, it may have been an *itseke*.
  It did seem to be one of them.
It said, 'Wait. You'll soon get better: don't worry.'
I said, 'You're not lying to me, are you?'
It answered, 'No, I'm not lying to you.
  You'll soon know that I'm telling you the truth.'
The next day I felt better, and by the following day it was all over.

The manner in which these experiences are described suggests a contrast between the careful focus on material forms that is particularly characteristic of Kalapalo observation, and another consciousness that is less focussed and less material than it is illusional. Under these circumstances, what are first held to be doubtful apparitions – first appearing out of the corner of the eye and from a distance, or in the stupor of serious illness – assume a central and convincing place in rational discourse, serving both explanatory and rhetorical functions. While these types of experiences have been called 'alternative states of consciousness,' they are more exactly forms of self-enchantment, during which an illusionary state of consciousness is recognized as such and made valid through its meaningfulness. This kind of consciousness contrasts with the material consciousness of the Kalapalo, which is characterized not by an oblique kind of awareness, but by the closely held stare, the almost microscopic focus that is characteristic of their 'thirst for objective understanding.'[4] So, while the word *itseke* can be used to designate a specific category of entity, what is implied by its use here is a special mental experience that involves the weakening or actual loss of a form of material consciousness in which things are held to be concretely present outside the mind, and a substitution of apparitions.

The shaman's reports I have quoted suggest three specific causes for dreaming: remembering someone or something, a powerful being encountering the wandering self of the sleeper, and the wandering self experiencing an event in which it is an active participant. To use Peirce's (1932) semiotic language, things that are remembered are 'indexical' because the dreamer recognizes them as concrete aspects of familiar experiences. Encounters with powerful beings are also interpreted indexically, but in such cases this means that speech and other aspects of the experience itself are interpreted literally. Finally, the kind of dreaming in which the interactive self (*akũa*) is the focus of experience is interpreted metaphorically or 'iconically.' As the Kalapalo describe them, these do not appear as mutually exclusive interpretations. For example, the particular form taken by a powerful being may need to be interpreted as a metaphor. To answer the question why there are such different kinds of dreams, given semiotically different forms of interpretation, I shall have to examine more closely how the Kalapalo describe their dreaming experiences. But before turning to these matters, I would like to discuss in detail the crucial notion of the *akũa*, a concept that takes us from the immediate subject of dreaming to some fundamental aspects of Kalapalo world view.

Akũa as 'interactive self

Because the term *akũa* refers to the appearance of an entity in the shape of a human being, *active* manifestations in human shape of the essential properties of entities, I translate the Kalapalo concept 'interactive self.' I am especially concerned to emphasize by such a translation two distinctive features of this concept. First is the idea that *akũa* are manifestations, to a human person who is aware but not awake or materially conscious, of both human and other animate beings, of manufactured objects, and of powerful beings. Second, the *akũa* is an interactive concept in that a person's awareness of it is always achieved in a communicative context – one that may be verbal, visual, musical, or any combination of the three – that constructs a relation of *transitivity*. In this connection, it is because such 'selves' are making themselves visible to human consciousness that they take human shape.

While the interactive self has all the attributes of the sleeper, it has the additional, uncanny ability to reveal new implications, future actions, and relationships involving that person. Hence, the Kalapalo notion of the *akũa* partakes of ideas about bodily parts, but also those implied by the concept of the powerful being. As a 'self' that fortuitously rather than purposefully experiences, the *akũa* is a concept implying detachment from responsibility for what is dreamed. Although memory is important for some of the indexical imagery in dreams – and in private situations non-canonical interpretation of dreaming plays a role in interpretation – dreaming is mainly a consequence, the Kalapalo assert, of what the *akũa* does, not just what the dreamer is thinking, feeling, or remembering prior to falling asleep.

The word *akũa* is a noun that falls into the large class of entities called 'things' (*iŋko*) whose distinguishing characteristic is their possessibility and alienability from the possessor. These two qualities are indicated by the suffix *-gï-* (or its allomorphs) that must be used together with mandatory pronominal prefixes indicating the person status of the possessor. Most, but not all, body parts fall into this class, as do virtually all material possessions. It is interesting that things in this class can be used against the possessor by a witch if they should by some misfortune happen to fall into his hands. But similarly, a witch can be literally burned up from inside himself when grieving parents have a magical charm made, consisting of boiled body parts of the dead child. These practices suggest that there is felt to be some kind of essential connection – a connection of substance – between such objects and their owners, despite a condition of physical separation.

The *akũa* is part of the self much like the eye, head, or foot; but, in contrast with all other body parts, from time to time it enjoys an existence separate from, but not independent of, the physical body. This separation occurs temporarily during sleep, as a consequence of which a person dreams. During severe illness, an even more tenuous connection with the body results at which time the victim may be caused to do things by the *akũa*, now acting almost as an independent entity. For example, one man who ran shrieking around the house circle as if in a mad race against an invisible partner told me upon recovery that he had done this because his *akũa* was pulling him by the wrist (normally a gesture for guiding or leading people). The separation of physical body and *akũa* is permanent when a person dies and the *akũa* travels to Añafïtï, the 'Place of Many Dead' located in the sky in the direction of the rising sun.

The word *akũa* also is used to refer to the shadow of an entity cast by the sun, and to its reflection as in a mirror – for example. The idea of the 'shadow' (and before their knowledge of mirrors, the 'reflection' as well) seems to be an apt metaphor for this kind of 'envisioned self,' since both are dim, somewhat mysterious images (*futofo*) in silhouette whose outlines bear no clearly perceivable detail. A person's *akũa* had dimensions that are equally dim and unfocussed, but these are dimensions of a conceptual image, rather than a visual one. During dreaming the visual experience of a concept is associated directly with the acquisition of knowledge, 'seeing' – rather than 'watching' – being a form of 'understanding.' Hence, dreamers learn about themselves by literally seeing their *akũa*.

There are several verbs formed from the noun stem *akũa*. The first is the form *-akũapïte-* ('to endow with the self or essence of' something). An example of the use of this verb in a sentence taken from a myth is: *Isifeke figey akũapïtega atïfigï, timitofoi*, 'It was his mother who had been endowing his *akũa*, his shooting instrument.' This sentence describes how a mother whose son (a master fisherman) was killed by a fish in turn took revenge upon his murderer by creating fishing equipment from various parts of his body. She thereby endowed those instruments of revenge with the essential quality of her son's interactive self, his remarkable ability to kill fish.

Another verbal construction involving *akũa* is the form *-akũaki-*, meaning to be excited, startled, or tense, or perhaps more exactly, hyperanimated. Kuju told me: 'When we are frightened, our *akũa* jump inside us with alarm.' Together with *-akũapïte-*, *akũa* is used here to refer to a person's 'animacy.' While the first expression refers to the specific essence of a life, the present verbal form has a sense that is at once more general and more intensive, referring to that which endows something with life itself.

A third form incorporating the noun *akũa* is the verb *-akũatë-*, meaning to replace a person's interactive self during a curing ritual. This refers to the notion that during severe illness, no matter what the specific diagnosis, the *akũa* may separate from the victim's body, necessitating recapture by ritual curers. The particular condition of severe illness necessary for such a separation of the self is fainting or loss of consciousness, which is labeled by the same term used to refer to dying. In fact, such a state is mid-way in intensity between that of sleeping and final death.

The Kalapalo have several words for the process of death. Only one, *tsitsi-*,[5] refers specifically to death in the sense of cessation of life 'on earth,' that is, since a dead person continues to exist in a non-earthly settlement. The other words used are a negative form of the copula, as in *afiti anïgila* ('he or she no longer exists'), and the verb stem *apuŋu-*, which has the general sense of undergoing a permanent transition from one state or condition to another. In death the human interactive self manifests its powerful being attributes; it can change appearance, commonly to that of the maned wolf,[6] and causes the death of living persons who have the misfortune to see it.

To summarize, the term *akũa* is used by Kalapalo in reference to anything (including oneself) apprehended in human form during a state of lessened consciousness. While its existence is not simply a function of someone's awareness of it when in such a state, under those circumstances *akũa* appear to people and engage them in some kind of mental adventure. Hence, the idea of *akũa* participates in the notion of an experience shared between a particular human being and some other entity, and this kind of shared experience can occur only when that entity takes, or is apprehended as taking, human form. Human form is somehow necessary for a certain kind of communication to take place, a type of communication that involves the mingling, with intense consequences, of the powers inherent in human language and in the musical spells of powerful beings. The *akũa* is not so much a 'thing' as an interactive phenomenon, a special kind of perceptual and conceptual experience for which 'soul' seems a very crude, offhand gloss. Also, in English, the word has been used to suggest a person's connection with God, our means of perceiving the good and the source of our rationality. Hence in translating the Kalapalo word *akũa*, I deliberately avoid using the English word 'soul,' because the moral implications of the term are absent in the Kalapalo usage. The staleness of this translation is compounded when we remember that *akũa* are the human manifestations of material objects as well as of living things and of powerful beings. To use 'soul' in connection with such entities is to distort the English sense of the word severely. On the other hand, 'self' seems more appropriate because in English it can be applied to many different kinds of entities, living and non-living; we can say, for example, 'itself' as well as 'herself.' Furthermore, 'self' is appropriate because the notion of *akũa* involves the entire entity, governing its being and thus pervading its entirety. The *akũa* is something more than the immaterial essence of a thing. It is an interactive *relation*.

Dreaming images as relations of transitivity

The resources drawn upon when Kalapalo interpret their dreaming are active images that also express relations of transitivity, in which the dreamer's self experiences either an agentive or patientive role. The Kalapalo theory of dreaming, the means of interpreting these transitive dreaming experiences, is one that makes explicit reference to the future of the dreamer. Just as their myths do, dreaming provides them with useful models for the formation of new roles and relations, or more simply, new and different feelings towards some problem. Kalapalo interpret their dreaming as a way the self *creates* a goal, rather than as a means of arriving at some satisfactory solution to a distressing problem or the conclusion of some goal, as Jung believed. Through dreaming, a Kalapalo dreamer experiences the self as an actively motivated, symbolically created entity. Finally, the link between dreaming and interpretation is metaphorical.

The fundamental idea that dreaming is both an intransitive process effected by the dreamer and a transitive experience of the dreamer's self, which should best be interpreted metaphorically rather than literally, is part of a more general native ontology, a theory of existence in which ideas about animacy, including the nature of feelings, motivation and processes involving creativity, invention, and transformation play a central role.[7]

Indexical and iconic interpretation of dreams

Indexical dreaming signs are said to be caused by memory or by the vision of a powerful being, and they are interpreted with reference to incidents in the recent past of the dreamer. Iconic dreaming signs (such as crossing a log bridge, or being nibbled at by minnows while sitting at the water's edge) are explicitly associated with the wanderings of the self. They are iconic insofar as they constitute metaphorical relations between images of the dreamer's own self as imagined in contexts of the future, and those of the self's active participation in the event of the dreaming. The particular images of the dreamer's own self that are created from the symbolism of the dreaming are verbalized concepts, whereas the self is a visual concept. While a dreaming can incorporate both iconic and indexical signs, only iconic images and the vision of self signifying the future of the dreamer are treated as significant in public dream reports. So, although the Kalapalo recognize that recent experiences of a person can influence what is dreamed, only those images that refer to the future of that person are considered socially meaningful.

The Kalapalo look to the totality of the agentivity relationship for significance before deciding that dreaming is worth paying public attention to. In fact, Kalapalo do not necessarily tell their dreams freely unless the dreaming is marked by the presence of some canonical metaphorical formula, is about a powerful being, or is considered ridiculous and trivial (*taloki*, 'without significance') by the dreamer. Furthermore, the fact of having dreamed in such a canonical manner may be used post hoc in explanation for some troublesome event that has just occurred. For example, when Agifuti cut his foot badly with an axe, his father, Kakaku, immediately asked him whether he had dreamed badly the previous night, and, receiving a reply in the negative, insisted to his son that he must have forgotten he had recently dreamed about wounding himself.

The Kalapalo associate their canonical dreaming, dreaming of images (*ifo*), with states of psychological tension (*-akũaki-*) that are associated with critical times in the life-cycle when people seclude themselves and are most focally concerned with the biological processes of life. Hence, most canonical dreaming is said to occur during the early stages of a shaman's training, during the first few months of puberty seclusion, during the onset of mourning seclusion, just before childbirth, or when a person is seriously ill. For young men, and to a lesser extent, young women in puberty seclusion, canonical dreaming is considered a crucial and integral part of the process of acquiring knowledge of one's biological and characterological self.[8] After earpiercing, or while attempting to acquire the powers of the wrestling master or bow master, a young man's dreaming is monitored by his elders for significant meanings about his future.

The appendix consists of a list of canonical dreaming imagery, together with the meanings given by various Kalapalo men and women. This list is by no means complete, for such imagery is limited only by concrete experience, and as one's experience of the world changes, so must the dreaming icons. In all cases the imagery of the dreaming is associated with a particular effect having important consequences for the dreamer. The form of sentences asserting the connection between a particular set of images and a consequential effect typically includes the use in the initial conditioning clause of the unmarked tense/hypothetical punctate action marker *-olï-* ('if' or 'when') to mark the verb stem. Appearing in the concluding clause is one of the two possible verbal suffixes indicating future action: *-uiŋo-* (the unmarked tense/punctate potential suffix) or *-ni-* (the unmarked tense/continuous potential action suffix). Such a construction expresses the idea that an effect is, or has been, directly caused by the action of the dreaming. We see this put into practice when Kalapalo athletes refrain from sleeping before a major wrestling match or spear-throwing ritual, 'lest they dream that something bad will happen to a visitor.' To keep awake, hosts sing and dance throughout the entire night before such events.

The Kalapalo can therefore be said to have a theory of iconic dreaming that we can call 'performative' (Austin 1962). In other words, dreaming is described as an event that *produces* a certain effect by means of its simply having occurred. Dreaming, interpreted by the Kalapalo as the visual awareness of a sleeper of activities engaged in by the interactive self, is understood as a kind of mental operation on current situations that changes a person's feelings, psychobiological motives, or goals.

The changes that are said to occur as a consequence of such canonical dreaming may take place through analytic self-interpretation, by means of which some important aspect of the dreamer's contemporary character is implicated in what is to happen in the personal future. And, since the performative future in a dreaming context has to do with goals, not actual events, there is a possibility of their being subverted by staying awake so as not to dream, a practice that deliberately thwarts the formation of goals. Finally, that dreaming is associated directly with shifts in moods and goals is also suggested by the discourse structure of myths, wherein reference to a character's sleeping is used as a marker of such shifts in the text.[9]

That canonical dreaming can be experienced throughout a person's lifetime suggests the Kalapalo desire to extend and redefine constantly the qualities of the self in keeping with changing circumstances, and especially with their perception of how knowledge of the world is developed throughout a lifetime. Concern with all aspects of the self and one's biological relations with the rest of the community is an expression of interest in the future potential of the self; what it can do, and be, given what it now seems to be. Finally, because the Kalapalo associate different aspects of human thought with different parts and regions of the body – emotions with the organs and viscera of the body cavity, vision and knowledge with the eyes, hearing and understanding with the ears, sexual passions with the genitalia – it is no accident their notion of the self should correspond to the entire person.

Kalapalo dreamers thus receive metaphorically encoded visions of themselves, metaphors that need to be interpreted through linguistic and cultural conventions, the canons of dreaming interpretation being preserved in oral tradition as a set of conventional iconic correspondences tied to life-crisis situations. During these times, dreaming has to be interpreted metaphorically, suggesting a certain idea of the distinctiveness of human beings in relation to other entities, in the world of their experience.

SOUND SYMBOLISM AND THE INTERPRETATION OF DREAMING

In Kalapalo cosmology, human beings are classed with other life forms (*ago*) as living things and as such are capable of producing calls (*itsu*) which we can refer to as expletives, following the English speaker's practice of distinguishing human and animal sounds in a way the Kalapalo do not.[10] These human utterances are, like animal calls, constructed indexically and are also indexical symbols in that they are associated in time and space with the feelings from which they arise. In this way, human beings express truthful and empirically motivated feelings.

However, humans are different from other living things because of their linguistic abilities. It is through language that they are most commonly symbolized and distinguished from other categories of entities. In narrative texts, the quoted speech of human beings is the most important sound symbolism of all and is the characteristic way of representing them as distinct characters in stories. But language allows people to do something very different from animals. Because human beings were created by Trickster, whose name Taugi means 'lies about himself,' they are preeminently deceitful beings whose deception comes from their ability to speak. Because they speak they are capable not only of truthfully expressing their feelings, but (and this is the unmarked understanding of human speech for the Kalapalo) of creating verbal illusions about them. The verb for this illusory speech is *augï-*, which subsumes both malevolent and relatively benign speech acts, including our ideas of lying and of joking. Truthful speech is always marked by verification particles such as the assertive emphatic *-ketsaŋe*, or lexemes like *augïndafïŋï*, 'it isn't a lie.' Human speech is thus understood to have a kind of creative power that extends human consciousness far beyond that of living things in general.

While human beings are capable of goal-oriented action like all living things, what is important for their distinctiveness among these living things is the fact that they are capable of deception in these relationships, of the expression of fantasy, and of imaginatively creating their goals. Since they are relatively more animate in their ability to construct imaginative images of themselves, they serve as patients of transitive verbs only when the agent is also human or is a powerful being.

Because people are understood to be different from what they appear to be and especially deceptive linguistically, iconic interpretation is the most suitable means of understanding what they are saying. By implication, what is being said about them must also be interpreted iconically. This follows from the fact that there is an understanding of the inherent ambiguity of speech. For this reason, the interpretation of Kalapalo dreaming must involve seeing dream images as metaphorical symbols, for dreaming is in the Kalapalo view a visual message from the interactive self to the dreamer, a person's mind seeking understanding and knowledge of what he or she will become in the future.

Turning now to the problem of why dreaming indicates something about the future of the self, we can see a solution in their notion of human beings as goal-oriented and linguistically inventive or creative. Creative goal-orientation involves using language to speculate about the future, or to use the present self as an armature linking one's past experiences with the unknown (that is, unconceived) future. The work of dreaming is here the work of the process of orientation towards goals by the self. Thus, the Kalapalo explanation of the process of dreaming as the wandering of the interactive self should be taken as a metaphor for the goal-search of the self. What actually happens to the *akũa*, what is seen during the dreaming, is the fixing upon some future goal.

CONCLUSIONS

I have shown how the language of Kalapalo dreaming interpretation constructs an image of the future by combining the sense of a hypothetical dreaming situation with performative functions that are given to the particular images of the dreaming. There is a linking of the dreaming subject with the consequential event in the dreamer's life to create a causal proposition. It is by now certain that Kalapalo understand their dreaming, at least interpretable dreaming, as performative in Austin's terms. The reason this can be so has to do with the Kalapalo's having grasped a profound implication of the human ability to create and use linguistic symbols. The Kalapalo understand that our ability to speak is intimately linked with our ability to fashion in sensory images an illusionary future for our selves – to fantasize. Since these images are concerned with the future, they must be doubly illusionary. Hence, for the Kalapalo interpreting a dream is a process of acquiring illusionary (but not inaccurate or deluded) self-knowledge, which is imaginative understanding of one's unconscious motives and proclivities. It is, in other words, acquiring knowledge of the interactive self. Dreaming is also a performative event because it causes the future by revealing the dreamer's life as it is encapsulated in current aspirations, moods, and inchoately understood motivations and fears of an individual. The dreaming is thus less a matter about what will happen to a person than about the self becoming. Since dreaming is considered an experience of the *akũa*, not of the sleeper directly, it is an experience of a hidden personal reality (the mind, perhaps) that is only inchoately perceived in waking life. Hence dreaming is interpretable through imaginative understanding in the mode best suited to meaning that is concealed and known to be so, metaphor.

It is only when we interpret the imagery of the dreaming process by means of the most unimaginatively literal concepts, like that of the 'soul,' extracted from our storehouse of nineteenth-century evolutionary models, that we create the impression of peoples outside our own tradition as non-rational and animistically motivated. Rather than implying by the use of the word 'soul' that the *akũa* is a 'thing' having an existence independent of the physical body, we can best understand the *akũa* as an hypostatization of the principle of imaginative awareness of some being or 'essence,' the 'interactive self' of an entity as engaged with the mind of a human being. The idea of 'interactive self' suggests how the careful perception of the independent existence of things, each understood to be motivated by internally generated goals and feelings, can be concretely represented by a human figure when engaged with human beings, but appear as natural life forms or inanimate 'things' when unconcerned with their relations with human beings. This separation of the self from the concrete manifestation of the entity further requires an understanding of how an entity changes over time, or somewhat more abstractly, the differences between the past, present, and future character of a person, which is the experiencing of life itself.

While Tylor's (1871) famous theory treated the universality of the dream experience as the ultimate origin of religion, we see in Kalapalo dreaming theory and its implications that religion, or rather the basic ontological propositions of a people's world view, can just as easily govern the manner of dream interpretation. The specific content of that world view – upon which the daily fears, anticipations, and joys of participants avidly feed – in turn affects the manifest content of the dreaming experience and conditions how it is to be communicated.

NOTES

1. My research among the Kalapalo during 1978–80 was supported by a National Science Foundation Research Grant (BNS 78–00849) and the University of Arizona. Research during 1982 was supported by the Wenner-Gren Foundation for Anthropological Research. I am grateful to the officials of the Conselho Nacional de Desenvolvimento Cientifico e Technologico, of the Fundação Nacional do Indio, and to my colleague Professor Roque de Barros Laraia of the University of Brasilia, for their considerable assistance. Robert M. Netting and all the participants in this seminar kindly provided helpful and incisive comments on earlier drafts of the paper.
2. The following phonetic symbols (deviations from standard written English) have been used to write Kalapalo terms. Stress

is normally on the penultimate syllable. Vowels – ï: as in sh*ou*ld (a middle open vowel) and ë: no English equivalent (a middle closed vowel); consonants – *ŋ*: pronounced 'ng' as in 'si*ng*.'

3. The word *akũa* is also used as a proper noun referring to a small species of piranha. Evidence that this usage is homophonic concerns the fact that, unlike a common noun, it cannot take the possession suffix or the required pronominal prefixes indicating the person status of the possessor (as does *akũa* when used to mean 'interactive self').
4. 'Cet appetit de connaissance objective,' an expression used by Lévi-Strauss in writing of the 'science of the concrete' (Lévi-Strauss 1963:5).
5. The metonymic modal suffix *-lefa-*, indicating a contiguity relationship in time and/or space, is usually attached to this verb. The resultant form *tsitsilefa* normally concludes a line or a longer discourse segment describing events that end in a subject's death.
6. *Chrysocyon* sp., a nocturnal canid scavenger associated with death and witchcraft.
7. I am not sure that 'dreaming' constitutes a semantic domain in an ethnosemantic sense. I am chiefly concerned here with the implications of the Kalapalo use of specific words in their explanation of the dreaming process.
8. That biology is important is suggested by the emphasis upon how medical practices affect the future statuses of persons in puberty seclusion; future bow masters, wrestling masters, and desirable women. Elsewhere (Basso 1985: ch. 6) I have described in detail how these practices affect not only the physical appearance and strength of a person (his or her 'beauty') but the equally important moral attributes of the adolescent, which are actually indicated by the person's physical appearance.
9. See Basso (1985) for an extended discussion of narrative segmenting procedures in Kalapalo, as well as other features of narrative discourse outlined in this paper, especially the symbolism of sound.
10. Some examples are '*akam*,' a cry indicating muscular or skeletal pain; '*aataa*,' an expression of pleasure; '*etse*,' expressing mental confusion.

APPENDIX: DREAMING METAPHORS

a. When a jaguar or a powerful being eats our *akũa*, we wake up and say we will die soon. But when we see a rock, or we see the sun setting, we will live a long time. When we see the sun rising, we will die soon, we won't live long.

Look – my older brother, Dyakua's father, dreamt when his ears were pierced that he saw the sun rising. When he awakened he said, 'I'm going to die soon.'

b. When we dream we are burnt by fire, later we will be bitten by a wild thing, by a spider or a stinging ant, for example.

c. When we dream we are cutting open a piqui fruit with a knife, later we will cut our foot on a stick of wood while traveling somewhere.

d. When we are making love to women, we will be very successful when we go fishing.

e. When there is a crowd of people, during a trading ceremony for example, but we are hidden – we can't be seen by them – we will kill monkeys if we later go hunting.

f. When we are throwing a log, we will be successful in our wrestling.

g. When we dream of a monkey, our son will be a wrestling master. When we dream of a macaw, we will have a beautiful child. When it's a parrot, it will be a somewhat less beautiful child; a large parakeet, or a miniature parakeet, is a beautiful daughter.

h. When a boy is in seclusion and he dreams of climbing a tall tree, or another one sees a long path, they will live long. This would also be true if we dreamt of crossing a wide stream in the forest.

i. In order to become the maker of *ataŋa* flutes, he has to have dreamt of the jaguar's call, and the call of the black locust after his ears are pierced.

j. When a maiden in seclusion sees a long path, she will live long.

k. When a man dreams of monkeys, he will be a good wrestler. The monkey moves its arms swiftly.

l. When a secluded maiden dreams of small fish nibbling at her body while she sits in the water, she will be desired by many men.

m. When we dream of painting ourselves, we'll be wounded later. The blood is *urucu* [a brilliant red paint]; they're both red.

n. A witch can make us dream of our hammocks being completely devoured by leaf-cutter ants. Also, of our being bitten by a jaguar or a dog. And so later on we'll be killed by the witch.

o. When we dream of someone else, our *akũa* is visiting with an *akũa* of that person.

p. You're asleep and the *akũa* of the main house post emerges from itself. You see someone and later you get sick. You're dizzy, perhaps. We say: 'That's the main house post.'

q. Unfortunately my dreaming was never anything like such an image. [In a story about some people seeking to kill jaguar monsters, a father is asked to prepare his young son to be a bow master. The quoted sentence is his response. Madyuta (a man in his forties) commented on this: 'If he had dreamed of a pet sparrowhawk, his son would have become a bow master who could kill the jaguars with a single shot.']

5
Zuni and Quiché dream sharing and interpreting

BARBARA TEDLOCK

Early one morning during our fieldwork with the Quiché Maya,[1] my husband, Dennis, reported to me that he had dreamed of receiving an ear of corn from an unknown person at a party; when he opened the husk the corn was already roasted, with butter, salt, lime juice, and chili powder on it. It occurred to me that if he had the dream interpreted by a Zuni from New Mexico (a people we both knew much more about at that time than we did about the Quiché) it would be considered very bad, indicating that he would die unless he were cured of having had it. The unknown person would be interpreted either as a witch or as a dead person who was trying to poison him, and he would be told that he should not have accepted the corn ear and opened it. Luckily he did not complete the dream by eating the corn; otherwise he might be destined to die soon.

If he had reported this dream to a Zuni medicine man, he would have been draped with a blanket while he inhaled the fumes of a burning piñon stick. Next the curer would have put the burnt stick into a glass of water, then fished it out and marked Dennis's chest over his heart with it, instructing him to drink the water. Finally, he would have told him that it was a good thing he had reported this bad dream; otherwise he would have shortened his life road. In a case where this dream was part of a series of bad dreams, the curer would have had to decide whether the patient should be whipped publicly and initiated into the Kachina Society, the tribal ancestor cult group, or else into one of thirteen secret curing societies.

What happened instead was that Dennis reported his dream to Don Andrés, a man with whom we were undergoing a formal apprenticeship in Quiché divination and dream interpretation in Momostenango, Guatemala. Don Andrés said it was an extremely good dream, but that since Dennis had not eaten the unknown ancestor's gift, it was not yet completed. In order to complete it, the next time Dennis dreamed of a food gift of any sort (which Don Andrés predicted he would), he was to accept the gift and eat it on the spot. Exactly twenty days later Dennis reported dreaming of receiving a green banana from an unknown person and, upon opening it, being surprised to find that it was ripe. He then proceeded to eat it, finding it very sweet. Don Andrés smiled and said that our apprenticeship was going very well, since we were being accepted by the ancestors. He added that if he had not already taken us on as apprentices, he probably would have begun thinking about it.

If these two dreams had been presented to a psychoanalyst, the phallic shape and size of both the corn ear and the banana, with their coverings that must be pulled back in order to eat them, could have been used to translate the manifest food content into a latent sexual content. But this is only an hypothesis; in checking out some of the standard psychoanalytic texts on dream interpretation I find an almost total neglect of the subject of food and the act of eating (Freud 1900, 1901, 1916–17, 1923b, 1925a, 1933; Abraham 1909; Róheim 1945, 1950, 1952; Jones 1951). Even Jung all but ignores the topic of food in dreams, with the exception of a rather brief discussion of the possible significance of black versus white bread (Jung 1929:170–3). Since eating is more basic in humans than either sexuality or aggression, it is astounding to notice this neglect of the analysis of eating within Western depth psychology. An exception is James Hillman (1979), who suggests that eating in dreams actually has very little to do with the hunger instinct, but is rather an expression of the psychic need for nourishing images. This interpretation would fit rather well with Quiché notions, but not at all with Zuni notions.

Ethnographers who have worked intensively in more than one society often confront such radical divergences in meaning systems. Nevertheless the present difference startled me, given that Zuni and Momostenango have a number of general similarities. Both communities practice maize horticulture, both have religious specialists who visit sacred springs and mountains that have directional orientations, and both locate themselves in the very center of a four-cornered world. In both cases the initial response to the arrival of Europeans was armed resistance. Today, more than four centuries after conquest, although both communities are ethnic enclaves under the domination of modern nation states, they have earned reputations for fierce independence and traditionalism. Both groups underwent a process of forced acculturation long ago, particularly focussed on their 'pagan' religions; in more recent times, as then, their strategies for dealing with Christian missionization range from polite indifference, through interest in economic advantages offered by missionaries, to the open hostility of nativistic revolts and revivals.

There are also important differences between these two societies. The Zunis, with a little less than 8,000 people living in a single nucleated village, are matrilineal and matrilocal. The Quiché Maya, with over 500,000 people located in twenty-six separate communities, are patrilineal and patrilocal. As a group Zunis are substantially better off in matters of economics, education, and health, but they lack the occupational class stratification of the Quiché, in which there is a small affluent upper level.

For both groups the ancestors are central beings, greatly respected and greatly feared. All Zuni males must join a tribal organization known as the Kachina Society, in which they spend a great deal of time, money, and creative energy impersonating their ancestors (*aalhasshinaawe*) in complex masked dances (B. Tedlock 1980).[2] With rare exceptions, however, Zunis do not speak the names of individual dead persons, and they describe visitations of these persons in night dreams as horrifying experiences that call for a cure through the performance of specified religious rituals including, in serious cases, initiation into either the Kachina Society (for women who are not normally members of this Society) or else into a medicine society (for both men and women). For the Quiché, generic ancestors (*nantat*, 'mothers-fathers') are also important beings, but the visitation of an individual and nameable deceased relative in a dream is often described as a positive experience, though it too may demand a cure in the form of religious rituals and eventual initiation into a religious organization. Members of this organization are burners (*poronel*)[3] and daykeepers (*ajk'ij*), who make offerings to the deceased, cure, divine, and practice dream interpretation.

Zuni and Quiché dream theories present a subtle blending of the metaphilosophy of being and essence with the metapsychology of affect and cognition. Because of this complex mixture of what we segment off as separate philosophical, religious, and psychological systems here in the West, it is crucial to the understanding of dreaming and dream interpretation as a cultural system in these two non-Western societies to set out the basics of their philosophy and psychology.

COMPARATIVE ONTOLOGY AND PSYCHOLOGY

A comparison of the ontological dimension of Zuni and Quiché metaphysics reveals major conceptual differences between these two cultures with respect to being, substance, and essence. Likewise a comparison of Zuni and Quiché psychology reveals major differences in affective-cognitive categories. These differences, in turn, structure lower-level contrasts in Zuni and Quiché ethos and world view.

Being, essence, and emotion at Zuni

According to Zuni ontology people are of two kinds, raw (or soft) beings (*ky'apin aaho"i*) and cooked (or ripe) beings (*akna aaho"i*); the latter are also known as daylight beings (*tek'ohannan aaho"i*). Cooked or daylight beings depend on cooked food and are under the special protection of the Sun Father. Raw beings – including (for example) deer, ants, rainstorms, corn plants, snakes, and the dead – eat food that is either raw or else has been sacrificed to them by cooked or daylight people.

Within the category of cooked or daylight beings there are two classes: poor (*tewuko'liya*, literally 'without religion') and valuable (*tehya*). Women have some value by virtue of their gender; men do not become their equals until their initiation into the Kachina Society. To exceed an ordinary level of value either sex may undertake initiation into one of the thirteen medicine societies or fourteen rain priesthoods. A member of such a group is 'valuable' by virtue of esoteric knowledge and because of the individual personal icon,[4] known as a *mi'le*, which is received at initiation. Each icon, which is considered a person in its own right, consists of a perfectly kernelled, unblemished ear of yellow corn, in which there is a hollowed-out central cavity filled with seeds, including corn of all colors, wheat, squash, melons, beans, and piñon nuts. Around the outside are parrot, macaw, downy eagle, drake mallard, bluejay, and turkey feathers. The base of the ear of corn is nestled in a rawhide cup, wrapped in cotton cloth and then fitted into an oat-straw basketry holder that is ornamented with a necklace of olivella and abalone shells, turquoise nuggets, and branch coral. The butt end of the icon is sealed with a cement of black earth brought from the underworld, mixed with piñon gum and yucca fruit. The icon is made individually for a novice and is given life by the maker. Each one is the opposite sex of the novice and is referred to as either 'mother' (for a male) or 'father' (for a female). Upon receiving them at initiation, novices breathe from them four times; for the remainder of their lives they will periodically blow on and breathe from them. Whenever the medicine society or rain priesthood meets, the icons of the individual members must be present in the miniature social and psychic world of the religious altar.

The living human or animal body is referred to in Zuni as the *shi'nanne* (literally 'flesh'), while the life force, essence, breath, soul, or psyche is the *pinanne* (literally 'wind' or 'air').[5] So, although breath is ultimately lodged in the heart and is thus a body-soul, under certain circumstances – such as during trancing, curing, singing, and dreaming – it can behave as a free-soul and leave the body.

All persons, regardless of species, also have thoughts and emotions, expressed with the same noun (*tse'makwiiwe*). Thus to think well or clearly and to feel happy is to have good thoughts (*tse'makwi k'okshi*), while to experience sadness, sickness, and confusion is to be 'filled up with thoughts' (*tse'makwi pottiye*). And though both *tse'makwiiwe* ('thoughts' and 'emotions') and *pinanne* ('wind' and 'breath') might be translated as Greek 'psyche' or English 'soul,' Zuni thoughts-emotions embody individualist self-expression and act as a free-soul leaving the body at will, causing the person no harm, while breath-wind embodies a combination of cosmic wind with personal breath and thus behaves either as a free-soul or spirit, or else as that combination of body-soul, breath-soul, and ego-soul defined by Scandinavian ethnologists as the 'life-soul,' which if it were gone from the body for long would cause the death of the person.[6] Although the *pinanne*, or breath-soul, arrives at birth and departs at death, it is never solely possessed by the individual during his or her lifetime. Rather, it remains closely connected to the sacred power suffusing the 'raw' world from which it came and because of this constant contact it acts as a strong moral agent.

Being, essence, and emotion at Momostenango

Quiché-speakers lack a single term analogous to the Zuni concept of 'being' or 'person,' with its reach beyond humans into animals, plants, and natural phenomena. Instead, humans, whether living or dead, are classified as *winak* and are totally distinct from all nonhumans. Articulate speech is the most important single feature separating humans (*winak*) from animals (*chicop*). Living humans and most other animals consist materially of a skeleton (*ubakil*) and flesh (*utiojil*). However, there is a metaphor for the entire body (specifically human), *ujuyubal*, literally 'one's mountain,' which also serves as an epithet for the earth deity (B. Tedlock 1982:189).

Each individual, depending on his or her day of birth on the Maya calendar, has one of twenty faces or destinies called *uwäch uk'ij* (literally 'face of his or her day'). The Nahua (Aztec) concept of the *nawal* is also used in Momostenango, in a way that overlaps with the Quiché concept of 'face' or 'destiny,' for the part of a person that can leave the body without causing death and is thus a free-soul or guardian spirit. While plants, animals, and even places lack a face or a destiny (*uwäch uk'ij*), they all have a guardian spirit (*nawal*), which they can impart to people. Thus, a child born on the day Ik', which is an extremely violent day, may be whipped by his or her parents with a branch of the 'shame bush' (*xibirib*) whenever he or she first displays a violent nature. This plant, whose leaves withdraw and fold up when anything brushes against them, imparts its timid guardian spirit to the child when it comes in contact with the child's body.

A Quiché person also has a life-soul, known by two names: the indigenous term *uxlab* (literally 'breath') and the borrowed term *ranima* (a combination of Spanish *ánima* with the Quiché definite article *ri*). This soul, by either name, arrives at the moment of birth according to traditional Quichés, but for those who follow Catholic doctrine more closely and think of it as the unitary and moralistic Christian soul, it arrives some time after baptism (see B. Tedlock 1982; 1983). Either way it is lodged in the heart, and if it should leave the body for any reason for very long a person would die.

In indigenous belief there is a second and more important type of life-soul, lightning-soul (*coyopa*, literally 'sheet lightning') which is automatically possessed by persons born on the days Ak'abal, Can, Came, Quej, K'anil, E, Aj, Ix, Tz'iquin, and No'j and which can be ritually acquired by a person not born on one of these days (B. Tedlock 1982:133–50; 1983). This extra life or body-soul is simultaneously a gift of the ancestors which moves about within the blood and muscles, leaving at death and, like Zuni wind, is a link to the moral power of the cosmos. In order to interpret these movements correctly as messages, a person must be trained and initiated as a daykeeper (*ajk'ij*), a calendrical diviner.

During an apprenticeship as a daykeeper the novice is taught a complex system of meanings for specific movements of the lightning-soul in the blood (B. Tedlock 1982:133–50) and will also be given an important personal icon that enables him or her to connect internal soul lightning to external sheet lightning. This sacred being consists of a small bag of approximately 260 red seeds from the coral tree and about a dozen crystals. Both teachers and novices project part of their life-soul into the *bara*, just as Zunis project part of their own life-souls into the *mi'le*. But where the Zuni personal icon with its internal cosmic wind is always kept dressed or closed, Quiché curing and dream interpretation sessions require that icons be undressed or opened in full view of all participants. The seeds and crystals are spread out on a table or rock so that part of the daykeeper's destiny (*uwäch uk'ij*), which is projected into the guardian spirit (*nawal*) of the *bara*, can be contacted and activated by cosmic sheet lightning (*coyopa*), which brings the necessary insights to cure clients of illness and nightmares.

For the Quiché the personal icon is a person of the same generation as its recipient, with whom it is joined in a metaphorical marriage, while for the Zuni it is a person of the parental generation, to whom one has been given in adoption. Quichés openly talk about the *bara* as a spouse, a jealous spouse that one cannot touch if one has had sexual relations with one's flesh-and-blood spouse in the past day; it has to be kept away from one's sleeping area. Zunis think of the *mi'le* as a stern parent who is always watching and judging their behavior; it is most properly kept in one's sleeping area. Quichés take their icons apart at will in order to seek knowledge of distant and hidden things through divination, while Zunis keep their icons intact, interpreting any outward change of appearance as an omen. The Zuni *mi'le* serves moralistic functions of the type Freud described for the adult superego, while the Quiché *bara* does not.

The Quiché superego is located elsewhere in their symbol system, taking the form of one of two external guardian spirits (*chajinel*), specifically the good one (*utsilaj chajinel*).[7] These two stand invisibly on either side of the person, sometimes sitting on the shoulders and constantly whispering good and bad ideas into one's ears.

Quichés, like Zunis and many other non-Western peoples, do not make a sharp dichotomy between affect and cognition. One form of combined thought-emotion, labeled *no'jinic*, is calm, cool, creative, intuitive, and meditative, while the other, *chomanic*, is calculative, willful, argumentative, or troubled. A person's moral qualities, or character, are lodged in the former kind of thought-emotion and are revealed by the public, talking ego-self, which may tend to be creatively good (*utsilaj no'j c'o ruc'*) or creatively evil (*itsel no'j c'o ruc'*). When a baby is named it receives these characterological qualities from a same-sex grandparent or great-grandparent, living or dead, for whom it is named. From this point on, the grandparent (if living) and his or her namesake take on a closer relationship, addressing each other by the reciprocal term *nuc'exel*, 'my surrogate,' from the transitive verb root *-c'ex-*, 'to exchange, repay, or replace one object for another.' Although it is expected that children will have the same personalities as their namesakes, since they are literally their replacements, some children do not share in the same strength of character as their *c'exel* (see Mondloch 1980). A willful side may be revealed later in life in angry argumentation (*chomaj c'o ruc'*). A good balance of the two thought-emotion processes is displayed in the process of divination (including dream interpretation), which is known as *ch'obonic*, 'understanding,' and is considered the highest possible mental and social performance.

DREAM THEORIES AND CLASSIFICATION

Both Zuni and Quiché dream theories, as codified epistemologies and symbolic systems, are closely connected to, even partly nested within, ontological and psychological systems. Important aspects of their respective dream theories are predictable on the basis of these systems; for example, for a knowledgeable Zuni, who has but one soul or essence known as the breath (*pinanne*), dreaming is a more dangerous activity than for a Quiché, whose body always has its breath-soul (*uxlab*) present during the dream wanderings of the free-soul (*nawal* and *uwäch uk'ij*). This predictability in symbolic thinking is brought about by the rhetorical principle of *entelechy*, by which particular symbol systems implicate other symbol systems in the inherent unconscious movement of symbolic action towards finishedness (Burke 1950:14,19; 1966a:69–70). Since dream theories and classifications are, as it were, 'rooted differently' (in Kilborne's sense, this volume) in Zuni and Momostenango, they take different shapes.

Dreaming at Zuni

In Zuni dreaming a segment of the dreamer's self travels outside the body and has experiences in past, distant, or future times and places. Although this part of the dreaming code is shared by all Zunis, there are conflicting theories concerning precisely which part of the dreamer is traveling. One notion is that one's mind or emotions leave the body and wander (*an tse'makwi allu'a*, 'his or her thought/emotions are wandering') outside into the night world. The second notion is that one's breath wanders (*an pinanne allu'a*, 'his or her wind or breath is wandering') out into the world. These two theories roughly correspond to a particular person's social and psychological status as 'poor' or 'valuable' in terms of initiatory religious and psychological knowledge. The theory that one's thoughts wander is more likely to be stated by poor Zunis, especially highly acculturated Zunis who, although they are aware of the other theory, verbally subscribe to the materialist mind/body dual opposition and state that if one's 'wind,' or 'breath,' which is an internal part of one's body, actually left during sleep, then one would simply die. Nevertheless, those who hold to this theory express anxiety about dying while dreaming.

In contrast, valuable Zunis express no fear of dying while dreaming, or at any other time, since their initiation involves the strengthening of their essence, composed of a combination of breath and heart, by projecting part of it into their personal icon (*mi'le*). Unlike ordinary Zunis, these medicine society members and rain priests have intimate knowledge of various altered or alternative states of consciousness (ASC), whether medicine knowledge of what is 'passed through to the other side' (*pikwayina*) or priestly knowledge of 'seeing ahead' (*tunaa ehkwi*). Thus, they have little difficulty in imagining dreaming, along with receiving omens, fainting, trancing (including trances induced by Jimson weed ingestion), and possession trancing (becoming possessed by wild animals during medicine society performances), as forms of 'death,' albeit deaths that are 'miraculous' or 'passed through to the other side,' imaginal and reversible, not to be confused with irreversible literal deaths.[8]

The Zuni verb stem for dreaming, *halowa*, is intransitive, glossed by Newman (1958) as a simple morph meaning 'to dream,' 'to fall short.' However, two other stems left unanalyzed by him suggest an etymology in which present-day *halowa* derives from a combination of a stem **haloow-* with the conditional suffix *-a*. The two forms in question are *haloowtina-*, 'sacred cornmeal' (the commonest Zuni offering to the dead), and *haloowilli*, 'to be lucky.' If the hypothetical common stem *haloow-* meant something like 'luck,' then *haloowtina-* (with *-ti*, inchoative, and *-na*, static) would mean 'that which becomes lucky,' *haloowilli* (a compound form with *illi*, 'to have or possess') would mean 'to have luck,' and **haloowa* would mean 'could or would be lucky.' In the present-day *halowa* it is the unfulfilled sense given by *-a* that persists in the meaning 'fall short'; as a term for dreaming, *halowa* suggests that dreams have something to do with future luck.

Zunis classify all dreams as either 'good' (*k'okshi*) or 'bad' (*pocha*), depending on their emotional reactions upon waking from a dream.[9] Within the bad, or nightmare, category there is a subcategory of violent dreams (*halowa samu*), including sleep-onset hallucinations (HH) and sleep paralysis (SP), in which the dreamer can perform no voluntary movements. In long conversations with Tenas, a Zuni veteran, about his experiences as a witness to atrocities and a prisoner of war in Korea, I learned that for years afterward he had been deeply bothered by excessive daytime sleepiness and by sleep-onset visual and auditory hallucinations of dying from which he could not escape because of extreme pressure on his chest. This combination of daytime sleepiness, hypnagogic hallucinations, and sleep paralysis fits the narcolepsy syndrome (Brock and Wiesel 1941; Guilleminault, Dement, and Passouant 1976; Hufford 1982:149–54). Tenas had bad luck in his family life, farming, and jewelry business until he confessed these violent dreams to medicine people. He had such a bad case of narcolepsy that after repeated ceremonial whippings and a medicine-society initiation he was initiated into a second society, a rarity at Zuni, where a cure should come through initiation into a single society.

Fear of death is rather strong at Zuni, with parents especially fearful for their children. When young children wake up crying from a nightmare parents rub dampened embers on their chests, over their hearts, and give them water with embers in it to drink. Adults actively try to prevent children from having bad dreams about Kachina Village, the Land of the Dead. During all-night kachina dancing, they tickle and force-feed soft drinks, bread, and candy to youngsters in order to keep them from drifting asleep and dreaming, lest they follow the dancers to Kachina Village. Zunis of all ages are also fearful of the dark, when witches and the dead are abroad; they accompany one another even on short nighttime trips to the outhouse or the car.

Dreaming at Momostenango

Quichés, like Zunis, recognize a close connection between dreaming and dying. As Don Andrés told us, 'When one dreams one's *uwäch uk'ij* (face or destiny) leaves and goes out of the body, and it is as if one were dead. It is the same. One does not feel.' But Quichés, quite unlike Zunis, have so little fear of the dark that they may visit one another and even initiate long journeys in the middle of the night, and they express noticeably less anxiety about dreaming. Underlying the contrast in affective attitudes toward the dreaming experience is an important linguistic difference. In the Quiché language the verb for dreaming (*wachic'aj*) is transitive, indicating that *the dreamer acts upon something while dreaming*, while in Zuni the verb for dreaming (*halowa*) is intransitive, indicating that *dreaming is simply a state of being*.

There are two main Quiché theories concerning precisely what is happening when one is dreaming. One is that the dreamer's luck or destiny (*uwäch uk'ij* or *nawal*), or what I have labeled the 'free-soul,' leaves the body and goes about in the world, meeting other people's and animals' free-souls. The other is that the gods or ancestors approach the sleeping dreamer's body and awaken the lightning-soul (*coyopa*), which then struggles with the visitors until they give the dreamer a message (*ubixic*). While everyone has a free-soul that wanders outside the body during dreaming, a daykeeper's lightning-soul can receive complex messages from the cosmos and the ancestors at any time, whether during dreaming or not, without ever leaving the body. Thanks to a combination of their seeds and crystals and their own internal lightning, daykeepers readily fall into the trance state, receiving important messages from the gods and ancestors about past, present, or future events for themselves or their clients.[10] These people have no fear of dreaming or trancing, which they consider to be similar states.

With or without a lightning-soul, the dreaming experience is described as a nightly struggle between the dreamer's actively engaged free-soul, which ought to be in search of knowledge, and the free-souls of the deities and ancestors who have important messages concerning the future but seldom say exactly what they mean. As Don Andrés expressed it, 'Dreams want to win and not to be remembered clearly. Instead, you must learn to fight in order to win them, to remember whatever they advise.' Since the dream messages from the gods and ancestors concern the future, which Quichés see as a projection of the good and evil here on earth in the past and still here now, it is only natural that there would be both good dreams (*utsilaj wachic'*) and bad dreams (*itsel wachic'*), the latter including vivid, emotionally charged, unpleasant nightmares (*c'ulwächic*, literally 'to have something suddenly appear'). Don Andrés described *c'ulwächic* as: 'When one is in bed, not yet really sleeping but in the white sleep (*sak waram*), then comes the apparition; it is represented. A person comes right up to touch one, one feels they are coming to touch one directly, but one can neither move nor cry out.' As at Zuni, dream experiences that include sleep paralysis and hypnagogic hallucinations are recognized as a special subtype of bad dream, which is treated as a sickness.

DREAM SHARING

Dreams are shared both informally among family members and friends and formally in social groups at Zuni and Momostenango. However, the precise social situation, the number and type of dreams shared, the discourse frames in which they are shared, and the outcomes of the sharing process are remarkably different in these two societies. At Zuni only 'bad' dreams are normally reported to anyone, while 'good' dreams are withheld for some time even from the closest of relatives, if they are reported at all. Bad dreams are often reported in both public and private discourse frames and may eventually be reported within a secret discourse frame to medicine society members, who are the official dream interpreters of the community. (See Herdt in this volume for a full discussion of the importance of discourse frames in dream sharing in cultures that have secret societies.) In Momostenango all dreams, whether 'good' or 'bad,' even including small dream fragments, are shared immediately in public and private discourse frames with relatives and friends; important dreams involving the gods are referred to a private frame and discussed at length with initiated daykeepers, who are the official dream interpreters. These variations in behavior between the two societies are rooted in differences in both cultural theories about dreaming and attitudes toward the dreaming process itself.

Dream reporting and performing at Zuni

Dream sharing in Zuni may occur among members of the matrilocal extended household, as well as among friends, on the day following a dream experience. Not all dream experiences are immediately reported, but even dreams that are kept secret may eventually be shared with one's family, sometimes many years later. Accounts of old dreams consist of a mixture of dreams which are labeled by their narrators as bad dreams, including nightmares, and good dreams. Reports of recent dream experiences, on the other hand, always concern bad dreams.

Not only bad dreams and bad luck, but also good dreams and good luck are closely connected in Zuni thought, as the following dream story illustrates:

> A woman dreamt she was out under a piñon tree and a deer walked right up to her and spoke, saying, 'Tie me up!' The next morning at breakfast she told her husband, 'Maybe I'll be lucky and you'll bring me a deer today.'

When one hears of a good dream at Zuni it is nearly always an account of a dream that occurred some time ago rather than an immediate sharing the morning after, but once told, the story of a good dream may even be disseminated through third-person accounts like this one. Since Zunis are unwilling to give away their luck by careless talk or bragging before it can be completed, all good dreams (which are by definition good omens) are discussed with others only after the good things foretold in the dream have been realized. Thus, although the woman in the present story knew that her husband would be lucky because of her dream, she withheld the dream itself from him, silently thinking about it and reviewing it over and over again in her mind the entire time he was out deer hunting. Of course her indirect statement that perhaps she would be lucky and he would bring her a deer cued him to the fact that she must have had a good dream, but he followed Zuni conversational etiquette in not directly questioning her about it.

Bad dreams, including hallucinations in which dead people appear, should be reported because, unlike good dreams, they must not be allowed to run their course and 'become realized' or 'become completed' (*yuk'iis mowa'u*). Joe, an official in the tribal government, told us that when his cousin was seventeen years old he dreamt he was going by the cemetery at night and saw an old woman with long white hair, wearing a black blanket and carrying prayer sticks in a basket. He thought she was a dead person, and when he told his parents they warned him that he would have to report this dream to a medicine society member and be ceremonially whipped. If he had continued to have bad dreams he would have had to join a medicine society in order to be cured. According to initiated medicine people, chronic bad dreams literally *cause* serious illness, followed by death. Thus they qualify, in our terms, as 'pathogenic dreams' (Devereux 1966).

The most common way of curing (or preventing the completion) of bad dreams at Zuni is for the dreamer to tell the dream while inhaling the fumes of burning piñon gum (Parsons 1916:254) and then plant prayer sticks to the dead, asking them not to present themselves to the living (Ladd 1963:24). In more serious cases the dreamer, and sometimes a person dreamed about, receive a ceremonial whipping (*shuwaha*, literally 'make circular motions') at the hands of a kachina, as part of the formal Kachina Society initiation, during a kachina dance, or else in a kiva on the final night of the winter solstice ceremonial (Parsons 1922:203). Zunis say that a whipping removes bad thoughts or turns them around and reverses their meaning, releasing good thoughts and good luck. After striking the dreamer four times on each forearm with a yucca whip, the kachina makes a heliacal movement with the whip while raising it over his own head.

A kachina appears not to be saying anything while carrying out a whipping, but in fact he is praying silently in his heart, saying over and over again *To' toowshonanne anikchiyatu* ('May you be blessed with all kinds of seeds'). When a boy is initiated into the Kachina Society, and after he has been ceremonially whipped, he is given a bowl full of seeds to plant in a cornfield; the results of this planting are closely watched as omens concerning his future. When the whipped dreamer is given seeds, in this case seeds that exist only in the thoughts of the whipper, the course of his life is watched. If bad dreams or hallucinations persist, formal initiation into a medicine society becomes necessary in order to cure the dreamer. It is at this time that he or she receives the personal icon (*mi'le*) filled with seeds, seeds that have been instilled with the words of prayers that ask for good thoughts.

Zunis, like Quichés and Kalapalos (see Basso, this volume), view dreams as actions in themselves and not as mere statements of possible actions. Dream actions are not complete until their waking-life counterparts have taken place, but there is a complementary sense in which waking-life actions require a preceding dream. When faced with an unexpected turn of events but unable to recall an appropriate dream, Zunis are nevertheless given to saying 'I must have dreamt it.' In other words, dreams are seen not merely as a source of incidental and randomly occurring glimpses of future actions but as a necessary part of the total stream of actions. Nevertheless, a dreamer can and should attempt to influence the course of the waking side of these actions. In the case of 'good' dreams, they should keep them inside their hearts silently, but nevertheless verbally, dreaming them along in order to help continue dream actions in the waking world. In the case of 'bad' dreams they should tell them and then undergo ritual catharsis so as to reverse the meaning and thus block the waking completion of the actions already started within the bad dream.

Zuni dream sharing by strictly verbal means might be described as simply 'reporting' or 'describing' a dream rather than 'performing' it; to qualify as 'performative' in Austin's original sense (1962:5), the expression of a dream would have to take the form of an utterance that is, in itself, the doing of something rather than just the saying of something. But the communicative system that is Zuni dream sharing involves various actions other than spoken dream narratives; in order to account for it we must go beyond both Austin's 'performative' and the folkloristic notion of spoken 'performance' (Bauman 1977). When Zunis withhold a good dream by not reporting it, but nevertheless act upon it – for example, by placing a bet during kick-stick races on the basis of favorable dream imagery – or when they report a bad dream and then receive a ceremonial whipping for the report, they might be said to be 'performing' the dream in both cases. The performance itself takes a form other than that of a narrative of the dream: on the one hand the dream is transformed into the action of testing one's good luck, and on the other into that of being whipped and thus seeking to transform bad luck into good. Either way, Zunis are performing their dreaming, carrying dream actions forward into the waking world. In both cases, the *verbal* expression of the good luck is hidden, staying in the thoughts of the dreamer on the one hand or in those of the whipper on the other. Here it should be noted that Zunis regard secret discourse, including silent thinking, praying, and singing, as more powerful than speaking, praying, and singing aloud, since language kept in the heart is the most potent of all performative language, causing the outer world to conform to the inner world. That is why the mere *reporting* of repeated bad dreams is not enough to stop the resultant bad luck; they must be *performed* by means of a public whipping that is paradoxically a blessing, bringing pain while at the same time removing all traces of the dream thoughts from one's body and replacing them with the silent seeds of good thoughts.

Dream reporting and performing at Momostenango

In sharp contrast with Zuni practice, daily sharing or reporting of *all* dreams, whether evaluated by the dreamer as 'good' or 'bad,' is the cultural ideal in Momostenango. Quichés insist that everyone dreams every night; children who have no dream report after a night's sleep may be told that they did indeed dream and that they should try 'to catch the dream,' since dreams are lucky. Infants, who are said to dream much more than adults and who are too young to speak or to understand speech, do not yet have their external guardians (*chajinel*) and thus are believed to be in great danger from apparitions that may suddenly appear to them in dreams, causing them to cry out in their sleep. Because infants are unable to articulate these frightening dreams and night terrors, they are unable to defend themselves and may simply be taken away to the cold, dark underworld, dying in their sleep.

In accordance with the Quiché belief that the actions and experiences in dreams are those of the detachable free-soul (*nawal*) rather than of the more intimate life or body-soul (*uxlab*), Quiché speakers sometimes sprinkle their dream narratives with the quotative 'he/she/it says,' (*cacha'*), which is otherwise used when relating anecdotes and mythic narratives that do not deal with personal experiences.[11] Here is a literal translation of a dream report Don Andrés made early in our relationship with him; it has an unusually high number of quotatives, given the shortness of the text:

Yesterday I dreamt. I don't know what place we were, it says. We were all three [the author, her husband, and the dreamer] there. We were walking, it says, and then suddenly I was drunk, it says, and the drink did me harm, it says. I began to vomit. But what came out of my mouth was animals. They resembled lions, resembled tigers, I don't know what. They were very small, it says. They resembled cats.

Thus the dream as he reported it to us was placed in quotes as if the person who dreamt it were one 'I' and the dream narrator a second 'I,' giving a second-hand report of the experiences of the first 'I.' In the subsequent conversation he expressed uncertainty and anxiety concerning its meaning. Although he knew it wasn't 'good,' he wasn't sure just how 'bad' it might be. Since it might indicate illness for himself or for all three of us, he decided he would tell it privately, later that same day, to another dream interpreter at a shrine. Given that small and invisible but dangerous cats are the official guardians of earth shrines, protecting them from contamination by outsiders, it seemed clear to me that he was having a strong resistance to serving as our key informant. But at the time of this dream he was actually thinking of initiating us as daykeepers and introducing us to these shrines and their guardian spirits.

The quotative is also used in dream stories told long after the dream experience. Here is the beginning of a dream Don Andrés narrated to us nearly ten years after it happened.

I came out there in Chuwi Nima Juyub on to the road. I had almost entered the road when I saw a fleet of girls on bicycles coming on to the road, it says. Some ten or twelve girls, it says, and I was going along ahead of them.

He knew at the time that the women carrying him along could be a sign (*retal*), iconically indicating that he was to receive an important office, since the male elders who decide on community leadership roles all possess female personal icons (*bara*) which commonly manifest themselves in dreams as women. Indeed, by the time he told this dream story to us, he had already served out his four-year term of office as the head of the traditional government of the local community. This being so, why did he report the dream with the inclusion of the quotative? Because his lightning-soul moved in his blood during the narrative, indicating that this dream was still dreaming itself – it was not yet complete. But what would happen? What other office could he possibly receive? He expressed concern that he might have to assume a leadership role within the larger Guatemalan society, which he did not want, or else perhaps he was now going to fulfill the bicycle part of the dreaming image. Since busses, trucks, and cars are all conventionalized dream signs or signifiers sharing the same interpretant 'coffin or death' (see Mannheim, this volume), indicating that the dreamer is being taken away 'to another place,' he wondered aloud if bicycles might not also be in the same domain or signifier-interpretant set. Was his own death now being predicted? He was quite uncertain.

Not all dream narratives contain quotatives. For example, one morning during our official apprenticeship period, after first eliciting our dreams of the previous night, Don Andrés reported his own dream in the following manner:

> I had a dream today, at 2:00 or at 1:00 a.m., that I broke the big jars [a step in the initiation ritual]; when I had made one into four or five parts, it had pure honey inside, and I ate the honey. I think it is good. I took it and drank. Today is the day Came: *rutsil ri camelal,* it is the good [a favor or luck].

This dream was immediately clear and unambiguous to him since the jar, which simultaneously symbolizes the head of the novice and the world, broke properly into four or five pieces, indicating that our initiatory death and rebirth into the sacred cosmos of the Quiché world would be successful. The fact that there was something sweet rather than bitter inside the dream jar was also a good sign concerning our initiation. Finally, this dream occurred on 1 Came, an auspicious day in general and one of the key ritual days in our apprenticeship period. Since he had no doubt concerning the meaning of this dream, he was able to report his dream actions in the same way he would report his waking-life actions, without the use of the quotative.

At the time Don Andrés instructed us that whenever a dream gives a clear message (*ubixic*), the dreamer should thank the deities in the following manner: *Maltiox Nan, maltiox Tat. Ri wachic' xuya ri sak k'alaj, cajuljutic cakopkotic, par ri k'ekum pa ri ak'äb* ('Thanks Mother, thanks Father. The dream gave the white light [truth], gleaming sparkling, in the darkness in the night'). The 'mother' and 'father' here are deceased dream interpreters, who by communicating clearly with the dreamer brought the bright light of knowledge into the darkness of sleep. An unambiguously good dream such as this one is always shared without the use of the quotative and is thus reported as the *doing* of something rather than the mere *saying* of something; in effect, the 'I' of the dreamer and the 'I' of the dream reporter are one and the same. It could be said that the Quiché quotative drops away at the same point where Zunis abandon secrecy about a good dream, but there still remains a difference. A Quiché dream teller may abandon the quotative when the future event indicated by the interpretation seems inevitable, whereas the Zuni must remain silent until it has actually happened.

DREAM INTERPRETING

Both Zunis and Quichés say that nearly all dreams provide information about future events, thus sharing progressive rather than regressive dream theories (see Basso, this volume). However, their dream-sharing practices and their interpretive statements may properly be understood only in the context of their respective ontologies and religious and psychic lives. Thus, the eating of food or the recognition of a specific deceased relative by a dreamer, for example, are classified in terms of locally motivated symbolic action in each society and are interpreted quite differently.

Dream interpreting at Zuni

The key ontological concept of 'raw' vs. 'cooked' persons, based on the type of food eaten, underlies the Zuni interpretation of being served a meal in a dream by a dead person as foretelling the death of the dreamer. The living feed the dead small portions of 'cooked' food, but if the process were reversed and the dead were to feed the living instead, the food would be 'raw' and thus categorically inedible. When someone suddenly gets thin and sickly, the typical Zuni remark is 'He must be getting his meals over there at Kachina Village.' This line of thinking exemplifies the entelechical motive in Zuni symbolics, whereby a thing is classified in terms of its maturing future or end possibilities. So strong is the belief that the dead attempt to share inedible food with the living, followed by the death of the living, that when a person dies at Zuni relatives often wonder aloud if he or she did not perhaps have such an ominous dream and then fail to report it, bringing it to completion through a literal performance rather than turning it around with a curative metaphoric performance (see D. Tedlock 1975:250–1).

At Zuni, on the last night of the four-day mourning period for Otho, a teenager who accidentally shot himself, his grandmother, Rose, dreamed that she saw a line of Mixed Animal Kachinas and that he was in the middle of the line, holding a bundle of prayer-stick offerings for the dead. The kachinas filed out of the plaza and as they did so the last one in line gave a high-pitched deer call. Here, the interpretation was difficult. To dream of kachinas in their masks is a happy portent of rain, but to recognize a dead relative foretells the dreamer's own death. This dream was ambiguous because although her grandson had his mask on, Rose nonetheless did recognize Otho. However, since she reported the dream, it had no bad results and was not immediately followed by similar dreams. Several years later, however, after her husband, Daniel, and her second-born son had also died, she began having a series of dreams in which she saw all these male relatives dressed as kachinas, but without their masks on. When she reported these dreams to her children they became quite concerned about her and mentioned to us that they had noticed she was also given to dozing off during the day. They reasoned that during these short naps she might be visiting relatives over in Kachina Village. Finally, when her youngest daughter dreamed that she saw her mother laughing and talking with these same relatives, she arranged to have herself and her mother cured by being whipped by a kachina during a night dance. In other words, even though her mother was reporting these dreams to the family, they were continuing and even spreading to other family members, so that both of them needed to perform the dreams by receiving whippings for them. After these cathartic whippings neither woman was bothered by bad dreams for some time.

Dream interpreting at Momostenango

For the Quiché, since humans continue as humans (*winak*) after death, albeit in an altered form, to dream of being fed by an ancestor does not involve a conflation of ontological domains and would be interpreted purely in terms of the nature of the food offered. If it were sweet (honey or fruit) it would be a very good omen, while if it were smelly (eggs), rotten, or simply not edible (a bone or stone), it would be interpreted as a bad omen. These propositions are as true to the striving for coherence and perfection in terms of unconscious entelechic motives as in the Zuni case, but the symbol systems begin with different propositions and thus complete themselves quite differently.

Whether a dream encounter with an ancestor is 'good' or 'bad' depends on a combination of the status of the dreamer and what 'shows its face' (*wächinic*) in the dream. Initiated daykeepers and novices undergoing pre-initiation training often seek direct contacts with their dead relatives, deliberately following the downhill paths of reverie and active imagination (see Bachelard 1969; Hannah 1981; Price-Williams, this volume). At night before retiring such seekers purge themselves by drinking hot water and then pray to their ancestors by name, asking them for knowledge. Then they clear their minds and wait for what appears. If they are lucky during this early, half-waking stage of sleep, or white sleep (*sak waram*), a series of images such as a slowly opening or turning flower, or a long slow flight of a colorful tropical bird, will lead into a night of dreaming about and receiving knowledge from the ancestors. But the novice who clearly recognizes the face, body, or voice of a particular deceased individual in a dream will be urged by his or her teacher to think of this person as a generic ancestor rather than a close relative such as a namesake or surrogate (*c'exel*).

If the dreamer is neither initiated nor undergoing pre-initiation training as a daykeeper, a downhill path is never deliberately taken. In this case an encounter with an ancestor is interpreted as either a 'good' or a 'bad' omen, depending on other elements in the dream. For example, Don Andrés told me that his younger brother once reported a dream in which their dead grandmother embraced him, after which she walked with him, laughing and talking, down a steep mountain path. Don Andrés interpreted this encounter as a 'bad' dream, warning of his brother's death. If their grandmother had instead walked *up* a hill with his brother it would have been a 'good dream,' indicating that he still had a long life road. In this case the dream was reduced to a single up/down contrast and then interpreted by reference to the semantically coded sign system used for the interpretation of omens that come in waking life, in which the up/down dimension is always interpreted as good/bad.

Don Andrés remarked that if his brother had been an initiated daykeeper, like himself, or even if he were just being trained as one, then he would have interpreted this same dream as a good one, since it occurred in the mountains where the gods live, and an ancestor appeared and was talking and laughing with the dreamer. In the case of training, their grandmother would have been indicating her willingness to help. In this alternative interpretation the single semantic distinction of up/down became so unimportant that Don Andrés did not even mention it. But such an interpretation occurs only if the dreamer participates in a larger pragmatic context in which direct contacts with the ancestors are important. When this is so the dream interpreter might push the dreamer by asking 'Well, but what did she *say* to you in the dream? What message did she have for you?' Then, if the dreamer had nothing to report, the interpreter would tell him that he needed 'to complete the dream' (*ts'akanic ri wachic*') by repeating it on a day of the same name as that of the original dream, but this time asking the ancestor for a message. If Don Andrés's brother, on hearing such an interpretation of his dream, had asked to be trained by Andrés as a daykeeper, the dream could have been reinterpreted as a good one later on, when he had a similar dream with a message-bearing ancestor in it, this within the larger pragmatic context of apprenticeship. Unfortunately he did not request training and so never completed the dream; he died within a year.

The crossover between the interpretation of dream signs and the waking dream signs that are omens is common not only among the Quiché but at Zuni – and among the Quechua (see Mannheim, this volume) and many other non-Western peoples. At times it even becomes difficult to tell whether a Zuni is narrating a dream or an omen. During breakfast one morning in Zuni with Andrew, when he reported a dream of the previous night, I asked him whether he ever had dreams that foretold the future. He answered yes, but instead of telling one of his own dream experiences he told a third-person anecdote, and instead of a dream he told an omen. A herder found a dead rabbit whose body was badly torn up, and he cooked and ate it despite the objection of his partner. Later he was thrown from a burro and his foot caught in the rope stirrup. The burro dragged him around in some rocks and when his partner found him he was all torn up, dead. Though Zunis have different terms for dreaming (*halowa*) and for perceiving omens (*teli'una*, literally 'seeing the world'), the fact that the torn-up rabbit was eaten in life rather than in a dream seemed to be a matter of indifference to Andrew; either way, the incident of the rabbit would have been a portent of the incident with the burro. Here the torn-up rabbit, as though in an unreported bad dream, continued into waking conscious life, with the herder failing to stop the completion of the dream through a transforming ritual performance.

CONCLUSIONS

Differences in dream sharing and interpreting between Zunis and Quichés are traceable to a combination of ontological and psychological differences. Except for those Zuni laypersons who try to comfort themselves with the notion that it is only the 'thoughts' or 'emotions,' rather than the 'wind,' 'breath,' or life-soul, that wander during sleep, dreaming is a deathlike breach of the fragile boundary between daylight or cooked persons and raw persons. For the Quiché it is merely the free-soul that wanders in the first place, which makes dreaming a less threatening experience; animals, whether encountered in dreams or in the waking state, are never persons, while the dead, although they lose their corporeality, retain their personal names, thoughts, memories, emotions, and their membership in the human category of being. When a living Zuni recognizes the individuality of a dead person in a dream, it implies that the dreamer is as good as dead, whereas for the Quiché this dream would be a meeting of free-souls that might provide an opportunity to learn something of importance from the dead person.

This marked affective and ideological difference is underscored on the linguistic level by the Zuni use of an intransitive verb for the experience, which indicates *a state of being* while dreaming; the Quiché use of a transitive verb for the experience indicates that the dreamer *acts upon something* while dreaming. Dreaming seems to be a more intimate and personal experience for Zunis, in the sense of being directly bound to the individual dreamer's very existence; hence the conservation of good dreams and the desire to shake off or reverse bad ones. In the Quiché case, the nightly struggle of the active free-soul for a message allows dreaming to be a more social act even before it takes the form of a verbal narrative, placing the dreamer in a nocturnal community of other free-souls, both living and dead.

That Zunis are passive within the dreaming process itself and secretive with respect to good dreams, whereas Quichés are active and open, is consistent with their respective behaviors toward and affective responses to personal icons, into which they project parts of their life-souls. Zunis are reluctant to discuss their *miwe*, or metaphoric 'parents,' and normally they display them only by placing them on an altar during a ceremony. If there is any apparent movement or change of appearance, it will be taken as an omen concerning the outcome of a particular ritual or their own futures; such omens are not actively sought, but can only be awaited. Quichés, on the other hand, are open and expressive in talking about and playing with their *bara*, or metaphoric 'spouses,' kissing, fondling, opening, and caressing them, the better to receive life-giving knowledge for themselves or for a particular client.

A key ontological difference between the two cultures is that for the Quiché, the defining feature of humans (who include the dead) is the ability to speak articulately; for the Zuni, humans (who exclude the dead) are defined by dependency on cooked food. Zuni anxiety about dreaming focusses, above all, on the horrible thought of being given food by a dead person, thus being moved from the 'cooked' category into the 'raw' category. The Quiché anxiety is to control dreaming so as to understand, or put into human speech, the message of the dream, whether there was actual speech in the dream itself or not. If Zuni dreaming risks the very life of the dreamer, the first and foremost risk of Quiché dreaming is the loss of articulate human communication.

In the matter of dream sharing, one of the most general contrasts between Zunis and Quichés is in the treatment of good and bad dreams. At Zuni only bad dreams are (or should be) immediately reported and interpreted, performed (if that is necessary) through the reversal of a whipping, while 'good' dreams should be carried into waking life and kept unfolding by verbally-full but silent performance. The linguistically coded perception of the experience of dreaming is that the dreamer's future state of being is revealed while the dreamer is unable to act directly upon the presentation, but that the wakened dreamer may perform the dream by turning the intransitivity of its events into the transitivity of the acting out of these events. Quichés, on the other hand, since they are already 'acting out' during the dreaming itself, are encouraged to report all dreams, 'good' or 'bad'; only later are certain of these reported dreams further acted out or 'performed' through prayer or decision making. This means, among other things, that Zunis privately evaluate a dream before they decide whether or not to report it, finally telling a 'good' dream only when it has been proven good through actual results in waking life. In this latter case, it might be said that life itself is the interpretation of the dream, making possible a coherent dream narrative. Quichés, on the other hand, treat all dreams as immediately and necessarily open to reporting and interpretation by self as well as by others.

What this suggests, at a more general level, is that the problems with comparing the phenomenology of dreaming between cultures begin even before the telling and interpretation of the dream, at the level of dream sorting, or classification, which is linguistically coded and symbolically rooted in local epistemology and metapsychology. And the problems do not end when the dream comes to be talked about or performed; the outward dimensions of the performance may take nonverbal forms, and the meaning may be questioned all over again at a later time. From the perspective of possibilities like these, any attempt at counting and comparing the manifest content of verbal dream reports that have been deprived of their social and symbolic contexts appears groundless. Where symbolic actions are concerned, the move to the comparative level does not free us from the kind of research in which the fieldworker takes account of the indigenous language and develops intimate interpersonal communication, on both conscious and unconscious levels, with the members of a culture. We need to find a way to move not from surface to surface, but from depth to depth.

NOTES

1. The Zuni field research upon which this chapter depends began during 1969 and the work is still in progress and will continue, while the field research among the Quiché Maya of Momostenango began in 1975 and has been suspended since 1979. The fieldwork and write-up have been supported at various times by an NEH Summer Stipend, a Grant-in-Aid from the Wenner-Gren Foundation, a Research Fellowship from the State University of New York at Albany, a Summer Faculty Fellowship from Tufts University, and a Weatherhead Fellowship at the School of American Research in Santa Fe, New Mexico.
2. In the Zuni orthography used here, the five vowels (a, e, i, o, u) should be given their continental values. Double vowels (aa, ee, ii, oo, uu) should be held a bit longer than single ones, like the long vowels in Greek. Most consonants should be pronounced as in English, except that p and t are unaspirated. The lh sounds like English h and l pronounced simultaneously, something like the Ll in Welsh 'Lloyd.' The glottal stop (') is like the tt in the Scottish pronunciation of 'bottle.' Double consonants (cch, hh, kk, ll, llh, mm, nn, pp, ss, ssh, tt, ww, yy) are held a bit longer than single ones, like the double consonants in Italian. Stress is always on the first syllable, except in words marked with accents.
3. In the Quiché orthography ä is like the u in English 'much'; other vowels (a, e, i, o, u) should be pronounced as in Spanish. Consonants are also as in Spanish, with an equivalence between c (used before a, o, and u) and qu (before e and i), except for k, which is articulated with the tongue farther back than for c or qu; l, which is like Zuni lh; tz,

which is like German Zeit; w, which is like English w; x, which is like the English sh; and b, which is a glottalized p. Other glottalizations are indicated by an apostrophe ('). Stress is nearly always on the final syllable of a word.

4. I have chosen the English term 'icon' rather than 'fetish' to refer to both the Zuni *mi'le* and the Quiché *bara* out of respect for native points of view. According to the *O.E.D.* an icon is 'a representation of some personage . . . itself regarded as sacred and honoured with worship or adoration'; while a fetish is 'an inanimate object worshipped by savages on account of its supposed inherent magical powers.' Semiotically these sacred objects might be considered both as 'icons,' or signs that bear a resemblance of some sort – they are individual, have heads and bodies, wear clothes – of the person who possesses them, and as 'indexes,' or signs that point to or are connected with the individual object or person (Peirce 1932).
5. My use of 'soul' in translating the Zuni term *pinanne* 'wind' or 'breath' should not be misunderstood as referring to the moralistic doctrine of the Spirit or Soul of God (*spiritus*), brought by monistic Christianity to the indigenous peoples of the Americas. I have decided to use 'soul' here since many psychologists today are returning to the general use of the word without its Christian implications (see Hillman 1975a, 1979; Bettelheim 1983).
6. In making this body-soul/free-soul distinction I am following Hultkrantz (1952) and Paulson (1954), who were modifying Wundt's (1912) 'bound-soul,' the activating principle of internal organs, and 'free-soul,' which is composed of two parts, the breath-soul and shadow-soul.
7. For a less elaborated Quichean soul belief in which there are but two souls, one evil body soul (*jalajmac*) and one good guardian spirit (*chajenel*), see Duncan Earle (1982).
8. Although the evidence for possession at Zuni was reported in early ethnographic descriptions (Stevenson 1904) and continues to be reported today (D. Tedlock 1976), Zuni is erroneously abstracted in the H.R.A.F. files. Thus Erika Bourguignon (1973:359–76) lists Zuni as one of her Type 5 societies, with ritualized trance but with a belief in possession that refers to phenomena other than trance. In fact there are various kinds of trance states at Zuni, some explained by possession beliefs and others not, which makes Zuni a Type 7 society.
9. The Hopi, neighbors to the Zuni, share the dual classification of dreams in which only 'bad' ones are reported while 'good' ones are withheld until they come true (Eggan 1961, 1966). Nevertheless, when Dorothy Eggan discussed her content analysis of a particular Hopi's corpus of dreams and found a

high ratio of 'bad' to 'good' dreams (136 'bad' to 84 'good' plus 34 'indifferent'), she strangely concluded that this was 'evidence of unease in this dreamer's personality' (1952:482). Since many 'good' dreams concern a long and healthy life for the dreamer one is rarely able to collect them; any Hopi or Zuni sample of the manifest content in reported dreams will always be nonrepresentative of the entire dream corpus.

10. Bourguignon (1973) lists the Quiché as a Type 3 society, where ritualized trance behavior, labeled as possession, occurs, but where possession beliefs referring to experiences or trance states that have other than possession explanations do not occur. Like the Zuni, however, the Quiché actually fit Type 7; the divination trance is *not* explained as possession, whereas trances during séances are explained as possession by gods or ancestors (see B. Tedlock 1982).
11. The use of the quotative in dream narration also occurs in the Highland Mayan community of Zinacantán (Laughlin 1976:11), where the basic theory of the dream experience is similar to the Quiché one, namely that one's 'essence' or 'soul' (*ch'ulel*) leaves the body during sleep and visits other souls or appears before the ancestral deities and communicates with them (Vogt 1976:18). This is also true of the neighboring towns of San Pedro Chenalho and Chamula (Guiteras-Holmes 1961:296; Gossen 1975:455).

6
A semiotic of Andean dreams

BRUCE MANNHEIM

Á quanto sueñan le atribuien misterio, governándoce por ellos, dessifiando cada cosa en axiomas significatibos, en lo que son eximios.

PABLO JOSÉ ORCAIN, Andahuaylillas, 1790

You don't understand the meaning of your dreams. For me dreams are so clear.

ANONYMOUS RUNA, Andahuaylillas, 1979

At dusk in the Southern Peruvian Andes,[1] doors close, as much to mark the limits of nighttime sociability as to keep out the cold night air. The world of dusk is fraught with danger as it passes from the dominion of social beings, or Runa,[2] to grotesque beings: the bones of the long dead; the slaughterer who sucks Runa fat and processes it for the church and for business; mermaids with hair of seven colors who live in springs along with other water beings; condemned souls; headless souls. Encounters with any of these beings inevitably leads to debilitating illness and death. Since several of them are able to take human form, from dusk on social interaction is guarded, particularly with those you do not know well.

Twice during our stay in the highlands of Cuzco we arrived at dusk in the community of Lluthu, a Grupo Campesino up valley from the district center of Andahuaylillas located in the province of Quispicanchi thirty-two kilometers south of Cuzco. The second time was late in our fieldwork and, following the advice of an acquaintance, we walked with our tape recorder blaring dance music at full volume. But the first time, Diane Hopkins and I arrived in silence. We had planned to arrive in the early afternoon, but rounds of forced hospitality of soup and liquor had kept us in the district center. When we finally arrived at the house of our hosts, Mr Choque and Ms Paucar, it was dark when we knocked at the door. We were surprised by their startled reaction; they knew we were coming and had greeted us warmly on other occasions, including the first time when we arrived in Lluthu as unknown travelers accompanying another traveler as he walked the uphill path to the community. But this time Choque, Paucar, and several of their neighbors looked at us warily, crossed themselves, hesitated, and invited us in. After another round of exchange of presents and several rounds of drinks we were asleep.

It was still dark and cold at half past three in the morning when we were awakened by a blaring radio placed close to our heads. Mr Choque said, 'Let's go to the mountain. Let's go to the mountain to get my animals.' I was bewildered but got up and Choque and I went out into the night with his radio still blaring. I remembered the strange reception of the night before and was worried. Walking along in near darkness, I finally broke my companion's single-minded crankiness to get an answer about why we were going to the mountain. He had had a dream: Diane Hopkins appeared to him calling '*papáy, papáy*.' She had a sack of potatoes which she had brought to exchange with him for a sack of dry maize. Choque explained the dream: 'maize (*sara*) is money (*qolqe*); potatoes (*papas*) are my animals. She came to warn me that a thief was planning to steal the animals which I left grazing on the high grasslands on Mount Hatun Saywa and sell them to butchers in Urcos, the provincial capital.'

What did Choque's dream mean? How did he know what it meant? The two questions, one concerning the structure of dream signs in Quechua culture and the other concerning the structure of the interpretive process, are closely linked. The purpose of this essay is to explore the nature of the linkage. I shall treat dreaming and dream interpretation as a cultural system; that is, a conventional, directively organized system of signs which is articulated with, but structurally autonomous from, other cultural media such as narrative (which I shall refer to as 'myth'), several genres of song, dance, and ritual.

When I refer to dreams as 'structurally autonomous' from other cultural media, I do so in order to treat the relationship between dream signs, their interpretations, and non-dream signs as problematic. While Quechua dreams clearly have peculiarly Quechua manifest content, we would trivialize the question of the relationship between dreams and the rest of the culture by attempting to explain them away in terms of other cultural media in a reductive and atomistic fashion. The stock of signs, their mutual connections and their interpretation are proper to dreams. By 'conventional' I mean that signs and their interpretants as well as the process of interpretation are intersubjective constructs which are, to some extent, shared by members of a cultural community. They are appropriated by individuals, not created, however subconsciously, *ex nihilo*, and therefore exhibit historical stability. Dream signs are historically stable insofar as they refer to culturally constituted objects and activities which are themselves signs. On the other hand, no matter how palpably motivated by their *designata*, dream signs are historical products and subject to change. The question of their historicity, that is, the extent to which they, among cultural systems, are subject to change over time, is a question which must be posed.

I propose to do so by examining two corpora of dream signs and interpretations from the highland Andean parish of Andahuaylillas which were collected three and one-half centuries apart. The older material was collected by the parish priest, Juan Pérez Bocanegra, and reported in a priest's manual which he published in 1631. The modern material is from my fieldwork in Andahuaylillas during the period 1976–9 and from subsequent work with a Quecha-speaking consultant from the area during the period 1980–1 in the United States, in which we examined and discussed the 1631 texts and worked with her own dreams and dream interpretations on a regular basis.

Confrontation of the two sets of data shows a virtually complete replacement of signifier-interpretant complexes despite the fact that they are drawn from a general cultural stock for which persistence over the entire time span has been so often noted by ethnologists and ethnohistorians that it has become a cliché of the field. The relative transience of dream signs contrasts especially sharply with the relative persistence of mythic and ritual forms. Custred (1978), for example, shows the durability of the thematic elements of a myth of social transformation from the early seventeenth century to the 1960s. Hopkins (n.d.) demonstrates the temporal invariance of a single mythic sign through superficial iconic reinterpretation in the process of showing its recording in a formally related myth which likewise is attested since the early seventeenth century. Hopkins (1982), again, points out the perdurance of the cluster of ritual activities surrounding moiety battles from Inkaic Cuzco until the present. Isbell (1978) demonstrates continuity in the organization of the ritual calendar and in related cosmological structure since the European invasion of the sixteenth century. Finally Hocquenhem (n.d.) has recently proposed a novel interpretation of the entire corpus of Moche ceramics which will push continuity of ritual calendrics and activity yet further. The near-total replacement of the lexicon of dream signs thus represents something of an anomaly for Andean systems of thought.

Sign systems carry meaning by virtue of three primary relationships: (1) the *semantic* relationships of signs to their objects by means of other signs (their *interpretants*); (2) the *syntactic* relationships of signs to other signs with which they are combined; (3) the *pragmatic* relationships of signs to their users.[3] Interpretation of signs relies both on perceptible cues supplied by the culturally conventional sign medium itself and on a conventionalized interpretive framework. Since a successful act of interpretation, be it by a user of the sign system or by an outside observer, requires taking account of all three dimensions, the interpretive framework must include conventions for interpreting the syntactic and pragmatic contexts of signs as well as their semantical dimension.[4] On the other hand, the medium itself might specify or encode one or two of the dimensions, placing a correspondingly larger burden on the interpretive system in the nonspecific dimensions.

In Southern Peruvian Quechua culture, dreams, myths, and rituals do in fact vary with respect to the semiotic dimensions which each encodes. Dreams mean, as we shall see, by virtue of an immediate relationship between signifier and interpretant. They encode the semantical dimension and leave the syntactic and pragmatic dimensions unspecified. Mythic signs are taken account of by way of encoded relationships with other signs. Quechua myth primarily encodes the semantical and syntactical dimensions. A 'taking account' of ritual signs is mediated both by their codified existential relationship to other signs and their codified relationship to ritual participants.

Such codified contiguity relationships index signs to their syntactical and pragmatical contexts.[5] These contexts, in effect, act as anchors on the semantical interpretation of signs. We may now account for the variable historical resilience of the three sign systems as follows. The signifier-interpretant relationship in ritual is anchored into coded syntactic and pragmatic contexts with which the ritual activity becomes an emergent structure of structures. Likewise, the syntactics of mythic discourse contribute to the emergent properties of particular texts and in the process anchor the signifier-meaning relationship of its component signs. The importance of narrative syntactics to mythic interpretation and of both syntactics, 'positional meaning,' and pragmatics, 'operational meaning,' to ritual interpretation has been pointed out numerous times in the anthropological literature (Lévi-Strauss 1967 and T. Turner 1969 for myth, and V. W. Turner 1973 for ritual). There is no need to belabor these points here, although since the problem was posed in culture-specific terms it will ultimately be necessary to demonstrate them for Southern Peruvian Quechua.

The specific mode of interpretation of dreams in Southern Peruvian Quechua culture involves a disaggregation of signs from any narrative sequence or pragmatic context by means of either selection of individual signs during the process of interpretation or suppression of all but a single conventionally interpretable sign. The taking account process focusses on individual signifier-interpretant complexes which may eventually be recontextualized in a different form, but often are not. Because dream signs are interpreted primarily by means of the immediate semantical relationship, signifier and meaning are, as it were, adrift in culture-specific terms it will ultimately be necessary to demonstrate intersubjectively less resilient to change. The characteristics which account for the relative permanence of ritual and mythic signs are, by dint of the mode of interpretation, absent from the dream code.

The following sections establish the context for the 1631 dream lexicon and further describe the specific mode of interpretation of dreams. I shall conclude with some general remarks on the locus of laws of structure for the three semiotic media and on their interpretation.

HISTORICAL PERSPECTIVE

We mistakenly think of the early colonial evangelical priests as doctrinal hairsplitters who contented themselves with baptismal body counts and administration of church properties. We underestimate their effort when all we see in it is the imposition of a formal Catholic overlay on a bedrock of indigenous beliefs. Besides being counters of baptisms and *reales*, missionary priests were the cultural soldiers of the conquest (Duviols 1971). Their job was not merely one of substitution of saints for sacred places, but the ideological conquest of the militarily vanquished. 'Bring me your sacred things,' they were instructed to say, 'and I will stomp them' (Tercer Concilio Provincial, 1585:242). While the colonial economy was still in the process of consolidation they campaigned against virtually any distinctly Andean cultural practice as 'idolatrous.' They admonished against offerings to the earth (ibid.:233), but also fought coca chewing, first haircutting, communal drinking, eating seated on the floor, and the Quechua language (Mannheim 1984). How could Runa expect to talk to god in their own tongue? (Tercer Concilio Provincial, 1585:405).

The evangelists observed the widespread Andean preoccupation with dreams and dream interpretation and enjoined its practice (Polo 1571:31; Cobo 1636,2:234).

Ama moscoyta yupaychanquichicchu,
caytam chaytam mosconi,
ymapac mosconam ñispa
ama tapucunquichicchu:
moscoyca yancallan
manam yupaychaypacchu
(Tercer Concilio Provincial 1585:255)[6]

Don't be keeping dreams:
'I dreamt this or that,
why did I dream it?'
Don't ask:
dreams are just worthless and
not to be kept.

There is some evidence that in preconquest Peru alongside popular lay concern with dream interpretation, there were ritual specialists whose dreams were considered particularly significant and other ritual specialists who interpreted dreams, much in the way in which organized specialists practice side-by-side with lay dream interpretation in contemporary Mesoamerica (see B. Tedlock 1981). Reports from the early-seventeenth-century campaigns against 'idolatry' identify both female dream ministers (*ministra soñadora*) and dream interpreters (*que daba respuesta de los sueños*) as *moscoc* ('who dreams') (Hernández Príncipe 1622:25ff; Arriaga 1621:206). Hernández Príncipe identified both types of dream specialists as women; Arriaga does not identify the sex of the *moscoc*.[7] State-level chroniclers (e.g. Cieza 1550:102) mention male state dreamers and interpreters. An early Augustinian report mentions the case of an indigenous priest whose recruitment was preceded by three dreams in which he was chasing an eagle. The Augustinians, of course, attributed the entire affair to the devil (Primeros Agustinos 1865:18).

Cobo (1636,2:227) observed that indigenous curers, known as *camasca* ('ordered') and *soncoyoc* ('with essence'), attributed their callings to dreams:[8]

> Preguntados quién les dió o enseñó el oficio que usaban los más daban por principal causa y respuesta haber soñado, diciendo que estando durmiendo se les apareció alguna persona, que doliendose de su necesidad, les dijo que les daba facultad para curar de aquellas enfermedades que curaban; y siempre que empezaban la cura, sacrificaban algo a aquella persona que afirmaban habérseles aparecido entre sueños y enseñandoles el modo de curar y los instrumentos con que lo habían de hacer.
>
> When asked who gave them or taught them their occupation, the majority gave as primary cause and response that they had dreamt, saying that while dreaming some person appeared to them who suffering from need told them that they were being given the ability to cure those diseases which they cured; and whenever they began a cure, they sacrificed something to the person who they claimed appeared to them in dreams and taught them the method of curing and the instruments with which they were to do it.

Dream specialists were employed by the state for prognostication. Garcilaso (1609:lib. IV, cap. xxii) reported that:

> particularmente miraron mucho en sueños, y más si los sueños acertaban a ser del Rey o del príncipe heredero o del Sumo Sacerdote, que estos eran tenidos entre ellos por dioses y oráculos mayores, a los cuales pedían cuenta de sus sueños los adevinos y hechiceros para los interpretar y declarar, cuando los mismos Incas no decían lo que habían soñado.
>
> they particularly divined using dreams, especially if the dreams turned out to be

those of the king or the crown prince or the high priest, for these latter were held to be gods and important oracles, who were asked to render account of their dreams for interpretation by diviners and sorcerers when the Inkas themselves didn't declare what they had dreamt.

Indeed, prognostication by dreaming figures prominently in Inka dynastic mythology (Jiménez 1961).

Only two colonial sources mention specific dream signs and their interpretations, both as accounts of early-seventeenth-century rural life. Felipe Guaman Poma de Ayala (*c.* 1615:282), an early-seventeenth-century indigenous local-level lord, political reformer, and ethnographer of sorts, listed eight or so dream signs in the context of a discussion of rural prognostication and omens in his 1,200-page letter of protest to the king of Spain.[9]

> quando suenan urunina dizen que ade caer enfermo y
> quando suenan de chicollo y uaychau y de chiuacoc
> dizen q' ade rrinir quando suenan acuyraqui mayuta
> chacata chinpani: yntiquilla uanun dizen q' ade murir
> su pe osu madre; quando suenan quiroymi lloccin q'ande
> murir su pe osu ermano llamata nacani lo propio cuando
> suena rutuscamcani que ade ser biuda moscospa yana
> pachauan pampascamcani, callampatam riconi, zapallotam
> paquini moscuypi enestos suenos abuciones creyan
> q'abian de murir ellos o sus pe. o madres o los dhos
> ermanos o enbida [a]vian de partirse de la tierra cada
> uno o ausentarse . . .

> When they dream 'firefly'
> they say they are to fall sick
> and when they dream *chicollo* and *uaychau* and *chiuacoc*
> [birds]
> they say that they are to get angry;
> when they 'dream *acuyraqui* ['misfortune'?]
> I cross a bridge over a river,
> sun-moon die,'
> they say that their father or their mother is to die;
> 'I butcher a llama'
> the same;
> one dreams 'I am sheared'
> one is to be a widow;
> dreaming 'with dark clothing I am buried
> I see *callampatan* [a mushroom of sorts]
> I break up a squash'
> in a dream

in these dreams,
  omens
they believed that they
  or their fathers
  or mothers
  or the said brothers
were to die
or that each one must leave the earth
or absent themselves . . .

Andean dream signs fade imperceptibly into omens or premonitions much as Tedlock (this volume) reports for Quiché and Zuni. Guaman Poma, as virtually every other colonial commentator, integrates dreams into a premonitory cluster including omen signs and divination, and though 'dream' (*mosqoy*) is the only named category among them we are likely dealing with a single system, for they share a characteristic focus on interpreting isolated signs by strictly semantical criteria.[10] It is not coincidental that Guaman Poma's dream signs are exclusively negative. Guaman Poma worked as translator for the idol-smasher Cristóbal de Albornoz, and was influenced by the published works of the Third Council of Lima. An unabashed Christian (albeit an Andean one), he considered dreams to be the work of the devil, and so relabeled the dream ministers 'dream witches' and 'lying witch sorcerers' (*llulla laica umi*) (see figure 6.1).

A curious final point about Guaman Poma's dream signs is that he reports a number of them in Quechua, in all cases using the affirmation suffix *-mi* ~ *-m*, which marks the narrated event as the verifiable, personal knowledge of the speaker. The suffix is entirely inappropriate for narrating dream events. Use of an affirmation marker is avoided in the unmarked tense. In the past tense a special form (*-sqa*) is used for dreamt events, and for delirium, drunkenness, and mythical and historical events which could not possibly be the personal knowledge of the speaker. Guaman Poma's use of the *-mi* suffix is likely intended as ironic ridicule of people who believed in dream interpretation.

The second colonial source with specific dream signs and interpretations is a priest's manual written by a contemporary of Guaman Poma, Juan Pérez Bocanegra, the parish priest in Andahuaylillas, the very village with which I began this paper. Pérez Bocanegra also served as a singer in the Cathedral of Cuzco and as choir book corrector and held the position of *examinador general* of Quechua and Aymara for the

Figure 6.1 Top: Guaman Poma's rendering of a 'dream witch.' Reproduced from Felipe Guaman Poma de Ayala, *El primer nueva coronica y bve gobierno*, facsimile edition (Paris, 1936)

bishopric of Cuzco. His *Ritual formulario* includes crucial data on Inkaic and early colonial Quechua culture and society as well as the first vocal polyphony composed in the New World, an untranslated hymn to the Virgin which identifies her with the Pleiades and praises her for her fecundity (Mannheim 1983:214–15). The *Ritual formulario* includes two texts, one in Southern Peruvian Quechua and the second a non-facing paraphrase in Spanish which purports to be a translation but varies from the Quechua often in subtle but telling ways.

Pérez Bocanegra observed the preoccupation with dream interpretation in the village and included it among a number of cultural practices which he regarded as idolatrous or sinful, most of which are still practiced in the parish today. His dream texts appear in the form of yes/no questions which are designated to allow a confessor to fish for sins from a parishioner with whom he is barely able to communicate.

Moçcoscaiquicta lñecchu canqui?
allintam moçconi
manallictam moçconi,
moçcoscaimã tupu chayapuan ñispa
ñecchu canqui?
Pimampas villacchu canqui,
vnanchapuay moçcoscaita ñispa
Puñuspa moçcoiñijquipi
chacacta purispa,
raquipacmi moçconi ñispa
ñecchu canqui?
Chai hinatacchu moçcopi,
challhuacta hapispa
cunã punchaumi machasac ñispa
ñecchu canqui?
Chaihinatac, moçcoyñijquipi,
tarucacta ricuspa,
runap uman coroscacta,
coro maquicta,
machachuaita
yutucta ricuspa,
puñucuspa yuyascaiquicta,
collom,
raquim,
acoiraquim ñispa
ñecchu cãqui,
chaita Iñispatac?

Are you a believer in what you dream?
'I dream well,
I don't dream well,
What I have dreamt has arrived to me in measure.'
Do you say it?
Do you tell someone
'understand me my dream?'
While asleep, in your dream
crossing a bridge
'it's for separation I dreamed'
Do you say it?
And like that, in a dream
catching a fish
'today I'll get drunk'
Do you say it?
And like that, in your dream
seeing a deer,
a headless person,
a handless one,
a snake
Seeing a partridge,
your remembrance, while sleeping,
'wrecked plans,
separation,
disaster,'
Do you say it,
Do you believe that?

Pérez Bocanegra's dream texts continue listing additional dream signs and interpretations without discursive shift into descriptions of omens (see Table 1). As Guaman Poma did, Pérez Bocanegra presents a lexicon of dream signifiers and conventional interpretants. Where signifier and interpretant are linked by more than simple juxtaposition it is with the suffix *-paq*, 'for': *chacacta purispa, raquipacmi* ('crossing a bridge, it's for separation').[11] Yet the use of the verbal expression *unancha-*, 'understand, interpret,' leads one to wonder whether both colonial sources are not in fact casting Andean dream interpretation into a Christian mode: Pérez Bocanegra was, after all, a priest and Guaman Poma the former assistant to Albornoz and an avid student of colonial religious texts. And *unancha* is the expression missionary preachers used to explain the Catholic doctrine of 'sign.' Their sermons emphasized that the cross and the saints were not idols, but *unancha*,

Table 1. *Signifiers and interpretations in Pérez Bocanegra's dream lexicon*

Signifier	Interpretation
condor, hawk	birth of a male child
wool, spider web	extreme sorrow
woody *quinua* plant	'clothing of pain' (lack of clothing?)
quinua	crestfallen, cast out
appear lit by sun or moon	death of a neighbor or companion
small birds	fear
dark person, pig, dog	some kind of disaster
person with change of clothing	someone will die
trip	defeat
trip with the left foot	thoughts will not come true
trip with right foot	thoughts will be reality
two-headed serpent*	great disaster

*See López-Baralt (1980) for a discussion of the symbolism of the two-headed serpent in Andean iconography.

which stood for holy entities. On the other hand, the two primary colonial sources on dreams are unusual in that they were both written by people with solid first-hand experience in rural Quechua-speaking communities. Guaman Poma was himself a first-language Quechua speaker whose native tongue is evident in his use of Spanish. His letter to the king is by far and away the best source on traditional local-level Andean practices. Pérez Bocanegra's superb command of the language (of which he was likely *not* a native speaker) is evidenced by his stylistic virtuosity. His priest's manual shows a detailed understanding of rural Andean life which similarly goes beyond that of his clerical colleagues. Both are close to unimpeachable as sources. But there is no independent corroboration of the interpretive practices which their descriptions imply were used by Quechua speakers of the early seventeenth century. But there is continuity between the mode of interpretation in the colonial descriptions and contemporary practices of interpretation.

CONTEMPORARY DREAMING

The Andean world of dawn, 'emergence,' or 'just from the night,' returns to Runa and they often discuss a dream of the past night as they awaken.[12] Dreams are premonitory of the day's events and are valid only for the day on which they are dreamed. Under normal circumstances one arises by standing first on the right foot. But in the case of a bad omen appearing in the dream, one stands first on the left foot. Before informing anyone of your dream you must find a young sheep or camelid, recount the entire dream to it and then spit in its mouth three times saying: *qolluy*, *qolluy*, *qolluy* ('disappear, disappear, disappear').

Dreams are world-creating (as in Kalapalo, see Basso, this volume), either by literally forecasting an event or by means of individual oblique signs. In the first case no further interpretation is required; in the second the dream is treated as a narrative from which an element or occasionally elements are singled out and interpreted from a lexicon of dream signs. Consider the following dream narrative:

Ch'isi mosqokurani terremotomanta. Manan reqsisqay llaqtapi terremoto pasaran. Chay llaqtapi kasqa huq mayu. Chay mayu t'aqasqa llaqtata iskayman. Huq lado llaqtapi terremoto pasasqa huq ladunpitaq mana. Chayñataq lluy pampakuna kicharirukuran. Mallkikuna kumpakamuran. Hinaspañataq lluy runakuna qaparispayku eshkapamuyku huq ladu llaqtaman. Chayñataq huq iskalera wichanapaq kasqa rumimanta. Chayta wichayman lluy wichayku. Nuqa ultimullataña wicharani. Hinaspa chay pataman chayaqtiy. Chaypi rumimantakama wasikuna pirqasqa kasqa. Chaymanta *MUNAY* ñawpa q'erokuna kasqa lluy q'erokuna t'urumanta allpamanta ruwasqa. Chaypi rixch'apurani.

Last evening I dreamt about an earthquake. The earthquake passed through an unknown village. There was a turbulent river in that village, and it split the village in half. (One part was in a pampa and the other half on a hill.)[13] The earthquake took place on one side but not on the other. All the pampas opened. Trees tumbled over. So all the people, we [including the speaker, excluding the addressee] screamed, and we escaped to the other side of the village. There was a stone staircase for climbing [to the other half]. We all climbed to get up. *But I was just the last to climb.* So I got to the top. There the houses were there, all made of stone (and without roofs). And there were *beautiful* old *q'eros* [Inkaic ritual drinking vessels], all the *q'eros* made of earth, made of mud. I woke up then.

For the narrator, the most significant element was the turbulent river, which indicated an imminent obstacle or problem. The climb suggested to the narrator that he think of his work, but no more definitive interpretation was made of it. Two days later I was told that the earthquake had forecast a storm that took place. I found the narrative so symbolically loaded in Andean cultural terms that I was surprised at the poverty of the interpretation. More curious still, the narrative was linguistically marked by a repeated switch between the unmarked past and a past form used for narrated events to which the speaker cannot attest (*-sqa*). The latter is the most frequent of the tense-mood markers in both dreams and myths. Scene descriptions were marked by the dream past (*-sqa*), whereas actions took the unmarked past (*-ra*). Although the tense-mood alternation functioned to highlight actions over scene descriptions, it was a feature of the telling itself and played no part in the interpretation. Highlighted actions had no special significance above background scenes. The significant element in this case was, in fact, drawn from the background marked by the dream past.

The interpretation begins by 'recalling' the dream in a narrative form. The narrative is scanned for individual signs drawn from a conventional lexicon of dream signs. The lexicon supplies a general conventional meaning for each signifier. The general meanings are narrowed into a more specific interpretation by taking individual situational factors into account. The interpretations may have absolutely nothing to do with the manifest content of the narrative apart from the interpreted signs! When more than one sign is selected from a given narrative, they need not have anything to do with the others, but may. If they are joined in interpretation, a second narrative is constructed. Mr Choque's dream of the potato–maize transaction with which I began this paper is a case in point. Hopkins came to Choque with a sack of potatoes which she brought to exchange for a sack of maize. The exchange of potatoes for maize is the prototypic Andean commodity transaction. Potatoes are emblematic of the higher-altitude *puna* zones in which they are produced. Maize is emblematic of the more temperate and lower-altitude *qheswa* zones. Here the activity is interpreted in terms of the conventional readings of maize as 'money,' and potatoes as 'meat.'

The relationship between maize and money is polarized by Hopkins's presence in the dream as a non-Runa exchanging with a Runa. Runa, who consider maize to be the basis of subsistence, often use the most general word for food, *mihuna* (the material nominalization of 'to eat'), to designate maize alone. NonRuna (*q'ara*, 'naked, uncivilized') are criticized because they, by inverse analogy, 'live from money.' This observation has been made by Runa at least since the seventeenth century. For example, a hilarious drawing in Guaman Poma's (1615:369) letter to the king shows a Runa handing a Spaniard some gold asking 'Do you eat this gold?' (*Cay coritacho micunqui?*). The metaphorical relationship between potatoes and meat is iconically heightened by the perceptual similarity, within Quechua culture, of the pulp of each. The relationship is supported by a metonymic relationship between the two: potato cultivation and grazing both take place in higher-altitude lands.

The two signs are now reintegrated taking individual situational factors into account. Choque left his animals grazing in *puna* lands on Mount Hatun Saywa. He interpreted the sack of potatoes to mean that 'there is meat on the mountain' and therefore thieves were planning to cut up his animals in the field in which they were grazing and take the pulpy parts to the provincial capital, Urcos, where they could exchange meat for money.

INTERPRETATION

Contemporary dream interpretation involves codification of the dream experience in narrative form; reduction of the narrative to one or a few pivotal signifier-interpretant complexes drawn from a conventional lexicon; and recontextualization of the pivotal signs taking into account personal situational facts and occasionally other pivotal signs. This process can be represented as follows:

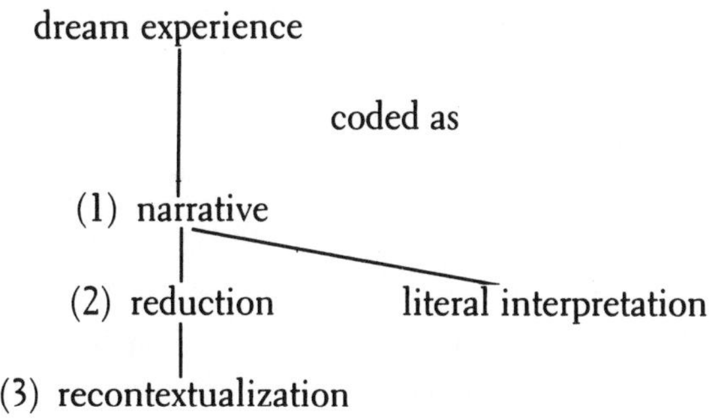

Each step in the interpretive process is a level of sign activity unto itself. A codified narrative may, in rare circumstances, be treated as a literal portent of the narrated events. The normal mode of interpretation, however, is to refer individual signs taken out of their context in the codified narrative to a conventionalized lexicon. The interpretation is figurative with respect to the narrative level but literal with respect to the conventionalized lexicon of dream signs. It is precisely the routinized and conventional nature of the maize-money sign relationship to Mr

Choque's dream which permits the sign to act as a pivot in the construction of a metaphorical interpretation of the narrated situation as a whole.

The crux of the interpretive process is the reduction step, in which the narrative is scanned for signifiers which might match a signifier-interpretant pairing from a conventionalized lexicon of such pairs. This much is in accordance with the seventeenth-century observations of Guaman Poma and Pérez Bocanegra. The signifiers may be objects, objects in certain states, attributes, events, or even individual people. All but individuals are intersubjectively accepted and fully conventionalized. Individuals may be interpreted by a dreamer after they appear repeatedly in dreams and are correlated with the following day's events: they are ultimately treated as indices of the events. Thus, if you repeatedly dream of your cousin and become ill, your cousin will come to signify illness.

All of the following are contemporary conventionalized dream signs:

green	sadness
fat cow or bull	*wayra* ('wind-soul')
old shoe	remain with the same partner
donkey	good luck
rope	walk on foot
cat	the devil
taxi or private car	coffin
Guardia Civil (police)	God
thirst	the soul needs food (confession or mass)
onions	sorrow

Consider now Pérez Bocanegra's dream lexicon from seventeenth-century Andahuaylillas in contrast to the modern conventional interpretation of the same signifiers in the same village. The signifiers are listed in the left-most column of Table 2 followed by the 1631 interpretant and the corresponding modern one. 'NI' indicates that no modern interpretation was available, even when I pressed the point. Since dream interpretation is a frequent topic of morning conversation, 'NI' likely indicates the absence of a signifier from the conventional intersubjective lexicon.

I have already suggested that in spite of considerable resilience in comparable sign systems such as ritual and myth the reason for the lack

Table 2. *Comparative dream signs (1631–1979)*

signifier	interpretations 1631	1979
cross a bridge	separation	fortunate day
catch a fish	luck	NI
deer	wrecked plans	NI
headless person }	separation	NI
handless person }	disaster	NI
snake }		devil, bad wind, problematic sex
partridge }		NI
condor (if birth imminent)	birth of male child	NI, replaced by 'eating orange'
wool	extreme sorrow	NI, replaced by 'turbulent water'
spider web		NI
woody *quinua* plant	'clothing of pain'	NI
appear lit by sun or moon	death of a neighbor	good fortune (darkness is death)
small birds	fear	fear
dark person }		NI
pig }	some kind of disaster	*soq'a* (ancestor bone causes painful illness and death)
dog }		theft
change of clothing	death	death
trip	defeat	miss an appointment
toad	fear	witchcraft
two-headed serpent	great disaster	NI

of correspondence between the seventeenth-century dream lexicon fragment and its modern counterpart is that dream signs lack the codified syntactic and pragmatic contiguity relationships which in myth and ritual index signs to their contexts of discourse and use. Dream interpretation involves taking account of an immediate semantical relationship between signifier and interpretant torn from syntactic and pragmatic context, if only to recontextualize the sign into both at another level of semiosis. It is the pivotal stage of interpretation, the reduction of narrative to isolated signs, which determines the characteristic non-syntacticity and non-pragmaticity of the dream code in Southern Peruvian Quechua culture.

CONCLUSIONS

There is a fundamental difference between the way signs function in Andean dreams on the one hand, and in Andean ritual and myth on the other. But students of Andean ritual and myth have all too frequently concentrated on the interpretation and historical exegesis of individual signs taken out of context without a corresponding return to the whole through a careful examination of the narrative, syntactic, and pragmatic structures of these events. In brief, it has been common to treat myth and ritual signs as if they were organized as are dream signs. By examining a sign system which does in fact encode only a semantic dimension we can see more clearly that the emergent characteristic properties of the other systems exist by virtue of the coded non-semantical semiotic dimensions.

I have argued that the relative speed with which sign systems change is a function of the way in which they are interpreted. The argument rests crucially on the assumption that cultural practices are patterned, regular, and law-governed. From this point of view a central goal of cultural analysis is to discover *laws of structure* which govern the composition of particular sign systems. Such laws of structure may be constructed on the basis of cross-cultural typological comparison between systems, as for example Roman Jakobson's (1941) search for laws governing possible natural-language phonological systems and Lévi-Strauss's (1949) typology of alliance systems. But laws of structure may also be discovered on the basis of detailed comparisons between sign systems in a single culture, that is by means of an *intersemiotic* typology. An intersemiotic typology setting Southern Peruvian Quechua dreaming against myth and ritual was implicit in the present essay.

Where are the laws of structure located? Are they located in the minds of actors? In the 1960s, it was fashionable for structuralists to speak of the 'death of the subject.' By 'subject' they referred to the traditional Western 'individual,' who had been treated as the irreducible and indivisible source of cultural practices: as the author of texts, as the dreamer of dreams – in general, as the actor of actions. Structuralism opposed itself to a humanistic discourse in which the ultimate forms of explanation were to be posed in terms of individual motives, moods, intentions, and wills. Cultural anthropology itself was torn on this point. Alongside a seventy-five-year-old tradition of treating culture as an emergent whole, there were repeated efforts to locate culture in the minds of individuals or in individual behaviors.

The death of the subject had an immediate payoff in analytic rigor. If cultural practices and forms have a social existence independent of the wills and intents of participants (or *exteriorité*, to use Mauss's 1954:76 expression), practices cannot be taken apart and reduced piecemeal to intentions and wills. The analysis can only be accountable to the particular details of a given situated practice. Moreover, one goal of structural analysis was to show how invariant cultural forms could be used in distinct ways under distinct circumstances by many different individuals; such forms acquired an objective reality that was independent of any individual subject (Lévi-Strauss 1964:19; cf. Derrida 1977:180 ff). With the recognition that cultural forms have an existence independent of any particular subjects – be they individuals or cultural collectivities – the laws of structure were located in the cultural forms themselves. Thus Lévi-Strauss professed to show 'not how people think in myths, but how myths are thought in people, without their being aware of it' (1964:20). Much the same rhetoric – without the stabilization of laws of structure – has been maintained by post-structuralists, particularly deconstructionists. The anti-humanist rhetoric of the death of the subject is one of the sources of vehement opposition to present-day deconstructionism as it was to structuralism.

But if we continue to grant that it is both feasible and desirable to account for cultural systems in terms of laws of structure (and this is no small matter), the banished subject reappears in another form. As we have seen from Southern Peruvian Quechua dreams, laws of structure – the structural properties which distinguish dreams from myth and ritual and give each its own historicity – are not to be found in the narrative structure of dreams or in the dream lexicon, but rather at the interface between the sign medium and the interpretive system. The subject in question is no longer the transcendental, non-cultural, non-historical subject ('human nature') of some approaches or the individual actor in an individual context in an individual culture of other approaches, but rather a historically and culturally situated *interpretive* subject. The forms that cultural practices take, and the ways in which they change, depend on the ways in which they are understood. Cultural analysis must aim at elucidating the ways in which they are understood, for in the last analysis, the interpretive system determines the nature of the sign system. A theory of culture without an active subject is a vain dream indeed.

NOTES

1. I wish to thank Ellen Basso, Gilbert Herdt, Diane Hopkins, Barbara Tedlock, Waud Kracke, Margaret J. Traywick, and

Harriet Whitehead for valuable criticism of an earlier draft. Work on Pérez Bocanegra's dream texts was undertaken with the assistance of Rosa Chillca Huallpa. Members of the Grupo Campesino de Lluthu offered their kind hospitality and support. The research on Southern Peruvian Quechua language, culture and text reflected herein was supported by the National Science Foundation, the Organization of American States, the Wenner-Gren Foundation for Anthropological Research and a grant from the Tinker Foundation administered through the University of Arizona Latin American Center. To each and all, *Dios se lo pague*.

2. Southern Peruvian Quechua speakers refer to themselves as *Runa*, 'human being.' I follow this usage here. Thus 'Runa' is the name of the people and 'Southern Peruvian Quechua' (or *Runa-simi*) the name of the language.
3. Charles Sanders Peirce distinguished between critical logic, speculative grammar, and rhetoric, respectively, for these three dimensions of semiosis. For an earlier formulation of the terms used here see Morris 1938 sections 3, 5, and 7.
4. I use the less familiar form 'semantical' to emphasize that I mean it in the specifically semiotic sense in which I defined it earlier rather than as a synonym of 'meaning.'
5. For a general discussion of the importance of indexical sign relationships to cultural analysis see Silverstein (1976).
6. The Quechua texts of the sermonal of the Tercer Concilio Provincial and the *Ritual formulario* of Pérez Bocanegra show careful attention to formal rhetorical structure which I have attempted to reproduce by a division into lines both in the presentation of the original texts and in their translation. The principle criteria for the line division were grammatical parallelism, illocutionary markers and quoted versus direct speech. Punctuation in the sermonal appears to mark intonational units in such a way as to make fairly respectable rhetorical performance possible even for the novice speaker (which was indeed the condition of many colonial rural priests). I have therefore also respected the punctuation of the original texts in determining the line division. The English translation was made line-by-line from the Quechua texts, with care taken to preserve the rhetorical structure of the original as much as possible in the translation.
7. On Andean female ritual specialists see Silverblatt (1980).
8. Diane Hopkins (personal communication) reports a contemporary case of calling to midwifery through dreams.
9. The quote from Guaman Poma is a transcription of the facsimile edition published by the Institut d' Ethnologie from the holographic manuscript. Guaman Poma's Spanish appears

to calque traditional Southern Peruvian Quechua rhetorical structure, perhaps to a greater extent than morpho-syntax. I have followed the same criteria in formulating the line structure of the translation as for the religious texts. In general, attention to rhetorical patterning in Guaman Poma's Spanish would do much to reduce the syntactic ambiguities which many commentators have observed and account for the 'syntactic barbarisms' noted by Euro-centric observers (e.g., Porras 1948:83; see Adorno 1974 for corrective discussion). Rolena Adorno (1978) noted contentive influence of the Third Council's sermonal and other colonial religious works on Guaman Poma, raising the question of possible influence of rhetorical style as well.

10. I shall continue to phrase my discussion in terms of dreams, however, as other premonitory activities are not presently understood.
11. The suffix *-paq* usually appears as *-pac* in colonial orthographies.
12. Dream interpretation has largely gone unreported in the literature on contemporary Andean peoples. Noteworthy exceptions include Paredes (1920:26–8), La Barre (1948:178–80), and Delgado (1968, ch. 8:5–6) for Jaqi speakers; and Gifford and Hoggarth (1976:60), Zorrilla (1978), and MacDonald (1979, ch. 6) for Quechua-speaking peoples. Deborah Poole (personal communication) reports a system of dream interpretation for Paruro (Department of Cuzco, Peru) consistent with that described here for nearby Andahuaylillas.
13. The details in parentheses were added later by the speaker.

7
Ropes of sand:
order and imagery in Aguaruna dreams

MICHAEL F. BROWN

> He understood that modelling the incoherent and vertiginous matter of which dreams are composed was the most difficult task that a man could undertake, even though he should penetrate all the enigmas of a superior and inferior order; much more difficult than weaving a rope of sand or coining the faceless wind.
>
> JORGE LUÍS BORGES

Analysis can very easily impoverish the things it sets out to explain, especially when the subject is dreams. How can we hope to make sense of something as complex and alien as another person's dream without trivializing it, without rendering it lifeless? This enterprise, daunting enough when the dreams are recorded in a familiar cultural setting, becomes an order of magnitude more difficult when one crosses into cultural *terra incognita*. Yet it may be more than the very real difficulties of the task that impedes progress in the anthropological interpretation of dreams. Perhaps some favorite assumptions about dreams hinder rather than help the advance of dream theory.

Consider, for example, the question of dream symbolism. In general, psychological studies of the symbolism of dreams have been informed by the assumption that dreaming is a discrete kind of thinking that operates by rules that are sui generis and possibly universal. Thus Freud (1900:506) states that 'dreams are nothing more than a particular form of thinking, made possible by the conditions of sleep.' Since dreams take place without the conscious control of the dreamer, this argument goes, they must be an ideal window to the unconscious. Recent experimental evidence, though, reveals how much at variance dream experience, as indicated by measurable neurophysiological events, and 'dream thoughts' or recall may be (Cohen 1979:178–80). The 'primary process' of dreaming appears to be converted into 'secondary process' the instant the dream is recalled, which means that cultural forces are brought to bear at a very early point. Dreams may have a universal neurological substrate, but the dream itself is primarily constituted by a 'symbolic praxis' (Sahlins 1976:196) unique to each society. Dreams must therefore be analyzed with reference to the other symbolic forms in a culture: myth, ritual, art, and so forth (cf. Herdt, Kracke, Tedlock, this volume).

Moreover, the boundaries between dreams and other altered states of consciousness are becoming ever more elusive as scientific research in this field advances. There is mounting evidence that (1) certain kinds of dreams occur in non-REM sleep, thus casting doubt on the supposedly unique physiological correlates of dreaming (Cohen 1979:184); (2) people in our own society regularly experience dream-like states while awake, yet do not acknowledge these as such because of our cultural bias against hallucinations (Davidson 1980:37); and (3) dreams and other altered states of consciousness share common neurophysiological features (Mandell 1980:426). The supposed uniqueness of dreams may thus be an artifact of Western ethnocentrism, a reflection of the fact that the dreams of sleep are the only legitimate, non-pathological hallucinatory experiences permitted by our society. Charles Tart (1980) has noted that all societies attempt to arrive at stable, discrete definitions of altered states of consciousness in order to facilitate communication. We must not assume, however, that our own definitions are necessarily applicable elsewhere, or that 'dreaming' (in the restricted scientific sense of the word) is anything other than an arbitrary unit of analysis (Bourguignon 1972).

Some of these problems can be circumvented by taking advantage of insights provided by cognitive anthropology, especially now that it has earnestly embarked on a rapprochement with symbolic theory (Colby,

Fernandez, and Kronenfeld 1981). If dreaming is a kind of thinking, then it might profitably be studied in terms of its place in the total knowledge system of a culture. What role do dreams play in the acquisition, validation, modification, and transmission of knowledge? Or, to put it in the terms proposed by Dougherty and Fernandez (1981:416), what can dreams tell us about 'principles that recur in the active processes of sense making?' If dreams are seen as symbolically charged, to what extent does dream symbolism resemble other forms of symbolic production found within the dreamer's society? Finally, what connections are there between the symbolic force of dreams and processes of personal empowerment in the waking world? The following analysis of the uses to which dreams are put by the Aguaruna of the Alto Rio Mayo, Peru, addresses some of these critical issues.[1] My general goal is to define the role of dreams in Aguaruna notions of causality. More specifically, I wish to call attention to certain formal similarities between manipulative dreams and magical utterances in Aguaruna thought.

DREAMS IN JIVAROAN THOUGHT

More than 20,000 Aguaruna inhabit Peru's northern *montaña*, a region where Andean foothills and Amazonian forest effect an uneasy merger. In this rugged terrain the Aguaruna have traditionally supported themselves by a combination of root-crop horticulture, hunting, fishing, and collecting. Like their close relatives the Shuar (or Jívaro proper) of Ecuador, the Aguaruna are known to the outside world chiefly for their belligerence, which in the past took the form of both intertribal and intratribal hostilities as well as vigorous resistance to incursions by foreigners. Today they are shifting their attention from warfare to the only slightly less Hobbesian arenas of commercial agriculture and resource extraction (Brown 1984). This transformation is producing profound changes in Aguaruna culture, among them what appears to be a declining interest in the systematic search for dreams and visions. Although I use the ethnographic present in the following discussion, it should be understood that some of the beliefs and practices I describe – especially those concerned with warfare – have not played a central part in Aguaruna life for a decade or more. They are, however, still fresh in people's minds, and they continue to play a role in the Aguarunas' response to contemporary problems.

Much has been written about the importance that Jivaroan peoples, such as the Aguaruna, attach to dreams and other altered states of consciousness. Half a century ago, Rafael Karsten (1935:444) stated that 'the Jibaros . . . are of the opinion that *only* in dreams is true reality revealed to man,' an assertion that Michael Harner (1972:134) repeats in his ethnography of the Untsuri Shuar. This view of Jivaroan dream theory has even made its way into commercial film: A missionary in Werner Herzog's movie *Fitzcarraldo* (1982) laments that his work among the Jívaro and Campa (who are juxtaposed geographically in the fanciful script) is hindered by the Indians' dogged adherence to the idea that 'their everyday life is only an illusion, behind which lies the reality of dreams.'

Although these statements have a romantic appeal, they vastly oversimplify a complex set of dream concepts. Dreams do indeed figure prominently in day-to-day decision-making, but they have no monopolistic hold on reality. It is more accurate to say that the Aguaruna think of dreams as experiences that reveal emergent possibilities or likelihoods, events that are developing but which are not yet accomplished facts. When, for example, a woman finds a stone that she suspects may have the power to assist the growth of her manioc plants, she searches her dreams for signs that confirm this suspicion. Once the stone's power has received dream confirmation, the woman can complete the procedures that transform it into a usable *nantag*[2] or growth-promoting charm (Brown 1985). Similarly, a man who dreams that he is embracing an attractive woman believes that the dream portends a successful hunt. After having such a dream (which is called *kuntúknagbau*), he will set off after game at first light. A reverse logic applies to dreams of misfortune; if a man dreams of snakebite, he spends the next day or two at home to prevent this emergent possibility from becoming a real and tragic event.

Precisely how or why dreams offer this glimpse of future possibilities was never made clear to me by my informants in the Alto Mayo. Some people asserted that we dream when our soul (specifically the shadow soul or *iwanch*) travels during sleep, encountering other souls and discovering their intentions. Others vigorously denied this explanation, arguing that soul loss of any kind inevitably results in sickness. The observed lack of consensus about how dreams take place may reflect confusion caused by the recent exposure of the Aguaruna to Christian soul concepts. In any case, people care less about the cause of dream revelations than they do about their implications. It should also be noted that the Aguaruna construe 'dreaming' in a broader sense than we do. The verb *kajamát*, usually glossed as 'to dream' (Larson 1966), denotes both the dreams of sleep and visions or hallucinations that occur in the somnolent state induced by psychotropic plants. 'Dreaming,' then, is a state in which a drowsy and usually recumbent person experiences events that cannot be seen by others. The role of the dreamer may be one of passivity, or it may encompass the sort of 'active imagining' identified by Douglass Price-Williams (this volume).[3] The importance of a given dream depends on the extent to which it falls within the established dream canon and on whether it is spontaneous or intentionally sought, the latter being more significant than the former.

SELFHOOD, INNER EXPERIENCE, AND THE USES OF IMAGERY

Among the Aguaruna, a person is, or strives to be, an autonomous agent who partakes of a unique identity and who compels recognition of that autonomy and unique identity by others.[4] This fierce and characteristically Jivaroan spirit of independence, an important aspect of the 'complete natural liberty' to which the nineteenth-century Bishop of Cuenca (cited in Stirling 1938:26) found the Shuar so devoted, manifests itself in a thousand ways, great and small. Etiquette requires, for example, that a man taking leave of a social gathering say goodbye to every other adult man, as well as all close female relatives. To do otherwise – to deliver a collective farewell, for instance – would be to insult the others by failing to acknowledge both their unique importance and the dyadic bond that links speaker to hearer. When naming children, people in the Alto Mayo go to great lengths to avoid names currently in use in the village or the immediate network of kin. 'Each person needs his own name,' they say. In the group singing that often occurs during beer-drinking parties, everyone performs his or her own personal song, trying to make it heard above the din. The resulting cacophony prompted one early chronicler of Jivaroan life to wonder 'how they have a head for so much noise, a throat for so much exclamation, and a tooth for so much liquor' (cited in Stirling 1938:45). These examples and the many more that could be adduced suggest that the Aguaruna idea of self has more in common with that of the industrial West – where, according to Geertz (1976:225), people see themselves as 'a bounded, unique, more or less integrated motivational and cognitive universe' – than it does with that of many other Amazonian societies.[5]

To move from these notions of self to theories of how the self acts upon the world is to advance more deeply into what is implicit rather than explicit in Aguaruna thought. It is, of course, obvious that people recognize the importance of physical acts, based on competence in essential crafts, in projecting their wills. Aguaruna child rearing practices, like those of most societies, emphasize the transmission of practical knowledge that allows a child to become a functioning adult. But one cannot live in an Aguaruna village without noticing something else: a marked concern with the ordering of inner experience so as to effect change in the external world. Customarily, young men (and to a lesser extent, young women) are expected to engage in rigorous fasting and sexual abstinence for weeks at a time. The general goal of these practices is to acquire strength through the avoidance of polluting or debilitating contacts, for instance, sweet foods, utensils associated with non-native society, or intimate encounters with the opposite sex. A more immediate goal is to create conditions favorable for the acquisition of life-giving visions. In the following account, here much abridged, a man remembers the privations he suffered during the vision quest:

> I took a lot of *datém* [the hallucinogen *Banisteriopsis* sp.] and continually went to a forest shelter. I also took *baikuá* [*Brugmansia* sp.]. My mother served me bland manioc soup because one can't drink much manioc beer. I took more *datém*, one day, then another. And when I felt exhausted, ready to die, I left it for a while.
>
> When looking for a vision, one can't eat chicken with manioc, or boiled peccary or the fish *kagka* and *wakámpi*. Salted fish can't be eaten. Nothing is eaten from metal plates or bowls, nor are spoons used. A young man can't have intercourse or play around with women. I was never interested in women because I lived to take *datém*, *baikuá*, and tobacco water. I took them day after day, for five days. Then I rested for scarcely a month before beginning all over again.

A major purpose of the dietary restrictions is to banish sweetness from the vision-seeker's body, replacing it with the strength-inducing bitterness of hallucinogens. This changes a person's heart from a pale, watery color to a deep red. The transformation of the heart, the organ regarded as the seat of thought, enables a person to think 'straight' or well. High-quality thought allows one to perform effectively both at the level of physical skills and in ritual operations.

Let me illustrate the links between inner experience and external control by describing how the Aguaruna approach one small area of practical activity, the care of domestic fowl. I choose this as my example neither because of an abiding interest in chickens on my part nor because the Aguaruna themselves direct a great deal of attention to it. It is merely a convenient and relatively simple case that illustrates principles receiving more elaborate treatment in other activities.

Domestic fowl, especially chickens, have an important role in the internal economy of an Aguaruna household because they are a reliable source of meat and are readily converted into cash for emergency purchases. They are generally cared for and owned by women, who see to it that their flocks are fed, attended to when ill, and protected from predatory animals. Most of the techniques used to produce healthy flocks are comfortably accommodated within the Western concept of practical aviculture. Alto Mayo women do, however, make use of special songs, called *anen*,[6] that further improve their prospects of success in raising chickens. Like other *anen*, these chicken-raising songs are attributed an ancient origin, perhaps going back as far as the time when Nugkui, the powerful woman who introduced manioc and other cultivars to the Aguaruna, freely communicated with the ancestors. Since the power of *anen* comes from ancient sources of wisdom, the songs are learnt and performed by rote. To ensure that her songs will be efficacious, a woman who wishes to perform an *anen* will inhale a small quantity of tobacco water, putting her in a dream-like state of intoxication. She then sings the song aloud or silently in her thoughts alone. *Anen* are usually performed in complete privacy, although in some instances a woman will allow her young daughters to witness the performance.

The following are the words of one chicken-raising *anen*, presented in abridged form:

> The chicks of the bird *puush* [*Odontophorus* sp., wood-quail]
> Tiu, tiu, tiu, tiu, tiu [sound of many chicks]
> Tiu, tiu, tiu, tiu, tiu
> Tiu, tiu, tiu, tiu, tiu
> The blood of the bird *amúnte* [*Anhima cornuta*, horned screamer]
> Is flooding, flooding
> Is flooding, flooding

Is flooding, flooding
They do not become ill,
They do not become ill,
The blood of the anaconda
Is flooding, flooding
Is flooding, flooding
Is flooding, flooding.

This small fragment of a single *anen* suggests the density of images characteristic of the genre. Three animal species are mentioned in these stanzas, each of which has a symbolic connection with, or possesses a desirable trait that should be transferred to, the singer's chickens. The wood-quail (*puush*) is noted for its numerous chicks. The connection between the horned screamer (*amúnte*) and chickens was less clear to the people who interpreted the song for me, though it may be significant that this large, pheasant-sized bird lays its eggs in a nest on the ground, as do chickens. The allusion to the anaconda has multiple meanings. The Aguaruna associate the anaconda with Tsugki, the being who rules the aquatic realm and controls shamanistic power. Furthermore, the myth of Tsugki (see, for example, Akuts Nugkai *et al.* 1979:134) explains that the first chickens were obtained from Tsugki's underwater house. The woman who recorded the song remarked that this *anen* would cause the young chicks to become so numerous that they would 'move like a flood across the ground, like the flowing blood of the anaconda.' In a few short lines the song summons a powerful visual image (the flowing blood, the flowing chicks) and an auditory counterpart (the 'tiu tiu tiu' cries of the chicks), establishes a connection between chickens and two wild birds that possess desirable traits, and puts the enterprise in a mythic context by alluding to the primordial source of domestic fowl, Tsugki.

People in the Alto Mayo proved just as reluctant to speculate on how *anen* work as they did to account for why people dream. A few informants spoke of the songs as direct appeals to supernatural beings, although many *anen*, including the example presented here, mention no such beings at all. What all *anen* do share are vivid, densely constructed images that connote the successful completion of the activity to which the songs are directed. The logic implicit in the use of *anen* is that people can, through internal processes of thought, direct events by creating and controlling a more pervasive, multidimensional order than that which would otherwise exist. (Remember that *anen* work when they are simply *thought*, as well as when they are sung aloud.) The imagery deployed by performers of *anen* – this active structuring of internal experience – is considered to be as important a part of instrumental activity as direct physical intervention.

By now it should be clear that my interpretation of Aguaruna magic departs significantly from the approaches of Tambiah (1968) and Leach (1976), both of whom argue (albeit in slightly different ways) that magic is motivated by an expressive, rather than instrumental, intent. Tambiah (1968:202), for instance, asserts that the ritual acts associated with Trobriand gardening represent only a 'simulation' of technology and are not confused with empirically valid, instrumental acts in the minds of their practitioners. The Aguaruna data require a more literal interpretation, however, because people do not consistently distinguish 'magic' from 'technology,' nor do they deny the possibility that practical activities can be accomplished through magic alone, provided that one has the requisite knowledge.

The instrumental/expressive dichotomy upon which the symbolist interpretation of magic is based is, at best, a dubious one inasmuch as instrumental acts ('technology,' etc.) themselves contain an expressive aspect: 'The cultural order equally informs the technological components of an economic system . . . Tools [are] constituent elements of a meaningful labor practice' (Chevalier 1982:43). To penetrate Aguaruna magic one must analyze the dialectic between expressive and instrumental components of all acts and utterances, be they technological or ritual in nature.

THE INSTRUMENTAL EFFECT OF DREAMS

'I took *datém* to find game,' Kute Jiukám told me one day as we walked along the trail to his village. Kute's remarks were for me the first hint of the instrumental effect that dreams can have on practical activities. Prompted by my questions, he explained that some years earlier he had been afflicted by *shimpankámu*, a condition that manifests itself as a chronic inability to encounter game animals. After trying several traditional remedies with no success, Kute took the hallucinogen *datém* in the hope that it would help him see the animals that had for so long eluded him. In his *datém*-induced dream, he did see animals – scores of them, he said, of all the desirable species – and shortly thereafter his hunting ability was restored. He stressed that it was seeing the animals in this dream-like state that effected the cure.

Karsten's (1935) description of Jivaroan culture, more than forty years before my conversation with Kute, provides a nearly identical account of a hunting vision:

> When a Jibaro Indian for instance drinks a narcotic at some of the feasts, his visions have special reference to his domestic and economic life. . . The Indian sees all sorts of game, wild turkeys, toucans, parrots, wild pigs, etc. When the sleeping Indian has such visions, it may happen that he suddenly starts up in excitement, points with his fingers at the birds and animals he fancies he sees, and exclaims: 'Behold, behold! Give me a blowgun, I want a blowgun, I want arrow-poison, I am shooting game to eat it, I am eating pig's flesh, I am eating hen's flesh, I am eating the flesh of the hog [peccary], the flesh of the hare [agouti]' etc. At such moments he must be held down on his bed by his comrades, but the fact that he has experiences of this kind is interpreted as a favorable omen by them. (Karsten 1935:446–7)

Although Karsten calls this dream an 'omen,' the term is altogether inadequate. The Aguaruna regard this dream as a virtual prerequisite for a successful hunting career, and it is periodically renewed by older men when they find that their hunting performance falters. It bears pointing out that the dream, rather than being the spontaneous event implied by the term 'omen,' represents the culmination of an extended process that begins with a period of fasting and sexual abstinence, continues through the consumption of disagreeably bitter hallucinogens, and concludes with an unusual sensory experience: the sight, sound, and smell of numerous game species parading before the dreamer. The experience is thus the endpoint of a cultural recipe, an established set of procedures that are informed by an instrumental purpose. The parallels between this vision and *anen* are striking. In both cases the actor consciously enters a dreaming or dreamlike state and then orders his thoughts so that they consist of highly evocative images favorable to the accomplishment of the task in hand.

The dream experience most highly esteemed by Aguaruna men is the establishment of contact with an ancient warrior soul (*ajútap*). The dream is essential for any warrior who hopes to survive combat. Because of the dream's importance, men are willing to undergo the most extreme hardships – weeks of enduring a restricted diet, lonely vigils deep in the forest, and frequent use of psychotropic plants – to obtain it.

Ajútap dreams typically have two parts: an initial vision of a terrifying beast or comet-like blast of light that the dreamer must confront and touch, followed by a second dream (sometimes separated from the first by a day or more) in which the *ajútap* presents himself to the dreamer in human form and tells him of his future victory in battle. A man who receives such a vision is called *kajintin*, 'owner of a dream,' or *waimaku*, 'one who has had a vision.' His outward manner becomes forceful and self-assured because he knows that his enemies cannot kill him (cf. Harner 1972:139).[7]

The songs of vision-seekers tend to portray the singer as a pathetic figure who will die if an *ajútap* does not appear soon. 'Grandfather, how can I find you?' goes one song. 'Sadly leaving my little forest shelter, I weep. How will it be done?' (See Pellizzaro 1976:101–60.) It appears that a successful vision depends more on the response of a capricious *ajútap* than on the purposeful acts of the vision-seeker. Yet most men apparently do succeed in their quest, if necessary by taking powerful solanaceous hallucinogens such as *Brugmansia* to speed things along. Aguaruna narratives frequently mention men who, by dint of extraordinary efforts, are able to accumulate ever more powerful visions so that they become renowned warriors and leaders of raiding expeditions. By means of immense personal effort, a warrior establishes control over his dream imagery and thereby increases his ability to structure events in the world.

I have already noted the similarities between magical songs and hunting visions, and there is evidence that *ajútap* visions share many of the same qualities. Men reveal their *ajútap* visions in a formal dream declaration (*kaja tigbau*) that occurs prior to a raid on an enemy house. I have never had an opportunity to record a dream declaration, but fortunately an excellent dream text has been published by Mildred Larson (1978). Below is a free translation of the entire declaration, followed by a brief sample of the original Aguaruna text:

Free translation 1. This is about a vision which was seen while sleeping. 2. Oh, I saw a powerful vision and I felt its greatness. 3. It said, 'Where someone is always killing my relatives, right there I will kill in revenge, wiping out the tracks on his abandoned trail. 4. Perhaps he is my relative. 5. Taking that very one, I will perhaps actually choose a relative. 6. I will change his trail into an abandoned trail. 7. Forming a single file of the children, happily I will lead them to where I will condemn them. 8. Giving each of them a sip of manioc soup, with great joy I will lead them single file, to where I will kill in revenge.' 9. As he was saying this, the wind was blowing, 'Whoooo, whoooo,' over me again and again. 10. He was standing in a whirlpool of dust and leaves, like smoke, over and over again making a sound like a dried skin (being folded back and forth) 'Boom, boom.' (Larson 1978:398–9)

Literal translation, lines 9–10 9. *taku, taku / dase, dase / tupuu, tupuu / awajtakua, awajtakua* 'saying, saying / wind, wind / whoooo, whoooo / doing-over-and-over-to-me, doing-over-and-over-to-me.' 10. *Tsakaipia, tsakaipia / imanun, imanun / bukui, bukui / awajtakua, awajtakua / duwapea, duwapea / imaanaa, imaanaa / kikug, kikug / awa awajtibi, awa awajtibi* 'whirlwind-of-dust-and-leaves, whirlwind-of-dust-and-leaves / like-that, like-that / smoking, smoking / doing-over-and-over-to-me, doing-over-and-over-to-me / skin, skin / equal-to, equal-to / boom, boom / he-did-this-very-much-to-me, he-did-this-very-much-to-me.' (ibid.:397–8)

Although the dream declaration is spoken in a loud, rhythmic style, as opposed to the soft, sinuous quality of a magical song, the two share a similar structure. Both consist of repeated phrases, a highly compressed vocabulary, and a series of evocative images related to the intended goal. In the case of the *ajútap* vision, these images include the metaphors 'wiping out tracks,' and 'abandoned trail,' augmented by the onomatopoeic words *tupuu* and *kikug*, which suggest wind and drum-like percussion respectively.

Any analysis of this dream declaration must take into account the fact that, unlike magical songs, it is presented in a public setting. Unfortunately, detailed information on the social circumstances surrounding Aguaruna dream declarations is not available. Harner (1972:139–40) reports that in the evening prior to a head-taking raid, Shuar warriors reveal their dreams to one another. One may then assume that an important function of the declaration is to enhance a warrior's reputation while at the same time helping other members of the raiding party feel confident about the expedition's ultimate success. That this particular speech act has a persuasive intent need not, in my view, dramatically change our interpretation of it. Indeed, it is the evocativeness of the dream text's imagery that makes it both effective in the practical sense (i.e., by giving the dreamer power to prevail over enemies) and persuasive in the social sense.

I suggest, then, that the most powerful dreams known to the Aguaruna, those concerned with hunting success and warfare, exercise control over the world in much the same way as do magical songs. The efficacy of both is based on the proposition that human beings influence events by creating order and simultaneously avoiding or neutralizing sources of disorder. One creates order by bringing the appropriate material objects and evocative imagery to bear on the task being undertaken. Dreams are a particularly potent field for the exercising of human control because they take place in an area of direct contact between people and powerful beings such as the *ajútap*. If a person can by force of will structure the events that take place in this arena – in a sense, domesticating the ineffable – then he or she will have succeeded in imposing order in a domain that is critically important to the outcome of an activity. Magical songs, requiring as they do some slight intrusion into the dream-world through the consumption of tobacco water, represent a safe but only moderately effective means of intervening in the dream-world. Intentionally sought dreams and visions, by contrast, require more of a personal sacrifice yet offer greater rewards with respect to their manipulative potential.

CONCLUSIONS

The people of the Alto Mayo often speak of a mythical hero named Bikut, a man who so obsessively consumed hallucinogens that he became both a visionary and a warrior possessed by an insatiable desire to kill (see Chumap and García-Rendueles 1978:297). Bikut and other mythical warriors used their vision-derived power to lay waste to entire tribes. In more recent times, the ability of men to exterminate their foes has declined to more modest proportions, but it is no less dependent upon the power of visions. Warriors will voluntarily participate in raids only when they have succeeded in seeing an *ajútap*; to do battle without such a vision is tantamount to suicide. Men who repeatedly demonstrate an ability to acquire visions and then translate them into successful raids become local war leaders, or *kakájam*.

Dreams and political leadership are similarly linked in many Amazonian societies. Quichua shamans, whose status depends upon the successful integration of practical knowledge and visionary knowledge obtained from dreams, wield considerable influence in local and regional decision-making (Whitten 1978, 1982). Watson's (1981) recent account of Guajiro dreaming notes that political crises are sometimes resolved when someone's dream reveals the proper course of action to be taken. Among the Makiritare, both shamans and chiefs have special expertise in dream interpretation and manipulation (Guss 1980). Many other such examples could be cited. Why is it, we might ask, that the ability to interpret and control dreams is so commonly linked to power relations in Amazonia?

Richard N. Adams (1975), in an extended meditation on the nature of social power, states that the kind of power characteristic of small-scale, unstratified societies is 'allocated' power, that is, the power which many individuals grant to one. People grant allocated power with the implicit understanding that it may be withdrawn at the grantor's pleasure. Adams further argues that in these small-scale societies (i.e., foraging bands and tribal villages) there is very little power to grant. Domestic units tend to be relatively independent of one another. There are few durable goods that can be accumulated. Exchange relations are too simple to offer much in the way of political leverage. What power there is tends to be based on what Adams calls 'skill authority,' demonstrated ability to perform essential tasks. The Aguaruna *kakájam* is typical of this pattern. His authority comes from known fighting skill and control over visions, often complemented by a developed sense of diplomacy that helps him suppress internal conflicts within a raiding party until the raiding expedition is successfully completed. His formal leadership role lasts only for the duration of the expedition, and his followers are free to withdraw their support if they oppose his decisions.

In these circumstances of power scarcity, the acquisition, interpretation, or control of dreams may be an important means of demonstrating competence beyond that which is required by immediate practical necessity. Through dreams, leaders amplify their skill authority by extending their abilities into the realm of altered states of consciousness. And since dreams are common currency, people in positions of power can accumulate potent dreams without taking from others; they can hoard without being stingy. Dreams are not, I hasten to add, the only source of authority beyond practical competence: rhetorical skill and ritual knowledge are alternative sources that come immediately to mind. But dreams have several qualities that make them likely vehicles for the expression of authority. Their complexity invites interpretation by people who have accumulated experience in this field. Their mysterious nature suggests a link to the numinous; by extension, control of dreams implies control of obscure but powerful forces. Nor can we disregard the possible connection between dreams and the psychological functions of leadership (Kracke 1978:191–205). Through a special sensitivity to the meaning of dreams, a leader may be able to give voice to unconscious concerns that his followers are unable to articulate. This adeptness ultimately contributes to his ability to mobilize the support of others.

In more complex societies, dreams play a reduced role in power relations. Here power can be exercised by other means: accumulation of durable goods, control over exchange relations or strategic resources, the use of military force, and so on.[8] People may still turn to dreams for guidance in personal matters, but dreams figure less prominently in the allocation or delegation of power at the highest levels. There may be instances in which rulers consult diviners or priests who derive information from dreams, but the power of the ruling elite exists independently of such functionaries, and the influence of their pronouncements is sharply circumscribed. Indeed, in stratified societies dreams become a subversive force associated with social protest and messianic movements. In such instances dreams empower the weak, not the strong.

The dream concepts that I have described here do not by any means exhaust all Aguaruna thoughts on the subject, and this essay must be considered a preliminary account only. Yet the data do provide a convincing demonstration of what Lévi-Strauss is driving at when he speaks of the 'complete and all embracing determinism' of preliterate thought (Lévi-Strauss 1966:11). Rather than viewing dreams as subjective mental phenomena bearing little relation to events outside of the dreamer's mind, the Aguaruna use dreams and altered states of consciousness as bridges between self and other, as sources of imagery that can be consciously appropriated to alter the dreamer's world. With typical energy, they have learned to shape what Borges (1956) calls the 'incoherent and vertiginous matter of dreams' into a powerful instrument of the human will.

NOTES

1. The field research on which this chapter is based was conducted between December 1976 and September 1978 in several Aguaruna villages in the Department of San Martín, Peru. I gratefully acknowledge the financial support of the Henry L. and Grace Doherty Charitable Foundation, the Wenner-Gren Foundation for Anthropological Research, and the Centro Amazónico de Antropología y Aplicación Práctica, Lima. Colleagues who were kind enough to evaluate critically an earlier draft include the participants in the School of American Research Advanced Seminar, as well as Kenneth M.

Kensinger, Gillian Feeley-Harnik, Robert Crépeau, and Howard Norman. Special thanks go to William L. Merrill for his perceptive comments during our many conversations about dreams and visions.

2. The orthography of Aguaruna words cited in the text follows the system now in use among the Aguaruna themselves. All letters are pronounced more or less as in Spanish except e (which represents the high central vowel **ɨ**), g (pronounced like ng in 'ring'), and b and d (pronounced like mb and nd, respectively). Accents fall on the first syllable unless otherwise noted; they have not been marked in the Aguaruna passage quoted from Larson 1978.
3. This brief account of Aguaruna concepts of altered states of consciousness cannot do justice to the complexity of the subject, about which there is still much to be learnt. For the people of the Alto Mayo, ASCs seem to be defined in terms of three axes: 'dreams' (*kaja*), 'visions' (at least three specific categories unmarked by a general cover term), and 'intoxication' (*nampét*). Significant visionary or dreamlike experiences may occur when one is sleeping, while one is intoxicated by psychotropic plants, or both; they may also occur spontaneously during an ordinary waking state. How shamanic trance fits into this pattern is still unclear. Shamans definitely seek 'intoxication' to treat patients, but their trance is not thought of as a kind of dreaming. See Kracke (1982) for an illuminating discussion of similar issues among the Kagwahiv of Brazil.
4. Newborn infants represent a notable exception to the idea of a bounded, autonomous self, since they retain an intimate link to their parents for the first months of life. This link is expressed in the belief that a neonate may be adversely affected by contacts between its parents and certain dangerous species of animals and plants. If the father of a newborn child encounters a snake or some other taboo species while walking along in the forest, the infant may contract *tapikbáu*, a potentially fatal condition caused by the snake's attack on the infant's soul. Similarly, parents do not eat varieties of food that may induce *tsuwapágamu*, a severe form of diarrhea, in their baby. Implicit in these beliefs is the notion that a baby's experience is somehow tied to that of its parents until it is old enough to move independently of them, i.e., at about eighteen months.
5. The similarity between Aguaruna and Western ideas of self may be partly responsible for the enthusiasm with which the Alto Mayo Aguaruna have entered into extractive activities, commercial agriculture, and the regional market system in general.
6. The similarity between the word *anen* (*aneg* in Larson's

Aguaruna–Spanish dictionary [1966] and *anentáimat*, 'to think'/*anentái*, 'heart,' suggests that magical songs are closely associated with the basic process of thinking.

7. The Aguaruna description of the effects of an *ajútap* vision differs in certain respects from the Shuar interpretation of *arutam* visions reported in Harner (1972). The Shuar hold that the *arutam* soul actually enters the body of the dreamer, residing there until it is released by the formal dream declaration. The Aguaruna, however, deny that the *ajútap* enters their body. Rather, it is the dream *of* the *ajútap* that enters them. The dream is, in a sense, reified, and supposedly shamans are able to see it inside a warrior's chest, 'shining like a string of white beads.' Whether the dream exists from the body during the dream declaration is unclear from Alto Mayo accounts. People do say that when a dream-possessor dies, the dream leaves his body with a thunderous roar to become an *ajútap* in its own right.
8. By arguing that control over economic affairs and military force is a more important aspect of political power in state-level societies than are ritual and symbolic activities, I clearly traffic in what Geertz (1980:123) calls the 'worn coin of European ideological debate'. Although Geertz makes a powerful case for the central importance of liturgy in Balinese state politics, his suggestion that similar conditions obtain in most states needs to be supported by much more evidence than he is in a position to present.

8
On classifying dreams[1]

BENJAMIN KILBORNE

> Your young men shall see visions, and your old men shall dream dreams.[2]
>
> ACTS 2:17

The quoted lines from the New Testament call attention to the important differences between dreams and visions as linguistic, perceptual, and cognitive categories. Furthermore, they remind us that in many societies dream classification has a great deal to do with social hierarchy and status. It is a fact eminently worthy of investigation that whereas it is commonly believed that thought systems have evolved from simple to complex, according to some sort of progression toward increasing complexity, dream classification apparently is most elaborate in cultures other than those associated with the modern Western rationalist tradition.

It is a fair question to ask what the absence of an elaborate system of dream classification in our own tradition might mean when compared with the presence of elaborate systems in the ancient Near East, in ancient Greece, and in modern Morocco. Can the absence of such a classificatory schema imply that classification is in all cultures subordinated to human concerns about areas of experience perceived to be of importance?[3]

In this chapter I will argue that classificatory systems and principles of dream interpretation can provide a wealth of material concerning not only rational, explanatory, and logical thought processes but also material revealing unconscious emotions, wishes, and irrational forces. Moreover, the attention required to establish and maintain an elaborate classificatory system of dream interpretation may be analyzed in terms of the principle of the investment of psychological resources. When it is assumed that the amount of psychic energy is limited, then where and how this energy is generated, how ideas and feelings become elements of a system, and how these systems of individuals are regulated through interactions all become pertinent questions for the elucidation of systems of dream classification.

In the pages that follow I will examine three systems of dream classification and the relations each bears to its cultural context. I will also demonstrate how an analysis of these systems can be carried out, and suggest some implications for the understanding and exploration of all classificatory systems, both scientific and religious. The three systems of dream classification to be analyzed are those of (1) ancient Mesopotamia; (2) second-century Greece, as represented by Artemidorus' famous dream book, the *Oneirocritica*; and (3) modern Morocco, where I did my fieldwork.

This selection presents several advantages. First, the Mesopotamian tradition studied by A. Leo Oppenheim influenced our biblical sources on dreams, as well as the tradition on which Artemidorus drew. Furthermore, the dream book of Artemidorus, translated into Arabic, has influenced dream interpretation right up to the present day in Morocco. Therefore, I will be analyzing three traditions related not only to one another but also to our own. Second, the sources used in each case are significantly and, I trust, instructively different. What we know of dream classification in ancient Mesopotamia has come to us in the form of cuneiform tablets written by scribes for purposes both political and religious. These purposes of course affect the choice of materials which were noted. In the second case, the dream book of Artemidorus, the author is a Lydian writing in the early Christian world dominated by Rome. Since he dedicates the book to his son in order to pass on the principles and tricks of his trade, dream interpretation is perceived as a profession, a craft that can be taught and learnt, and upon which a son can be expected to survive. Finally, in the case of the Moroccan materials, while I can say I had the advantage of being able to question living people, I cannot claim that my materials are influenced any less by my own preoccupations, my own motivated ignorance as a European fieldworker in a non-European society, or my own limitations. I trust, nonetheless, that my attempts to elucidate these inevitable obstacles will provide the interested reader with some insight into the nature, purpose, and function of the organization and presentation of Moroccan materials (see Kilborne 1978, 1981).

In short, we will be examining three different kinds of sources about three different cultural traditions of dream interpretation. In each case I will argue that dream classificatory principles indicate something about cultural values and individual experience, that the nature and purpose of the writers who provide us with sources suggest paths of exploration, that each case can usefully be seen in the light of the other two, and finally that all three cases bear some relation to our American and European ideas today about dreams and dream classification. They can therefore be profitably and intelligibly compared precisely because there is a framework within which all are relevant to our concerns and ideas.

DREAM CLASSIFICATION

Only certain types of classificatory systems have been studied, a fact that surely has much to do with vogues for particular subjects and the desire that anthropological research be consonant with American and European values. The frame of reference according to which classificatory systems are isolated for specialized study is seldom examined. Likewise, the theory of classificatory principles is neither consistent nor very well explored. For one thing, to study such a frame of reference touches upon the limits of classification as an analytic method and upon the problem of belief; for another, it raises the specter of controversies over 'primitive thought,' both issues which many social scientists find it more comfortable to ignore.

Dream classifications as collective representations are, generally speaking, conspicuously absent from our Western tradition. Of course, there are dream theories, but it seems fair to say that we do not invest as much culturally and psychologically in dreams as, for example, Mediterranean peoples do, or as did the ancient Greeks, Assyrians, or Egyptians. To some extent, then, the very existence of an elaborate classificatory system of dreams is a manifestation of the importance accorded to dreams. For us, dreams are either objects of superstition (another manifestation of our European problem with belief) or an individual experience (as in psychotherapy or psychoanalysis). For the same individual to compare and classify his dreams is rare in the West; for him to compare his dreams with those of his neighbor by means of a classificatory system is rarer still.

Elaborate systems of dream classification are inseparably bound up with cultural belief systems and are essentially related to religion (Kilborne 1985). Thus, dream classification is one of those instances of a classificatory system rooted in belief systems. Its existence and persistence testify to the meanings and perceived importance attached to dreams by social actors.

DREAM FUNCTIONS AND CULTURAL USES OF CLASSIFICATION

Psychoanalysts have contributed to the following lines of investigation concerning theories of dream functions: (1) dreams are a point of departure for secondary associations and the technique of free association; (2) they are a way of dealing with conflict; (3) they are an element in the design of a case history; (4) they are an expression of unconscious desires and defense mechanisms; and finally (5) they are an expression of varying capacities for ego synthesis and reality testing during the course of therapy (see, for example, French and Fromm 1964; Natterson 1981; Bonime 1962).

A functional analysis of dreams in psychoanalytic writings, however, does not touch upon the important matter of dream classification, upon questions of collective representations and cultural values. Furthermore, whereas one can describe a butterfly and assign it to a particular genus and species, the same cannot be done for a dream. Thus, dream classification is significantly different from classification in the natural sciences. Although dream classification does not have the 'scientific' functions of, for example, the classification of mollusks, where observation and classification go hand in hand, it does have social functions. Closer to linguistic models and classification in language (thought categories), dream classification necessarily deals with psychodynamic processes.

The important question in dream classification concerns the perception of the dream and the way in which, for specific individual and social reasons, it becomes associated with certain kinds of experiences;

with its role in the formulation of thinking and social consciousness. Dreams and dream interpretation have, broadly speaking, at least seven functions: (1) divinatory, (2) political, (3) religious, (4) artistic or formal, (5) therapeutic, (6) psychodynamic, and (7) expressive. Naturally, these functions overlap and interlock in most societies in which dreams are believed to be important.

DREAMS AND DIVINATION IN ANCIENT MESOPOTAMIA

According to A. Leo Oppenheim (1966:341), divination was the subject of greater and more sustained interest in ancient Mesopotamia than in any other civilization. To analyze the dream in ancient Mesopotamia, Oppenheim holds, it is necessary to examine dreams in divination and science. 'I propose to see in the divination aspect of the dream a "scientific" attitude, while I consider as falling under the heading of folklore the aspect that derives no predictions from dreams but accepts them as psychological phenomena' (ibid.:342). Then to emphasize his position he continues, 'I am prepared to say that predictions derived from such dream contents as, for example, seeing certain animals, eating certain foods, and so forth, are based on a "scientific" attitude of the Mesopotamian interpreters, whereas dreams that the modern psychologist could characterize as nightmares, or as typically symbol-affected dreams, belong in Mesopotamia to an "unscientific" view of the world; they are vestiges of dream explanations on a folklore level' (ibid.).

Whether or not one agrees with Oppenheim's opposition between scientific and folkloric attitudes, the distinction does indicate a fundamental proposition that theories of dreams imply ideas about thinking and culturally significant conceptions of evidence and knowledge. If this proposition is accepted, then it becomes possible and worthwhile to examine the cultural, religious, folkloristic, scientific, economic, and political as well as the psychological (in this instance, the 'individual,' i.e., psychodynamic and cognitive) functions of dream theories. However, any assessment of the cultural and psychological functions of dream theories depends not only on the analytic theories available but also on the character of the evidence.

The first feature of ancient Mesopotamian dream theories to consider is that all we know about them is filtered through written documents and other materials, since the culture is today inaccessible to observation. If there were aspects of dream interpretation which were not written down, we cannot know them except perhaps by inference. Thus, the first difficulty lies in gaining some idea of the full context of dream theories; the second lies in understanding what we *do* have access to.

Mesopotamian divination practices were recorded in highly formalized one-sentence units known as 'omens.' There are large numbers of these omens available to scholars. Because of their emphasis on observation and systematic analysis, Oppenheim (ibid.:343) holds that 'these omen texts reflect a consistently rational approach which is hardly paralleled in Mesopotamian literature.'

It would appear, then, that in ancient Mesopotamia, not only was there a considerable body of knowledge about divinatory dreams but, equally significant, this body of knowledge reflects careful observation and is treated systematically. Moreover, those social and political forces in ancient Mesopotamia which gave dreams a prominent role in divination may be expected to be reflected in these omens. And, as Oppenheim demonstrates, indeed they are. Finally, the classificatory approach to dreams and divination in ancient Mesopotamia itself would appear to be rooted in social attitudes towards the dream. The appearance of dream classification is itself a social fact worth considering rather carefully.

In Oppenheim's analysis the 'message dream' is clearly not associated with the systematic, analytic, observational approach. Such dreams are reported in a stylized fashion and use as their hallmark narrative conventions which he calls 'the dream frame.' Typically the dreamer is a king, a hero, or a priest. In the dream a deity appears to this dreamer and conveys a message. No sooner is this done than the dreamer awakens suddenly. Interestingly, such dreams are generally not interpreted.

So far, then, we have one major official class of dreams dreamt by socially, politically, and/or religiously important individuals: message dreams in which the deity communicates with the dreamer, and the dreamer then appears as spokesman for divine beings communicating 'their' message to the people. If message dreams are not interpreted, one can infer that this is because of the prominent position of the dreamer and the less prominent position of the interpreter. For, as Oppenheim (ibid.:347) remarks, only message dreams are recognized by the ancient Mesopotamians to be theologically acceptable. If the dreamer/king is graced with a divine communication, then how can a lesser man tell those around him what the god really meant?

Oppenheim identifies a second category of dreams, 'symbolic' dreams. Like message dreams, these conform to strict conventions and are subjected to minimal interpretation. Examples of symbolic dreams are Joseph's two dreams which foretell of his own supremacy over his brothers (Gen. 37:5–9). The sheaves, sun, moon, and stars made obeisance before a single sheaf, which Joseph interpreted as symbolizing himself. Joseph's interpretation of Pharaoh's dream (Gen. 41:25–36) is another example of a symbolic dream dreamed by a king and interpreted by a religious man in touch with the deity.

But we are here faced with trying to assess the cultural meanings attributed to stereotyped categories and dreams. Interpretable religious messenger and symbolic dreams are stereotyped to the extent to which: (a) dreamers are predictably important persons and (b) dreams (as reported in the literature) conform to explicit literary conventions. But not only religious dreams are stereotyped. Interpreted dreams and interpretation itself may also be relegated to the profane (i.e., rational and 'scientific') realm of the political and social spheres. And categories of interpreters would appear to reflect this division. On the one side we have the 'inspired interpreter-artist, the wise man,' and on the other, the 'diviner-scientist' (ibid.:349). Each class of interpreters as it were takes its cut of the dreams which can be interpreted. And criteria for interpretability would seem to depend upon conventional definitions of dream perception.

In Oppenheim's analysis, symbolic dreams are distinctly less official (and therefore less religious?) than messenger dreams. For there is a significant difference in the way in which the two are reported. 'In the Bible, "symbolic" dreams are reported solely by gentiles – the Pharaoh of the Exodus and Nebuchadnezzar – for whom the Lord very conveniently provides the services of Joseph and Daniel – who are his pious interpreters. In the cuneiform literature, Sumerian and Akkadian alike, "symbolic" dreams occur only in mythological texts and are interpreted there by gods and heroes' (ibid.). If I understand this passage correctly, Oppenheim says that messenger dreams are in effect direct communications from the deity, not texts in need of exegesis; and the more in need of exegesis is the dream, the less inspirational and/or the less powerful the dreamer.

A third major category of dreams can be called 'realist' or 'physicalist.' These dreams, capable of being linked to physical causes, are believed not to warrant interpretation precisely because they come from the body. Examples of such dreams include themes with hunger, sexual intercourse, and pain. Such 'physicalist dreams' are perceived to be what they seem, extensions of waking perceptions which do not call for 'interpretations.' The 'absent' symbolic (i.e., negative social) value attached to such dreams is, of course, meaningful. But their meaning is left to individual dreamers to determine. Such meanings are perceptually unintelligible to interpreters, precisely because they are not defined to be socially symbolic. In other words, they are not collective representations in the Durkheimian sense. Because certain dreams can be meaningful only to their dreamers, they are 'transparent' and therefore invisible to interpreters. Because these are dreams perceived to be what they appear, there is no stereotype to which the physicalist dream can be compared in interpretation.

Logically, we would expect that the dreams on which interpretation would concentrate would be those which are neither so stereotypical that there is little room for interpretation nor those which are physicalist and therefore idiosyncratic, in which case the interpretive art of comparison has no play.

The kinds of dreams on which interpretation concentrates are likely to be dreams which are clearly neither 'religious' nor 'secular,' but rather which deal with the ambiguities of common experience. According to Oppenheim, what seems to make a dream a 'message dream' has to do more with the person who has it than with either any absolute standards by which dream content can be judged or criteria for putting it in a particular category. What makes a dream an ordinary dream attributed to body functions and not credited with any divinatory value is the dreamer's feelings that the dream is not important, or that it represents no communication, rather than any specific content or theme associated with the class of ordinary dreams. Their cause tends to be sought in the body.

In the light of the Mesopotamian materials, we can suggest several propositions about dream classification and interpretation that need to be explored cross-culturally. First, the apparatus of cultural systems of dream interpretation will not be brought to bear on *all* dreams. Dreams at both ends of the spectrum, whether spiritual – royal, messenger-type dreams – or physical – grumbling-stomach dreams – will be set apart as too important and too unimportant respectively. The fact that neither type of dream was interpreted in ancient Mesopotamia indicates that perception of the significance or insignificance of dreams is, to a large extent, dependent upon cultural conceptions of dreaming rather than upon any objective taxonomy of the entity one might call 'the dream.' Otherwise why would some dreams rather than others be exempt from interpretation?

Second, the belief that dreams are objects of a science of divination is as significant in determining the perception of the dream as the belief that some dreams are important because their dreamers are important. Moreover, beliefs about classes of dreams and beliefs in true dreams in no way preclude what Oppenheim calls a 'scientific' or 'rationalist' approach towards dream classification. Thus, supernatural beliefs, classificatory principles, and political benefits may all be considered an integral part of conception of dreams in the minds of the ancient Mesopotamians.

Third, there is a relationship between the spectrum of dream categories and the cultural theories of the self and of thinking. This, of course, raises the issue of what sort of role dream classification plays in folk dream-theories, as well as how and to what extent interpreters actually follow either the classifications or the dream books available to them. In the case of the Babylonian and Assyrian dream books, we can only guess what the ancient Mesopotamian experience and perception of dreams were like. For, as we have seen, a number of cultural and individual elements determined what sort of dreams were written down, and we can only go by recorded materials. Nonetheless, if one wishes to understand more about ancient Near Eastern notions of self and personhood it is highly instructive to study ancient Near Eastern dream theories. And, as Oppenheim well shows, a careful examination of dream books reveals a great deal about belief systems in the ancient Near East.

DREAM INTERPRETATION IN SECOND-CENTURY GREECE: ARTEMIDORUS

The popular tradition of dream classification and interpretation which persists in the Islamic world and in the Mediterranean[4] has its roots in one extremely important work: the *Oneirocritica (Interpretation of Dreams)* of the second-century Greek, Artemidorus. Between the messenger (supernatural) dreams and the grumbling-stomach (natural) dreams, both relegated to the general category of dreams which for different reasons are not interpreted, we find the richest tradition of dream classification. Moreover – and this is the point to be emphasized – this tradition of dream divination and classification is linked to popular lore and to the attempt to find meaningful patterns in the here-and-now of daily experience. To scrutinize dreams for Artemidorus and those who follow him is to look into the commonality of daily experience, to probe the human mind, rather than to attest to the existence of a divine spirit. It is to provide the appearances of dreams with mundane, psychological meanings in order to enable dreamers to deal better with daily existence.

Artemidorus lived in the second century A.D., the century of the emperors Hadrian and Marcus Aurelius, the orator Aelius Aristides, the writer Pausanias, and the scientists Ptolemy and Galen. Widely traveled himself, Artemidorus was a keen observer, a quality which stood him in good stead as the most brilliant exponent of a long oneirocritic tradition which was to influence European thought and literature and with which Freud was to become familiar seventeen centuries later.

The *Oneirocritica*, composed of five books organized in a systematic fashion, displays a 'rational, practical approach' (White 1975:7). It is helpful to dwell on the organization and classification of the first two books to understand better what kind of 'scientific' approach White and others have perceived in the *Oneirocritica*, to compare these books with the description of categories found in ancient Mesopotamia, and to assess the importance of Artemidorus' work for the Mediterranean tradition of dream interpretation and temple sleeping still very much alive today.

The first book concerns the self and the body and is to be contrasted with the second, which deals with the natural world. In Book I mention is made of internal as opposed to external relationships and of the relation between dream and dreamer which the interpreter needs to know (ibid.:20). Whole dreams are discussed, and what is meant by 'whole' in this context is highly suggestive. From these the sequence of subjects roughly includes birth (of oneself), pregnancy, and children, the coming into being of the notion of self, and then a series of subjects focussing on the head (ibid.:13–17). This is particularly significant because, as Onians writes, 'in Greek popular belief the head is an organ of life, a seat of the psyche, an organ of generation, and a symbol of the continuity of life and family' (1954:93). We still speak of the 'head' of state and the 'head' of the household. Onians mentions the Greek idea according to which the doctor acts as a brain to the patient. That such an idea gained acceptance implies the considerable extent to which suggestion and authority must have been used in healing. Finally, there is the analogy of the philosopher to the brain; the philosopher-king acts as a brain to his people.

The sequence of themes dealing with the head in the *Oneirocritica* includes hair, forehead, ears, eyebrows, vision, nose, cheeks, jaws, beards, teeth, tongue, vomiting, abscesses in head region, beheaded, back headedness, animal-headed, head in hands, and horns on head (White 1975:26–36). Two features of this sequence are worth noting: the fact that the various themes begin with the hair on the head (i.e., at the top) and then proceed downwards more or less straightforwardly until one comes to vomiting. From there on all themes deal with illness or abnormality. Significantly, one finds two categories of features, the first normal and healthy, the second abnormal and associated with illness. This sequence implies culturally grounded perceptions and conceptions of the self, the body and body parts, together with their relations to political and social organization on the one hand and to physiology and medicine on the other.

The systematic fashion in which Artemidorus organizes his considerable volume of material and the ways in which he also uses the older popular tradition of auspicious and inauspicious meanings of certain dream symbols are among the most fascinating features of the *Oneirocritica*. Moreover, in the light of the distinction mentioned above between scientific and status-oriented interpretations of dreams, Artemidorus' approach is of particular interest. No longer is there that emphasis on position and hierarchy, whether political or social, which characterized dream interpretation in the ancient Near East. Rather, much depends upon context and the systematic consideration of the field of dream interpretation generally. To Artemidorus, symbols are a language of their own, to be decoded through the method of dream interpretation. In contrast to methods of dream interpretation in ancient Mesopotamia, the scientific (i.e., systematic and classificatory) method of dream interpretation used by Artemidorus has egalitarian overtones: Dreams are phenomena to be explained with reference to the everyday life of the folk rather than with reference to symbols of social, political, and/or religious status.

For instance, consider the discussion of food in Book I. Dry and wet (rather than the Lévi-Straussian raw and cooked) are principles according to which nourishment is divided into two basic categories. Artemidorus first discusses drinks. Drinking cold water is good luck for all, but drinking warm water brings bad luck except to those used to it (it is an unnatural practice); drinking moderate amounts of wine is auspicious but drinking mead, honeyed quince wine, hydromel, myrtle wine, and prepared wines means bad luck to all but the rich, to whom it is natural to drink them (ibid.:50). Drinking vinegar presages a quarrel with a member of the household 'because of the contraction of the mouth' (ibid.), while drinking olive oil means poisoning or illness. 'It is always auspicious for a thirsty man to drink . . . for thirst is nothing but a longing for something, and drinking releases a person from that craving' (ibid.).

After a brief discussion of drinking cups Artemidorus passes to dry nourishment beginning with vegetables, specifically 'vegetables that give off a smell after they are eaten as, for example, radishes, endive, and cut leeks indicate that secrets will be revealed and signal hatred for one's associates' (ibid.:51). Also, 'beets, mallow, dock, curled dock, and orach are only auspicious for debtors, since they stimulate the stomach and relax the bowels' (ibid.). Any reader here is a bit perplexed. And, as is often the case reading Artemidorus, the explanation which follows is more suggestive than helpful. 'For the stomach and entrails especially are like a money-lender' (ibid.). Presumably this is because money 'passes through' them. Plants with a head (carrots, etc.) are good luck and signify success. This seems in keeping with the importance attributed by the Greek and Roman world of Artemidorus to the head. But dreams about cabbage are 'entirely inauspicious' since 'the cabbage is the only vegetable around which the vine does not curl' (ibid.), yet another empirical observation incorporated into the 'science' of dream interpretation. After an elaborate discussion of cereals and breads Artemidorus notes that 'it is good for a man to dream that he is eating the kind of bread to which he is accustomed. For to a poor man, black bread is appropriate and to a rich man, white bread' (ibid.:52). He goes on to discuss meats and fish, then concludes the section on edibles with fruit, having followed in his presentation the order of courses. The transition to the following section is made with the phrase: 'Since household articles naturally [*sic*] come next after food, I think that it is fitting to deal with them also' (ibid.:54–5).

I have dwelt on Artemidorus in some detail here in order to

demonstrate the kind of careful observation of the real world that characterizes his *Oneirocritica*. Significantly, the order of presentation often reflects not so much immutable natural sequences, as with the seasons, but rather customary social procedures. For instance, he begins his discussion of food not with apples (because A is the first letter of the alphabet) or with milk (because that is what newborn infants eat first), but rather with vegetables. The sequence is: (1) vegetables, (2) meat and fish, and (3) fruit, the common order of courses in an ordinary meal.

In other words, Artemidorus bases his classificatory principles on the organization of human behaviors he sees around him. There is no preoccupation with Platonic forms or ideal order. His is a mundane (profane) system of dream interpretation rooted in the customs, habits, and psychological motivations and symbolic meanings which he has observed at first hand, collected and compiled in 'meaningful' systems. The systematics of Artemidorus' approach may seem to us oddly incompatible with the 'superstitious' meanings of the symbols. But this incompatibility should not blind us to the richness of his classificatory system, or to the many ways in which his book can profitably be studied by all those interested in cultural systems of dream interpretation. Our very difficulties in confidently tagging the work of Artemidorus as either scientific or religious, profane or sacred, point up its significance.

Finally, Artemidorus' discussion of dream symbolism effectively calls attention to what has been referred to as the multivalence of symbols or what Freud (1900) called 'overdetermination,' one symbol having a variety of complementary meanings. In Artemidorus the same symbols have different meanings for different people (e.g., dreams of white and black bread for rich and poor dreamers). In working out the interpretive principles of comparative dream interpretation, Artemidorus articulates a symbolic language which retains many of the characteristics of linguistic systems. In fact, dream interpretation for Artemidorus is a discourse on the language of dreams; rather than distancing the dreamer and interpreter from the here-and-now, dream interpretation brings them closer. The principles of interpretation are to be discovered not in any divine messages or exegesis of texts, but in the world of daily experience. Thus by calling attention to the depth and richness of everyday existence, by applying the methods of observation to the behaviors of those around him, Artemidorus can be seen as having developed what Freud is now known for: a method of relating dreams to the various hidden meanings of social and individual life.

It is worth emphasizing that the prosaic, concrete system of

Artemidorus in which meanings vary depending upon the dreamer and the dream situation is quite unlike the more idealized system of dream interpretation which Islam and other religions appear to encourage. Other-worldly truths are less relative than those with which our daily lives confront us. The very relativity of the meanings of dream symbols in Artemidorus lends itself to systematizing them as a language, to contextualizing them. And the context in turn then needs describing and understanding. Hence the importance of social context, social status, sex, age, and all the variables which enter into the interpretation of a dream for Artemidorus. In short, dreams serve as a prism which concentrates and encodes the hidden meanings of daily experience; they depend upon interpretation to decode them and make them intelligible.

Because Artemidorus addresses many kinds of dreamers and consequently takes into account a far more variegated, realistic social spectrum than do the message dreams of the ancient Near East and of ancient Greece, one can argue that his system of dream interpretation reflects a more complex and diverse society than do the dream books studied by Oppenheim. Indeed, there is certainly much evidence to substantiate such a claim. Artemidorus' mundane search behind dream symbols for meanings in daily experience may be opposed to the more ethereal thrust of rationalist religious theology, particularly Christian theological dogma. The influence of the dream book of Artemidorus was profound throughout the Mediterranean primarily because it articulated cultural notions of and attitudes towards the dream and dream interpretation. The Christian tradition discredited dreams, relegated them to a secondary place, and treated them with suspicion. By contrast, within Islam the situation was rather different. Whereas Christ gained a reputation as a doctor because he healed the sick, Mohammed gained a reputation as a visionary prophet. In Islamic texts it is stated that there can be no truthful dreams since Mohammed, because he had them all. For Mohammed, dreams were the vehicle of revelation essential for his role as prophet and visionary, whereas Christ laid no substantive claims to prophecy. Since he was the son of God, there was automatically a hotline, so to speak, established between Father and Son. More than that, since they were one, their communication could not be 'symbolic.'

MOROCCAN DREAM CLASSIFICATION AND INTERPRETATION

There persists in Morocco today a rich tradition of dream interpretation (see Kilborne 1978). In addition to reflecting daily experience, Moroccan dream interpretations and dream classifications reflect also the domains of folk Islam and classical Islam, popular as well as orthodox beliefs, attitudes, and doctrines.

Moroccan dream classifications indicate a split between truthful, divinity-inspired dreams (i.e., dreams that square with the orthodox written tradition) and deceitful dreams coming from all other sources. However, characterizing Moroccan dream books in this way does not do justice to the wealth of material they contain about the world view of Moroccans and the meanings of daily experiences. Indeed, it would seem that the basis of Moroccan dream interpretation is akin to the dream book of Artemidorus: it has its roots in the complexity of interpersonal situations, however much interpreters and dreamers would wish it to be prescriptive.

Interested readers may wish at this point to consult the appendix to this chapter in order to acquire some familiarity with specific schemata of dream classification on which subsequent discussions are based. Of the questions that come to mind when comparing the various similarities and differences among these classes, one stands out: that between truth and falsehood in dreams. Generally speaking, we in our modern tradition assume that only waking experience is truthful, and that all dreams are deceitful – an attitude consistent with most Christian doctrine. Luther, who one might have thought was not unduly preoccupied with dreams, begged God not to send him any, because he was so afraid he could not tell a true dream from a false one.

Even if, in principle, the truth of the religious category of veridical dreams is assumed, there are a variety of meanings in terms of which dreamers in Morocco perceive and interpret their dreams. Thus distinctions made between categories of dreams tend to reflect ideals and values, not simply to describe realities, like classifications in the natural sciences. As Moroccans are fascinated by the social life around them and are often extremely perceptive and keen observers of their fellows, and as these traits find expression in folk Islamic beliefs and practices, it would indeed seem odd if the category of 'bad dreams' always drew universal condemnation. What matters for our purposes is how the various categories are *used*, how they *function* in social contexts and for individual actors.

One cannot help suspecting that the residual category of deceitful dreams (because they are mundane and not God-sent) is somewhat like Satan in Milton's *Paradise Lost*: of far more interest psychologically than the divine veridical counterpart. Milton makes Satan in many respects more attractive than God, who is flat and boring. Similarly, deceitful dreams afford a kind of interest which 'veridical' dreams do not have. The question is: What kind?

I suggest that an exploration of deceitful dreams will enable us to understand some rather fundamental elements in the Moroccan world view. Consider the widespread beliefs in the evil eye, and in jealousy, envy, and rivalry as explanations for conflict. Consider also the Islamic ideal of the good man, who has truthful dreams. Consider thirdly the ways in which Moroccan beliefs in *djinn* (spirits good and bad who oversee daily social interaction) articulate experiences interpreted as relating to 'goodness' and 'badness.' They provide a way both of projecting unwanted hostile feelings on to spirits and of attempting to deal with an inner world of suspicion and jealousy. In the light of this, it is hardly surprising that the vast majority of dreams should be thought potentially dangerous. Indeed, dreams in the ancient Near East had been so regarded.

If, as I am arguing here, such defensive projective mechanisms are indeed an essential part of the beliefs in the *djinn*, then dreams in which these *djinn* appear, and dreams believed to be produced by the *djinn*, need to be considered together, as do dream interpretations that depend upon these evil-intentioned spirits and men. Because dreamers are uncomfortable with feelings of hostility, rivalry, and suspiciousness, it is far more convenient to have dreams in which these emotions play a major part interpreted. In this way it appears that there really *is* an enemy there and thus the suspiciousness is justified; since reality *is* full of evil intentions, the hostility is self-defense.

Furthermore, truthful dreams are associated with safety, as deceitful dreams are associated with harm, revealing the evil intentions of spirits, family, friends, and enemies. Only God-sent dreams can really be trusted. But two difficulties arise here: first, how does one know whether a particular dream is a God-sent dream and not a fake sent by Satan? Second, how can it be that many actors who have never been sure of experiencing truthful dreams persist in believing in them?

Both questions indicate individual mistrust, which motivates reliance on an external authority figure who can assert and judge knowledge in dreams. Ideas about dream interpretation in Morocco, so it would seem, express real, experienced and basic mistrust. But they also underlie beliefs in truthful dreams, beliefs which go counter to experience. These beliefs in dreams rely upon idealization, a process analogous to the construction of heaven, which is believed in even if nobody has ever been there and returned to describe it.

Interpreted this way, Moroccan perceptions of dream categories appear quite consonant with the tendency to perceive enemies when interpreting dreams. Most dreams, indeed virtually all dreams, cannot be trusted any more than people can, and this mistrust is itself one powerful motive behind taking dreams to be interpreted, telling them, and using them in different ways in communication. In fact, one method of interpreting dreams in Morocco is to spell out to the dreamer specifically what is not to be trusted. And it does appear that Moroccan dreams tend to confirm feelings that the world is not to be trusted, not to be taken at face value, and that there is much psychological saliency to valuing dreams as deceitful.

Thus, I suggest, Moroccan perceptions of basic categories of dreams – what we might consider a dichotomy of truthful versus deceitful dreams – are understood by Moroccans in several ways. Whereas on the surface, good, truthful, or God-sent dreams logically are more important in religious dogma (in terms of ideals), psychologically and experientially it is the deceitful dreams which have more psychological salience. Deceitful dreams correspond to the basic sense of mistrust which is expressed in beliefs in *djinn* and in the use of envy to explain social relationships. These deceitful dreams reflect the social fabric of the life in Morocco and various levels of daily experience. It is therefore on their interpretation that *fqih* and other professional dream interpreters naturally concentrate. In short, because Moroccans value deceitful dreams as expressions of psychological realities and everyday experiences, the category is equally as important as God-sent, truthful, or good dreams. 'True' might mean 'better' or more valuable in terms of what the dreamers wish, but 'deceitful' would seem to square far better with the world as experienced.

I have argued that to Moroccans deceitful dreams are culturally and psychologically as important as God-sent dreams. The argument has proceeded from a re-examination of the more obvious interpretations of the basic dual categories, *ruya* and *ahlam*, God-sent and deceitful dreams respectively. That a dream is believed to be God-sent does not explain how it is understood by Moroccans to be good, nor does it enable us to understand how it is used in social interactions. One of the psychological functions of beliefs in the possibility of 'true' dreams (which few people have) is to allow for the maintenance of ideals in the face of experienced mistrust and uncertainty. Moreover, if one looks at the overwhelming proportion of deceitful dreams, and at the interest in deceit generally, the meanings of true as well as of deceitful dreams in Moroccan experience become considerably clearer.

Furthermore, in view of the confusion, moral repugnance, and indignation felt by most Europeans when confronted with problems of lying and truth in Morocco (and the Near East generally), it seems paradoxical that in dreams Moroccans should make such a clear distinction. I have suggested that the classification reflects a *wish* for clarity, a clarity which simply does not exist in waking experience. Given then the prevalence of what appears to us as lying and deceit, it is psychologically plausible that the emphasis on the category of truthful dreams corresponds to wishes that there be areas of experience which, at least in principle, are thoroughly trustworthy.

It would appear therefore that the very categorization of dreams into good (*ruya*) and deceitful (*ahlam*) is part of a belief system in the Weberian or Durkheimian sense; that this is not a structural opposition experienced as evidence of a split between official and folk Islam; and that individuals are motivated to perceive dreams as they do because of their experience as Moroccans. Deceitful dreams are psychologically salient because they correspond to, and make palpable, Moroccan beliefs in the evil eye, the presence of enemies, and in easily offended, revengeful *djinn*.

There is yet another consideration which further strengthens my arguments concerning Moroccan dream classification and some of the basic meanings of the *ruya/ahlam* distinction. This is the tendency to split dreams into those that come from a divinity and those that come from inside (i.e., from the body or the self).

Thus, in Nabulsi's two categories, 'God-sent dreams' and 'deceitful dreams' (see the appendix to this chapter), the latter are rooted in internal individual wishes, ambition, or confusion; they are sexual dreams, dreams sent by Satan the deceiver. In Hadj Brahime's three categories, 'God-sent dreams,' 'warning dreams,' and 'dreams coming from self and body,' dreams are also categorized depending on their origin or their cause. Thus each type of dream bears its own trademark. Ahmed reproduces essentially the same classification: messenger dreams, warning dreams, preoccupation dreams, and sexual dreams. Consequently, the classification is essentially between dreams from outside (from the divinity, immortal messages or divinatory signs) and dreams from inside (deceitful dreams sent by Satan). Furthermore, dreams originating in the self are deceitful.

One might interpret the mistrust of what comes from within in relation to the projective beliefs in evil beings (*djinn*) and in the jealousy (evil eye) of friends and neighbors. Significantly, internal mistrust is frequently interpreted by dream interpreters as symbolic of external threats. In short, Moroccan notions of the self, particularly those persecutory ideas that depend upon evil and envious family and neighbors to validate individual denial, are seen to be part of the context in terms of which basic dream classification belief systems are maintained, interpreted, and understood.

CONCLUSIONS

If dream classification expresses world view, and if it is likely to change both with the cultural context and with the kind of place dreams have in cultural belief systems, then it can be of far more use to anthropologists than it has been in the past. I have argued here that in ancient Mesopotamia, dreams which come down to us (i.e., those that were recorded) reflect above all the political, social, and religious status of the dreamers, who were kings and prominent figures. By contrast, in the Graeco-Roman world of Artemidorus the meaning of dreams is far more dependent upon context than upon the dreamer's place in the social order (i.e., his rank per se). Indeed, the very cosmopolitanism of the period and the secular, methodical approach used by Artemidorus provides a strikingly different view of the world from that of Mesopotamia, one which is far more complex and diverse. This is of course due partly to the difference in the nature of the documents and partly to the social importance of dream interpretation in the world of Artemidorus where interpretations of message dreams could be subordinated to other concerns. For Artemidorus, context and the weave of daily experience are extremely important in determining the meaning of a dream; for the inhabitants of ancient Mesopotamia, the status of the dreamer is relatively more important. In sum, the popular preoccupation with the social fabric of daily life is one of the motives behind the interest in classification and observation reflected by the dream book of Artemidorus. By contrast, in ancient Mesopotamia, where dreams are seen to be related to the status of the dreamer, social context is less prominent. To use an analogy, it seems somewhat as though when one 'pulls up' a dream in ancient Mesopotamia, one gets a long tap root and relatively little soil; but when one does the same thing in the world of Artemidorus, the root system is vast and the ramifications far-reaching.

In Morocco there is a deferential system of attitudes and wishes – orthodox, idealized, and Islamic – built into images of 'good dreamers': they are pious men, generally known as such already in the society, and often have political power and social visibility. As such, these men are venerated. In this respect, dream interpretation in Morocco may be compared to that of ancient Mesopotamia. But the folk system of dream interpretation feels very similar to that of Artemidorus, and attends to the interests and concerns of daily life while interpreting them. Alongside the more stereotyped – because less realistic, less familiar – idealized category of 'good dreams' we find those which express the popular tradition of examining the here-and-now for evidence substantiating internal mistrust projected as beliefs in *djinn*, in saints, and in the evil eye. Hence the psychological saliency of the Moroccan system of dream classification and interpretation. Dream interpretation provides an arena in which real and imaginary spades can be called spades.

In short, examinations of dream classification cannot be expected to reveal the same kinds of cultural features or provide the same kinds of insights in these three societies because they are rooted differently in each one. In each, an understanding of the functions of dreams and dream interpretation provides us with essentially different, although comparable, insights into cultural processes. No two systems of dream classification can be expected to reflect the values, beliefs, and behaviors (i.e., the cultures) of their members in the same way.

When dream classification is approached not as a reflection of logical 'scientific' thinking, or in terms of Durkheim's dichotomy of sacred and profane, then it is no longer necessary to understand or evaluate it as absolute or universal. The classificatory system of dreams and dream interpretation may be grasped in relation to the motivations of the authors whose perceptions we conceptualize collectively as world view or behavioral environment. When dream classification is approached in relation to beliefs and substantive epistemological issues, then anthropologists can see dream classes as social facts, study their functions, and better comprehend relative and universal meanings of the cultural experience and belief systems involved. Rather than indicating the 'unscientific' character of non-European thought, studies of dream classification underline the importance of assessing the cultural and psychological functions of the scientific organization of superstitious beliefs, as these reflect perceptions of the world.

My emphasis throughout this chapter has been on the cultural and psychological functions of the classificatory schema of dreams. I have argued that identifying or describing such systems, however important, is never sufficient. It is necessary to examine the ways in which these schemata are *used* by members of the culture, the ways in which these classificatory systems themselves represent the world view of the actors. In other words I am suggesting that classifications of dreams serve psychological and cultural functions relative to the conscious and unconscious purposes of the actors. In this respect they can be compared to teleological belief systems. However, that they are motivated does not mean that they are to be dismissed as unscientific or non-rational; it does not mean that we can assume an epistemological gap between rational, logical, scientific thought on the one hand, and teleological belief and superstition on the other. Indeed, I would suggest in closing that *all* classificatory systems, scientific and religious, Western and non-Western, have psychological and cultural functions that we, as students of human nature, need to understand.

NOTES

1. This chapter has been immeasurably improved by suggestions from various colleagues and friends including Melford E. Spiro, Jeffrey Alexander, and Barbara Tedlock. To these and other friends I am grateful.
2. 'Your old men shall dream dreams, your young men shall see visions' (Joel 2:28). 'And your sons and your daughters shall prophesy, and your young men shall see visions, and your old men shall dream dreams' (Acts 2:17).
3. There is a copious literature on classification within anthropology: the standard work is that of Durkheim and Mauss (1963). A modern work which synthesizes for the

general reader much work done since is Needham (1981). In much of the recent anthropological literature on classification attention has been drawn to rather specific subjects: kinship, color categories, plant and animal taxonomies, and social stratification. The success of such studies in promoting a 'scientific' image of anthropology has not been inconsiderable. It is also worth noting that, structuralist methods and binary oppositions notwithstanding, religious belief, psychodynamics, and individual motivation have been relegated to a secondary status as objects of anthropological investigation.

4. Dream theories and methods of interpretation in Mediterranean countries, related to ancient Mesopotamian dream theories, have several distinctive features: the appearance of the tall man as a messenger figure, the practice of incubation, or temple sleeping, the obedience of directives given in dreams, and the performance of activities in certain sacred places. It is tempting to speculate that theories of the state – combined with political realities from Mesopotamia to ancient Greece and modern Mediterranean states – have fundamentally influenced the representation of authority, and might, in part, help to account for the similarity of dream theories and methods of interpretation in the Mediterranean.

APPENDIX

Basic Islamic dream categorization

1 *ruya*: message dreams sent by Allah (clear and important); prophetic dreams demonstrating righteousness of dreamer

2 *ahlam*: deceitful dreams coming from other sources

Nabulsi (1641–1731)

1 *God-sent dreams*: appearance of Mohammed or one of his messengers, clear and unconfused, 'good' and truthful

2 *deceitful dreams*: rooted in individual wishes, ambition or confusion; sexual dreams (nocturnal emission) requiring ablutions and not needing an interpretation; dreams sent by sorcerers (both *djinn* and human) and which are as painful for dreamer as those sent by Satan; dreams sent by Satan; dreams produced by humors when they are liquid and cloudy; the 'return' – the old dreamer sees himself as a young man

Hadj Brahime (Moroccan informant from the Souss)

1 *bouchra min Allah*: God-sent dreams, peaceful and happy

2 *takouif*: fearsome dreams, warning dreams (do not do this or that)

3 *hadith en nafs*: dreams rooted in physical needs and day residue (*nafs* are passions or appetites); Hadj Brahime added 'each *nafs* must die'

1 *messenger dreams*
2 *warning dreams*
3 *preoccupation dreams*: problems and day residues
4 *'normal' (sexual) dreams*

Mohammed (Moroccan informant in rural town near Meknes)

1 *message dreams*: dreamt at sanctuaries (marabouts) and other saintly or divinatory places

2 *warning dreams*: advice, recommendation about the future; ghosts of the dead returning from their tombs to deliver messages

3 *preoccupation dreams*: from within the self caused by love or hate; explained by the dreamer or if complex a seer (*fqih*) interprets

4 *'normal' (day residue) dreams*: problem solving; disturb a parent when told; expectable dreams

9
The Rarámuri stereotype of dreams[1]

WILLIAM MERRILL

The Rarámuri Indians of northern Mexico consider dreams to be the activities of a person's principal soul during sleep. They value dreams highly, for it is primarily through dreams that they communicate with their deities, diagnose illness, and acquire information about the future.[2]

I first noticed this attitude toward dreams while listening to Rarámuri men talk about their dreams in the mornings. Dreams are a frequent topic of conversation, and 'What did you dream last night?' is rivaled only by 'How many times did you have sex?' as the most popular morning greeting among men. These dream discussions ranged in complexity from single sentences to detailed recountings. But what struck me was the fact that men who claimed not to have dreamt the night before consistently responded to this inquiry with a standard phrase: 'I didn't dream at all. I slept very peacefully.'[3]

Given the importance of dreams to the Rarámuri, I was puzzled that they would portray dreaming and sleeping peacefully as mutually exclusive activities. I asked several men why people said this about dreams. Among the comments I received were the following:

People say 'I dreamed unpleasantly last night,' when their souls encounter evil people and other things like coyotes. These things are from the devil and our souls fight with them. If we don't fight, they will grab our souls. People say 'I didn't dream, I slept well,' because they sleep well when their souls don't encounter bad things. When our souls don't meet anyone or anything while we sleep, then we don't dream at all.

Further, from an interview with a Rarámuri doctor:

Anthropologist: Why is it said 'I slept well, I didn't dream?'
Doctor: It is good if one doesn't dream, very good.
A: Where are the souls when you don't dream?
D: Here, peacefully sitting inside [the body]. But then if someone should appear to challenge me then I dream, I dream instantly. He hates me. He hates me, that's how it is. Then I completely wake up. It would be dangerous to sleep then. That's how this thing is. When you don't dream, things are very peaceful. You sleep well.
A: All the souls are inside?
D: All are inside, as long as no one challenges me. If someone challenges me, then I dream right away. God himself alerts me so that I will think well and will not die [will protect myself]. If a strong opponent should attack me and I do not wake up, I will fall ill right away. Not dreaming is good, a person is very content. If I dream of a woman, I will fall ill. That's an ugly thing. For three days my head will hurt and feel as if I were drunk. I'll have a bad cold and cough. Dreaming of a woman is bad. She is illness, that's what she is, a bad illness. That's how it is.

Both of my interlocutors proposed that dreaming precludes peaceful sleep because malevolent beings – evil people, coyotes, and personified illnesses were specifically mentioned – attack or otherwise attempt to harm the dreamers or their souls. They emphasized, in other words, the threats that occur in dreams. This rather fearful picture of dreams, however, represents accurately neither the Rarámuri actual dream experiences – that is, their memories of them – nor the bulk of their ideas about dreams.

Between 1977 and 1984, I collected dream accounts and commentary on the dream experience from over twenty different Rarámuri men, residents of the Ejido of Basíhuare, situated in the Sierra Madre Mountains of southwestern Chihuahua, Mexico.[4] Of a sample of forty-eight dream accounts exactly half involved threats to the dreamer. The other half, all innocuous, featured such things as visits to friends in distant places, the receipt of unexpected gifts, and the revelation of impending rain or other future events.

While my sample is limited, the ratio of threatening to non-threatening dreams it displays is about the same as or *lower* than that recorded from other societies, many of which do not view dreams as negatively as the Rarámuri. Hall (1951), for example, reports from a sample of 1,320 American dreams that hostile acts by or against the dreamer outnumbered friendly acts by over two to one. In a later study of American college students' dreams, aggressive acts occurred in 457 of the 1,000 dreams in the sample, while friendly acts appeared in 302 (Hall and Van de Castle 1966). These results are echoed in Schneider and Sharp's (1969) survey of thirteen different societies in which dreams involving aggression consistently appeared more frequently than any other kind, with the dreamer as victim much more often than as aggressor.

An important conclusion that can be drawn from these studies is that, while the amount and nature of aggression in dreams is remarkably consistent cross-culturally, societies vary in their general attitude toward dreams from very positive to very negative. Phrased differently, the attitude that the members of a society maintain toward dreams cannot be assumed to reflect in a direct and uncomplicated fashion the content of their dreams. This conclusion certainly applies to the Rarámuri, and I will argue that the converse also is true: that the attitude toward dreams does not determine – indeed, has little impact on – the content of dreams. Given the fact that there seems to be no necessary relation between a society's general image of dreams and the content of the dreams of its members, why should the Rarámuri have adopted such a negative view of dreams?

I must emphasize that the Rarámuri focus on the threatening aspects of dreams primarily when they consider them in the abstract. When they discuss dreaming in detail, it is clear that they do not think that dreams must necessarily be unpleasant, nor do they consider all their dreams to be threatening or negative. The view that dream events are threatening is the Rarámuri stereotype of dreams and, like all stereotypes, it simplifies reality. It reflects neither the diversity of individual dream experiences nor the many other more positive ideas about dreams held within the society. It represents what they consider to be typical and critical about dreams, not the totality of their dream experience.

Why the Rarámuri should subscribe to this particular stereotype of dreams is the focus of this chapter. After providing background information on the Rarámuri and the place of dreams in their lives, I propose that this stereotype is but one of many manifestations of an idea that pervades their world view: the notion that insiders are threatened by outsiders. The explanation of the Rarámuri stereotype of dreams thus hinges on accounting for the presence of this more general idea in their world view. I present historical evidence from the seventeenth century to argue that the Rarámuri maintained this view prior to the European conquest. I then suggest that its existence and persistence are directly linked to the manner in which the Rarámuri establish and maintain social relations and only incidentally to the psychological processes of any individuals.

THE RARÁMURI

The people who call themselves Rarámuri have been known to outsiders since the seventeenth century as the Tarahumara.[5] Most famous for their endurance as long-distance runners and their proximity to the spectacular Barranca del Cobre, the Rarámuri, who number over 50,000, live in small hamlets scattered across 20,000 square miles of rugged sierra and canyon country in southwestern Chihuahua and adjacent Sinaloa and Durango, Mexico, approximately 275 miles south-southwest of El Paso, Texas. Most settlements are found along stream drainages where they cultivate crops of maize, beans, and squash, collect wild plant and animal foods, and herd goats, sheep, and cattle. They secure cash and manufactured goods by working for their Mexican neighbors and by selling agricultural products and crafts to them.

They reckon descent bilaterally, but kinship plays only a minimal role in the organization of social action beyond the limits of the immediate family and household. Most inter-household interaction takes place during drinking parties, held on average several times a week all year round. The vast majority of these parties are sponsored by individual households, typically to attract their neighbors' assistance in completing some work project or performing a ritual. Rarámuri social and economic life revolves around these parties. In fact, Kennedy (1963) proposes that the complex set of linkages among households that emerges from the participation of their members in these drinking parties constitutes the fundamental form of Rarámuri social organization above the household level. He labels this set the 'tesguino network,' *tesgüino* being the Spanish name for their maize beer.

The diffuse tesguino network contrasts sharply with the centralized pueblo organization imposed during the seventeenth and eighteenth centuries by the Spanish colonial administration, in particular Jesuit missionaries. Attempts to settle the Rarámuri in compact mission towns for the most part failed, but the newly erected churches became the foci of much of their political and religious life. In each pueblo a hierarchical political organization was established together with a set of religious offices, all filled by Rarámuri, to direct the activities of the people affiliated with the pueblo (Dunne 1948; Pennington 1963; Sheridan and Naylor 1979; González 1982). These pueblo political organizations persist today and have substantial influence on community life. There is, however, no effective political organization that unites all the various Rarámuri pueblos.

Although the Jesuits had an enormous impact on many areas of Rarámuri life, their main efforts were directed toward converting them to Christianity. Today, Christian ritual and belief pervade Rarámuri religion, but the people are not orthodox Catholics. Their Catholicism, like their way of life in general, is a synthesis of Indian and European elements (Merrill 1983a). This blend of indigenous and introduced is perhaps no better exemplified than in their view that the universe is composed of seven levels, the Earth being the fourth, or middle, level. The three levels above the earth belong to God, who is identified with the Sun, and to God's wife, associated with the Moon and the Virgin Mary. The three levels below the Earth are the domain of the devil, said to be God's elder brother and bitter enemy. This contemporary figure of the devil possibly combines European Christian notions of Satan and pre-contact ideas about a wolf described by a seventeenth-century Jesuit as the 'lord of the underworld' (Ratkay 1683:40–1).

The Rarámuri employ the opposition between God and the devil to structure their thinking about many other topics, especially ethnicity. They consider themselves and other Native Americans to be God's children, while non-Indians, whom they call *chabóchi*, meaning 'whiskered ones,' are the devil's children. Rarámuri and Chabóchi are protected by God and the devil respectively, and join their parents at death in heaven or in the underworld, as the case might be.

Ranchers and miners began settling in southwestern Chihuahua during the sixteenth century, but not until the twentieth century has their population, now numbering around 200,000, exceeded that of the Rarámuri. These Chabóchi people control the area's government and most of the commerce, including the exploitation of its natural resources, chiefly timber and precious metals (Pennington 1963, 1983; Champion 1962; Lartigue 1983). Rarámuri and Chabóchi often live near one another and interact with some frequency, particularly in the economic and political spheres. However, while each group has adopted some of the ways of the other, relations between them are not always amicable. The settlers have often displaced the indigenous people from their land, leading in some instances to violent confrontations. Each group also maintains a negative stereotype of the other. The Chabóchi view the Rarámuri as uncivilized, dirty, and superstitious, and they in turn characterize the Chabóchi as violent, dishonest, and shameless. Few deep friendships develop between Rarámuri and Chabóchi individuals, and intermarriage is discouraged by both groups.

DREAMING IN THOUGHT AND LIFE

For the Rarámuri, dreams are events, not things; they have no noun that can be glossed as 'a dream,' only the verb *rimúma*, 'to dream.' Dreams are understood as the activities of a person's principal soul while the person sleeps. Each individual is composed of one body and many souls, which are identified with the breath. The souls, which range in size from large to small, are distributed throughout the body, with at least one soul located at each part of the body that can move. The smallest souls are found in the joints of the fingers and toes, the largest in the chest and head.

The Rarámuri rely on their concept of the soul to explain all deviations from a waking, sober, sane, and healthy state (Merrill 1978, 1981). People sleep when their souls sleep and wake up when the souls as a group awaken. If while they sleep their largest souls wake up, they dream.[6] If the souls should be harmed by evil beings, either while inside or away from the body, the dreamers will be seriously ill upon awaking. When people drink, their largest souls leave because they dislike the smell of the beer inside the body. They remain near the drinkers to care for them from outside, but the smaller souls assume the major responsibility for watching over the body, just as children care for their homes when their parents attend drinking parties. Because these souls are small, like children, people act like children when they are drunk, joking, laughing, crying, playing, and fighting. When all the souls abandon the body, people die and their bodies decompose into clay.

At first glance, it seems that the Rarámuri associate the separation of people's souls from their bodies primarily with undesirable things, such as interpersonal violence, serious illness, and death. One might suggest, in fact, that they maintain a negative stereotype of dreams precisely because dreams entail the departure of the principal soul from the body. Such a conclusion, however, is difficult to sustain. Souls are perhaps a bit more vulnerable when they are outside the body, but evil beings like sorcerers can attack them regardless of where they are. Besides, such attacks are best defended by a soul that is awake, in other words, when the person is dreaming. All my evidence indicates that the Rarámuri do not consider the act of dreaming itself to be threatening, and they do nothing to prevent dreams.[7] Dreaming is their principal avenue of communication with beings like God and the devil, who have a substantial impact on their lives. Despite the dangers that potentially await a dreamer's soul, dreams are crucial to the preservation of the individual's and community's well-being.

The reality of dreams

For the Rarámuri, dreams are real events. On numerous occasions, people would describe to me quite incredible personal experiences but fail to mention that the events had taken place in dreams until I asked. This does not mean that they do not distinguish between their waking and dreaming lives but that they attribute comparable reality to both. The main difference between dreaming and waking events is that during dreaming people's souls operate independently of their bodies, while in waking life they act in conjunction with them. The Rarámuri do not consider dreams to be periods of impaired perception or loss of control. For them, dreaming begins when the large soul 'wakes up' (*busuréma*). The verb *busuréma* literally means 'to open the eyes,' but also, more figuratively, 'to sober up,' 'to regain health or consciousness,' 'to begin thinking well,' 'to be alert,' and 'to learn.' Dreams occur when the soul primarily responsible for a person's thoughts and actions is awake and alert.

Rarámuri thinking about the reality of dreams ties in with their more basic ideas about the ultimate nature of the universe. They distinguish conceptually and lexically among various sorts of things they encounter in the world: water, dirt, sounds, rocks, souls, wood, words, wind, flesh, bone, and so on. But they do not assume that the perceived or conceived diversity of the world can be reduced to a more fundamental level, to an underlying unity or dichotomy such as material and spiritual. They also do not postulate the existence of separate, qualitatively different, and more or less mutually exclusive realms of the universe, like natural versus supernatural, among which communication and interaction are restricted or impossible. For them, the world is decidedly pluralistic but there is only one, and both waking experience and dreams take place within it.

The reality they ascribe to dreams extends to waking experiences that from a certain Western perspective might be classified as hallucinations or, as Price-Williams (this volume) proposes, 'waking dreams.' Examples that I recorded include one in which a Rarámuri woman named Rosaria[8] spotted a Catholic priest and nun playing in the sand near a hot spring downstream from her home. She ran to get her husband and children but when they returned the priest and nun had disappeared, leaving no trace. The family concluded that they were water people who had slipped back beneath the surface of the adjacent stream. In another example, around dusk one evening, Rafael was returning from work at the sawmill. As he passed the cemetery, Ventura, who had died only a few weeks before, started chasing him up the road. Rafael escaped by running at top speed but almost dropped the flour and other provisions he was carrying home. Although such experiences are considered unusual and remarkable, no one would question either the reality of the experience or the sanity of the people who have them. The Rarámuri would not say that the person dreams (*rimúma*) them, since dreams take place only during sleep. They also would not characterize them as hallucinations, visions, or fantasies; I encounted no terms for these notions among the Rarámuri of the Basíhuare area.[9]

D'Andrade (1961:315–16) proposes that in societies where dream experiences are considered to be 'real,' dreams and the events of waking life tend to be more alike than in societies where dreams are viewed as fantasy. While this observation possibly holds for Rarámuri dreams as a whole, these dreams often differ in some particulars quite radically from occurrences in waking life. A review of Rarámuri dream accounts suggests that these differences are of three types: (1) the actors in dreams are capable of doing things, such as flying, that people cannot do while awake; (2) people often encounter strangers or wild animals in their dreams but seldom in their waking lives; and (3) the level of violence reported for dreams far exceeds that of waking life, where the ethic of inter-personal harmony is seldom violated outside the context of drinking parties.

The Rarámuri interpret these discrepancies as evidence not of the unreality of dreams but of the limitations of waking life. The abilities of souls, they say, are far superior when they are unencumbered by the bodies in which they live. They can travel very fast and even fly; the small whirlwinds that speed across the countryside are said to be souls in transit. Souls are intrinsically alive and thus capable of visiting places, like the underwater settlements of the water people, unavailable to waking people. Many of the beings who appear in dreams but rarely in daily life live in regions of the world too distant or marginal to be reached except by souls. In addition, most of these beings are active only or primarily at night when most dreams take place. Since they tend to be the devil's allies, they often attack the Rarámuri, so dreams are much more violent than waking life.

Dreams in Rarámuri life

Bennett and Zingg, who conducted research among the Rarámuri in 1930 and 1931, summarized the place of dreams in their lives in the following way:

> As already mentioned, the soul and its escapades constitute dreams. When one dreams of the dead, it may mean that the soul is helping the dead with their planting. If one dreams of sowing, the soul is sowing on that day of the moon. The soul may fall in love with women and have relations with them in dreams.
>
> If a man dreams that his wife has relations with other men, he may wake up very angry and beat her. She may admit her fault. If a man is on a trip and his wife has relations with another, he may dream of it. His animals get sick, and he has bad luck. He may get sick, too. Upon his return, he will reprimand her, although, if she denies her guilt, he probably will not beat her.
>
> A man may dream that his granary is being robbed, and the next day move his valuables to another place. Dreams are not sufficient evidence for damage suits or punishments, however.
>
> If one listens carefully to his dreams, he can learn many things. The shamans are especially instructed to respect and heed the things that dreams tell them. Dreams may predict smallpox (symbolized by a man covered with sores) or drought. The souls of the dead may inform the man when to dance to avoid disasters. (Bennett and Zingg 1935:324)

Fifty years later, I encountered many of these same ideas and attitudes.

Two fundamental features in the Rarámuri's approach to dreams have persisted: (1) the tendency not to initiate action on the basis of dreams alone, and (2) a near-exclusive concern with the manifest content of dreams, which they interpret literally. In my experience, a Rarámuri man would not beat his wife for being unfaithful if the only evidence of her infidelity appeared in a dream, and I doubt that he would move his valuables on the basis of a dream if more than a few, easily transported items were involved. In both cases, however, he would be more attentive and cautious, looking for additional indications of his wife's adultery and checking his granary for signs of suspicious activity and to ensure that the lock was secure.

Their reticence to act upon dream experiences, despite considering them to be real, can be attributed in part to the fact that they distinguish between a person and his or her souls. An individual may dream that his wife commits adultery, but the transgressor he observes is not his spouse but her principal soul. On the other hand, since this soul directs her waking behavior, its dream activities are worthy of attention, for they may reveal propensities that will find expression in waking life. An individual also may hesitate to act if a dream bears no apparent connection to his present circumstances or if he lacks the resources to undertake the indicated action, such as sponsoring a major ceremony.

The Rarámuri value dreaming primarily for the insights provided into the activities and inclinations of other beings in the universe, all of whom potentially have an impact on their welfare. Dreaming reveals, for example, what God expects an individual or the community to do if a neighbor is practicing sorcery, or if dead relatives are hungry or in need of clothing or tools. This information enables them to fine-tune their behavior with respect to these entities so as to act in the most advantageous fashion.

Not surprisingly, dreams are a subject of considerable interest to the Rarámuri, often being the first topic of conversation within a household as well as among the members of different households during morning visits. In fact, because they tend to sleep for a few hours, awaken, and then sleep again, they frequently discuss dreams during the course of the night. The role of dream interpreter is not institutionalized within the society, but children are encouraged from an early age to remember their dreams and to recount them to older members of their households, who aid in interpreting them. Such discussions, combined with those among members of different households, are an important means of transmitting and standardizing ideology in the absence of formal institutions, such as schools, for doing so.

By comparing what one is taught with what one dreams, an individual develops an interpretive framework that both influences the contents of dreams (at least what one remembers of them) and is influenced and confirmed by them. One result is vivid cosmological images built up over many sessions of informal dream interpretation, such as the following example:

Doctor: Many people live below the stream over there, near the bridge. There are many of them, just like here, just like in Creel [the closest Mexican town]. They are Chabóchi people. The houses are made of boards very precisely cut like planks from a sawmill. There also is a fine store and a large and beautiful church. This is over near Lirio's house, where the fiesta was just held. The water in the little creek is evil there. This is below the water but actually there is no water there. It is dry land there. I have seen it well.

Anthropologist: While you were dreaming?

Doctor: Yes, while dreaming. I passed right through the water. In my dreams I go there to retrieve a soul, a small child perhaps. A water serpent (*walúluwi*) captures the soul and takes it there, putting it inside a large house. The soul becomes the peon of the water serpent, who sends it out to herd his goats. There are large numbers of goats and cattle there, very beautiful spotted cattle. I have seen all this in my dreams. There is a bell in the church which they ring. A priest comes out; he is fat and healthy. The church is quite beautiful, just like the ones above. A saint stands inside. This is near where Salomena lives, not far at all from here. There are some Rarámuri down there, too, but they do not enter the church because they are afraid. It is evil inside. If you go inside you will die. This church belongs to the devil, not God. It is totally different from the churches here.

I have heard equally elaborate descriptions of inaccessible regions of the universe from people who are not doctors, but the ability to travel to such places at will and to retrieve lost souls from them distinguishes doctors from ordinary people. Pastron (1977:102ff) reports that the Rarámuri of the Samachique area consider the abilities to dream well and to cure to derive from a power inherent in some individuals from birth. In nearby Basíhuare, where I lived, the Rarámuri say that God bestows these abilities upon people, usually males but sometimes females, in a specific type of dream, what Lincoln (1935) might have called a 'culture pattern dream.' In this dream, God offers the individual three (or four if the dreamer is female) light-colored pieces of paper. If one takes the paper, then God provides the knowledge to cure and will assist in future curing endeavors. Sometimes the devil stands beside God in such dreams, holding three (or four) dark-colored papers. The person then can choose to become a doctor, a sorcerer, both, or neither, according to whether he or she accepts a set of papers and the color of the papers selected. The role of doctor is the only position in the society that requires legitimization through a dream.

Every night, the souls of doctors join God and his assistants in watching over the other members of the community, preventing the devil and his cohorts from hurting them. If a person should fall ill, the doctor discusses the symptoms with him and inquires about recent events, including dreams, to determine what might be responsible. If soul loss is indicated, the doctor concentrates his attention on locating the soul in his dreams on that or subsequent nights. The task is considered potentially quite arduous, requiring lengthy journeys through little-known and often dangerous territory; as one man put it, it is like searching for a thief whose location is unknown.[10]

While all doctors must be accomplished dreamers, not all good dreamers are doctors. In 1981 in the community where I lived, ten individuals out of a total adult population of sixty were noted for their dreaming ability, of whom seven practiced as doctors. The remaining three people were recognized as good dreamers primarily because they could predict future events on the basis of information they acquired in their dreams.

The Rarámuri publicly acknowledge the value of this ability to society during their Palm Sunday and Holy Week ceremonies (Merrill 1983a, Kennedy and López 1981). At several points in the proceedings, pueblo officials line up outside the church and members of the community assemble facing them. The officials then call before them five or so men known to be good dreamers and ask each in turn what he has learnt in his dreams that bears upon the events of the coming weeks and months. The dreamers respond with brief statements describing their dream experiences. They speak rapidly in a style rich in metaphor and allusion similar to that of formal speeches, but softly, with the result that only the officials and the other dreamers actually hear their words. An example from Palm Sunday 1978:

> God told me, 'The devil offered me beer to drink but I did not want any so he hit me on the nose. Blood flowed from my nose so I drank with him and now I still am a little drunk.' God is lying down telling me this. He says 'Tell all the good people who gather at the church to have strength. I will recover slowly, little by

little. I will think well when I drink again. Tell the Rarámuri to have strength and fortitude. Tell this to my children. Tell all the good people who gather here to have strength.' This is the way it is. I have no more to say.

When all the dreamers have spoken, one of the officials delivers a speech to the crowd, based in part upon what the dreamers tell him. These reports and suggested courses of action conform to what the Rarámuri expect at Easter time, namely, that they must protect God in his weakened state by performing their Holy Week ceremonies, or the devil will destroy God and the universe.

Dreams are felt to anticipate but not infallibly predict the future. This position is in keeping with the Rarámuri view that the future is not predetermined and also that souls can travel in space but not through time. There are three basic ways in which dreams can reveal something about the future. First, God may simply tell dreamers what he plans to do, or he may 'cause them to encounter' (*riwiríma*) an event comparable to the one that will occur in the future, such as a rainstorm. Second, a dream event may be linked to a future waking event in some causal or anticipatory way: dreaming of people absent from the community means that their return is imminent because their souls are near enough to home to be encountered by the principal soul of the dreamer. Third, dreaming and waking events may be related in a categorical fashion. For example, when people dream of an unknown old woman, they expect hail soon because such a woman, whom they call Grandmother (*u'sú*), forms hailstones with her frigid hands and sends them to destroy the crops (see Burgess 1985:99, 169). In this case, the old woman metonymically represents the hail storm, but the Rarámuri rarely propose such connections in understanding their dreams. They favor as literal an interpretation as possible rather than the more symbolic or iconic approaches adopted in many other societies (see Kracke 1979a:130–1).

Because dreams often twist the reality of waking life, they do not invariably lend themselves to literal interpretation. The Rarámuri acknowledge that some dream events are inexplicable and that what is seen in dreams may be deceiving, but they consider such challenges to the literal interpretation of dreams as only confirming their belief that certain aspects of their world are beyond understanding. Such minor inconsistencies in their theory of dreams reflect the fact that it is more than just a set of ideas and logical relations: it is a framework which individuals manipulate to fit their unique circumstances and desires in order to understand their experiences and determine their actions in the world.

THE RARÁMURI STEREOTYPE OF DREAMS

Despite the positive values they attach to dreaming, the Rarámuri maintain the negative stereotype that dreams typically involve threats. Coyotes and strangers, often identified as the devil's soldiers, are the figures they mention most frequently as attacking them in dreams. The following examples, from a single individual, are typical of the threats the Rarámuri expect in dreams. A coyote chased the dreamer at a settlement called Wisaróchi, about fifteen kilometers from his home. He escaped by fleeing inside his father's brother's house. When he awoke the following morning he ached all over and decided that he had been bewitched because a sorcerer probably owned the coyote. In a second dream, a naked Rarámuri man, who was a complete stranger, told the dreamer to bathe in the deep pool below the waterfall at Basáchi, a spot identified as the home of a water serpent. Realizing that the stranger was a demon who wanted to force him below the water, the dreamer climbed a pine tree and flew away. In another almost identical dream the aggressors were four Chabóchi men, all strangers but clothed.

The Rarámuri postulate the existence of many other threatening beings, all of whom can appear in dreams. Perhaps most dangerous of all are sorcerers, who kill and eat the souls of people with whom they are angry, although they can attack complete strangers. They also put objects such as knives, bottles, and stones inside their victims' bodies to cause them pain. Rather than threatening people personally, sorcerers sometimes send one of their animal helpers, such as a coyote or an *oromá*, large birds with long pointed beaks and glowing tails identified with shooting stars. Less dangerous but more devious are illnesses (*nawirí*), which afflict people by appearing in human form in their dreams and seducing them into accepting offers of food, drink, and sex.

Serious threats also emanate from beneath the surface of streams. The water people (*bawichí piréame*) include large snakes called *walúluwi*, comparable to the Hopi water serpent, Palulukon, discussed, by Eggan (1966) in connection with Hopi dreams; rainbows (*konomí*), also conceived to have serpent form; and Chabóchi and Rarámuri people whose homes are below the water. Rainbows rise to the sky to prevent the rains from falling and pursue women and domestic animals to have sexual intercourse with them, as well as to steal their souls and those of children. The other water people tend to be threatening only when a person is startled at or near water, at which point they try to capture his or her principal soul and convert it into their peon.

Four other potentially threatening beings are associated with plants that grow in or near the Rarámuri homeland (Bye 1979; Merrill 1981:98–101). *Bakánawi*, probably a bulrush (*Scirpus* sp.), and *híkuri*, various peyote cacti including *Lophophora williamsii*, will protect people from harm and help them, particularly in competitive games, if they give these plants food and observe a few taboos. If they fail to do so, these beings will capture their largest souls and hold them for ransom. *Uchurí*, identified with several kinds of spiny ball cacti, and *rikúhuri* (jimsonweed, *Datura inoxia*) never help the Rarámuri. They will, however, attack them if they should step on or otherwise harm them, arriving when the offenders are sound asleep to guide them to the tops of tall cliffs from which they will fall to their injury or death.

The dead also endanger the living, appearing in dreams to request the food and goods the living are obliged to give them, to visit with friends and loved ones, or simply because the soul of the dreamer happens to encounter them. Often they try to convince the souls of the living to join them in the afterlife or offer them food and maize beer. Except when angry over unfulfilled obligations the dead intend no harm, but dreamers' souls must resist all overtures from them. If they eat or drink with the dead, they will fall ill and if they go with them rather than returning to their own homes (i.e., the dreamers' bodies), they will die.

I recite this list of threatening beings to indicate the diversity of threats that the Rarámuri perceive to confront them. These threatening beings do not appear invariably in Rarámuri dreams; it will be remembered that only half of the dreams in my sample involved threats. But understanding the nature of their stereotype of dreams requires recognition that all these various threatening beings share one important characteristic: they reside beyond the bounds of Rarámuri society. The one exception is members of the community who practice sorcery, but even they are portrayed, using a spatial metaphor, as thinking and working 'apart' (*waná* or *chakéna*) from their good neighbors. Except for the dead and possibly *bakánawi*, all these beings are classified as the devil's allies against whom God, aided by his soldiers and Rarámuri doctors, endeavors to protect the Rarámuri. The opposition between God and the devil thus structures Rarámuri thinking about threats confronting them, just as it does so many other domains of their thought. Dreams become the arena within which the conflict between God and the devil is most vividly played out.

To proceed with the analysis, it is necessary to rephrase the Rarámuri stereotype of dreams. This stereotype does not simply propose that dreams involve threats but that these threats emanate from beings who are outside local society and personally unknown. I want to emphasize that this stereotype focusses upon only one dimension of Rarámuri dreams and their ideas about them. Dream reports include a wide range of experiences, many of which are pleasant and others no more than the mundane events of daily life. Moreover, Rarámuri thinking about dreams and their evaluations of them are much more complex than the stereotype suggests. The problem, then, is not why they have a remarkably large number of threatening dreams or why they dislike dreaming, because they do not. The problem is why they stereotype dreams in this fashion.

The solution will not be found by focussing strictly on Rarámuri ideas about dreams and the dream experience but by moving to a more general perspective. All stereotypes, including those of dreams, must be understood within the context of the larger sets of ideas of which they are a part. For example, if Euro-Americans were asked to select the single feature of dreams most striking to them, many would point to the way that dream events deviate so markedly from those of waking life yet seem so real while they are involved in them. This aspect of dreams is especially salient because it directly challenges our materialist world view, which rejects the reality of experiences like dreams. Threats, which seem to be a universal characteristic of dreams, are regarded as unimportant because they are considered imaginary. In a comparable fashion, the Rarámuri emphasize the threatening aspects of dreams – that is, they stereotype dreams as involving threats from outsiders – because this is the feature of dreams most consonant with their general world view.

The image of insiders threatened by outsiders is pervasive in Rarámuri world view. At the level of the local community, relations among the members of the same household are envisioned to be supportive and non-threatening, while those between individuals of different households (particularly if they are not kinsmen) are thought of as potentially hostile. When people believe they have been attacked by a sorcerer, for example, they almost never look within their own households for the culprit, even when a household member is reputed to be a sorcerer. Instead the suspicion is directed outside the household, either toward other members of the local community or toward strangers (see Kennedy 1978:136–9 for some contrary findings).

This image is most elaborately developed at the boundary between local society and the remainder of the world. The majority of threatening beings live in distant settlements or just beyond the margins of the human domain, under the water, in the mountains and forest, or below the ground. On an even broader scale, the earth as a whole is conceived to be an island surrounded by apparently limitless oceans that are restrained by dikes. Animals that live in these waters constantly attempt to breach the dikes and flood the world, but they are driven away by the diminutive but fierce 'people of the edge' (*suwé piréame*).

To suggest that this image of outsiders threatening insiders pervades Rarámuri world view because it reflects in a more or less straightforward fashion their actual historical experience is not very convincing. Kearney (1976:187) adopts this approach when he proposes that the Spanish conquest engendered among the members of many New World societies what he calls a 'paranoid world view.' I would not deny that during the past four hundred years Europeans and their descendants have deprived the Rarámuri of their land, their crops, their freedom, and their lives. In the nineteenth century, Apaches also raided in their country, plundering and killing. Today the Rarámuri are surrounded and outnumbered by non-Indians who control the region's politics and economy, but have little respect for them. Through the centuries they have both fought back and withdrawn farther into the mountains, but neither strategy has proven very successful (Champion 1962; González 1982; Lartigue 1983). The adverse impact of these outsiders is evident in much of their thinking, including certain of their ideas about the dreams. Chabóchi people, for example, are among the assailants in dreams, and the descriptions of the settlements of the water people visited in dreams are based on experiences in Mexican towns. The fact that the water people convert captured souls into their peons and demand ransoms for their return also may reflect forced labor situations of the past.

However, although the impact of Europeans upon them has been substantial and pervasive, there is sufficient evidence to suggest that the image of insiders threatened by outsiders predates European contact. First of all, if this view emerged principally as a reaction to European conquest, the threatening beings should be primarily from the conquering society. Instead Rarámuri people and wild animals, particularly coyotes, figure prominently as aggressors. The distinguishing feature of the humans who threaten the Rarámuri is their status as strangers, not their ethnic affiliation. Secondly, a seventeenth-century document attests to the antiquity of this image. In 1683 the Croatian Jesuit Johannes María Ratkay described the Rarámuri's 'religion of former times,' by listing a series of 'gods' and 'demons' (Ratkay 1683:40–1; González 1982:111–12, 182–9). Of the thirteen beings he mentioned, three were characterized as being favorably inclined toward the Rarámuri, and the inclinations of three others were not indicated. The remaining seven clearly threatened people by preventing sleep, causing gastro-intestinal disorders, or killing children and adults. The domains of three of these threatening beings were revealed and all fall outside the human realm: the Tetsani and their wives, called Uribi, who lived in the forests and mountains and killed people, and Teregori, 'said to be the lord of the underworld; they believed that he was a wolf who killed men' (Ratkay 1683:41).

Although admittedly circumstantial, this evidence does imply that Europeans, rather than being responsible for the emergence of the image of insiders endangered by outsiders, were simply integrated into it as the threatening outsiders that they were. Assuming that this image predates European contact, its persistence over the centuries is not surprising. The Rarámuri's overwhelmingly negative experience with Europeans certainly has confirmed its accuracy. Moreover, as Bateson (1968) and many others have noted, such views of the world tend to be self-perpetuating. In the case of dreams, by subscribing to the view that insiders are threatened by outsiders the Rarámuri are inclined to take particular notice of those dreams in which unknown beings attack them, thereby reinforcing the general image.

Historical experience and self-perpetuation help explain why an idea persists, but do not necessarily reveal anything about how it was established in the first place. The specific circumstances within which their image of insiders threatened by outsiders first appeared cannot, of course, be reconstructed. But certain features of Rarámuri social relations – which, unlike many other areas of their culture, seem to have changed very little since European contact – can be suggested as having played a role in the emergence and persistence of this image.

Rarámuri society is better described as obligation-based than as kin-based. Kinship, while important in their thinking about social relations, plays a significant role in structuring social interaction only at the household level. Each household is composed of members of at least one nuclear family and many include two (rarely more) related nuclear families, usually parents and their married children or less frequently siblings with their respective spouses and offspring. Positive relations among household members are based on bonds of immediate kinship and a history of helping, caring for, and sharing with one another.

To a large degree, relations within households correspond to Sahlins's (1972) model of generalized reciprocity in that people do not expect or demand compensation for goods given or shared and assistance rendered, the transactions being 'putatively altruistic.' In contrast, relations among individuals of different households are established and maintained primarily through balanced reciprocity, in which a direct, equal, and often immediate return is expected for goods or services. The Rarámuri feel that a person should help one's neighbors when asked, even when doing so requires postponing one's own work. At the same time, individuals expect compensation for labor or favors they perform for the members of other households, even those of close kinsmen. People will not solicit the assistance of individuals outside their households if they are not in a position to reciprocate with food or alcoholic beverages. Conversely, people seldom offer their assistance until asked because to do so would require reciprocation which the beneficiary might be unprepared to make.

The principal contexts within which the members of different households express their obligations to one another are drinking parties. Most of these parties involve the completion of some work project or ritual for the benefit of the sponsoring household, the members of which express their appreciation to their guests by providing them with food and intoxicating drinks, usually maize beer. Messages about the obligations between the hosts and guests are pervasive. For example, people outside the host household who helped prepare the beer are called to drink first, and individuals to whom the hosts are especially indebted – perhaps a doctor who cured the family or the owner of a yoke of oxen loaned for plowing the household's fields – are given jars of the beer to distribute to the others.

These parties take place all year round, and a person begins participating in them as an adolescent. Over years of helping and being helped, the members of a community develop deep feelings of obligation to one another, reinforced by the practice of offering food to all visitors to one's home. The Rarámuri's devotion to their drinking parties derives as much from their sense of obligation to help their neighbors as from their desire to get drunk and socialize with them.

In such a situation, the failure to fulfill one's obligations is an extremely serious transgression because it is upon these relations of obligation that society and an individual's ties to it are based. Unfulfilled obligations of one form or another are cited more often than any other factor as instigating interpersonal violence. Violent confrontations almost invariably take place during or after drinking parties, but seldom involve blood kinsmen of the same household. The relationship between spouses, in contrast, is the most volatile in the society because it is so close yet is felt to rest almost entirely upon the performance of complementary tasks for one another and the household in general, principally cooking and child care for women, farming and providing firewood for men.

The connection the Rarámuri make between positive interpersonal relations and fulfilling obligations is indicated in the way they talk about these relations. They refer to the individuals with whom they exchange drinking invitations and generally enjoy good relations as people who 'help' (*kuwírama*) them, while often characterizing those who do not fall into this category with the verb 'to oppose' (*saérama*). For the Rarámuri, who often structure their thinking dualistically, a person with whom one does not share obligations of mutual assistance is a potential enemy.

The recognized procedure for transforming actual or potential enemies into friends is offering them food or inviting them to drinking parties, that is, establishing relations of obligation with them. They adopt this strategy when dealing with visitors from other settlements, whom they regard almost without exception as potential sorcerers. They also resort to offerings of food, alcoholic beverages, and other items to encourage positive relations with all the beings who live outside society and potentially threaten them, except for wild animals.

The nature and frequency of these offerings vary according to the kind of relation the Rarámuri envision to exist between themselves and each of these beings. They regularly offer God large quantities of food and beer to petition his continued benevolence because their survival depends upon it. If they fail to do so, God is likely to send sickness, withhold the rain upon which their crops depend, and cease protecting them from the devil. Almost as frequently they give the devil and personified illness (*nawirí*) smaller portions to encourage them to refrain from harming the members of the community. They also present food or goods to placate angry dead and offended plant-people and to ransom souls captured by the water people.

Yet, despite the possibility of establishing relations of obligation with these beings, such relations must always be partial because these beings can never fully participate in Rarámuri society. Positive relations with them must remain tentative, and they must be viewed as potential threats. Phrased from a Rarámuri perspective, the good intentions of people outside one's household can be insured only by establishing and maintaining relations of obligation with them. When this is impossible, as it is to a large degree with the beings outside their society, the entities in question represent potential enemies.

CONCLUSIONS

Before discussing the more general implications of this Rarámuri material, I would like to recapitulate my argument. The Rarámuri stereotype of dreams is that dreams involve threats, specifically threats from beings outside society. I proposed that they maintain this image not because their dreams are inordinately violent but because the threats that do occur during dreams resonate more than any other feature of their dreams with their world view. The stereotype of dreams, then, is best construed as emerging not from the Rarámuri's reflections on specific dream experiences but from their consideration of dreaming within the context of their more general ideas about the universe.

This stereotype of dreams represents one expression of the image, pervasive in Rarámuri world view, of insiders threatened by outsiders. I argued that this image emerges from certain features of Rarámuri society and social process. The principal means by which the Rarámuri create and maintain positive relations with one another is by establishing obligations through balanced reciprocity. The failure or inability to produce such obligations results in a situation of potential confrontation. Beings who are believed to reside beyond the bounds of society can never fully participate in such relations, so they are viewed as threatening those inside. Many of the figures who appear in dreams fall into the category of outsiders because they are unknown. Their presence, even when they do not actually threaten the dreamer, tends to reinforce the stereotype.

Ideas like these about the nature and significance of dreaming mediate between the personal dream experiences of the members of a society and public ideology. On the one hand, these ideas have an impact on how people remember and report dreams; on the other hand, as socially constituted commentary on dreams, they are influenced by processes of social interaction and interpersonal negotiation of meaning. Not all of these ideas, however, will be equally connected to both the private-psychological and public-social dimensions. The Rarámuri stereotype that dreams involve threats from beings outside society appears to relate primarily to social process and to exert little influence on the content of their dreams. Otherwise, they should report a substantially higher percentage of threatening dreams than people who maintain a more positive view of dreaming, particularly since the stereotype presumably affects how they remember their dreams.

Despite the fact that there is considerable individual variation in Rarámuri world view (Merrill 1981), all the Rarámuri I questioned maintained the image of insiders threatened by outsiders. Yet very few seemed to feel threatened in any personal or immediate way; in most cases these were individuals who were in fact disliked and somewhat marginal to the larger community. To argue that such images are widely held within a society only because they directly express some shared psychological trait, such as paranoia, is fallacious. The image is embedded in the society's ideology but the degree to which it is internalized and integrated into the emotional life of the individual varies from person to person. Phrased differently, the Rarámuri may rely on the opposition between insiders and outsiders to create an image of their society and universe and to determine proper courses of action within them, but few consider themselves in serious or proximate jeopardy. Thus, the statement 'I didn't dream last night; I slept peacefully' is not an expression of relief, but a cliché.

The dream stereotype and the image of insiders threatened by outsiders are two of a fairly limited set of ideas that constitute a simplified, in fact schematic, view of the world. These ideas are what the Rarámuri consider to be typical about the world and as such are separate from both the ideal and what might be called the empirical. The stereotype of dreams is that dreams typically involve threats, whereas dreams ideally should include no threats and empirically some dreams do while others do not. Saying that dreams typically involve threats is not a statement about the actual frequency of threatening dreams but a judgment about the fundamental nature of the world within which dreams take place, that it is characterized by a series of confrontational relations between insiders and outsiders. The typical, while appearing to be more objective, is no less value-bound than the ideal.

Most of the Rarámuri's ideas about the world presented in public – in speeches delivered by community leaders, in diagnoses of illnesses announced during curing ceremonies, and in casual group conversations during drinking parties – are conveyed at the level of the typical. Consequently, the typical, which represents a very restricted portion of the complex and detailed system of ideas that makes up the world view of each individual, is widely shared.

The schematic view of the world, of which the dream stereotype is a part, provides the fundamental understandings in terms of which the Rarámuri initiate and justify much of their social action. Basically it proposes that they are confronted by a benevolently inclined but easily angered God and a universe full of threatening beings, whose behavior depends upon human actions with respect to them. This view encourages the Rarámuri to rely upon their doctors for protection against these beings and upon one another for assistance in staging the rituals crucial to their continued well-being. Such reliance almost inevitably entails establishing relations of obligation with individuals outside one's household; these are the relations upon which their society is founded. I have suggested that because their society is obligation-based, the Rarámuri's inability to establish relations of obligation with beings outside society inclines them to think of these beings as potentially threatening. The existence of threats encourages relations of obligation while the absence of these relations implies threats. Thus, the system is circular and self-reinforcing.

The stereotype of dreams emerges from social process and its main implications are for that social process. I am not suggesting, however, that Rarámuri thought as a whole is determined, or even influenced, by the nature of their social relations. Rather, I am proposing that they have applied the same logic that orders their relations with one another – the logic of reciprocity – to structure another, related but circumscribed domain, that of their relations with beings outside their society. Presumably the Rarámuri would have postulated the existence of these beings regardless of the nature of their society, but they would not necessarily have given the same tone to their relations with these beings. The logic of reciprocity suggests why they should regard all of these beings as potentially threatening. Obligations established through reciprocity insure friendly relations just as the failure to fulfill obligations guarantees hostility. The inability to establish such obligations, however, renders a relationship ambiguous at best and therefore possibly hostile (see Gouldner 1960; Schieffelin 1980).

The relations they envision between themselves and these beings are far from uniform, ranging from the benevolence of God sustained through balanced reciprocity, through the ambivalence of the dead, plant, and water people addressed on an ad hoc basis, to the nearly implacable hostility of the devil and his allies only partially deflected by offerings. The logic of reciprocity by itself cannot account for the specific differences in these relationships. On the other hand, the diversity of these relations encompasses most of the forms that relations of reciprocity can assume. It is as if the Rarámuri have taken the theory of reciprocity and mapped it out for all to see.

Reciprocity in one form or another is a feature of social relations in all human societies. Yet not all societies maintain the stereotype that dreams typically involve threats from beings outside society. Such a view would not be expected in societies that are not based on relations of obligation established and sustained through reciprocity or where dreams are regarded as fantasy or interpreted figuratively. The fact that Rarámuri assumptions about the reality of dreams are themselves made reasonable by a whole set of other ideas to which they subscribe, such as their complex concept of soul, lessens the likelihood that this same image of dreams will be found anywhere else. Nonetheless, remarkably similar attitudes toward dreams are reported from societies very distant and, superficially at least, very different from the Rarámuri, for example, the Fulagan Fijians (Herr 1981) and the Ixil Maya (Colby and Colby 1981:50). Such instances of ideological convergence offer excellent opportunities for determining more precisely how relatively independent social, psychological, and ideological processes impinge upon one another.

NOTES

1. I am grateful to the University of Michigan, the National Institute of Mental Health, and the Smithsonian Institution for financial support of my research among the Rarámuri. I also appreciate the helpful comments on this chapter provided by Cecilia Troop, Arturo Salinas, Don Burgess, John Kennedy, Martha Graham, Bob Hard, Ivan Karp, and the participants in the School of American Research Advanced Seminar.
2. Bye (1979) reports that some Rarámuri ingest hallucinogenic plants to such ends, but I did not encounter this practice in the area where I lived and worked.
3. In Rarámuri this phrase is *tási namúti rimúri nihé. wéni kaníre kochíre*. The phonemes of Rarámuri are: (voiceless stops and affricate) p, t, ch, k, '; (voiced stops) b, g; (voiceless fricatives) s, h; (nasals) m, n; (liquids) r (flap), l; (semi-vowels) w, y; (vowels) i, e, a, o, u; (stress) v́ (Pennington 1983:276).
4. I know practically nothing about the dreams of women because it is improper in Rarámuri society for unrelated men and women to talk at length.
5. Major ethnographic treatments of the Rarámuri include Lumholtz (1902), Bennett and Zingg (1935), and Kennedy (1970, 1978). Shorter overviews are those of Fried (1969), González (1982), Pennington (1983), and Merrill (1983b). Kennedy (1978) details the differences between the majority of Rarámuri and the members of those few 'gentile' communities who have rejected any affiliation with the Catholic church. Rarámuri settlements in Durango, Sinaloa, and Sonora are reported by Passin (1943:361), in Durango and Sinaloa by Pennington (1963:Map 2), and in Sinaloa by Boudreau (personal communication). Brouzés (personal communication) also notes the seasonal migration of Rarámuri agricultural laborers into Sinaloa and Durango.
6. Some people claim that the souls never sleep, and there are other individual variations in Rarámuri explanations of sleeping and dreaming (Merrill 1981). Here I report only what appears to be the most widely shared views.
7. Brambila's (1980:476) suggested but mistaken translation of *rimugápuma* as 'to conjure away, to cut away dreams of evil portent' (*conjurar, cortar los sueños de mal agüero*) is based on a confusion between *rimugá*, the gerund form of the verb *rimúma* 'to dream,' and *rumugá*, a white thread that grows from the crown of a person's head that must be ritually cut or burnt to prevent it from causing illness and attracting lightning and hail (Merrill 1981:241–2; 1983b:302).

8. To protect the privacy of the residents of Basíhuare, I use fictitious names throughout.
9. Burgess (personal communication) informs me that in the western dialect of Rarámuri, the word *sayé* means 'to have a vision or visions' and that *sayéme* means 'one who has a vision or visions.' *Sayé* is used instead of *remú*, 'to dream,' to refer to the visions that doctors have during their sleep as they search for lost souls. He discovered similar usage among central dialect speakers from the Samachique area (which borders Basíhuare on the south), where *sayé* also means 'to sense or feel' as, for example, when a coyote senses the presence of a dog. Brambila (1980:510–11) defines *sayéame* as *listo, perspicaz, que se da cuenta de las cosas* ('alert, acutely perceptive, aware of things').
10. Kennedy (1978:134–6) provides accounts of several dreams from Seledonio Inápuchi, a Rarámuri doctor of moderate accomplishments. For a description of the recovery of a soul from the water people, see Merrill (1981:187–8).

10
The mystic revelation of Rasta Far-Eye:
visionary communication in a prophetic movement

JOHN HOMIAK

Dreaming has always been a key source of religious inspiration in prophetic and millenarian movements. While previous authors have noted the importance of dreaming to charismatic authority, there are no ethnographic accounts which document, describe, and analyze the communicative situations in which self-revealed prophets relate their dreams to others. This is unfortunate given the constitutive role of verbal communication in religious contexts where language not only signifies and communicates but also creates and articulates social reality (Fabian 1974). Furthermore, even though it is recognized that accounts of dream experience may become enshrined in the oral tradition of a movement, the link between the imagery situation of dreams, the social context in which they are verbalized, and the linguistic and rhetorical devices by which they are made socially meaningful remains largely unexplored.

In this chapter I am concerned to illustrate how dream experience is rendered as oral performance and to analyze the role this plays in the reproduction of Rasta ideology. I will present and discuss transcripts of three dialogues which include dream accounts, interpretations, and the resultant social actions undertaken by a leader in the Rastafari movement of Jamaica. These visionary accounts (Rastas use the term 'vision' to refer to both their waking and sleeping dreams) were collected during a one-year period of fieldwork in 1980–1 plus a short visit in 1982.

Although these 'visions' (all of which occurred in night dreams) were tape-recorded as excerpts from dialogues, they were generated by using neither traditional ethnographic techniques of direct elicitation or depth interviewing nor electronic eavesdropping. Rather, they are records of face-to-face communicative interactions in which I was both a present and engaged participant, and all took place within the proper communicative context, known as 'reasoning.' Reasoning is a ritual context accompanied by the sacramental smoking of 'the herb' – Rasta argot for marijuana. For the brethren, the ingestion of this sacred substance induces visionary sight and movement associated with the 'Far Eye' – the inspired capacity which allows the Rastaman to be 'far seeing' when compared with the limited sight of the non-Rasta. Suffice it to say that a learned response to the ingestion of cannabis aids a cognitive dynamic within reasoning that promotes 'active imagination' through which visionary communication is generated (see Price-Williams, this volume). The brethren participate in a form of intersubjective visionary communication that is central to their religious experience and to the continuing creation of a powerful ideology of racial protest. This has enabled them continuously to interpret the historical and sociopolitical processes affecting black people in a colonial situation.

My acceptance and participation in 'reasoning' with various circles of brethren involved me in a profound learning process in which I gradually moved from being largely 'spoken to' to progressively 'speaking with' others. From both Rasta and modern ethnographic perspectives my progressive participation in these intersubjective communicative events is the basis for the objectivity of my account (Fabian 1974; Jules-Rosette 1975). My presentation and discussion of these transcribed verbal interactions is a contribution to dialogical anthropology in which the ethnographer is an active participant in the continuing process of the construction of the data rather than totally replacing field data with his own discourse (D. Tedlock 1979).

THE RASTAFARIAN MOVEMENT OF JAMAICA

The Rastafarian movement is a decentralized, polycephalous, and predominantly black form of social protest that originated in the British

Crown colony of Jamaica in the early 1930s. Viewed historically, it is a politico-religious response to the legacy of widespread plantation slavery and subsequent proletarianization of an inchoate peasantry. This legacy includes racial discrimination and the class-color values embedded in a Creole society, the manipulation of the black masses by an Anglophilic political elite, and the manifestations of capitalist-imperialist domination.

Rastafarian religion is a form of black Zionism,[1] a complex ideational synthesis based on a distinctive fundamentalist approach to the Bible, selected aspects of an Afro-Christian revivalism, and a racial eschatology embodied in the ideology of Ethiopianism. In the Bible, the Rastafari have discovered a series of metaphors through which the struggle between good and evil is portrayed in largely racial terms. Likening the historical struggle of Afro-Jamaicans against European domination to the bondage of God's Chosen People in Babylon, Rastas assert that black people are the true Israelites. They have awaited the return of the Messiah, Jah Rastafari, to fulfill their providential destiny of repatriation to Africa, their ancestral Zion. In Rasta conception, Jah[2] is the godhead who reigns over Zion and is manifest in the person of Emperor Haile Selassie I of Ethiopia. By contrast, the Pope in Rome is the Anti-Christ incarnate who reigns over Babylon, the white-ruled European world and its colonial outposts. This proposition reflects a condemnation of white Christianity as an ideological weapon used by the colonial state to subjugate black people and, more specifically, of the reputed complicity of the Vatican in the Italo-Ethiopian conflict during the mid 1930s (Asante 1979).

Rasta world view treats time as a repeating cycle and assimilates discrete historical personages and nations to categorical biblical identities.[3] Since it was Queen Elizabeth I who originally commissioned British pirates to carry Africans into captivity in the West, both she and her contemporary successor are identified as 'The Great Whore of Babylon,' who will be destroyed in the final judgment. While the British are held primarily accountable for the forced enslavement of Africans, it is understood that they were simply following their forebears – the Romans – and before them the Babylonians, who subjugated and persecuted Israel. The symbolic opposition between 'Zion' and 'Babylon' thus represents a cosmological paradigm which embraces racial, geopolitical, moral, and metaphysical referents.

In addition to this potent biblical imagery, Rasta ideology is based

Figure 10.1 Artistic rendition of Emperor Selassie, eyes charged with spiritual energy, in coronation regalia. The imperial scepter and golden orb identify him as the Creator, the 'Alpha and Omega.' Reproduced from *Blackheart Man* (Island Records), courtesy Neville Garrick

upon the philosophy of Marcus Garvey, the Jamaican-born father of modern Pan-Africanism. Garvey revived the long-standing vision of an African homeland for the scattered black people of the West and established an international movement in the early twentieth century that mounted political opposition to the hegemony of European colonialism. His message of African cultural conservation and 'racial upliftment' was proclaimed under the banner of 'Africa for the Africans at home and abroad' and his preaching appealed to redemptive passages in the Bible mentioning Ethiopia (see Psalm 68:31). In the early 1920s, it was allegedly Garvey who prophesied the coming of a black Redeemer, instructing his followers to 'Look to Africa, where a black king shall be crowned, for the day of deliverance is near' (cf. Hill 1983:25–7). In 1930, the crowning of a young Ethiopian nobleman, Ras Tafari Makonnen,[4] as successor to the Throne of David in Addis Ababa was interpreted by a number of Jamaicans as the fulfillment of the prophecy.

Many of those who entered the movement in this formative period did so by claiming direct visionary inspiration from Garvey or Haile Selassie. This generational cohort and their immediate successors have established themselves as 'elders' – the local charismatic leaders of the movement who are the principal expounders of ideology and architects of its cultural expressions.

REASONING AS VISIONARY COMMUNICATION

Reasoning is the principal form of Rastafarian ritual activity. It is central to both the conceptual tenets of Rasta life and the social organization of the movement. This activity repeatedly brings together members of a non-localized speech community who share a loosely codified system of signs, symbols, and understandings. As the communicative event in which elders typically attempt to formulate truths about various social situations, diverse sources of data can become grist for speculation in reasoning, including historical and contemporary events, biblical prophecy, and dream experience. With regard to the latter, elders may draw upon recent as well as long-past visions to authenticate their tutorial roles for those 'coming up' in the faith.

There is no set liturgical format, agenda, content, or length to a reasoning. Typically reasoning is initiated and accompanied by the sacramental use of 'herbs' smoked communally in a water-pipe known as a 'chalice' which is prepared for smoking, lit, and passed through an assembled group of brethren according to a flexible ritual protocol. A given session may canvass a wide range of issues and the content or propositions generated in any reasoning can be seen as a product of communicative processes which reflect the concerns and relations of those assembled. While reasoning reflects a mutual quest for divine inspiration based on egalitarian principles, in circles of brethren who 'ground' (reason regularly) together it is common for a select few to serve as the principal expositors of ideology and interpreters of events. These communal speech acts are not only the basis for formulating, reshaping, and disseminating movement ideology but are the context in which a Rastaman validates his role, at least provisionally, as a source of inspiration for others.

Performance criteria in reasoning encompass such factors as knowledge and intellectual ability, personal biographical attributes, and the situated use of rhetorical and linguistic resources that are part of a stylized speech code. Central to this code is the pronoun 'I' with its sound symbolism related to 'high,' 'eye,' and the idea of vision. It is also formative in the concept 'I-and-I' or 'I-n-I,' which expresses both Rasta collective identity and the interdwelling between Jah and man, the source of visionary power that lives within the 'Internal' of the Rastaman. As the foundation upon which all spiritual experience and knowledge rests, it is through the 'Internal' or 'Far I/Eye' that brethren remain in constant spiritual contact with Zion despite being physically exiled in the modern Babylon of Jamaica. This paradoxical proposition is mediated through a complex iconography and lexicon that link the word 'I' and other sacred symbols. These include dreadlocks – the knotted rope-like hair style emblematic of Rasta identity which serves as psychic 'antennae' – and herbs, the spiritual food that 'opens up' the Internal to spiritual communication from Zion.

In Rasta speech 'I/Eye' not only connotes a pronounced emphasis on the relationship between visualization in thinking and knowing, but is also assimilated to varied characteristics of the sacred, the domain of Zion. These include references to life, righteousness, height, heat, interiority, purity, spirituality, illumination, timelessness, and ancestral remembrance, all of which are implicitly contrasted with their Babylonian opposites such as death, evil, lowliness, coldness, exteriority, pollution, fleshliness, blindness, ephemerality, and forgetfulness.

In Rasta discourse, these contrasts are continuously reiterated through an appropriate use of metaphor and/or a process of word formation in which the pronomial 'I' is substituted for key syllables in various words. (For example, 'I-nity' [unity], 'I-ditation' [mediation], 'I-bs' [herbs], and 'I-ses' [praises].) It also includes neologisms such as 'dynasity' for race and 'precept' for beard as well as reconstructed words made to bear the precise weight of their phonological representation such as '*down*pression' for oppression and '*over*standing' for understanding. In reasoning, this code is internally generated from the overall philosophical stance associated with the concept of 'I,' and the metaphysical and cosmological implications of this sound/concept give a thick complexity and potency to the metaphors that find frequent expression in Rasta discourse.

Knowledge of this linguistic code is important in appreciating Rasta cognitive dynamics in visionary communication and in understanding the social construction of a mythopoetic reality among the brethren. In introducing the term 'mythopoetic,' I am following a long line of scholars beginning with Frederick Myers, who coined the concept of a 'mythopoetic function' (Price-Williams, this volume), down to Leib (1983:3), who has used it to describe Rasta interpretations of historical processes.

I am, however, concerned to point out that the term 'mythopoetic' as used here does not prejudge the truth value of interpretations evolved in reasoning but simply takes as given that metaphorical processes predominate and that the factual and evaluative processes are entangled in this form of thought. If the 'mythos' is taken as the interpretive framework defined by the opposition between Zion and Babylon, the polarized struggle between these domains is given 'poetic' interpretation through the creative use of metaphor, metonymy, analogy, and other forms of symbolic communication. Following Burke (1966b:145) it is emphasized that poetic meaning cannot be evaluated on a true or false basis but can only be assessed in terms of the scope, range, relevancy, and accuracy which a given metaphorical perspective can advocate. As in other systems of classification, the analogical contrast between Zion and Babylon functions as a true paradigm in which sets of figurative terms are related to one another so that the distinction between figurative field and literalist ground tends to be obliterated or obscured (Crocker 1977:55).

One can view on a continuum the kinds of metaphorical processes inherent in dreams and the use of these same processes within the culturally shaped intrapsychic state induced during the communal smoking of marijuana. And this state is crucial in grasping traditionally incompatible idea associations which lead to new insights or express widely held ideological propositions in fresh and inspirational ways. Another way of describing this state is to say that it promotes a communal process of active imagination by which communicants linguistically map their subjective experiences upon the external world in a meaningful intersubjective way.

RAS MOBUTU'S VISIONS

I first encountered Ras Mobutu after moving into a coastal community east of Kingston, the capital city of Jamaica, which I had chosen because it was the site of two important Rasta 'camps' dominated by a number of leading elders. During the early months of my fieldwork, I became a regular visitor to the camp where Mobutu lived and, despite being a white man, I established congenial relations with several of its leading figures.[5] Mobutu, however, remained distant during this period, cautiously eyeing my activities with other brethren before allowing me to penetrate his confidence. At the time I met him he was seventy-six years old and had established himself as a leading historical figure in the movement. I learnt from one of his cohorts that both he and Mobutu had heard Garvey preach to enthusiastic crowds in Kingston during the early 1930s and that Mobutu was one of thirteen brethren to have been singled out for exemplary work and awarded a gold medal by Emperor Selassie during his state visit to Jamaica.[6] From others I learnt that Mobutu had been involved in nearly every significant Rasta confrontation with Jamaican authorities during the 1950s and 1960s concerning protests for repatriation to Ethiopia.

Late one afternoon as I was leaving the settlement Mobutu appeared in his doorway and hailed me with a customary greeting. When I approached he inquired if I could 'put some herbs on the board,'[7] an indication of his desire to initiate a reasoning. Following some initial probing on his part in order to determine 'how my head stayed,' whether or not I was liberated from Babylonian thoughts, and whether my movements among brethren were sincerely motivated, Mobutu began to explain his 'calling' to me. In so doing he was simultaneously offering a testimony about himself as an instrument of the divine and acknowledging me as a candidate for salvation. He told me that during the mid

1930s he had received a vision in which the emperor appeared to him 'seated on a white horse with a sickle to reap in one hand and a fire to burn in the other hand' (see Post 1970:200). Before I left that day he had emphasized that he was an 'elect' among brethren, a prophet specially chosen by Jah to 'work through vision.'

After this encounter, I began to 'ground' with Mobutu, and in the course of our association he has recounted more than twenty visions. A few, however, stand out for a variety of reasons: (1) their association with crucial historical points in the movement and key junctures in Mobutu's ritual career, (2) a wealth of symbolic details linking pervasive themes in the Rasta mythos, and (3) the context and style in which he chose to relate these experiences. The three dialogues and interpretations that follow are intended to provide a glimpse of the communicative interaction in which Ras Mobutu revealed himself to me as a visionary prophet. Although the visionary accounts presented here are in the chronological order in which they occurred during Mobutu's career, the second vision was related to me at a much later stage of my fieldwork than the other two. By this point I was able to respond appropriately to the symbolic markers set forth in the account, thus intersubjectively validating at least one of the meanings conveyed by Mobutu's imagery. In order to share the texture and feeling-tone of these interactions with you, I have chosen to present these dialogues in as close to the native *patois* in which they were spoken as possible.[8]

A *private reasoning*

One of the first visions Mobutu related to me concerned Garvey's role in the Rasta genesis and occurred during a 'closed door' or private reasoning between ourselves. This private context was important because Mobutu was simultaneously testifying to his status as a prophet and testing to see if I-n-I was 'conscious' and could 'catch' his meanings.

Mobutu: Concerning dis ensign [flag], de Red-Black-and-Green, in 1929, Elijah de prophet, Marcus Mosiah Garvey, mek forth a Convention in Jamaica. After de convention, Britain gather we and said ta we dat de Union Jack is no emblem feh us. In case of hostility between de black and de white, we must consider ourselves aliens and prisoners of war. Well, I see Marcus Garvey rise in power. Him stand before I [and] seh, 'De Union Jack are no emblem feh us. We are a people and a nation 'pon de earth and we suppose ta have our own emblem.'

Jakes: Prophecy dat, Jah, Yes-I.

Mobutu: I see Marcus rise in power and guh ta de Vatican where him pass 11,000 priest an guh down ta de bottom a de Vatican where de Pope rest. When de Pope see de black M'Adonai [Garvey] approach before him, him stretch him hand forth feh shook him hand, but Marcus give him de head a de black crook stick [instead]. Head of de wha . . .?

Jakes: Of de black crook stick.

Mobutu: An argument arise, and Marcus Garvey seh, 'Eighty million scattered black people are sending feh der ensign [flag].' Well, being de Pope seh he is God of de Earth feh all people, him have all nations' flags. So de Pope run ina de flag room and stir, and stir, and stir. But him couldn't find de flag. Him come back ta de throne and turn up de throne seat, and it der him tek up de Red-Black-and-Green and give it ta Marcus Garvey. When I see Garvey leave, him mek forth de proclamation, 'De Golden Hammer have rattle 'pon de St Peter door and thousands of Angels? [Ethiopians] gone home.'

Jakes: Mi bredrin, on a point of reasoning, de Golden Hammer, is those said words?

Mobutu: De Golden Hammer is de man [Garvey], feh de gold was black before it purified. Only Garvey, as a 'scientist,' could understand dat and know what it mean. Dat interpret so, dat flag, Red-Black-and-Green, was teken from Jerusalem when de ploughshares were over Zion [an era of peace and prosperity]. Den, all nations pass through Jerusalem: de Syrians, and de Mede, and de Persian army. Well, afta a time, de Ethiopian start ta mingle [cohabitate] wid de Syrian woman, because now deh have woman up der which is not of der race. Jah seh ta de prophet Jeremiah ta guh an tell Hezekiah [King of Israel] dat deh must not allow de Ethiopian ta mingle wid de Syrian woman feh deh will led dem away ta idol worship. But deh nah tek heed! From dat, de Mede and Persian army come up through de River Euphrates and hold [imprison] Hezekiah, dig out him two eye [blind him] and tek off him two son's head, and tek I-n-I [Ethiopians] away ta Babylon. Dem tek 'way de scepter, de golden sword, de filigree robe, and de encrusted diamond ring [monarchial symbols of the Solomonic dynasty restored to Haile Selassie at his coronation: see figure 10.1].

Jakes: So, it a [racial] mix-up business dat really cause de exile of Israel?

Mobutu: True, true. Well dis knowledge come through de ages from Marcus Garvey ta I. Now dat wise-man [wisdom] put forth with overstanding [understanding], we know all things concerning de good and welfare of a nation. De Red-Black-and-Green is our first ensign. Dat ensign is a dangerous weapon!

By the time of the reasoning I already knew that I had to be a participating listener and thus I was prepared to respond to Mobutu's sudden interjection of a direct question into his narrative, 'Head of de wha. . .?' with 'Of de black crook stick.' I was also aware that although elders are not averse to providing clarifying remarks at various points in a reasoning, a mechanical combing of a narrative would imply that I was a dull person who could not 'see.' To one prepared to 'see,' however, the symbolism of the vision and the reasoning in which it is embedded encode an important sociopolitical perception which runs throughout Rasta thought; namely, that the exploitation and suffering of black people has been perpetuated by a forcefully imposed alien system which, by promoting racial and cultural amalgamation, has caused them to forsake their true African identity and consciousness. This truth is symbolized by the opposed figures of Garvey and the Pope, respectively representatives of Zion and Babylon. These two, together with the imagery which surrounds them, are an allegory of black struggle against white domination and the preservation of African identity through religious means.

The structural simplicity of the text is in striking contrast to its metaphorical richness, which enlists the attention of the listener and adds to the impact of the vision (cf. Fernandez 1966:51–8). This use of metaphor with multiple meanings is actually a rhetorical technique used by various elders. Since the relationship between imagery and meaning must be inferred from knowledge outside the reasoning itself, an ambiguity is maintained which plays upon what speakers and listeners share intersubjectively. This lends the vision some of its mystic aura and imbues a prophet with charisma. For example, the symbolic inversions in the imagery of Garvey the black M'Adonai risen in power passing 11,000 priests to reach the *bottom* of the V*at*ican are implicitly opposed to the iconic allusion commonly made by brethren to Mt Zion, the abode of Jah which, at 11,000 miles *up*, is the highest spot on earth. This up/down semantic inversion is further juxtaposed with Mobutu's description of the black man's 'first ensign' which 'flew over Zion' and its retrieval by Garvey from '*underneath* the throne seat of the Pope. Likewise the banner of Ethiopian identity, the dreadlocks convenant, is said to 'fly' upon the head, or 'heavens,' of a Rastaman and is the tangible symbol of cultural and spiritual recovery. By contrast, reference to the 'bottom' or buttocks as evoked by the 'underside' of the Pope's throne seat is steeped in the imagery of racial pollution, 'fleshliness,' and moral blindness. Thus the concern with violation of divine command and the fall into spiritual blindness contrasts with the emphasis of Garvey upon black liberation and racial upliftment.

All of these themes are summed up by Mobutu's allusion to Garvey's philosophy concerning the 'good and welfare of a nation' [black people] with its demands for racial purity and cultural conservation embodied in the prophetic injunction that blacks come to see God 'through the spectacles of an Ethiopian' (Garvey 1974:44). In the vision, the Rasta rejection of the white man's Christianity is symbolized by Garvey's recovery of the black man's ensign which portends racial redemption: 'thousands of Angels have gone home.' Tied to concerns with moral duty, this symbol reflects the inherent problems of existing as realized 'Ethiopians' in the Anglophilic Jamaican context.

The two-fold image of Garvey as the black M'Adonai [Adonai in Hebrew is the ineffable name of God] and as the 'Golden Hammer' is a reference to black people as the gold stolen from Africa by Europeans. This alludes to the captivity and racial exile of blacks caused by their infidelity to Jah. This explicit liminality which lends Rasta symbolism much of its sacredness is related to another potent and historically significant symbol featured in the vision: the crook stick wielded by Garvey. Known also as a shepherd's crook, it is a symbol of spiritual authority associated with the leaders of Afro-Christian revival sects that flourished in Kingston during the height of the Garveyite period. Many of these sect leaders were later to become key figures in the Rasta movement. Today, these crooks, rods, or prayer sticks continue to be carried by elders of the movement (see figure 10.2). These ceremonial objects are known as 'power keys,' or control points through which spiritual power and visions can be 'drawn' or directed (Cassidy 1974:240; Moore 1965:64). They are related to re-Africanized religious beliefs and practices that emerged after emancipation and became focal points for black resistance to Christian missions seeking to dominate the spiritual and cultural lives of Afro-Jamaicans (Simpson 1956:334–7; Bilby and Leib 1983:3).

It is from within this cultural context that Mobutu qualifies Garvey as a 'scientist,' a spiritually empowered African who uses this icon to insulate himself from the pernicious influences of the Vatican and, by extension, from the exploitative influences of white colonialism. This both reflects the generalized concern in Rasta thought to keep the mutually antagonistic domains of Zion and Babylon from mixing and provides an appropriate perception of Garvey's role in the history of black resistance in the Diaspora.

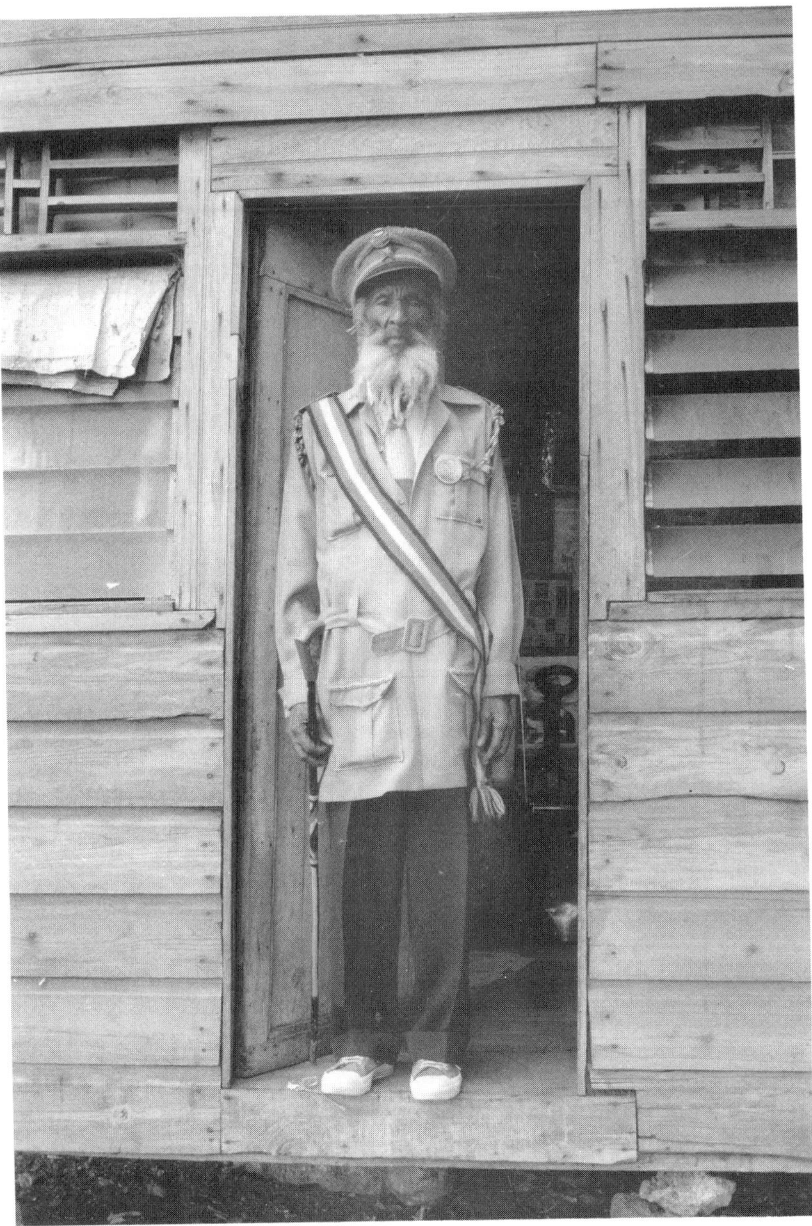

Figure 10.2 Ras Mobutu arrayed in the type of military dress in which Emperor Selassie was frequently photographed. In his right hand Mobutu holds his crook stick with three-cornered head, symbolic of the power of the Trinity. Photo: John Homiak

A visionary duty

In the late 1950s, prior to the official end of colonial rule, Mobutu had another vision, in which Garvey commissioned him to carry the Red-Black-and-Green ensign into the Jamaican House of Parliament as a symbolic demand for repatriation and a spiritual duty which would eradicate the last vestiges of colonialism. In this instance, the symbol linking Mobutu and Garvey was not only the ensign, but a 'Kaska Rico [Costa Rica] potato' which was to be 'roasted.' In a reasoning with myself and an elder by the name of Jah Nago, Mobutu related the vision and then described the duty he and Nago performed together as a result of his vision.

Jakes: So, mi bredrin, de man had mentioned a vision pertaining to that duty –

Mobutu: Yes, I coming ta dat –

Nago: Him wanna burn a likle more *kali* [marijuana] first. Gwann, rub it up now, Jakes. It [the chalice] soon set up.

Mobutu: Yes, him [Jakes] a capable morale. Yes, man, knowledge open up, man. It open up. It seal up ina de Most High [pause while chalice is relit]. Garvey give I as a 'Kaska Rico potato' when I see I gwaan guh get dis flag. Garvey give I de ensign, de Red-Black-and-Green, and I found miself carried ta a precipice. Around thirty feet below in a yard I hear a voice seh 'Police after yuh.' I shuv dat sound right out until I come 'pon a road and I 'member dat de voice seh 'Police after yuh,' and I leap over a draw rail, which is Trinity [three rails]. And next ta de gate where de draw rail is, I see Garvey stand up 'gainst it. Him seh 'Here, tek dis [potato]. Anywhere yuh ketch fiya [find fire], roast it! Anywhere yuh step where der fire, yuh must roast it!'

Jakes: A Kaska Rico potato?

Mobutu: Kaska Rico potato, Garvey's works –

Jakes: Seen. [I understand.]

Mobutu: I tek it and I travel [spiritually] through a common. Since I guh through a draw rail, I must guh through a common –

Nago: Yes, feh yuh passed a draw rail inta a pasture –

Jakes: So, is over a draw rail which is Trinity and through a pasture?

Mobutu: Yes, and going on, I face toward de North and come ta a crossroads. And when I look, I see a tangerine tree before I [which] is around four or five chain [100 feet] in circum-fence [circumference]. And de tangerine tree, it bear [ripe], it red like cherry, wid bunch-and-bunch. Dat mean ta show de number of people [for repatriation]. And when I look toward de East [Zion], I see two lime skil [limekilns] wha dem use feh burn white lime 'pon [kilns for melting limestone]. I guh round it, but I haven't seen no fiya. And when I come back ta de tangerine tree, deh all gone, deh close off.

Jakes: De tangerines drop a ground, de harvest reap.

Mobutu: De interpretation of dat is, 'De harvest [of people] is ripe feh repatriation and de old colonial government, de two brick houses dat Britain leave in Jamaica [Parliament and the Governor General's residence] are de two political parties. De two party is de two lime skil, cause dem burning Israel upon lime skil.

Jakes: Iyah, why *two* lime skil?

Mobutu: De two lime skil are de two party.

Nago: PNP and Labour.

Jakes: Sight. [I understand.]

Shortly after his vision, Mobutu with a small group of brethren, including Nago, carried Garvey's Red-Black-and-Green flag into the Jamaican House of Parliament. As the chamber was about to convene Mobutu unexpectedly unfurled the flag and made a speech demanding repatriation to Africa. For this he was arrested and jailed. When he was arraigned before a local magistrate, the judge offered to allow his conditional release if he agreed to create no further disturbances, to which Mobutu confidently replied, 'I don't need two shots for one bird.'

The vision that inspired this important duty not only demonstrates the way that visions are used strategically to assert claims to prophetic empowerment, but also illustrates how a Rastaman can communicate aspects of movement history and creatively articulate the Rasta mythos as part of his own inspiration. To be 'roasted' draws upon the powerful symbolism of fire and its manifold biblical and cultural meanings for Jah prophets.[9] Thus, while the Costa Rica potato iconically refers to the kind of 'roasting' or sacrifice demanded of a prophet it also indexes, or points toward, the very beginning of Garvey's Pan-Africanist work. It was in Costa Rica in 1912 that Garvey first grasped the plight of his race in a more global perspective. Incensed by the brutal exploitation of black workers in Costa Rica, Garvey filed official protest with the British Council against the deplorable working conditions to which his countrymen and fellow blacks were subjected (Garvey 1974:34). On his return to Jamaica, two years later, Garvey founded the Universal Negro Improvement Association (UNIA), a powerful social movement which threatened the hegemony of European interests in both the West Indies and Africa. In the reasoning the Costa Rica potato evokes both an episode in the history of colonial oppression and a point of resistance to that oppression, thus identifying Mobutu with the works of Garvey.

Mobutu's vision is also linked to the charismatic authority of Emperor Selassie. The metaphor of the draw rail as 'Trinity' is a reference to the Amharic interpretation of the name Haile Selassie, 'The Might of the Trinity.' The draw rail as 'three rails' is a reference to a metaphorical fence setting off Mobutu's commission as a prophet and is thus conspicuously juxtaposed with a warning signaling his dangerous task, 'Police after yuh.'

The ripe tangerine tree represents the faithful awaiting repatriation, and the two 'lime skil' are Jamaica's two-party political system controlled by a brown elite which has traditionally manipulated the black masses [Israel]. Together these polarized symbols express the contrast between the possibility of the ultimate redemption of blacks and the false consciousness imposed upon blacks through the deceptions of a culturally alien brown political elite. The fruit tree refers to biblical portents of the redemption of blacks as the 'first fruits unto God and to the Lamb' to be redeemed when the 'harvest is ripe' (Rev. 14:4; Joel 3:13). The theme of deception by the brown elite is linked with the symbolism of the limekilns, facing East toward Zion, upon which blacks are being 'burnt' [exploited]. These elements encode a critique of Jamaican politics, including reference to the messianic language and symbolism by which its leaders have posed as 'deliverers' of the black masses while actually keeping them at odds with each other and dependent upon these heirs to colonial privilege by the infamous colonial strategy of 'divide and conquer.' Mobutu's vision placed him within the crucial context when this social critique, which is now generally shared within the larger Jamaican society, was collectively authored by Rastas. This amounts to a further claim to prophetic stature.

From a Rasta perspective, the full significance of Mobutu's duty would become clear in the years immediately following. Thus, in 1961, amidst deteriorating relations between Rastas and the larger society, Jamaican authorities began to take Rasta protest seriously enough to send a mission, including three Rasta delegates, to Ethiopia in order to explore the possibility of repatriation. In 1962, colonial rule officially ended in Jamaica and before the decade was out, Norman Manley, one of the leaders of Jamaican politics, died an untimely death, and another, Alexander Bustamente, was forced into retirement because of blindness.

Throughout the 1960s political violence in Jamaica increased with the difficult struggle for survival faced by the urban proletariat in Kingston. With independence in 1962, 'multiracialism' became the official ethos for national identity, proclaimed by the elite. Political patronage remained critical to the urban poor for both housing and jobs, especially as their ranks were swelled by an accelerated rural-to-urban shift in the island's population. The frustrations of this growing urban proletariat were directed at each other by the two parties through mercenary relationships with roving 'lumpen youth bands.' Inevitably, the toll of this conflict fell most heavily upon poor blacks, most of whom shared the squalor of shanty-town life with the Rastafari. From a Rastafarian perspective, black people, or the nation of Israel, were at war with themselves, exploited by a divide and conquer policy that had existed since slavery. The Rastafari remained outspoken in their condemnation of the island's brown power-structure, insisting that independence was a sham and that this elite continued to pay primary allegiance to the British Crown.

Another visionary duty

In early 1966, when news of a state visit to the island by Queen Elizabeth II circulated throughout Jamaica, Ras Mobutu received a vision which inspired another spiritual duty. He chose to relate this particular vision one afternoon in 1980 when he, I, and another young Rasta were reasoning together. Earlier that morning, this youth, the son of one of Mobutu's age cohorts who periodically made special trips from the country to reason with him, arrived in camp with a high quality 'draw' [batch] of marijuana. After the three of us had been reasoning upon the likely outcome of the upcoming general elections, Mobutu introduced the following vision, emphasizing to us that he was a 'mystic' who 'worked through vision.'

Mobutu: Yes, man, I-n-I move ina mystic, ina cosmic. One balm-yard night I mount [fly spiritually] up ta mi house and see Marcus Garvey put down a brand new key at de doorway. And I balance it and mount up ta Spanish Town Road next ta Coronation Market and I hear de people seh, 'See him der, see him up der 'pon de job.' Den I find I reach ta de park and I see de statue of Victoria and I perform a duty right der. Feh [because] when I pass by de statue, I saw dat Victoria was in a family way [pregnant]. And I seh, 'What is dis?' So I guh up ta her closer and look up under her and der was some likle [little] thing, like a blinkey-blinkey [an object used for *obeah*] underneath her. And I seh, 'So dat's de "science" Babylon plant wid we!'

Jakes: De 'science'?

Mobutu: De 'science' Babylon try feh work 'pon we. Well, from [when] I see dat, I pass by de statue again and when I look upon her again I see de scepter in her right hand. Dat interpret like Genesis 49:10, 'De scepter shall protect de just.' But when I look into it, I seh, 'Wait, I-n-I are not protected.' And when I look in her left hand I saw a round ball and a tube dat run from her left breast [heart] down into de ball [the earth]. Dat interpret, 'to suck lust as a mother.'

Jakes: To suck de blood of de righteous.

Mobutu: To suck lust, feh she [the Queen] seh she a protector, but de black man is not suckled, not wanted. So, from [when] I see dat, I solve out de science of de likle thing I see underneath her. Jah show I dat when deh [the government] was putting up dat statue, deh tek a census and deh stick a black-head pin ina parchment paper and roll it in Lamb-skin and shuv it up underneath de statue's belly [vagina] and den deh put it down 'pon de stone [a power object used in *obeah*]. So dat is de science.

Jakes: But what is de meaning of a de black pin in de parchment paper?

Mobutu: Deh tek de census of us and to every one of I-n-I deh stick a black pin, feh in dat time we not so plentiful.

Jakes: Dat come like *obeah*.

Mobutu: Yes, 'science,' but Jah show I how to unlock de 'science' of dat [Garvey's key].

This vision inspired another symbolic political duty for which Mobutu has become well known among both his cohorts and latter-day brethren. Reasoning upon this event with us, he explained that another Rasta had crafted him a replica of the key he had visioned and that in the midst of a political rally prior to the Queen's visit, he drew the attention of the crowds in Victoria Park. In his testimony Mobutu recollected the following scene.

Three day afta I get de key made, Elizabeth come ta Jamaica feh her second visit. I dress in de robe and regalia and went wid de key ta East Queen Street on a duty. I tek up de duty de 24th March [1966] at Victoria Park. Bustamente [then Prime Minister] have thousands of black man gathered a King Street and down Harbour Street deh guh. Den de Manley procession come and deh have we [black people] divided. When Busta and Manley come on [arrive] and see I up 'pon de statue of Victoria wid de Bible ina mi hand, he marvel. I turn 'pon de Governor and seh, 'Look, dis day above all days set out feh de British Empire. Dis day I haven't seen an ensign, or a star, or stripe ta represent de people and I therefore bring deliverance unto de people wid dis sound: BAP, BAP, BAP.' I lick [strike] Victoria's belly three times wid de key and bust de 'science.' Dat duty fulfill Isaiah chapter 47, 'Come down Ye virgin daughter of Babylon and be no more called tender and delicate. Der is no more throne feh thee.'

In mystic and prophetic imagery this duty provides an apt reading of the events of the day. As noted, Jamaican political leaders had consolidated their hold on colonial privilege by manipulating the masses with a litany of empty promises. The language of the narrative again characterizes the political strategies used to manipulate or divide the masses as 'science' (i.e., sorcery) and alludes in a potent symbolic way to the sociopolitical situation in which blacks found themselves during the 1960s when increasing internecine street warfare came to accompany politics, a situation which the Rastas have come to condemn as a 'vampire system' sucking the blood of black sufferers. For the Rasta, politics or 'poli-tricks,' as it has come to be known, represents the same kind of threat to communal values and harmony as the malicious forces of 'science' or *obeah* traditionally represented.[10]

The repugnant imagery of this evil is evoked here in a particularly effective way in relation to the political machinations of the island's brown leaders. A multivocalic link between Euro-Creole values, racial amalgamation, and black self-deprecation is expressed in magico-religious terms in which 'science' is 'planted' in Victoria's 'belly,' or vagina. Sympathetic magic, including pin-sticking, the writing of names on parchment paper, and the use of magical stones, all traditional *obeah* techniques, are believed to 'hold down the ability' of the victims against whom it is directed (Simpson 1956:389; Beckwith 1929:109–11). The 'science,' a metonym for Euro-Creole machinations, wrapped in lamb skin, a representation of Israel, reflects a confusion of cultural categories. The fact that it is used to put Victoria, the biblical harlot, in a 'family way' is a potent metonymic way in which to represent an historical process which has informed the cultural values of the Anglophilic brown middle class and at the same time represent the racial and cultural pollution of blacks. This process of racial and cultural hybridization, to which Rastas are so sensitive, is seen in their strident condemnation of multiracialism as the elite-proclaimed ethos for Jamaican cultural nationalism. From a Rasta perspective, this is merely a political sham to play down the economic hegemony of the native socially white minority and the true de facto apartheid policies which hold down the black masses. As a representation of 'science,' the potency of the iconic imagery surrounding Victoria is heightened by an implied association with blood; not only because of its obvious reference to political warfare but because of its sexual connotations. This aspect of the vision's iconography resonates with the ambivalent to negative evaluation of females in Rasta cosmology, particularly with the Rasta theory which emphasizes race-mixing as the 'original sin' and cause of a woman's polluting menses. 'Science' is thus a veiled allusion to racial amalgamation and to blood as a two-fold symbol of pollution and suffering.

At another level, Mobutu's description and interpretation of his vision serve to unmask in a powerful and dramatic way the false image of the Queen as a 'mother' figure, and the Crown as a 'protector.' In the Jamaican cultural context, these themes touch upon historically derived sentiments and perceptions toward the Crown carried over from emancipation and deeply embedded in the social psychology of the Jamaican masses. Blacks have always had a deep-seated hostility towards and distrust of colonial governors and the socially white upper class, yet could hold an affection for the Queen, who stood as a protective symbol and source of their liberation from slavery. It was, in fact, Queen Victoria I who freed the slaves in 1834. Paradoxical as it may seem, blacks have looked with some degree of hope to the British Crown to intervene periodically on their behalf in order to mitigate the excesses of local colonial rulers. This curious outlook, bound up in the racial ambivalence generated within a Creole hierarchy, was not seriously challenged until the advent of Garveyism and the Rasta movement. It should be appreciated that the monarchial symbols with which the Queen is depicted in Mobutu's vision are central to the scriptural interpretation cited by early Rasta leaders for the divinity of Haile Selassie. As Hill (1983:34) has observed, this biblical interpretation provided an important element of prophetic authority by which the Rastafari preached a withdrawal of political allegiance from the colonial state and postulated a counter political legitimacy in their version of black religious nationalism.

The iconography of the harlot with 'scepter in right hand, ball in left hand' is thus a corruption of the insignia of monarchial and divine office identified with Emperor Selassie as 'Earth's Rightful Ruler,' the 'Protector of Israel,' and is a critique of the deceptions behind colonial and neocolonial rule (see figure 10.1). This is indicated in Mobutu's claim that it 'interprets like Genesis 49:10,' which reads, 'the scepter shall not depart from Judah, nor a lawgiver from between his feet, until Shiloh [the Messiah] come; and unto Him shall the gathering of the people be.' Thus, those identified with colonial power and privilege have attempted to usurp the rightful symbols of authority which, from a Rasta perspective, are vested only in the King of Kings.

The interpretation of Queen Victoria as 'mother' and 'protector' holding the 'ball' [earth] in her left hand is not only a corruption of the monarchial symbolism identified with Emperor Selassie, but also a corruption of the earth as the sacred 'mother,' the organic life source associated with purity. In Rasta thought, this is a basis for positing the natural order as the model for the ethical life and is to be contrasted with Babylonian 'science' not only in terms of a political critique but also in the sense that the excesses of Western technological 'science' have abused and defiled the earth. The imagery of the tube running from the Queen's left breast [heart] into the ball [earth] is another corruption of Rasta symbols since in communal herb smoking the chalice is typically drawn through a length of tubing and the act of smoking is the means by which brethren draw spiritual sustenance communicating 'from earth to Zion.' In Mobutu's vision, the tube connected to the Queen's breast – to 'suck lust as a mother, – is a 'fleshly' version of this spiritual act.

The 'key' as the instrument by which moral confusion is undone or counteracted is not only a metaphor for Garvey's doctrine of racial patriotism and purity but a power object through which spiritual force can be directed. Mobutu's act of striking the offending figure of Victoria three times with the key portends the fulfillment of a biblical prophecy in which the ascension of Elizabeth II to a British throne of diminished imperial power signals the fall of Babylon for the Rastafari (Rev. 17:5; 128:10; Isaiah 47:1–9). Scriptural support which Mobutu links with his vision is also to be found in the biblical promise that in the final days, God's Chosen People would see through 'the multitude of [the harlot's] sorceries' (Isaiah 47:9). At a personal psychic level too the 'key' clearly has special meanings for Mobutu which go beyond the context of his vision and have become an established part of his customary regalia (figure 10.3).

As 'testimony,' the power of Mobutu's visionary narrative derives from the incorporation of a number of symbolic elements including key, scepter, ball, tube, *obeah* paraphernalia, Garvey, and the Queen. Conveyed is the view that race-mixing and the false hybrid values associated with Creolization are at the core of much suffering and conflict promoted by an alien cultural minority. The vision relates these symbols on multiple levels to central propositions and shared understandings in Rasta world view so that an informed listener can 'sight' or discover his own meanings.

For myself, and the other Rasta present, the impact of the narrative was accentuated by Ras Mobutu's multimedia presentation of his

Figure 10.3 Ras Mobutu in robes and regalia with his spiritual key. Photo: John Homiak

testimony in which he allowed me to photograph him for the first time, insisting that this picture be taken in 'full regalia,' part of which was the key. Between the narrative and ritual iconography he had produced an inspired account which enmeshed history, biblical prophecy, African mysticism, and fragments of his own life history to point up aspects of his role as a prophet called upon to defend the moral and cultural ethos of the Rastafari.

CONCLUSIONS

Three visionary dialogues with a leading Rastafarian elder have been presented, the communicative contexts in which they were related have been described, and selected aspects of their manifest meanings explored. These visionary narratives are not ineffable flights into fantasy but accounts that resound with the social and moral order and that have profound implications for understanding Afro-Jamaican cultural identity and sociocultural history. Mobutu's descriptions of blacks as 'aliens,' himself as a 'Costa Rica potato,' and of the British Queen as a 'mother' who 'sucks lust' are not merely decorative hyperbole but powerful rhetorical statements containing insights into the sociopolitical realities of colonial exploitation. Rather than confounding reality, a condensed mythopoetic interpretation of the type 'Marcus Garvey retrieved the black man's ensign from the Vatican' actually communicates a number of important truths about this apostle of black liberation and his influence on the Rastafari, particularly their understanding of the collusion between European church-and-state in the colonial context.

It should be apparent that Mobutu's visions have become incorporated into an oral tradition in which complementary understandings are negotiated or shared by speakers. Thus, they cannot be approached as separate from the social contexts and ritual processes through which ideology is reproduced. For Mobutu, they have become a way of engaging his own personal history and at the same time validating his informal tutorial role as an elder. And while they are culturally significant because they punctuate and illuminate specific points in Rasta history, their interpretation and received meaning by others must be seen as variable rather than homogeneous. This derives from the fact that reasoning is a process which is 'intertextual' and a given reasoning must be heard in the context of a previous reasoning and, at least in part, experienced as preparation for future communicative interaction.

Ras Mobutu's distinctive use of visions in his oral narratives is characteristic of the high degree of personal style that can prevail in reasoning as in other New World black oral traditions. As part of his technique for communicating oral history and 'grounding' other brethren, he was in my experience peerless in his ability to take the less initiated through a kind of 'guided imagery' (Price-Williams, this volume) during reasoning. These stylistic elements in his reasoning not only provide a metaprogam in reasoning for those he seeks to enlighten and inspire but also serve to enhance his stature as a mystic and prophet.

So situated, it is reasonable to conclude that Mobutu's revealing of his dreams has merged with the mindscape activated during reasoning and that over time their meanings have probably been multiplied and embellished by the metaphorical richness of Rasta language. Meaning in this oral culture draws upon a continuum of experience ranging from the intrapsychic experiences of dreams (no doubt themselves shaped by the figurative resources used to communicate these experiences) to the communal discourse of reasoning. The predominant emphasis upon the visual mode in which the speaker is linked with an imagery situation frequently serves to structure discourse by reiterating basic semantic and metaphorical contrasts internal to Rasta world view. At the same time it is the originality of metaphorical content that a brethren brings to visionary discourse that makes its interpretation by others such a personal experience. This intellectual and linguistic ability enables creative speakers to reveal accepted truths in new and other surprising ways that encourage others to 'sight' certain truths for themselves.

One day, after telling a vision in the presence of me and a number of other brethren, Mobutu suddenly announced that I had been sent to him by Jah and that he intended to 'use me up' upon Jah works (i.e., to use me to carry the Rasta message farther afield). Mobutu's proclamation not only indicates something of his own psychic investment in his visions, but casts the dialectic between ethnographic data and dialogue into sharp relief. In religious contexts where the telling of dreams can inspire oral performances which relate actors as speakers and listeners, ethnographers do well to attend closely to the interpersonal meanings that inform dream telling. That a researcher in such circumstances is a participant in the production of ethnographic knowledge should make us increasingly uneasy with traditional distinctions between observer and observed, theory and data, description and analysis.

NOTES

1. The designation of Rasta as a form of black Zionism is intended to emphasize the meaning of the Diaspora experience in Afro-American religious thought (Drake 1975; Leib 1983). This partly explains why the Rastafari have come to regard themselves simultaneously as Israelites and Ethiopians, a biblical link established by their identity as the exiled Sons of Ham.
2. Jah, as an abbreviation of Jehovah or God, is found in both the English Bible from 1539 to 1758 (Cassidy 1974:237) and in Psalm 68:4 of the King James Bible. The term acquired currency in the Afro-Christian tradition in the late nineteenth century (Simpson 1956:398) and is now used as a term of address between brethren, as well as to refer to Emperor Selassie as the Godhead.
3. The Rasta conception of a 'repeating cycle' fuses both historical and non-historical ideas about time and draws upon a diverse and complex set of ideas about reincarnation.
4. At his coronation Ras Tafari Makonnen was crowned 'His Imperial Majesty, Emperor Haile Selassie I, King of Kings, Lord of Lords, Conquering Lion of the Tribe of Judah, Elect of God, and Light of the World,' thus taking the divine titles reserved in scriptures for the Second Coming of the Messiah (see Rev. 5:5, 19:16 and Timothy 6:15). Fundamentalist Rastas, pointing to the absence of both a corpse and a state funeral, reject the claim that Haile Selassie died in 1975.
5. In a forthcoming paper, 'Testament of the Patriarchs: Race and Religious Experience in Rastafarian Culture,' I present an account of my immersion in Rasta culture, the process of establishing rapport with movement fundamentalists, and the social and psychological dynamics by which total outsiders can become candidates for participation within a predominantly black social movement.
6. When government officials learnt of Emperor Selassie's scheduled state visit to Trinidad in 1966, they invited him to Jamaica. This was a calculated maneuver to quell Rasta demands for repatriation based on the assumption that the emperor would publicly disclaim his divinity. Selassie neither made such a disclaimer nor claimed divinity. Rastas turned this to their advantage by pointing out that this repeated the example of Christ.

7. Mobutu's request to 'put some herbs on the board' reflects the Rasta view that a proper reasoning should not proceed without herbs. The elaborate preparation of this sacred substance is done on a type of bread board termed a 'suru board' on which the herbs are finely cut and kneaded into a resinous block through the addition of small amounts of water and tobacco leaf. This is an important part of the process of sacralization which surrounds the activity of reasoning.
8. This transcription follows a convention already established in Afro-Caribbean literature (Brathwaite 1974, 1978; White 1983). It also preserves the texture of the narratives and the elliptical leaps which they require of the listener or reader. In instances where native use of conjunctions or other terms, including historical or biblical allusions, is possibly confusing I have inserted standard English equivalents or glosses in square brackets.
9. On the biblical imagery of fire and its meaning for the Rastafari, see Isaiah 48:10 and Daniel 3:26. In more proverbial terms, Mobutu is enjoined to 'catch fire,' a phrase that connotes the position of danger in which protest has always placed the black man in Jamaica (White 1983). At the same time, it signals for the Rasta the impending fiery cataclysm which will ultimately engulf Babylon.
10. In Jamaican folk tradition, 'science' is a synonym for *obeah* or sorcery and obeahworkers are known as 'scientists.' These magico-religious practices are, however, used for both good and evil since a scientist is required to counteract the *obeah* 'set' or 'planted' by an adversary (see Curtin 1955:31–3).

11
The waking dream in ethnographic perspective[1]

DOUGLASS PRICE-WILLIAMS

In the 1800s Frederick Myers, a classical scholar who wrote on paranormal phenomena, coined the term 'mythopoetic function' (see Ellenberger 1970:314). The term was intended to refer to the tendency of some people, while in a trance or reverie, to weave fantasies. This might be done orally in mediumistic states or in literal form, as in automatic writing. The French psychiatrist Theodore Flournoy pushed the notion further, formulating the idea that there was a region of the unconscious that was continually engaged in creating fiction and myths, which could manifest in nocturnal dreams or in daydreams. Flournoy (1900) gave rich descriptions of a woman medium, called Hélène, in a book called *From India to the Planet Mars*. Hélène, from time to time, exhibited various personalities in her mediumistic trances. One of these spoke in a very detailed fashion of a supposed Martian environment. There were copious descriptions of the Martian people, flora and fauna, and even descriptions of the Martian language.

Freud's theories of the unconscious tended to usurp the attention given to the mythopoetic function, in the same way as his method of free association and emphasis on the transference situation tended to minimize interest in hypnosis and in imaginative productions (see

Ellenberger 1970:877). However, there was, mainly on the European continent, a continued interest in these matters. It can be traced back to the great figure of Pierre Janet, a contemporary of both Flournoy and Freud, who spoke of the *fonction fabulatrice* and who utilized fantasy in therapy. The main heritage of the mythopoetic function, however, could be found in two related streams of psychiatric interest. The first was the utilization of what Jung (1916) called 'active imagination,' and the second was the use of 'guided imagery.'[2]

ACTIVE IMAGINATION AND GUIDED IMAGERY

It is difficult for those who have not experienced it to grasp the emotional impact of active imagination from merely reading examples of it. In our age and time the term 'imagination' has come to mean a wispy and evanescent process that lacks flesh-and-blood substance. It was presumably to differentiate it from this notion that Jung called the process *active* imagination as opposed to our ordinary *passive* imagination. It is clear that active imagination is something quite different from what we usually regard as imagination. Good descriptions of the process have been provided by some of Jung's immediate students (von Franz 1975:111–12; Hannah 1981:16–17). The process consists of setting aside the critical faculty and allowing emotions, fantasies, and images to surface into awareness. It is not an easy task, and at first the productions are fleeting and vague. The process is not like watching an interior video screen, although it may begin like this. The images and emotions that emerge are encouraged to be identified with; to be treated as if they were objectively present.

In hypnosis one time I had a subject who saw a picture on the wall. It was of a house with a path, surrounded by country scenery. While hypnotized, the subject was in a room looking up at the picture. I encouraged this subject to get into the picture, and very soon the subject was walking up the path in the picture. The picture, in other words, was no longer a picture. The active imagination process is rather like that. The idea is to regard these interior events exactly as if one were in a similar exterior situation. The imaginative process is one of involvement; not merely a spectacle. Emotions are felt, not just noted. Jung once rebuked a patient who was doing this for not feeling fear when an imaginative lion appeared. A real lion would have elicited fear; an active imagination lion should do no less (von Franz 1976). Often personification of interior voices is encouraged, so as to build up the reality that one is dealing with an autonomous entity.

Active imagination is experienced throughout all the modalities. Visual images and auditions may be the most frequent, but movement is also a fairly consistent modality. Mindell (1982) has encouraged focussing on body cramps or tensions as a starting-point for more elaborate imaginative productions. It should be noted that the production of images cannot be divorced from the means of expressing them. In therapy the patient is encouraged to retain the images produced through a variety of expressive methods. The patient may verbalize the images; dance them, or merely move in certain ways; paint or draw the images, or utilize clay or stone. Writing is a standard method. It is, I suppose, well appreciated that such a process underlies fictional works. Aldous Huxley (1980) referred to the case of Robert Louis Stevenson, who revealed that all his short stories were provided for him by his unconscious, either in reverie or in nocturnal dreams. He thought of the mythopoetic faculty in a fanciful fashion as his 'brownies,' fairy people who inhabited his skull and produced the material, which on waking he simply wrote down.

In therapy the procedure is to encourage the imaginer to integrate these interior figures and events with the rest of life. What Jung (1916) called the 'transcendent function' was the process whereby imaginative productions are used as revelations of unknown parts of the self, which need to be confronted or worked through in the normal waking life. Otherwise, of course, imaginative productions become at best emotional diversions and at worst a psychosis. It can be readily seen that active imagination is a true knife-edge. Von Franz called it a voluntary psychosis.

In guided imagery, as the title suggests, the imaginer is given some structure. Desoille (1945) provided his patients with archetypal imaginary situations, such as a descent into the sea or into a cave, meeting with a dragon, and other elements common to fairy-tale or myth. Leuner (1969) had his patients start off with fairly common but positive images, such as a cloud or a brook, or a mountain or a meadow. He then escalated the imagery by having his patients imagine a person of the opposite sex, or borrowing an image from a nocturnal dream. Other techniques exist; for example, there is the application of guided imagery to dreams, the so-called oneirodrama, where dream and theatrical sense come together (Frétigny and Virel 1968). Or there are sculpting techniques, wherein patients make family figures out of clay after reflecting on early experiences (Keyes 1974).

In both active imagination and guided imagery, at least three principles stand out. First, we are not dealing with a cerebral ghost in the mind. The person feels and images in a realistic and involved manner. Second, the term 'image' need not be narrowly relegated to a visual picture. Auditions, sensations, feelings, movements, tensions, smells, and tastes are all included under the generic term 'imagery.' It might be better terminology to call the process 'imaginative representation,' thereby avoiding the classical battle in experimental psychology concerning whether there are really 'pictures in our heads' or whether there are just representations (see Block 1981). Third, the imaginative world is experienced as autonomous; the imager does not have the sense that he is making up these productions, but feels that he is getting involved in an already created process.

ETHNOGRAPHIC PARALLELS

If these methods have been extant and viable over half of a century in our own culture, and indeed can be found even in Western religious practices as in Loyola's meditative exercises (see Mottola and Gleason 1964), it would be surprising indeed not to find something similar in examples from other cultures. But when one starts to look for such 'waking dreams' in other cultures, at once it becomes quite plain that there is a confusion of terminology. First of all ethnographers themselves have not had the term 'waking dreams' (which almost seems a contradiction in our culture) uppermost in their minds when doing fieldwork. What might conceivably have been coded this way has been relegated to nocturnal dreams on the one hand or visions on the other hand. We see immediately the difficulty with respect to the well-known Australian dream time. As has always been appreciated (Stanner 1972, 1979) the aborigines themselves chose the English term 'the dreaming' or just 'dreaming' as the nearest approximation to the indigenous term *alcheringa*, used by the Arunta, or Aranda tribe. Despite what these particular aborigines said in finding the equivalent term in English, it seems that *alcheringa* is not precisely what we understand in English as 'dreaming,' as otherwise the aborigine who complained to Stanner in a lyrical way that 'White man got no dreaming, him go 'nother way' (Stanner 1972:270) would make no sense. Most of the commentators on 'the dreaming' realized that they were dealing with a concept that was difficult to understand. Stanner even admitted that 'why the blackfellow thinks of "dreaming" as the nearest equivalent in English is a puzzle.' The emphasis in the anthropological literature has always fallen on the end product of the myth, seeing the dream time as a kind of sacred or heroic time, that nonetheless is still present. It is true that some ethnographers have remarked on the mutual interaction of dreaming and waking with the aborigines. Berndt (1951:72) noted that the aborigines performed rituals in dreams, or made designs, or heard songs that were applied to these activities in later life. But the psychological status of the dream time has always been a puzzle.

As a matter of fact it is not only the ethnographer who may have trouble; sometimes the informant – in talking with a questioner from another culture – finds it difficult. Thus a Southern Cheyenne reported: 'It may be I was dreaming, but it does not seem like a dream' (Marquis 1931:52). Another informant was at pains to state to a white ethnographer that what he experienced wasn't like a dream. The material comes from an Oglala Sioux.

> It's like this: it isn't a dream. At night you go to bed and think hard on something. Like say, just anything, a car probably. Think hard on it, worry about it, and in a dream you will dream about a car. It's not like that, the visions come, whether you're thinking about a car, a horse will appear, or something different, you know what I mean. It's like looking out in space and suddenly somebody shows you a picture. It's like that. (Powers 1977:137)

If the waking dream cannot be assimilated to a nocturnal dream, then the term 'vision' is the alternative. The term is usually used for some highly idealized experience and reflects a value judgment. Some ethnographers, like Elmendorf with the Twana, have remarked on the waking, delusional appearance of a vision, and note that it 'was not sharply distinguished from a trance, an hallucination in a semiconscious state' (Elmendorf and Kroeber 1960:494).

There is an iatrogenic quality in all these reports. A psychiatrist will talk of 'hallucinations,'[3] or allow pseudo-hallucinations if there is no delusion present; a religionist will use the term 'visions'; the student of the paranormal will prefer the word 'apparitions.' And if we are accustomed to active imagination and guided imagery, then we employ the notion of 'waking dreams.' However, there is an important difference between visions and the use of active imagination. The latter method is used consciously, and can be construed in terms of learning. Visions, on the other hand, are usually spontaneous and characteristically burst through into an individual's ordinary consciousness.

Difficult though it may be there are one or two pristine examples of what I am talking about that can be found in the ethnographic literature. One comes from Elkin's book *Aboriginal Men of High Degree* (1977). An aboriginal informant is commenting to an ethnographer on the behavior of an old man lying on the ground:

> Do not play near him, because he is sitting down by himself with his thoughts in order to 'see.' He is gathering those thoughts so that he can feel and hear. Perhaps he then lies down, getting into a special posture, so that he may 'see' when sleeping. He sees indistinct visions, and 'hears' persons talk in them. He gets up and 'looks' for those he has 'seen,' but not seeing them, he lies down again in the prescribed manner, so as to see what he has 'seen' before. He puts his head on the pillow as previously so as to 'see' (have a vision) as before. Getting up, he tells his friends to strengthen the power (*miwi*) within them, so that when they lie down they will see and feel (or become aware of) people not present, and in that way they will perceive them. (Elkin 1977:56)

This was an instance where vision and audition play the major role. Other modalities also can become enacted. Lowie, in discussing Crow religion, indicated that motor imagery is sometimes prominent in visions, 'as when the Stars appearing to an Indian throw arrows, one of which comes wriggling back' (1925:12). Or else there are kinesthetic and tactile impressions,[4] as when a Crow woman said that on one occasion, 'a weasel came to her neck, causing a curious sensation and then entered her stomach' (ibid.). Evans-Pritchard's (1958) fieldwork with the Azande prominently indicated the role of movement and bodily disturbances.

He was also quite aware that 'witch-doctors' are fully conversant with local scandal, and are quite cunning characters to boot. Nevertheless, in the Zande identification of a witch, Evans-Pritchard considered that the determination was not solely attributed to the witch-doctor's reason, but that a measure of intuition must be allowed. What happens in the process of determining the identity of a witch in Zande society is that the witch-doctor and his client quite consciously select a number of people likely to have caused the client's sickness. The witch-doctor then engages in a dance with the name of these people in his mind until he comes to a decision about the true identity of the witch.

I believe that in this secondary process of selection he is very little influenced by logic. . . It is indeed almost impossible to be more explicit, but I am convinced that they select one of the names through what is largely unconscious mental activity. . . As far as I can gather from what witch-doctors have told me, they keep their minds a blank. Suddenly one of the persons to whom he is dancing obtrudes himself upon the witch-doctor's consciousness, sometimes as a visual image, but generally by an association of the idea and name of the witch with a physiological disturbance, chiefly in a sudden quickening of the heart-beats, which begin to pulsate violently, pit-a-pat, pit-a-pat, pit-a-pat. (Evans-Pritchard 1958:175–6)

One of the Zande witch-doctors well described his state of mind: 'Witch-doctor dances and begins to see men with his eyes; his eyes see a certain man and his heart shakes about him. He dances the dance of divination in order to consider him further, and his heart shakes and shakes about him. For this reason, a witch-doctor knows that this man is a witch' (ibid.).

As the French mathematician and philosopher Blaise Pascal would have commented: the heart has its reasons which reason knows nothing of. Evans-Pritchard's comment was less poetical. He concluded that a witch-doctor while dancing 'does not simply weigh up the advantages of denouncing this or that man. Doubtless he does this to some extent, but it is evident that there is also a measure of free and unconscious association' (ibid.).

THE SENSE OF REALITY

The rise of scientific method and better knowledge of psychotic conditions has accentuated the attention paid to what is meant by 'reality.' The subject has been the arena for Western philosophers for years. 'Ultimate reality,' 'reality versus illusion,' the nature of 'physical reality,' 'reality versus myth': there is no end of talk on the subject. At least from the day of Hume there has been a consensus among Western thinkers that unless a thing can be given ostensive definition and measured, then it cannot be placed in the domain of reality. It is only in recent years, from the direction of sociology and anthropology, that reality has been given the qualifier 'social,' to indicate a construction with a social consensus. With this exception all that was not in the field of ostensive definition and measurement was thrown into the garbage heap of 'subjectivity' and given second-class citizenship. It is here that imagination was located and more or less identified with the blanket term 'fantasy.' It comes then as a surprise to find out that back in the sixteenth century, alchemists were distinguishing 'imagination' from 'fantasy' (see von Franz 1975:204–5) and that the medieval figure of Paracelsus was contrasting 'true imagination' with 'fantasy,' which he identified as the 'madman's cornerstone' (see Watkins 1981:18). Furthermore, as Engell (1981, ch. 13) has so well documented, throughout the eighteenth century in English usage there was a growing distinction between fancy and imagination, formalized later by Coleridge. Clearly there was a psychological distinction being made here that escapes us now. Whatever the distinction may be, it seems to be the case that the factor of *perceived reality* is crucial. We have already noted this with the Jungian advocacy for successful active imagination. It is a commonplace observation that good hypnotic subjects are immersed in their internal reality.

Recently I hypnotized two young women into sharing a fantasy.[5] The excerpt given here is instructive for noting the sophistication that a perceived reality can extend to. One of the women had an alter ego in this altered state, and she was more experienced than the other in realizing, while being hypnotized, what was going on. The name of the alter ego of the first woman is Leyla, and the name of the other woman is Jean. The conversation between them and myself as the hypnotist occurred as they were both going down a tunnel. Jean remarked: 'There seems to be a red hue coming from somewhere.' I turned to the other subject, addressing her as her alter ego: 'Do you see that, Leyla?' 'Yes,' she answered and laughed. I asked her why she laughed, and she answered: 'Jean need only to relate cognitively to know that she is but seeing the inside of her mind – and her desires, and that part of herself that she calls the inner core of her being.' After this Buddhist blast from the imperious Leyla, I turned to Jean and asked her if she understood that: 'That this cave is inside your mind?' Jean struggled to grasp the idea. 'I can understand that, but it seems to have an existence in itself. I can feel the cold, the damp.' This naivety was too much for Leyla. She interrupted: 'It is totally external because you make it external. It has as much reality as a cave you'd walk into in – Appalachia.'

The seeming reality of internal events was a phenomenon that gripped Freud's attention for many years. Indeed it was almost the starting point of his new inquiry into psychological phenomena, when he began to realize that the incestuous memories of his hysterical patients were imagined and were not necessarily of actual events. At one time he wrote that 'psychical reality was of more importance than material reality' (Freud 1925b), although he immediately qualified this statement as pertaining to people with a neurosis.[6] It is interesting to note that when Freud looked at the anthropological material in his 'Totem and Taboo' (1913a) he was faced with the same concern. After noting that behind the guilt of the neurotic are always *psychical* realities and not *factual* ones (italics in the original), he asked whether this may not be true also of 'primitive men,' who 'overvalued their psychical acts to an extraordinary degree.' He came to the conclusion that 'physical reality' had a share in the matter as well. Hence he was led to the idea that 'primitive men actually *did* what all the evidence shows that they intended to do,' and thus went on to formulate his historical notion of the origin of totemism, which elicited so much concern with the anthropologists of his day.

What appears to heighten the sense of reality is the autonomous nature of the internal events, which marks it off from the more mundane experience of imagination that most of us share. People, animals, beings appear as if they had independent volitions. The situation is not like that of psychic puppetry, in which the puppet master is aware of pulling the strings. It is this sense of being plunged into or immersed in an already existing scene that heightens the sense of reality. In this connection I find it significant that Godfrey Lienhardt, in referring to what he termed the 'image' of the Dinka representations of divinities and powers, found difficulty in expressing in our Western idiom that which was experienced by the Dinka people. He made a revealing point: 'It is perhaps significant that in ordinary English usage we have no word to indicate an opposite of "actions" in relation to human self. If the word "passions," *passiones*, were still normally current as the opposite of "actions," it would be possible to say that the Dinka Powers were the images of human *passiones* seen as the active sources of those *passiones*' (Lienhardt 1961:151). Vincent Crapanzano, in his book on the Muslim Brotherhood of the Hamadsha, also commented on this quotation from Lienhardt, and followed him in the use of the term 'image,' but went further in stressing that the various elements of the religion of the Hamadsha – saints, *djinns*, and so forth – 'are not logical constructs . . . they are elements in what I would call the participational mode of explanation of illness as therapy' (1973:213). The term 'participational mode' betrays just this sense of involvement with and immersion in an already existing universe that so illustra *mundus imaginalis*, as Corbin (1972) called it. It will be remen of course, that *participation mystique* was a hallmark of Lévy-Bru (1923) pre-logical mentality.

We may suppose that tolerance of what is and what is not reality is itself a cultural projection. Recently the Native American artist Jamake Highwater has asked his contemporaries to accept that 'intuition is capable of existing as apparition, as virtual image . . . a *substance* independent of materiality' (1981:80). Highwater recognized that with this acceptance, we are entering an entirely different cosmos from the one in which the West exists, but then he goes on to exclaim inclusively that '*everything* that happens to us, everything we think, everything we envision, imagine, conceive, perceive, dream, and intuit, is a real and vital part of our lives' (ibid.:81).

The role of the social scientist is not, of course, to pass judgment on what should be the case. It is within the social scientist's mandate that analysis be made of the varieties of acceptance to reality, and its possible connections with other domains of society, such as social organization and, most notably, religion and myth.

THE THEATRICAL ELEMENT

The sense of reality is reinforced by not only participating in the imaginative productions 'in the head' so to speak, that is, not only ideationally, but by acting out the internal events. It would be too far from our theme to discuss the origin of the theater or the nature of tribal theater. But it is the case that there is a very thin line between treating an internal character on an 'as-if' basis and actually *being* that character. This would be further reinforced if two or three or more were acting out in this way. We know from our own Western theater that there are schools, such as the Stanislavsky (1937) school, which encourage thorough identification with the role. And we know from consideration of the morality plays in the Middle Ages, the *commedia dell'arte* movement in Italy, and the early days of pantomime that there was a thin membrane between the events on the stage and everyday life events. We may know little of the nature of empathy, but we do know that so-called role-playing or role enactment extends further than a charade.[7] The importance of role-playing in what has been called hypnosis has stretched to the point where the former term is considered a better choice than 'hypnosis' itself for the phenomena exhibited.[8]

Actually, the distinction between role-*taking* (as a psychological concept) as distinct from role-*playing* (as a sociological concept), due first to Coutu (1951), emphasizes the identity element even further. To return to the ethnographic literature, it is also the fact that hypnosis has been invoked for much of the phenomena of spirit possession (e.g., Walker 1972). This explanation does not really advance our knowledge of the subject, as hypnosis itself is in dire need of proper explanation. But there has also been noticed, in the literature on possession, the theatrical element. Sheila Walker in her book on African ceremonialism and spirit possession cites the French ethnographer Leiris's (1958:7–8) observations on the Zar cult to the effect that the spirit personalities offer ready-made attitudes and behavior, 'are half-way between real-life and the theater' (Walker 1972:85). The Bori cult of the Maguzawa Hausa provides a variety of institutional spirit personalities which the participants identify with and act out, possessed, in front of an appreciative audience. I witnessed this myself with Robert LeVine in 1969.

There are good accounts of the phenomena in Oesterreich (1966), who drew on the early ethnographers, and in Greenberg's (1946) monograph. Greenberg lists sixty-eight spirits, whose characteristics the participants of the Bori imitate. An excerpt from one of the earlier ethnographers indicates the pattern: '[the dancer] will continue to act up to his name [i.e. the spirit character], his words and actions being supposed to be due to the spirit by which he is possessed, and if it is not clear which spirit it is, the chief *mai-bori* [master of ceremonies] present will explain, or the performer may do so' (Tremearne, as cited by Oesterreich 1966:258–9). Oesterreich then goes on to state 'there is, for example, the Bori Malam Alhaji. He is a scholar and pilgrim. He pretends to be old and trembling, as if counting little pellets with his right hand, holding meanwhile in the left a book which he reads. He walks bent double, with a crutch, and is all the time tired out and coughing' (ibid.).

On the other side of the world we meet much the same in Haitian voodoo. In a well-known article Alfred Metraux remarked on the dramatic elements in ritual possession: 'The spirits, regardless of their sex, enter the bodies of either men or women. The subjects must, by their clothing or their behavior, indicate the change which has taken place in them' (Metraux 1957:22). Thus, 'the one visited by the serpent-god Damballah sticks out his tongue, slithers along the ground, or hangs head down from the roof-beams' (ibid.). Metraux made the point that unlike the hysteric, who exhibits idiosyncratic means of expression, 'the ritual of possession must conform to the classic image of a mythical personage' (ibid.:24). Elsewhere in this article Metraux pointed to occasions when the person fell into spontaneous possessions, in the street, in the market, but the normative occasion is during the ritual, which Metraux recognized as having all of the attributes of theater. Metraux, like other anthropologists, was plagued with the problem of what was 'sincere' or 'authentic' possession as distinct from a put-on. 'The . . . [possessed] person does not *play* a person, he *is* that personage throughout the trance' (ibid.:25), he wrote; but also acknowledged that it is not so easy to tell the difference. The same difficulty of distinction has been noted in the hypnosis literature and with Western mediums.

The question of authenticity turns on the concept of control. When the 'act' gets out of control, appears spontaneously, the tendency is to regard it as authentic. When there is control, the tendency is to view it as simulation. Peters and Price-Williams in their survey of forty-four shamanistic societies made the point that 'ideally, the shaman's ecstasy is controlled role involvement with intense organismic participation and communicative rapport' (1980:401–2). The mimetic quality of the shaman has long been noted. A clue to understanding this involvement may come from the active imagination literature. The unconscious often appears to speak in an oracular way, as if it were addressing an audience, and as von Franz said, 'these contents often express themselves in a solemn and pompous way, a hellish mixture of the sublime and ridiculous' (1975:111). Jung himself complained that 'archetypes speak the language of high rhetoric, even of bombast' (1965:178). In other words, we have the language of the mythopoetic function.

The further step to be taken is to recognize that the mythopoetic function need not be restricted to words. It can be expressed in action. Here again the psycho-therapeutic literature can help us. In Watkins's book *Waking Dreams*, there is a section devoted to the so-called oneirodrama (1976:67–8), mainly describing the therapies outlined by Frétigny and Virel (1968). The main point to be noted here is that the subject of oneirodrama does not only conceive of a scene; he or she participates in the scene via what is called the 'imaginary corporal ego.' This would mean the extension of active imagination from couch to theater, and from intra-individual to inter-individual. The state of mind is probably the same in each for the individuals concerned. It has long been our habit to associate this frame of mind with passivity and sleep so that the possibility of an imaginative behavior expressed in action has escaped us – except on the theatrical stage, where it is generally conceived as being 'put on.' The identification of hypnosis with sleep has reinforced this habit. Yet it is not necessary to elicit the phenomena of hypnotism by suggestions of sleep and relaxation.

The classical induction procedure used in hypnosis probably stemmed from the medical model of earlier times where the patient is presented with an authoritarian doctor, or at least is expected to submit passively to the active role of the practitioner. Mesmer's form of induction was, as a matter of fact, more active. It was quickly reformed by the medical men – such as Elliotson, Esdaile, and Braid – into a more passive form where the subject sat or lay down and was commanded by the doctor (see Bramwell 1903, ch. 3). In the 1960s Ludwig and Lyle (1964) got their subjects in hypnosis to walk and spin around, and encouraged alertness. Gibbons (1976) introduced a new hypnotic technique called 'hyperempiria' that directly instructed subjects to be wide awake. Banyai and Hilgard describe making their subjects ride a bicycle ergometer while giving them instructions of alertness: 'Just sit on the bicycle with your hands on the handlebars and pedal. I want you to pedal steadily and while pedaling, listen to what I say. Your ability to enter a state of alert hypnosis depends partly on your willingness to cooperate and partly on your ability to pedal the bicycle steadily, while concentrating on my words' (1976:219).[9]

Finally, we should take into account the emphasis that Josephine Hilgard (1979, chs. 4 and 7) placed on the theatrical component in hypnotic states. She stressed that hypnotically susceptible individuals 'are sensitive to situations and people, they react emotionally to the mood that is created, and they reenact situations with felt emotion, even though they modify the details' (ibid.:64).

INTERPRETATION

If we assume that perceived alternate realities through the medium of waking dreams can be found in diverse cultures, how may they be interpreted by the different folk groups themselves? I am not talking here about folk notions of symbols – what a cosmic tree might mean, and so forth. I am talking about the more generalized question about the relationship of two realities. If we are to suppose that as much reality is given to the inner world as to the outer world, how are the two related? We may allow that the distinction of inner and outer is founded on a certain philosophy of mind, and we may further suppose that the notion of 'mind' in the first place also requires a basic philosophy. But I am not referring to this either. I am referring to the simple question that arises when such entities of myth as flying horses and talking deer are encountered: How are they marked off from the daily routine of sense perception, where such entities are clearly not encountered? Failure to mark them off, and treat them differently than one would a neighbor's cow or dog, would mean psychosis, and we may suppose that indigenous people have, on the whole, quite clear notions of madness.

One way of distinguishing the two realities is by the use of ritual space. The reality of the imaginative leap, the entities and actions encountered in imaginal space, is carried out in the *temenos*, the sacred ground, the theater, the altar. This is what marks the process off from sense perception reality. Here I am emphasizing what seems to be the normative case. It would need a detailed analysis of every instance to find out if this is an invariant across cultures. In other words, the imaginative process – what I am calling here the mythopoetic function – is not carried on outside of the ritual space. It is not extended into the common domestic sphere, the market or the areas of ordinary work. Or if in some cases it is, then the idea of a special time is invoked. The subject is really discussed in Leach's essay on 'Time and False Noses' (1979), which relies on the Durkheimian notion of sacred and profane, and goes into the origin of festivals. My point here is that demarcating time in a special way is an alternative method to demarcation of space, of keeping the two realities separate and not confused. The classic distinction of sacred and profane is thus reached anew, on pragmatic psychological grounds and not religious ones.[10]

Similar reasoning can be applied to the interpretation given to the formulations of the imaginative process. Again, we may balk at the idea that everybody uses symbolism, in the specialized interpretive sense in which we have understood this term in the West. But we may not balk at the suggestion that everyone strives for *meaning*. Eliade, who incidentally was one of the first scholars to appreciate the importance of waking dreams in religious thought, in discussing Desoille's use of symbols in his type of psychotherapy, had this to say about symbols: 'In the frame of reference in which they were known to the historian of religions, these symbols express the *attitudes* taken up by man and, at the same time, the *realities* he is confronting, and these are always sacred realities, for, at the archaic level of culture, the *sacred* is the pre-eminently *real*' (Eliade 1960:117; italics in the original).

I am focussing now, quite simply, on symbols as attitudes, and am asking the question: How do various cultures which may practice this imaginative art regard the contents of their art? Do they take them in the same literal and functional way as the observation of everyday life? Or are they regarded in some special way, requiring interpretation? Again, an exhaustive inquiry would have to be made to answer this succinctly. In the meantime I suggest that there may well be variation here, especially when we deal not only with immediate perception but with the memory of the experience. We note for example in Lienhardt's work that when the Dinka refer to the activity of a Power, it is 'to offer an interpretation, and not merely a description, of experience' (1961:148). This would seem to suggest that the Dinka would go along with the psychologist Hillman's assertion that psychic images are not identical to sense images or pictures but are rather 'images as metaphors' (1979:272). Sociolinguists and ethnolinguists might assist here, to find out whether imaginative creations are discussed in a specific linguistic manner, prefixed with a specific tense, for example, or otherwise introduced in a manner distinct from how external events are discussed.[11]

However, I think that there is evidence to suppose that internal and external realities do get intertwined when they are remembered over time. This was the case of Freud's women patients with their incestuous memories. It was true for the Trobriand Islanders of Malinowski's time who pointed out the precise locales where the emerging clans of the Trobriand creation surfaced (Malinowski 1954:113–14). It was true of the Huichol hallucinogenic plants which were personified to mix in with actual historical trends in Huichol life (Furst 1976:137–8).

IMPLICATIONS FOR ANTHROPOLOGY

In a discipline already well endowed with terms in need of explanation, it is not my intention to add to its burden yet others – waking dream or the mythopoetic function. But if either of these terms alerts the discipline to the interface of waking and dreaming, a truly liminal state, they would have served their purpose. Our concern here is with the continuum between the dream in sleep and the dream in waking consciousness, suggesting emphasis be given to the activity of dreaming, as distinct from the noun 'dreams.' The interchange of dreams while asleep and the waking life of the culture has been remarked on by almost every ethnographer of dreams since Lincoln (1935). There is always a terminological difficulty in pinning down something which is inherently dynamic and elusive. Burridge (1960), for example, in his book on a New Guinean cargo cult, tried to introduce the concept of 'myth-dream,' which he felt to be important. Although he admitted that 'myth-dream' does not lend itself to precise definition, 'nevertheless, myth-dreams exist, and they may be reduced to a series of themes, propositions, and problems which are to be found in myths, in dreams, in the half-lights of conversation, and in the emotional responses to a variety of actions, and questions asked. Through this kind of intellectualization myth-dreams become "aspirations" ' (ibid.:148).

What I would like to emphasize is the transaction between dreams and waking life, which reaches its asymptote in the waking dream.

A further consideration is the determination of learning principles that are employed to elicit the waking dream, and the understanding of dispositional conditions in the individual that might promote their occurrence. Lengthy attention should be given to the nature of the transaction, to its content. The mythopoetic function can produce drivel as well as wisdom; it can be wholly idiosyncratic as well as culturally patterned; it can produce good stories and literature as well as acceptable myths. The problem for an anthropology of the imaginal is to find out why one imaginary production elicits social support and another does not. The social matrix is crucial, for on this depends the development of an institutional setting for what otherwise would be mere individual images. Asking what kind of social conditions can bring about this social support would take us into the domains of the historian of religions, sociologist, and political scientist. A study of the intertwining of psychic and physical realities covers a lot of territory.

NOTES

1. This chapter was supported in part by the Socio-Behavioral Research Group, Mental Retardation Research Center, School of Medicine, University of California, Los Angeles, California, and by an NICHD grant, HD 11944.
2. See Watkins (1976) for a good survey of these therapies.
3. The relationship of experiences that have been coded as hallucinations to waking dreams via active imagination is an

issue that would require a further article. In the cultural sphere, Wallace's (1959) treatment of the subject and La Barre's (1975) review cover the essential points of the anthropological perspective on hallucinations.

4. During our discussions at the seminar in Santa Fe, Barbara Tedlock provided an important reference to feelings of blood flow and tactility among the Quiché; a complex of sensations which had its own semantic system, which was shared among groups. For more detail about this see Tedlock (this volume and 1982, ch. 6).
5. Article in preparation with co-authors D. L. King and K. Mann. Some of the ideas in the present chapter and another article in preparation were first presented as an Invited Address to the Society for Cross-Cultural Research, Minneapolis, February 1982.
6. Freud first made a distinction between 'thought-reality' and 'external reality' in 1895. As the editors of the Standard Edition of his works note (see Freud 1895b), the distinction was first made between 'psychical' and 'factual' reality. In later discussions 'factual' was changed to 'material,' which reverted in his last writings to 'external.'
7. In our discussions in Santa Fe, Gil Herdt made the point that recent psychiatric work indicated that 'identity' and 'identification' should be seen as a continuum, to the extent that what at one point on the continuum could be designated as imposture of a character could at another point merge into belief in being that character.
8. There has been a lively debate in the literature on hypnosis for years (see Sarbin 1950, Barber 1972, and Hilgard 1977).
9. During our seminar discussions, Ellen Basso said that when she was in Brazil she was struck by the pattern repetition of dance among the Kalapalo as being congruent with this example of active hypnotic induction. She also made the important point that waking dreams required a channel of expression, tied in with specific dispositional learning processes.
10. In Santa Fe, Waud Kracke brought up the point that in some cultures the period of mourning stimulated involuntary visions. Mourning, then, in these cultures, would represent a 'special time.'
11. Three linguistically oriented anthropologists at our seminar discussed special grammatical elements and lexical items that are used by native speakers in distinguishing the imaginal from the real, for the Kagwahiv (Kracke, pp. 34-5), Cuzco Quechua (Mannheim, p. 146), and Quiché Maya (Tedlock, pp. 120-2).

References

Abraham, Karl. 1909. 'Dreams and Myths: A Study in Folk Psychology,' in *Clinical Papers and Essays on Psychoanalysis* (New York: Basic Books, 1955)

Adams, Richard N. 1975. *Energy and Structure: A Theory of Social Power* (Austin: University of Texas Press)

Adorno, Rolena. 1974. 'Racial scorn and critical contempt,' *Diacritics* 4 (4):2–7

1978. 'Las otras fuentes de Guaman Poma: Sus lecturas castellanas,' *Historica* 2(2):137–58

Akuts Nugkai, Tímias, *et al.* 1979. *Historia Aguaruna*, Primera Etapa, Segunda Parte, Tomo III (Yarinacocha, Peru: Instituto Lingüístico del Verano)

Amiotte, Arthur. 1982. 'Our Other Selves: The Lakota Dream Experience,' *Parabola* 7 (2):26–32

Antrobus, John S. 1978. 'Dreaming for Cognition,' in *The Mind in Sleep*, ed. Arthur M. Arkin, John S. Antrobus, and Stephen J. Ellman (Hillsdale, N.J.: Lawrence Erlbaum)

Antrobus, John S., and Howard Ehrlichman. 1981. 'The "Dream" Report: Attention, Memory, Functional Hemispheric Asymmetry, and Memory Organization,' in *Sleep, Dreams and Memory*, ed. William Fishbein, Advances in Sleep Research, vol. 6 (New York: Spectrum)

Applebee, Arthur N. 1978. *The Child's Concept of Story: Ages Two to Seventeen* (Chicago, Ill.: University of Chicago Press)

Arkin, Arthur M. 1981. *Sleep-Talking: Psychology and Psychophysiology* (Hillsdale, N.J.: Lawrence Erlbaum)

Arkin, Arthur M., John S. Antrobus, and Stephen J. Ellman. 1978. *The Mind in Sleep* (Hillsdale, N.J.: Lawrence Erlbaum)

Arriaga, Pablo José de. 1621. *Extirpación de la idolatria en el Perú*, reprinted in *Cronicas peruanas de interés indígena*, ed. Francisco Esteve Barba, Biblioteca de Autores Españoles, 209 (Madrid: Atlas, 1968)

Asante, S. K. B. 1977. *Pan-African Protest: West Africa and the Italo-Ethiopian Crisis, 1934–1941* (London: Longman)

Aserinsky, Eugen, and Nathaniel Kleitman. 1953. 'Regularly Occurring Periods of Eye Motility, and Concomitant Phenomena, during Sleep,' *Science* **118**:273–4

Assagioli, Roberto. 1965. *Psychosynthesis: A Manual of Principles and Techniques* (New York: Hobbs, Dorman)

Austin, J. L. 1962. *How to Do Things with Words* (Oxford: Oxford University Press)

Avens, Roberts. 1980. *Imagination is Reality* (Dallas, Texas: Spring Publications)

Ayer, A. J. 1960. 'Professor Malcolm on Dreams,' *Journal of Philosophy* **57**:517–35

Bachelard, Gaston. 1969. *The Poetics of Reverie*, trans. Daniel Russell (Boston, Mass.: Beacon)

1971. *On Poetic Imagination and Reverie* (Indianapolis: Bobbs-Merrill)

Banyai, E. E., and E. R. Hilgard. 1976. 'A Comparison of Active-Alert Hypnotic Induction with Traditional Relaxation Induction,' *Journal of Abnormal Psychology* **85**:218–24

Barber, Theodore X. 1972. 'Suggested ("Hypnotic") Behavior: The Trance Paradigm versus an Alternative Paradigm,' in *Hypnosis: Research Developments and Perspectives*, ed. Erika Fromm and Ronald Shor (Chicago, Ill.: Aldine-Atherton)

Barber, Theodore X., Nicholas P. Spanos, and John F. Chaves. 1974. *Hypnosis, Imagination, and Human Potentialities* (New York: Pergamon)

Barnouw, Victor. 1963. *Culture and Personality* (Homewood, Ill.: Dorsey)

Barth, Frederick. 1975. *Ritual and Knowledge Among the Baktaman of New Guinea* (New Haven, Conn.: Yale University Press)

Basso, Ellen B. 1973. *The Kalapalo Indians of Central Brazil* (New York: Holt, Rinehart & Winston)

1985. *A Musical View of the Universe: Kalapalo Myth and Ritual Performances* (Philadelphia: University of Pennsylvania Press)

Basso, Keith H., and Henry A. Selby. 1976. *Meaning in Anthropology* (Albuquerque: University of New Mexico Press),School of American Research Advanced Seminar Series

Bateson, Gregory. 1968. 'Conventions of Communication: Where Validity Depends upon Belief,' in *Communication: The Social Matrix of*

Psychiatry, ed. Jurgen Ruesch and Gregory Bateson (New York: Norton)
1972. *Steps to an Ecology of Mind* (New York: Ballantine Books)
1980. 'Some Components of Socialization for Trance,' in *Socialization as Cultural Communication*, ed. Theodore Schwartz (Berkeley: University of California Press)
Bauman, Richard. 1977. *Verbal Art as Performance* (Rowley, Mass.: Newbury House)
Beckwith, Martha W. 1929. *Black Roadways: A Study of Jamaican Folk Life* (Chapel Hill: University of North Carolina Press)
Bennett, Wendell C., and Robert M. Zingg. 1935. *The Tarahumara: An Indian Tribe of Northern Mexico* (Chicago, Ill.: University of Chicago Press)
Berblinger, Klaus W. 1960. 'The Quiet Hysteric and His Captive Respondent,' *Diseases of the Nervous System* **21**:386–9
Berensohn, Paulus. 1968. *Finding One's Way with Clay* (New York: Simon & Schuster)
Beres, David. 1960. 'Perception, Imagination, and Reality,' *International Journal of Psycho-Analysis* **41**:327–34
Berger, Hans. 1930. 'Ueber das Elektroen-kephalogramm des Menschen,' *Journal of Psychological Neurology* **40**:160–79
Berndt, Ronald M. 1951. *Kunapipi: A Study of an Australian Aboriginal Religious Cult* (Melbourne: Cheshire)
Berry, Patricia. 1982. 'An Approach to the Dream,' in *Echo's Subtle Body: Contributions to an Archetypal Psychology* (Dallas, Texas: Spring Publications)
Bettelheim, Bruno. 1977. *The Uses of Enchantment: The Meaning and Importance of Fairy Tales* (New York: Random House)
1983. *Freud and Man's Soul* (New York: Alfred A. Knopf)
Bilby, Kenneth, and Elliott Leib. 1983. 'From Kongo to Zion: Three Black Musical Traditions from Jamaica,' liner notes to the album *From Kongo to Zion* (Cambridge, Mass.: Heartbeat Records)
Billiard, Michel. 1976. 'Competition Between the Two Types of Sleep, and the Recuperative Function of REM Sleep versus NREM Sleep in Narcoleptics,' in *Narcolepsy*, ed. Christian Guilleminault, William Dement, and Pierre Passouant, Advances in Sleep Research, vol. 3 (New York: Spectrum)
Blau, Harold. 1963. 'Dream Guessing: a Comparative Analysis,' *Ethnohistory* **10**:233–49
Block, Ned J. 1981. *Imagery* (Cambridge, Mass.: MIT Press)
Bloom, Joseph D., and Richard D. Gelardin. 1976. 'Eskimo Sleep Paralysis,' *Arctic* **29**:20–6
Bock, Philip. 1980. *Continuities in Psychological Anthropology* (San Francisco, California: W. H. Freeman)
Bonime, Walter. 1962. *The Clinical Use of Dreams* (New York: Basic Books)

Borges, Jorge Luis. 1956. *Fictions* (London: John Calder)

* Bourguignon, Erika. 1972. 'Dreams and Altered States of Consciousness in Anthropological Research,' in *Psychological Anthropology*, 2nd edition, ed. Francis Hsu (Cambridge, Mass.: Schenkman)

1973. *Religion, Altered States of Consciousness, and Social Change* (Columbus: Ohio State University Press)

1976. *Possession* (San Francisco, California: Chandler & Sharp)

Brambila, David. 1980. *Diccionario Rarámuri-Castellano (Tarahumara)* (México: La Buena Prensa)

Bramwell, John M. 1903. *Hypnotism: Its History, Practice and Theory* (New York: Julian Press, 1956)

Brathwaite, Edward Kamu. 1974. 'The African Presence in Caribbean Literature,' in *Slavery, Colonialism, and Racism*, ed. Sidney W. Mintz (New York: Norton)

1978. 'The Spirit of African Survival in Jamaica,' *Jamaica Journal* **42**:45–67

Breger, Louis. 1980. 'The Manifest Dream and its Latent Content,' in *The Dream in Clinical Practice*, ed. J. M. Natterson (New York: Jason Aronson)

Bro, Harmon. 1979. 'Procedures to Increase Dream Recall,' *Sundance: Community Dream Journal* **3**:122–30

Brock, S., and B. Wiesel. 1941. 'The Narcoleptic-Cataplectic Syndrome – An Excessive and Dissociated Reaction of the Sleep Mechanism and its Accompanying Mental States,' *Journal of Nervous and Mental Disease* **94**:700–12

Brown, Michael F. 1984. *Una paz incierta: Historia y cultura de las comunidades aguarunas frente al impacto de la carretera marginal* (Lima, Peru: Centro Amazónico de Antropología y Aplicación Práctica)

1985. 'Individual Experience, Dreams, and the Identification of Magical Stones in an Amazonian Society,' in *Directions in Cognitive Anthropology*, ed. J. W. D. Dougherty (Urbana: University of Illinois Press)

Bruce, Robert D. 1975. *Lacandon Dream Symbolism*, vol. 1 (México: Ediciones Euroamericanas)

1979. *Lacandon Dream Symbolism*, vol. 2 (México: Ediciones Euroamericanas)

Bunzel, Ruth L. 1932a. 'Introduction to Zuñi Ceremonialism,' *Annual Report of the Bureau of American Ethnology* **47**:467–544

1932b. 'Zuñi Origin Myths,' *Annual Report of the Bureau of American Ethnology* **47**:545–610

Burgess, Don. 1985. 'Leyendas Tarahumaras,' in *Tarahumara*, ed. Bob Schalkwijk, luís gonzález Rodrígues, and Don Burgess (México: Chrysler de México)

Burke, Kenneth. 1945. *A Grammar of Motives* (New York: Prentice-Hall)

1950. *A Rhetoric of Motives* (New York: Prentice-Hall)

1966a. *Language as Symbolic Action* (Berkeley: University of California Press)

1966b. *The Philosophy of Literary Form* (Berkeley: University of California Press)

Burridge, Kenelm. 1960. *Mambu: A Melanesian Millennium* (London: Methuen)

Bye, Robert A., Jr. 1979. 'Hallucinogenic Plants of the Tarahumara,' *Journal of Ethnopharmacology* 1:23–48

Cahen, Roland. 1966. 'The Psychology of the Dream,' in *The Dream and Human Societies*, ed. G. E. von Grunebaum and Roger Caillois (Berkeley: University of California Press)

Caillois, Roger. 1956. *L'Incertitude qui vient des rêves* (Paris: Gallimard)

1966. 'Logical and Philosophical Problems of the Dream,' in *The Dream and Human Societies*, ed. G. E. von Grunebaum and Roger Caillois (Berkeley: University of California Press)

Cartwright, Rosalind D. 1977. *Night Life: Explorations in Dreaming* (Englewood Cliffs, N.J.: Prentice-Hall)

1981. 'The Contribution of Research on Memory and Dreaming to a 24-Hour Model of Cognitive Behavior,' in *Sleep, Dreams and Memory*, ed. William Fishbein, Advances in Sleep Research, vol. 6 (New York: Spectrum)

Cassidy, Frederic G. 1974. *Jamaica Talk: Three Hundred Years of the English Language in Jamaica* (London: Macmillan)

Champion, Jean R. 1962. 'A Study in Cultural Persistence: The Tarahumaras of Northwestern Mexico' (Ph.D. diss., Columbia University)

Chevalier, Jacques M. 1982. *Civilization and the Stolen Gift: Capital, Kin, and Cult in Eastern Peru* (Toronto, Ontario: University of Toronto Press)

Chumap, Aurelio, and Manuel García-Rendueles. 1978. *Duik Muun: Universo mítico de los Aguaruna* (Lima, Peru: Centro Amazónico de Antropología y Aplicación Práctica)

Cieza de Leon. 1550. *El Señorío de los Incas* (Lima, Peru: Instituto de Estudios Peruanos, 1967)

Cobo, Bernabe. 1636. *Historia del nuevo mundo*, reprinted in *Obras del Padre Bernabe Cobo*, vol. 2, ed. F. Mateos, Biblioteca de Autores Españoles, 112 (Madrid: Atlas, 1958)

Cohen, David B. 1974. 'Toward a Theory of Dream Recall,' *Psychological Bulletin* 81:138–54

1979. *Sleep and Dreaming: Origins, Nature, and Functions* (Oxford: Pergamon Press)

Colby, Benjamin N., and Lore M. Colby. 1981. *The Daykeeper: The Life and Discourse of an Ixil Diviner* (Cambridge, Mass.: Harvard University Press)

Colby, Benjamin N., J. A. Fernandez, and D. B. Kronenfeld. 1981.

'Toward a Convergence of Cognitive and Symbolic Anthropology,' *American Ethnologist* 8:422–50

Collins, Kathleen May. 1977. 'Secret Desires in Social Contexts: An Anthropological Approach to Dreams' (M.A. thesis, University of Illinois at Chicago)

1984. 'Anthropology of Dreaming in America,' *ASD Newsletter* 1(4):1, 3

Conrad, Joseph. 1910. *Heart of Darkness & The Secret Sharer* (New York: New American Library, 1950)

Corbin, Henry. 1966. 'The Visionary Dream in Islamic Spirituality,' in *The Dream and Human Societies*, ed. G. E. von Grunebaum and Roger Caillois (Berkeley: University of California Press)

1972. '*Mundus Imaginalis*, or the Imaginary and the Imaginal,' *Spring: An Annual of Archetypal Psychology and Jungian Thought* 1972:1–19

Coutu, Walter. 1951. 'Role-Playing Versus Role-Taking: An Appeal for Clarification,' *American Sociological Review* 16:186–7

Coxhead, David, and Susan Hiller. 1976. *Dreams: Visions of the Night* (New York: Crossroad)

Crapanzano, Vincent. 1973. *The Hamadsha: A Study in Moroccan Ethnopsychiatry* (Berkeley: University of California Press)

1975. 'Saints, *Jnun* and Dreams: An Essay in Moroccan Ethnopsychology,' *Psychiatry* 38:145–59

1981. 'Text, Transference, and Indexicality,' *Ethos* 9:122–48

Crick, Francis, and Graeme Mitchison. 1983. 'The Function of Dream Sleep,' *Nature* 304:111–14

Crocker, J. Christopher. 1977. 'The Social Functions of Rhetorical Forms,' in *The Social Use of Metaphor: Essays on the Anthropology of Rhetoric*, ed. J. David Sapir and J. Christopher Crocker (Philadelphia: University of Pennsylvania Press)

Curtin, Philip D. 1955. *Two Jamaicas: The Role of Ideas in a Tropical Colony 1830–1865* (Westport, Conn.: Greenwood Press)

Curtis, Homer C., and David M. Sachs. 1976. 'Dialogue on "The Changing Use of Dreams in Psychoanalytic Practice," ' *International Journal of Psycho-Analysis* 57:343–54

Cusihuamán, Antonio G. 1976. *Gramática Quechua, Cuzco-Callao* (Lima: Instituto de Estudios Peruanos)

Custred, Glynn. 1978. 'The Theme of Social Transformation in Andean Oral Tradition,' in *Amerikanistsche Studien: Festschrift für Hermann Trimborn*, ed. Roswith Hartmann and Udo Oberem, vol. 1 (St Augustin: Anthropos Institut)

D'Andrade, Roy G. 1961. 'Anthropological Studies of Dreams,' in *Psychological Anthropology: Approaches to Culture and Personality*, ed. Francis Hsu (Homewood, Ill.: Dorsey)

Davidson, Richard J. 1980. 'Consciousness and Information Processing: A Biocognitive Perspective,' in *The Psychobiology of Consciousness*, ed. J. M. Davidson and R. J. Davidson (New York: Plenum)

Delgado de Thays, Carmen. 1968. *Religión y magía en Tupe (Yauyos)* (Cuernavaca, Mexico: Centro Intercultural de Documentación)
Dement, William. 1960. 'The Effect of Dream Deprivation,' *Science* **131**:1705–7
Dement, William, and N. Kleitman. 1957. 'The Relation of Eye Movements during Sleep to Dream Activity: An Objective Method for the Study of Dreaming,' *Journal of Experimental Psychology* **53**:339–46
Dennett, Daniel C. 1977. 'Are Dreams Experiences?,' in *Philosophical Essays on Dreaming*, ed. Charles Dunlop (Ithaca, N.Y.: Cornell University Press)
Derrida, Jacques. 1976. *Of Grammatology* (Baltimore, Maryland: Johns Hopkins University Press)
1977. 'Signature, Event, Context,' *Glyph* **1**:172–97
Desoille, Robert. 1945. *Le rêve éveillé en psychothérapie* (Paris: Presses Universitaires de France)
1966. *The Directed Daydream* (New York: Psychosynthesis Press)
Devereux, George. 1956. 'Mohave Dreams of Omen and Power,' *Tomorrow* **4**(3):17–24
1966. 'Pathogenic Dreams in Non-Western Societies,' in *The Dream and Human Societies*, ed. G. E. von Grunebaum and Roger Caillois (Berkeley: University of California Press)
1969. *Reality and Dream: Psychotherapy of a Plains Indian* (New York: Doubleday Anchor, revision of 1951 edition)
Dittman, Allen T., and Harvey C. Moore. 1957. 'Disturbance in Dreams as Related to Peyotism among the Navaho,' *American Anthropologist* **59**:642–9
Dougherty, Janet W. D., and James W. Fernandez. 1981. 'Introduction [to the Special Issue on Symbolism and Cognition],' *American Ethnologist* 8:413–21
Downing, Jack, and Robert Marmorstein. 1973. *Dreams and Nightmares: A Book of Gestalt Therapy Sessions* (New York: Harper & Row)
Drake, St Clair. 1975. 'The African Diaspora in Pan-African Perspective,' *The Black Scholar* 7(1):2–13
DuBois, Cora. 1944. *The People of Alor* (Minneapolis: University of Minnesota Press)
Dunlop, Charles E. M. 1977. *Philosophical Essays on Dreaming* (Ithaca, N.Y.: Cornell University Press)
Dunne, Peter M. 1948. *Early Jesuit Missions in Tarahumara* (Berkeley: University of California Press)
Durkheim, Émile. 1961. *The Elementary Forms of the Religious Life* (New York: Collier)
Durkheim, Émile, and Marcel Mauss. 1963. *Primitive Classification*, trans. Rodney Needham (Chicago, Ill.: University of Chicago Press)
Duviols, Pierre. 1971. *La lutte contre les religions autochtones dans le pérou colonial* (Lima: Institut Français d'Études Andines)

Earle, Duncan. 1982. 'Night Time and Dream Space for a Quiché Maya Family,' Paper presented at the 17th Mesa Redonda, Sociedad Mexicana de Antropología, San Cristobal de las Casas, Chiapas, México

Eggan, Dorothy. 1952. 'The Manifest Content of Dreams: A Challenge to Social Science,' *American Anthropologist* 54:469–85

1955. 'The Personal Use of Myth in Dreams,' *Journal of American Folklore* 68:445–63

1957. 'Hopi Dreams and a Life History Sketch,' *Primary Records in Culture and Personality* 2(16):1–147

1961. 'Dream Analysis,' in *Studying Personality Cross-Culturally*, ed. Bert Kaplan (New York: Harper & Row)

1966. 'Hopi Dreams in Cultural Perspective,' in *The Dream and Human Societies*, ed. G. E. von Grunebaum and Roger Caillois (Berkeley: University of California Press)

Eliade, Mircea. 1960. *Myths, Dreams, and Mysteries: The Encounter Between Contemporary Faiths and Archaic Realities* (New York: Harper & Row)

Elkin, Adolphus P. 1977. *Aboriginal Men of High Degree* (New York: St Martin's Press)

Ellenberger, Henri. 1970. *The Discovery of the Unconscious: The History and Evolution of Dynamic Psychiatry* (New York: Basic Books)

Elmendorf, William W., and Alfred L. Kroeber. 1960. *The Structure of Twana Culture: With Comparative Notes on the Structure of Yurok Culture*, Monograph supplement no. 2:27 (Pullman: Washington State University)

Engell, James. 1981. *The Creative Imagination: Enlightenment to Romanticism* (Cambridge, Mass.: Harvard University Press)

Evans-Pritchard, Edward E. 1958. *Witchcraft, Oracles and Magic Among the Azande* (Oxford: Clarendon Press, 1937)

Evans-Wentz, W. Y. 1958. *Tibetan Yoga and Secret Doctrines* (New York: Oxford University Press)

Fabian, Johannes. 1966. 'Dream and Charisma, "Theories of Dreams" in the Jamaa-Movement (Congo),' *Anthropos* 61:544–60

1974. 'Genres in an Emerging Tradition: An Anthropological Approach to Religious Communication,' in *Changing Perspectives in the Scientific Study of Religion*, ed. Alan W. Eister (New York: Wiley & Sons)

Fernandez, James. 1966. 'Unbelievably Subtle Words: Representation and Integration in the Sermons of an African Reformative Cult,' *History of Religions* 6:43–69

Firth, Raymond. 1934. 'The Meaning of Dreams in Tikopia,' in *Essays Presented to C. G. Seligman*, ed. E. E. Evans-Pritchard, R. Firth, B. Malinowski, and I. Schapera (London: Kegan Paul)

Fishbein, William. 1981. *Sleep, Dreams and Memory*, Advances in Sleep Research, vol. 6 (New York: Spectrum)

Fisher, C., *et al.* 1975. 'A Psychophysiological Study of Nightmares and Night Terrors, I: Physiological Aspects of Stage 4 Night Terror,' in *Psychoanalysis and Contemporary Science*, vol. 3 (New York: International Universities Press)

Flournoy, Theodore. 1900. *From India to the Planet Mars: A Study of a Case of Somnambulism with Glossolalia* (New Hyde Park, N.Y.: University Books, 1963)

Foster, George M. 1973. 'Dreams, Character, and Cognitive Orientation in Tzintzuntzan,' *Ethos* 1:106–21

Foucault, Michel. 1980. *The History of Sexuality* (New York: Pantheon)

Foulkes, David William. 1966. *The Psychology of Sleep* (New York: Scribner's)

1978. 'Dreaming as Language and Cognition,' *Scientia* **113**:481–99

1982. *Children's Dreams* (New York: Wiley & Sons)

Franz, Marie-Louise von. 1975. *C. G. Jung: His Myth in Our Time* (Boston: Little Brown)

1976. *Confrontation with the Collective Unconscious* (Los Angeles, California: C. G. Jung Cassette Library)

French, Thomas M., and Erika Fromm. 1964. *Dream Interpretation: A New Approach* (New York: Basic Books)

Frétigny, Roger, and André Virel. 1968. *L'Imagerie mentale: Introduction à l'onirothérapie* (Geneva: Mont Blanc)

Freud, Sigmund. 1894. 'The Neuro-Psychoses of Defense,' in *The Standard Edition of the Complete Psychological Works of Sigmund Freud*, vol. 3, trans. and ed. James Strachey (London: Hogarth Press and the Institute of Psycho-Analysis, 1955)

1895a. 'Project for a Scientific Psychology,' in *The Origins of Psychoanalysis*, ed. Eric Mosbacher and James Strachey (New York: Basic Books, 1954)

1895b. 'Attempt to Represent Normal Psychological Processes (2),' in *The Standard Edition*, vol. 3

1900. 'The Interpretation of Dreams,' in *The Standard Edition*, vols. 4–5

1901. 'On Dreams,' in *The Standard Edition*, vol. 5

1908. 'The Relation of the Poet to Day-Dreaming,' in *Character and Culture*, ed. P. Rieff (New York: Collier Books, 1963)

1909. 'The Analysis of a Phobia in a Five-Year-Old Boy,' in *The Standard Edition*, vol. 10

1913a. 'Totem and Taboo,' in *The Standard Edition*, vol. 13

1913b. 'The Occurrence in Dreams of Material from Fairy-Tales,' in *Character and Culture*, ed. P. Rieff (New York: Collier Books, 1963)

1915. 'The Unconscious,' in *The Standard Edition*, vol. 14

1916–17. 'Introductory Lectures on Psycho-Analysis, in *The Standard Edition*, vols. 15–16

1923a. 'The Ego and the Id,' in *The Standard Edition*, vol. 19

1923b. 'Remarks on the Theory and Practice of Dream Interpretation,' in *The Standard Edition*, vol. 19

1925a. 'Additional Notes on Dream Interpretation as a Whole,' in *The Standard Edition*, vol. 19

1925b. 'An Autobiographical Study,' in *The Standard Edition*, vol. 20

1933. 'New Introductory Lectures on Psycho-analysis,' in *The Standard Edition*, vol. 22

Fried, Jacob. 1969. 'The Tarahumara,' in *Handbook of Middle American Indians*, gen. ed. Robert Wauchope, vol. 8, pt. 2, ed. Evon Z. Vogt (Austin: University of Texas Press)

Friedrich, Paul. 1985. 'The Poetry of Language in the Politics of Dreams,' *Dreamworks* **4**(4):265–78

Furst, Peter. 1976. *Hallucinogens and Culture* (San Francisco, California: Chandler & Sharp)

Galin, David. 1974. 'Applications for Psychiatry of Left and Right Cerebral Specialization: A Neurophysiological Context for Unconscious Processes,' *Archives of General Psychiatry* **31**:572–83

Garcilaso de la Vega, El Inca. 1609. *Primera Parte de los Commentarios reales que tratan del origen de los Yncas, reyes que fueron del Peru, de su idolatria, leyes, y govierno en paz y en guerra: de sus vidas y conquistas, y de todo lo que fue aquel imperio y su Republica, antes que los Españoles passaron a el* (Lisbon: Crasbeeck)

Garvey, Amy Jacques. 1974. *The Philosophy and Opinions of Marcus Garvey* (New York: Atheneum)

Geertz, Clifford. 1966. *Person, Time and Conduct in Bali: An Essay in Cultural Analysis*, Yale Southeast Asia Program, Cultural Report no. 14 (New Haven, Conn.: Yale University Press)

1976. ' "From the Native's Point of View": On the Nature of Anthropological Understanding,' in *Meaning in Anthropology*, ed. Keith H. Basso and Henry A. Selby (Albuquerque: University of New Mexico Press, School of American Research Advanced Seminar Series)

1980. *Negara: The Theatre State in Nineteenth-Century Bali* (Princeton, N.J.: Princeton University Press)

Gibbons, D. E. 1976. 'Hypnotic Versus Hyperempiric Induction Procedures: An Experimental Comparison,' *Perceptual and Other Skills* **42**:834

Gifford, Douglas, and Pauline Hoggarth. 1976. *Carnival and Coca Leaf* (New York: St Martin's)

Globus, Gordon G. 1972. 'Discussion of Periodicity in Sleep and Waking States,' in *The Sleeping Brain*, ed. M. Chase (Los Angeles, California: Brain Information Service)

González, R. Luis. 1982. *Tarahumara: La sierra y el hombre* (Mexico: Fondo de Cultura Económica)

Gossen, Gary H. 1975. 'Animal Souls and Human Destiny in Chamula,' *Man* **10**:448–61

Gouldner, Alvin W. 1960. 'The Norm of Reciprocity: A Preliminary Statement,' *American Sociological Review* 25:161–78

Greenberg, Joseph. 1946. *The Influence of Islam on a Sudanese Religion*, American Ethnological Society Monographs, no. 10 (New York: Augustin)

Gregor, Thomas. 1981. 'A Content Analysis of Mehinaku Dreams,' *Ethos* 9:353–90

Griffith, R. M., O. Miyagi, and A. Tago. 1958. 'The Universality of Typical Dreams: Japanese versus Americans,' *American Anthropologist* 60: 1173–8

Grunebaum, G. E. von, and Roger Caillois. 1966. *The Dream and Human Societies* (Berkeley: University of California Press, Los Angeles Near Eastern Center)

Guaman Poma de Ayala, Felipe. *c* 1615. *El primer nueva coronica y bve gobierno*, facsimile edition (Paris: Institut d'Ethnologie, 1936)

Guilleminault, Christian, William Dement, and Pierre Passouant. 1976. *Narcolepsy: Proceedings of the First International Symposium on Narcolepsy*, Advances in Sleep Research, vol. 3 (New York: Spectrum)

Guiteras-Holmes, Calixta. 1961. *Perils of the Soul: The World View of a Tzotzil Indian* (New York: Free Press of Glencoe)

Guss, David M. 1980. 'Steering for Dream: Dream Concepts of the Makiritare,' *Journal of Latin American Lore* 6(2):297–312

Habermas, Jürgen. 1971. *Knowledge and Human Interests*, trans. Jeremy J. Shapiro (Boston, Mass.: Beacon)

Hall, Calvin S. 1951. 'What People Dream About,' *Scientific American* 184(5):60–3

Hall, Calvin S., and Robert L. Van de Castle. 1966. *The Content Analysis of Dreams* (New York: Appleton-Century-Crofts)

Hall, Calvin S., and Vernon J. Nordby. 1972. *The Individual and His Dreams* (New York: New American Library)

Hall, James A. 1977. *Clinical Uses of Dreams: Jungian Interpretations and Enactments* (New York: Grune and Stratton)

1983. *Jungian Dream Interpretation: A Handbook of Theory and Practice* (Toronto, Ontario: Inner City Books)

Hallowell, A. I. 1966. 'The Role of Dreams in Ojibwa Culture,' in *The Dream and Human Societies*, ed. G. E. von Grunebaum and Roger Caillois (Berkeley: University of California Press)

Hannah, Barbara. 1981. *Encounters with the Soul: Active Imagination as Developed by C. G. Jung* (Santa Monica, California: Sigo Press)

Harner, Michael J. 1972. *Jívaro: People of the Sacred Waterfalls* (New York: Doubleday)

Hartmann, Ernest. 1967. *The Biology of Dreaming* (Springfield, Ill.: Charles C. Thomas)

1984. *The Nightmare: The Psychology and Biology of Terrifying Dreams* (New York: Basic Books)

Haskell, R. E. 1984. 'Empirical Structures of Mind: Cognition, Linguistics and Transformation,' *Mind and Behaviour* **5**:29–48

Herdt, Gilbert H. 1977. 'The Shaman's "Calling" Among the Sambia of New Guinea,' *Journal de la Société des Océanistes* **33**:153–67

1981. *Guardians of the Flutes: Idioms of Masculinity* (New York: McGraw-Hill)

1982a. 'Fetish and Fantasy in Sambia Initiation,' in *Rituals of Manhood: Male Initiation in Papua New Guinea*, ed. Gilbert H. Herdt (Berkeley: University of California Press)

1982b. 'Sambia Nose-Bleeding Rites and Male Proximity to Women,' *Ethos* **10**:189–231

Herdt, Gilbert H., and R. J. Stoller. 1983. 'The Effect of Supervision on the Practice of Ethnography,' in *Die wilde Seele, Aufsätze zur Ethnopsychiatrie George Devereux*, ed. Hans Peter Duerr (Frankfurt: Syndikat)

n.d. *Intimate Communications: Method and Interpretation in Clinical Ethnography* (in preparation)

Hernández Príncipe, Rodrigo. 1622. 'Idolatrías de Recuay,' *Inca* **1**(1):25–49, 1923

Herr, Barbara. 1981. 'The Expressive Character of Fijian Dream and Nightmare Experiences,' *Ethos* **9**:331–52

Hett, W. S., trans. 1935. 'Aristotle, "On Prophecy in Sleep," ' in *On the Soul; Parva Naturalia; On Breath* (Cambridge, Mass.: Harvard University Press)

Highwater, Jamake. 1981. *The Primal Mind: Vision and Reality in Indian America* (New York: Harper & Row)

Hilgard, Ernest R. 1973. 'A Neodissociationist Interpretation of Pain Reduction in Hypnosis,' *Psychological Review* **80**:396–411

1977. *Divided Consciousness: Multiple Controls in Human Thought and Action* (New York: Wiley & Sons)

Hilgard, Josephine. 1979. *Personality and Hypnosis*, 2nd edition (Chicago, Ill.: University of Chicago Press)

Hill, Robert. 1983. 'Leonard P. Howell and Millenarian Visions in Early Rastafari,' *Jamaica Journal* **16**(1):24–39

Hillman, Deborah Jay. 1983. 'Making Dreams Important,' *Newsletter of the Association for Transpersonal Anthropology* **5**(2):3

1985. 'On Cultural Anthropology, The Dream Work Movement, and Dream Research,' *ASD Newsletter* **2**(4):4–5

Hillman, James. 1972. *The Myth of Analysis* (New York: Harper & Row)

1975a. *Re-Visioning Psychology* (New York: Harper & Row)

1975b. 'Methodological Problems in Dream Research,' in *Loose Ends: Primary Papers in Archetypal Psychology* (Zürich: Spring Publications)

1979. *The Dream and the Underworld* (New York: Harper & Row)

Hiscock, Merrill, and David B. Cohen. 1973. 'Visual Imagery and Dream Recall,' *Journal of Research in Personality* 7:179–88

Hishikawa, Yasuo. 1976. 'Sleep Paralysis,' in *Narcolepsy*, ed. C.

Guilleminault, W. Dement, and P. Passouant, Advances in Sleep Research, vol. 3 (New York: Spectrum)

Hobson, J. Allan. 1980. 'Film and the Physiology of Dreaming Sleep: The Brain as a Camera-Projector,' *Dreamworks* **1**(1):9–25

Hobson, J. Allan, and Robert W. McCarley. 1977. 'The Brain as a Dream State Generator: An Activation-Synthesis Hypothesis of the Dream Process,' *American Journal of Psychiatry* **134**:1335–48

Hocquenhem, Anne-Marie. n.d. 'Contribution a l'étude des mythes et des rites dans les sociétés andines,' ms. in Mannheim's possession

Hodgson, A. G. O. 1926. 'Dreams in Central Africa,' *Man* **26**:66–8

Hofstadter, Douglas R., and Daniel C. Dennett. 1981. *The Mind's I: Fantasies and Reflections on Self and Soul* (New York: Basic Books)

Hogbin, Ian. 1947. 'Shame! A Study of Social Conformity in a New Guinea Village,' *Oceania* **17**:273–89

Holden, C. 1973. 'Altered States of Consciousness: Mind Researchers Used to Discuss Exploration and Mapping of "Inner Space,"' *Science* **179**:982–3

Homans, George C. 1941. 'Anxiety and Ritual: The Theories of Malinowski and Radcliffe-Brown,' *American Anthropologist* **43**:164–72

Hopkins, Diane E. 1982. 'Juego de enemigos: La interpretación de una batalla ritual en el sur del Perú desde una perspectiva histórica y simbólica,' *Allpanchis Phuturinqa* **20**:167–86

n.d. 'Symbols and Structure in Quechua Myth: *Sirenas* and Sunken Cities,' ms. in Mannheim's possession

Hufford, David J. 1982. *The Terror that Comes in the Night: An Experience-Centered Study of Supernatural Assault Traditions* (Philadelphia: University of Pennsylvania Press)

Hultkrantz, Åke. 1952. *Conceptions of the Soul Among North American Indians* (Stockholm: Caslon Press)

Huxley, Aldous. 1980. *The Human Situation* (Reading: Triad/Granada)

Isbell, Billie Jean. 1978. *To Defend Ourselves: Ecology and Ritual in an Andean Village* (Austin: University of Texas Press)

Jacobi, Jolande. 1973. *The Psychology of* C. G. *Jung* (New Haven, Conn.: Yale University Press)

Jaffe, Daniel S. 1968. 'The Masculine Envy of Women's Procreative Function,' *Journal of the American Psychoanalytic Association* **16**:521–48

Jakobson, Roman. 1941. *Kindersprache, Aphasie und allgemeine Lautgesetze*, reprinted in *Selected Writings* I (The Hague: Mouton, 1962)

1960. 'Linguistics and Poetics,' in *Style in Language*, ed. Thomas A. Sebeok (Cambridge, Mass.: MIT Press)

Jiménez Borja, Arturo. 1961. 'La noche y el sueño en el antiguo Perú,' *Revista del Museo Nacional* **30**:85–95

Johnson, Kenneth E. 1978. 'Modernity and Dream Content: A Ugandan Example,' *Ethos* **6**:212–20

Jones, Ernest. 1951. *On the Nightmare* (New York: Liveright)
1953. *The Life and Work of Sigmund Freud*, 3 vols. (New York: Basic Books)

Jones, Richard N. 1970. *The New Psychology of Dreaming* (Harmondsworth, Middlesex: Penguin Books)

Jouvet, M. 1962. 'Recherche sur les structures nerveuses et les mecanismes responsables des differentes phases du sommeil physiologique,' *Archives Italiennes de Biologie* **100**:125–206
1975. 'The Function of Dreaming: A Neurophysiologist's Point of View,' in *Handbook of Psychobiology*, ed. M. S. Gazzaniga and C. Blakemore (New York: Academic Press)

Jules-Rosette, Bennetta. 1975. *African Apostles: Ritual and Conversion in the Church of John Maranke* (Ithaca, N.Y.: Cornell University Press)

Jullian, Philippe. 1971. *Dreamers of Decadence: Symbolist Painters of the 1890s* (New York: Praeger)

Jung, Carl G. 1916. 'The Transcendent Function,' in *The Collected Works* of C. G. Jung, vol. 8, trans. R. F. C. Hull (Princeton, N.J.: Princeton University Press, Bollingen Series 20, 1959)
1919. 'Instinct and the Unconscious,' in *Collected Works*, vol. 8
1928. 'On Psychic Energy,' in *Collected Works*, vol. 8
1929. 'Lecture VIII Winter Term, March 13, 1929,' in *Dream Analysis*, ed. William McGuire (Princeton, N.J.: Princeton University Press, Bollingen Series 49, 1984)
1932. 'Everyone Has Two Souls,' in C. G. *Jung Speaking: Interviews and Encounters*, ed. William McGuire and R. F. C. Hull (Princeton, N.J.: Princeton University Press, Bollingen Series 47, 1977)
1934. 'Archetypes of the Collective Unconscious,' in *Collected Works*, vol. 9
1945. 'On the Nature of Dreams,' in *Collected Works*, vol. 8
1947. 'On the Nature of Psyche,' in *Collected Works*, vol. 8
1948. 'General Aspects of Dream Psychology,' in *Collected Works*, vol. 8
1965. *Memories, Dreams, Reflections*, ed. Aniela Jaffé (New York: Vintage Books)

Kalff, Dora M. 1980. *Sandplay: A Psychotherapeutic Approach to the Psyche* (Santa Monica, California: Sigo Press)

Kamiya, Joe. 1961. 'Behavioral, Subjective, and Physiological Aspects of Drowsiness and Sleep,' in *Functions of Varied Experience*, ed. D. W. Fiske and S. R. Maddi (Homewood, Ill.: Dorsey)

Karsten, Rafael. 1935. *The Head-Hunters of Western Amazonas*, Societas Scientiarum Fennica, Commentationes Humanarum Litterarum, vol. 7, no. 1, Helsingfors

Kearney, Michael. 1976. 'A World-View Explanation of the Evil Eye,' in *The Evil Eye*, ed. Clarence Maloney (New York: Columbia University Press)

Kennedy, John G. 1963. 'Tesguino Complex: The Role of Beer in Tarahumara Culture,' *American Anthropologist* 65:620–40

1969. 'Psychosocial Dynamics of Witchcraft Systems,' *International Journal of Social Psychiatry* 15:165–78

1970. *Inápuchi: Una Comunidad Tarahumara Gentil* (Mexico: Instituto Indigenista Interamericano)

1978. *Tarahumara of the Sierra Madre: Beer, Ecology, and Social Organization* (Arlington Heights, Ill.: AHM Publishing)

Kennedy, John G., and Raúl A. López. 1981. *Semana Santa in the Sierra Tarahumara: A Comparative Study in Three Communities*, Occasional Papers, Museum of Cultural History, no. 4 (Los Angeles: University of California)

Kernberg, Otto F. 1976. *Object Relations Theory and Clinical Psychoanalysis* (New York: Jason Aronson)

Keyes, Margaret F. 1974. *The Inward Journey: Art as Therapy for You* (Millbrae, California: Celestial Arts)

Khan, M. M. R. 1976. 'The Changing Use of Dreams in Psychoanalytic Practice: In Search of the Dreaming Experience,' *International Journal of Psycho-Analysis* 57:325–30

Kihlstrom, John F. 1984. 'Conscious, Subconscious, Unconscious: A Cognitive Perspective,' *The Unconscious Reconsidered*, ed. Kenneth S. Bowers and Donald Meichenbaum (New York: Wiley & Sons)

Kilborne, Benjamin. 1978. *Interprétations du rêve au Maroc* (Claix: La Pensée Sauvage, Bibliothèque d'Ethnopsychiatrie)

1981. 'Moroccan Dream Interpretation and Culturally Constituted Defense Mechanisms,' *Ethos* 9:294–312

1985. 'Religions and Cultural Functions of Dreams,' in *Encyclopaedia of Religion* (New York: Macmillan)

Kinder, Marsha. 1980. 'The Adaptation of Cinematic Dreams,' *Dreamworks* 1:54–68

Klinger, Eric. 1971. *Structure and Functions of Fantasy* (New York: Wiley-Interscience)

Kohut, Heinz. 1977. *The Restoration of the Self* (New York: International Universities Press)

Kracke, Waud H. 1978. *Force and Persuasion: Leadership in an Amazonian Society* (Chicago, Ill.: University of Chicago Press)

1979a. 'Dreaming in Kagwahiv: Dream Beliefs and their Psychic Uses in an Amazonian Indian Culture,' *Psychoanalytic Study of Society* 8:119–71

1979b. 'The Birth of Knowledge: A Psychoanalytic Approach to the Kagwahiv Myth of the Burning of Old Woman,' paper presented at the 18th annual meeting of the Northeastern Anthropological Society, Québec, Canada

1979c. 'Review of G. Róheim, *Children of the Desert* (1974),' *Journal of the American Psychoanalytic Association* 27:223–31

1980. 'Amazonian Interviews: Dreams of a Bereaved Father,' *The Annual of Psychoanalysis* 8:249–67

1981. 'Kagwahiv Mourning: Dreams of a Bereaved Father,' *Ethos* 9:258–75.

1982. 'He Who Dreams: The Nocturnal Source of Transforming Power in Kagwahiv Shamanism,' paper presented at the 44th International Congress of Americanists, Manchester, England

Kuper, Adam. 1979. 'A Structural Approach to Dreams,' *Man* **14**:645–62

La Barre, Weston. 1948. *The Aymara Indians of the Lake Titicaca Plateau, Bolivia*, American Anthropological Association Memoir, no. 68 (Menasha, Wis.: American Anthropological Association)

1975. 'Anthropological Perspectives on Hallucination and Hallucinogens,' in *Hallucinations, Behavior, Experience, and Theory*, ed. Ronald K. Siegel and Louis J. West (New York: Wiley & Sons)

La Berge, Stephen. 1985. *Lucid Dreaming* (Los Angeles, California: Jeremy P. Tarcher)

Labruzza, Anthony L. 1978. 'The Activation-Synthesis Hypothesis of Dreams: A Theoretical Note,' *The American Journal of Psychiatry* **135**: 1536–8

Lacan, Jacques. 1968. *The Language of the Self: The Function of Language in Psychoanalysis* (Baltimore, Maryland: Johns Hopkins University Press)

Ladd, Edmund J. 1963. 'Zuni Ethno-ornithology' (M.A. thesis, University of New Mexico)

Larson, Mildred L. 1966. *Vocabulario Aguaruna de Amazonas*, Serie Lingüística Peruana, no. 3 (Yarinacocha, Peru: Instituto Lingüístico del Verano)

1978. *The Functions of Reported Speech in Discourse*, SIL Publications in Linguistics, no. 59 (Austin, Texas: Summer Institute of Linguistics)

Lartigue, François. 1983. *Indios y bosques: Políticas forestales y comunales en la Sierra Tarahumara* (México: Centro de Investigaciones y Estudios Superiores en Antropología Social, Ediciones de la Casa Chata)

Laughlin, Robert M. 1976. *Of Wonders Wild and New: Dreams from Zinacantan*, Smithsonian Contributions to Anthropology, no. 22 (Washington, D.C.: Smithsonian Institution Press)

Leach, Edmund R. 1976. *Culture and Communication* (Cambridge: Cambridge University Press)

1979. 'Two Essays Concerning the Symbolic Representation of Time,' in *Reader in Comparative Religion*, 4th edition, ed. William A. Lessa and Evon Z. Vogt (New York: Harper & Row)

Lee, S. G. 1958. 'Social Influences in Zulu Dreaming,' *Journal of Social Psychology* **47**:265–83

Leib, Elliott. 1983. 'Churchical Chants of the Nyabingi,' liner notes from the album *Churchical Chants of the Nyabingi* (Cambridge, Mass.: Heartbeat Records)

Leiris, Michel. 1958. *La possession et ses aspects théatraux chez les Ethiopiens de Gondar* (Paris: Librairie Plon)
Leuner, Hanscarl. 1969. 'Guided Affective Therapy (GAT): A Method of Intensive Therapy,' *American Journal of Psychotherapy* **23**:4–22
LeVine, Robert A. 1966. *Dreams and Deeds: Achievement Motivation in Nigeria* (Chicago: University of Chicago Press)
1982. *Culture, Behavior, and Personality*, 2nd edition (New York: Aldine)
LeVine, Sarah. 1981. 'Dreams of the Informant About the Researcher: Some Difficulties Inherent in the Research Relationships,' *Ethos* 9:276–93
Lévi-Strauss, Claude. 1949. *Les structures élémentaires de la parenté* (Paris: Presses Universitaires de France)
1963. *La pensée sauvage* (Paris: Librairie Plon)
1964. *Le cru et le cuit* (Paris: Librairie Plon)
1966. *The Savage Mind* (Chicago, Ill.: University of Chicago Press)
1967. 'The Story of Asdiwal,' in *The Structural Study of Myth and Totemism*, ed. Edmund Leach (London: Tavistock)
Lévy-Bruhl, Lucien. 1923. *Primitive Mentality* (New York: Macmillan)
1926. *How Natives Think* (London: G. Allen & Unwin)
1928. *The Soul of the Primitive* (New York: Macmillan)
Lienhardt, Godfrey. 1961. *Divinity and Experience: The Religion of the Dinka* (Oxford: Clarendon Press)
Lincoln, Jackson S. 1935. *The Dream in Primitive Cultures* (Baltimore, Maryland: Williams & Wilkins)
Longrée, Georges H. F., ed. 1978. 'Voir et lire,' in *Essais sur l'art et la culture de la belle epoque* (Liège, Belgium: Editions Noël)
López-Baralt, Mercedes. 1980. 'The *Yana K'uychi* or Black Rainbow of Atahuallpa's Elegy,' ms. in the author's possession
Lounsbury, Floyd G. 1955. 'The Varieties of Meaning,' *Georgetown University Monograph Series in Languages and Linguistics* 8:158–64
Lowie, Robert H. 1925. *Primitive Religion* (London: George Routledge & Sons)
Ludwig, A. M., and W. H. Lyle. 1964. 'Tension Reduction and the Hyperalert Trance,' *Journal of Abnormal and Social Psychology* 69:70–6
Lumholtz, Carl. 1902. *Unknown Mexico*, 2 vols. (New York: Charles Scribner's Sons)
MacDonald, Theodore. 1979. 'Processes of Change in Amazonian Ecuador' (Ph.D. diss., University of Illinois)
Malcolm, Norman. 1956. 'Dreaming and Skepticism,' *Philosophical Review* **65**:14–37
1959. *Dreaming* (London: Routledge & Kegan Paul)
Malinowski, Bronislaw. 1927. *Sex and Repression in Savage Society* (New York: Meridian Books, 1955)
1954. *Magic, Science and Religion* (New York: Doubleday)

Mandell, Arnold J. 1980. 'Toward a Psychobiology of Transcendence: God in the Brain,' in *The Psychobiology of Consciousness*, ed. J. M. Davidson and R. J. Davidson (New York: Plenum)

Mannheim, Bruce. 1983. 'Structural Change and the Structure of Change' (Ph.D. diss., University of Chicago)

1984. '*Una nación acorralada*: Southern Peruvian Quechua Planning and Policy in Historical Perspective,' *Language in Society* **13**(3):291–309

Marquis, Thomas B. 1931. *Wooden Leg: A Warrior Who Fought Custer* (Lincoln: University of Nebraska Press)

Mauss, Marcel. 1954. *The Gift* (London: Cohen and West)

McCarley, Robert W. 1981. 'Mind-Body Isomorphism and the Study of Dreams,' in *Sleep, Dreams, and Memory*, ed. William Fishbein, Advances in Sleep Research, vol. 6 (New York: Spectrum)

McCarley, Robert W., and J. Allan Hobson. 1977. 'The Neurobiological Origins of Psychoanalytic Dream Theory,' *American Journal of Psychiatry* **134**:1211–21

McCarley, Robert W., and Edward Hoffman. 1981. 'REM Sleep Dreams and the Activation-Synthesis Hypothesis,' *American Journal of Psychiatry* **138**:904–12

McGuire, William. 1984. *Dream Analysis: Notes of the Seminar Given in 1928–1930 by C. G. Jung*, Bollingen Series 99 (Princeton, N.J.: Princeton University Press)

McLaughlin, James T. 1978. 'Primary and Secondary Process in the Context of Cerebral Hemispheric Specialization,' *Psychoanalytic Quarterly* **47**(2):237–66

McLeester, Dick. 1977. *Welcome to the Magic Theater: A Handbook for Exploring Dreams* (private publication)

Meggitt, Mervyn J. 1962. 'Dream Interpretation among the Mae Enga of New Guinea,' *Southwestern Journal of Anthropology* **18**:216–20

Melnechuk, Theodore. 1983. 'The Dream Machine,' *Psychology Today* November 1983:22–34

Merrill, William L. 1978. 'Thinking and Drinking: A Rarámuri Interpretation,' in *The Nature and Status of Ethnobotany*, ed. Richard I. Ford, Museum of Anthropology at the University of Michigan, Anthropological Papers, no. 67 (Ann Arbor: University of Michigan)

1981. 'The Concept of Soul Among the Rarámuri of Chihuahua, Mexico: A Study in World View' (Ph.D. diss., University of Michigan)

1983a. 'God's Saviours in the Sierra Madre,' *Natural History* **92**(3):58–67

1983b. 'Tarahumara Social Organization, Political Organization, and Religion,' in *Handbook of North American Indians*, gen. ed. William C. Sturtevant, vol. 10, *Southwest*, ed. Alfonso Ortiz (Washington, D.C.: Smithsonian Institution)

Metraux, Alfred. 1957. 'Dramatic Elements in Ritual Possession,' *Diogenes* 11:18–36

Millar, W. Malcolm. 1958. 'Hysteria: A Re-evaluation,' *Journal of Mental Science* 104:813–21

Mindell, Arnold. 1982. *Dreambody: The Body's Role in Revealing the Self* (Santa Monica, California: Sigo Press)

Moffit, Alan, *et al.* 1985. 'Individual Differences in the Interrelation of States of Sleeping and Waking,' paper presented at Eastern Psychological Association Meetings, Boston, Mass.

Mondloch, James L. 1980. 'K'e?sh: Quiché Naming,' *Journal of Mayan Linguistics* 2:9–25

Moore, Joseph G. 1965. 'Religious Syncretism in Jamaica,' *Practical Anthropology* 12:63–70

Morgane, Peter J., and Warren C. Stern. 1974. 'Chemical Anatomy of Brain Circuits in Relation to Sleep and Wakefulness,' in *Advances in Sleep Research*, vol. 1, ed. Elliot D. Weitzman (New York: Spectrum)

Morris, Charles. 1938. *Foundations of the Theory of Signs, International Encyclopedia of Unified Science*, vol. 1, no. 2 (Chicago, Ill.: University of Chicago Press)

Mottola, Anthony, and Robert Gleason. 1964. *The Spiritual Exercises of St. Ignatius* (New York: Image Books)

Muratorio, Lodovico. 1745. *Della forza della fantasia umana* (Venice: Giambatista Pasquali)

Natterson, Joseph. 1981. *The Dream in Clinical Practice* (New York: Jason Aronson)

Needham, Rodney. 1981. *Classification* (Santa Monica, California: Goodyear)

Neisser, Urlich. 1967. *Cognitive Psychology* (New York: Appleton-Century-Crofts)

Nettleford, Rex. 1970. *Mirror, Mirror: Identity, Race, and Protest in Jamaica* (Kingston: Sangster)

Newell, W. H. 1976. 'Good and Bad Ancestors,' in *Ancestors*, ed. W. H. Newell (The Hague: Mouton)

Newman, Stanley. 1958. *Zuni Dictionary*, Indiana University Research Center in Anthropology, Folklore, and Linguistics, pub. 6 (Bloomington: University of Indiana)

Noy, Pinchas. 1969. 'A Revision of the Psychoanalytic Theory of the Primary Process,' *International Journal of Psychoanalysis* 50:155–78

Oesterreich, Traugott K. 1966. *Possession: Demoniacal and Other* (Secaucus, N.J.: Citadel)

O'Flaherty, Wendy Doniger. 1982. 'Hard and Soft Reality,' *Parabola* 7:55–65

1984. *Dreams, Illusion and Other Realities* (Chicago, Ill.: University of Chicago Press)

O'Nell, Carl W. 1965. 'A Cross-Cultural Study of Hunger and Thirst

Motivation Manifested in Dreams,' *Human Development* 8:181–93

✱ 1976. *Dreams, Culture, and the Individual* (San Francisco, California: Chandler & Sharp)

Onians, Richard B. 1954. *The Origins of European Thought* (Cambridge: Cambridge University Press)

Oppenheim, A. Leo. 1966. 'Mantic Dreams in the Ancient Near East,' in *The Dream and Human Societies*, ed. G. E. von Grunebaum and Roger Caillois (Berkeley: University of California Press)

Orcaín, Pablo José. 1790. 'Compendio breve de discursos varios sobre diferentes materias y noticias geográficas comprehensivas á este Obispado del Cuzco escrito en la villa de Andaguaylillas del partido de Quispicanche,' in *Juicio de límites entre el Perú y Bolivia: Prueba peruana presentada al gobierno de la Republica Argentina*, vol. 11, ed. Victor M. Maurtua (Barcelona: Henrich, 1906)

Palombo, Stanley R. 1978. *Dreaming and Memory: A New Information Processing Model* (New York: Basic Books)

Paredes, M. Rigoberto. 1920. *Mitos, supersticiones y supervivencias populares de Bolivia* (La Paz: Biblioteca del Sesquicentenario de la Republica, 1976)

Parsons, Elsie Clews. 1916. 'A Few Zuni Death Beliefs and Practices,' *American Anthropologist* 18:245–56

1922. 'Winter and Summer Dance Series in Zuñi in 1918,' *University of California Publications in American Archaeology and Ethnology* 17(3):171–216

Passin, Herbert. 1943. 'The Place of Kinship in Tarahumara Social Organization,' *Acta Americana* 34:360–83, 471–95

Pastron, Allen G. 1977. 'Aspects of Witchcraft and Shamanism in a Tarahumara Indian Community of Northern Mexico' (Ph.D. diss., University of California, Berkeley)

Paul, Robert A. 1980. 'Symbolic Interpretation in Psychoanalysis and Anthropology,' *Ethos* 8:286–94

Paulson, Ivor. 1954. 'Swedish Contributions to the Study of Primitive Soul-Conceptions,' *Ethnos* 19:157–67

Peirce, Charles S. 1932. 'The Icon, Index and Symbol,' in *Collected Papers of Charles Sanders Peirce*, vol. 2, *Elements of Logic*, ed. Charles Hartshorne and Paul Weiss (Cambridge, Mass.: Harvard University Press)

Pellizzaro, S. 1976. *Arutam*, Mundo Shuar, Serie F. no. 1 (Sucua, Ecuador: Centro de Documentación e Investigación Cultural Shuar)

Pennington, Campbell W. 1963. *The Tarahumara of Mexico: Their Environment and Material Culture* (Salt Lake City: University of Utah Press)

1983. 'Tarahumara,' in *Handbook of North American Indians*, gen. ed. William C. Sturtevant, vol. 10, *Southwest*, ed. Alfonso Ortiz (Washington, D.C.: Smithsonian Institution)

Peters, Larry G., and Douglass Price-Williams. 1980. 'Towards an

Experiential Analysis of Shamanism,' *American Ethnologist* 7:397–418

Piaget, Jean. 1951. *Play, Dreams and Imitation in Childhood*, trans. C. Gattegno and F. M. Hodgson (New York: Norton)

Piaget, Jean, and B. Inhelder. 1971. *Mental Imagery in the Child* (New York: Basic Books)

Pitcher, E. G., and E. Prelinger. 1963. *Children Tell Stories: An Analysis of Fantasy* (New York: International Universities Press)

Polo de Ondegardo. 1571. 'Los errores y supersticiones de los Indios sacadas del tratado y averiguación que hizo el Licenciado Polo,' in *Informaciones acerca de la religión y gobierno de los Incas*, ed. Horacio Urteaga (Lima: Sanmarti, 1916)

Pontalis, Jean-Baptiste. 1981. 'Between the Dream as Object and the Dream-Text,' in *Frontiers in Psychoanalysis: Between the Dream and Psychic Pain*, trans. Catherine and Philip Cullen (London: Hogarth)

Porras Barrenechea, Raúl. 1948. *El cronista indio Felipe Huamán Poma de Ayala* (Lima, Peru: n.p., 1971)

Post, Ken. 1970. 'The Bible as Ideology: Ethiopianism in Jamaica, 1930–38,' in *African Perspectives*, ed. Christopher Allen and R. W. Johnson (Cambridge: Cambridge University Press)

Powers, William K. 1977. *Oglala Religion* (Lincoln: University of Nebraska Press)

Price-Williams, Douglass. 1975. 'Primitive Mentality – Civilized Style,' in *Cross-Cultural Perspectives on Learning*, vol. 1, ed. R. Brislin, S. Bochner, and W. Lonner (Beverly Hills, California: Sage)

1978. 'Cognition: Anthropological and Psychological Nexus,' in *The Making of Psychological Anthropology*, ed. George D. Spindler (Berkeley: University of California Press)

Primeros Agustinos. 1865. 'Relación de la religión y ritos del Perú hecha por los primeros religiosos agustinos que alli pasaron para la conversion de naturales,' in *Coleccion de documentos inéditos relativos al descubrimiento, conquista y colonización de las posesiones espanoles en América y Oceania*, vol. 3 (Madrid: Quiros)

Rahman, Fazlur. 1966. 'Dream, Imagination and 'Ālam al-mithāl,' in *The Dream and Human Societies*, ed. G. E. von Grunebaum and Roger Caillois (Berkeley: University of California Press)

Rank, Otto. 1909. *The Myth of the Birth of the Hero* (New York: Vintage Books, 1964)

Ratkay, Juan [Johannes] Maria. 1683. 'An Account of the Tarahumara Missions, and a Description of the Tribe of the Tarahumaras and of their Country,' ms., trans. Marion L. Reynolds, Bolton Collection, Bancroft Library, University of California at Berkeley

Reay, Marie. 1962. 'The Sweet Witchcraft of Kuma Dream Experience,' *Mankind* 5:459–63

Rechtschaffen, Allan. 1967. 'Dream Reports and Dream Experiences,' *Experimental Neurology* suppl. 4:4–15

1973. 'The Psychophysiology of Mental Activity During Sleep,' in *The Psychophysiology of Thinking*, ed. Frank J. McGuigan and R. A. Schoonover (New York: Academic Press)
Reina, Rubin E. 1966. *The Law of the Saints* (Indianapolis: Bobbs-Merrill)
Ribstein, Michel. 1976. 'Hypnagogic Hallucinations,' in *Narcolepsy*, ed. Christian Guilleminault *et al.*, Advances in Sleep Research, vol. 3 (New York: Spectrum)
Ricoeur, Paul. 1970. *Freud and Philosophy: An Essay on Interpretation*, trans. Dennis Savage (New Haven: Yale University Press)
Róheim, Géza. 1945. *The Eternal Ones of the Dream* (New York: International Universities Press)
1950. *Psychoanalysis and Anthropology: Culture, Personality, and the Unconscious* (New York: International Universities Press)
1952. *Gates of the Dream* (New York: International Universities Press)
Rothenberg, Albert. 1979. *The Emerging Goddess: The Creative Process in Art, Science, and Other Fields* (Chicago, Ill.: University of Chicago Press)
Rycroft, Charles A. 1977. 'Is Freudian Symbolism a Myth?,' in *Symbols and Sentiments*, ed. I. M. Lewis (London: Academic Press)
Sahlins, Marshall. 1972. *Stone Age Economics* (Chicago, Ill.: Aldine-Atherton)
1976. *Culture and Practical Reason* (Chicago, Ill.: University of Chicago Press)
Sarbin, Theodore R. 1950. 'Contributions to Role-Taking Theory, I: Hypnotic Behavior,' *Psychological Review* **57**:255–70
Schieffelin, Edward L. 1977. 'The Unseen Influence: Tranced Mediums as Historical Innovators,' *Journal de la Société des Océánistes* **33**:169–78
1980. 'Reciprocity and the Construction of Reality,' *Man* **15**:502–17
Schneider, David D., and Lauriston Sharp. 1969. *The Dream Life of a Primitive People: The Dreams of the Yir Yoront of Australia*, Anthropological Studies, no. 1 (Washington, D.C.: American Anthropological Association)
Schwimmer, Erik. 1980. 'Power, Silence, and Secrecy,' in *Toronto Semiotic Circle*, Monograph no. 2 (Toronto, Ontario: Victoria University)
Sears, Walter E. 1948. 'The Navaho and Yir-Yoront, their Primitive Dreams' (B.A. thesis, Harvard University)
Seligman, C. G. 1921. 'Note on Dreams,' *Sudan Notes and Records* **4**:156–61
1923. 'Type Dreams: A Request,' *Folklore* **34**:376–8
1924. 'Anthropology and Psychology: Presidential Address,' *Journal of the Royal Anthropological Institute* **54**:13–46
Sheridan, Thomas E., and Thomas H. Naylor, eds. 1979. *Rarámuri: A Tarahumara Colonial Chronicle 1607–1791* (Flagstaff, Arizona: Northland Press)
Shweder, Richard A., and Robert A. Levine. 1975. 'Dream Concepts of

Hausa Children: A Critique of the Doctrine of Invariant Sequence in Cognitive Development,' *Ethos* **3**:209–29

Siegel, James. 1978. 'Curing Rites, Dreams, and Domestic Politics in a Sumatran Society,' *Glyph* **3**:18–31

Silverblatt, Irene. 1980. 'Andean Women under Spanish Rule,' in *Women and Colonization*, ed. Mona Etienne and Eleanor Leacock (Brooklyn, N.Y.: Bergin)

Silverstein, Michael. 1976. 'Shifters, Linguistic Categories and Cultural Description,' in *Meaning in Anthropology*, ed. Keith Basso and Henry Selby, School of American Research Advanced Seminar Series (Albuquerque: University of New Mexico Press)

Simpson, George E. 1956. 'Jamaican Revivalist Cults,' *Social and Economic Studies* **5**:321–445

Singer, June. 1973. *Boundaries of the Soul: The Practice of Jung's Psychology* (Garden City, N.Y.: Doubleday, Anchor)

Smith, Alfred G. 1966. *Communication and Culture* (New York: Holt, Rinehart & Winston)

Soldatos, C. R., Anthony Kales, and Roger Cadieux. 1978. 'Narcolepsy: Evaluation and Treatment,' *Journal of Psychedelic Drugs* **10**:319–25

Somersan, Sembra. 1984. 'Death Symbolism in Matrilineal Societies,' *Ethos* **12**:151–64

Sperber, Dan. 1976. *Rethinking Symbolism*, trans. A. L. Morton (Cambridge: Cambridge University Press)

Sperry, Roger. 1968. 'Mental Unity Following Surgical Disconnection of the Cerebral Hemispheres,' *The Harvey Lectures*, series no. 62 (New York: Academic Press)

Spiro, Melford E. 1979. 'Whatever Happened to the Id?,' *American Anthropologist* **81**:5–14

Stanislavsky, Constantin. 1937. *An Actor Prepares* (London: Geoffrey Bles)

Stanner, William E. H. 1972. 'The Dreaming,' in *Reader in Comparative Religion*, 3rd edition, ed. William A. Lessa and Evon Z. Vogt (New York: Harper & Row). Reprinted from *Australian Signpost*, ed. T. A. G. Hungerford (Melbourne: F. W. Cheshire, 1956)

1979. *White Man Got No Dreaming: Essays 1938–1973* (Canberra: Australian National University Press)

Stephen, Michele. 1982. 'Dreaming is Another Power: The Social Significance of Dreams among the Mekeo of Papua New Guinea,' *Oceania* **53**:106–22

Steriade, M., and J. A. Hobson. 1976. 'Neuronal Activity During the Sleep-Waking Cycle,' *Progress in Neurobiology* **6** (3 & 4):155–376

Stevenson, Matilda Coxe. 1904. *The Zuñi Indians: Their Mythology, Esoteric Fraternities, and Ceremonies*, Annual Report of the Bureau of American Ethnology, vol. 23 (Washington, D.C.: U.S. Government Printing Office)

Stirling, Matthew W. 1938. *Historical and Ethnographic Material on the*

Jívaro Indians, Bulletin of the Bureau of American Ethnology, no. 117 (Washington, D.C.: U.S. Government Printing Office)

Stoller, Robert J. 1973. *Splitting: A Case of Female Masculinity* (New York: Quadrangle)

Stoyva, Johann. 1973. 'Biofeedback Techniques and the Conditions for Hallucinatory Activity,' in *The Psychophysiology of Thinking*, ed. F. J. McGuigan and R. A. Schoonover (New York: Academic Press)

Strachey, James. 1961. 'Editor's Introduction,' in *The Interpretation of Dreams* (New York: Science Editions)

Strathern, Marilyn. 1968. 'Popokl: The Question of Morality,' *Mankind* 6:553–62

Szasz, Thomas S. 1961. *The Myth of Mental Illness* (New York: Harper & Row)

Tambiah, S. J. 1968. 'The Magical Power of Words,' *Man* **3**:175–208

Tart, Charles T. 1972. 'States of Consciousness and State-Specific Sciences,' *Science* **176**:1203–10

1980. 'A Systems Approach to Altered States of Consciousness,' in *The Psychobiology of Consciousness*, ed. J. M. Davidson and R. J. Davidson (New York: Plenum)

Tedlock, Barbara. 1980. 'Songs of the Zuni Kachina Society: Composition, Rehearsal, and Performance,' in *Southwestern Indian Ritual Drama*, ed. Charlotte Frisbie (Albuquerque: University of New Mexico Press, School of American Research Advanced Seminar Series)

1981. 'Quiché Maya Dream Interpretation,' *Ethos* 9:313–30

1982. *Time and the Highland Maya* (Albuquerque: University of New Mexico Press)

1983. 'A Phenomenological Approach to Religious Change in Highland Guatemala,' in *Heritage of Conquest: Thirty Years Later*, ed. Carl Kendall, John Hawkins, and Laurel Bossen (Albuquerque: University of New Mexico Press)

1985. 'Anthropological Approaches to Dreaming.' Address given at the Second Annual Conference of the Association for the Study of Dreams. Audio tape (San Fransciso: ASD)

Tedlock, Dennis. 1975. 'An American Indian View of Death,' in *Teachings from the American Earth: Indian Religion and Philosophy*, ed. Dennis Tedlock and Barbara Tedlock (New York: Liveright)

1976. 'In Search of the Miraculous at Zuni,' in *The Realm of the Extra-Human: Ideas and Actions*, ed. Agehananda Bharati (The Hague: Mouton, World Anthropology Series)

1979. 'The Analogical Tradition and the Emergence of a Dialogical Anthropology,' *Journal of Anthropological Research* **35**:387–400

Tercer Concilio Provincial. 1585. *Tercer catecismo y exposición de la doctrina Christiana por sermones* (Lima: Antonio Ricardo, 1773)

Tholey, Paul. 1983. 'Techniques for Inducing and Maintaining Lucid Dreams,' *Perceptual and Motor Skills* **57**:79–90

Toffelmier, Gertrude, and Katherine Luomala. 1936. 'Dreams and Dream Interpretation of the Diegueño Indians of Southern California,' *Psychoanalytic Quarterly* 2:195–225
Tucci, Giuseppe. 1969. *The Theory and Practice of the Mandala*: With *Special Reference to the Modern Psychology of the Subconscious* (New York: Samuel Wiser)
Turner, Ralph H. 1976. 'The Real Self: From Institution to Impulse,' *American Journal of Sociology* 81:989–1015
Turner, Terence S. 1969. 'Oedipus: Time and Structure in Narrative Form,' in *Forms of Symbolic Action*, ed. Robert F. Spencer, Proceedings of the 1968 American Ethnological Society (Seattle: University of Washington Press)
Turner, Victor W. 1967. *The Forest of Symbols* (Ithaca, N.Y.: Cornell University Press)
1973. 'Symbols in African Ritual,' *Science* 179:1100–5
1978. 'Encounter with Freud: The Making of a Comparative Symbologist,' in *The Making of Psychological Anthropology*, ed. G. Spindler (Berkeley: University of California Press)
Tuzin, Donald F. 1975. 'The Breath of a Ghost: Dreams and the Fear of the Dead,' *Ethos* 3:555–78
Tylor, Edward B. 1870. *Researches into the Early History of Mankind and the Development of Civilization* (London: John Murray)
1871. *Primitive Culture: Researches into the Development of Mythology, Philosophy, Religion, Language, Art and Custom* (London: John Murray, 1903)
Ullman, Montague, and Nan Zimmerman. 1979. *Working with Dreams* (New York: Dell)
Vogel, Gerald. 1960. 'Studies in the Psychophysiology of Dreams III: The Dream of Narcolepsy,' *Archives of General Psychiatry* 3:421–8
1978. 'An Alternative View of the Neurobiology of Dreaming,' *The American Journal of Psychiatry* 135:1531–5
Vogel, Gerald, David Foulkes, and Harry Trosman. 1966. 'Ego Functions and Dreaming during Sleep Onset,' *Archives of General Psychiatry* 14:238–48
Vogt, Evon Z. 1976. *Tortillas for the Gods: A Symbolic Analysis of Zinacanteco Rituals* (Cambridge, Mass.: Harvard University Press)
Wagner, Roy. 1967. *The Curse of Souw: Principles of Daribi Clan Definition and Alliance* (Chicago, Ill.: University of Chicago Press)
1972. *Habu: The Innovation of Meaning* (Chicago, Ill.: University of Chicago Press)
Walker, Sheila S. 1972. *Ceremonial Spirit Possession in Africa and Afro-America* (Leiden: E. J. Brill)
Wallace, Anthony C. 1958. 'Dreams and the Wishes of the Soul: A Type of Psychoanalytic Theory Among the Seventeenth Century Iroquois,' *American Anthropologist* 60:234–48

1959. 'Cultural Determinants of Response to Hallucinatory Experience,' A.M.A. *Archives of General Psychiatry* **1**:74–85

Watkins, Mary. 1976. *Waking Dreams* (Dallas, Texas: Spring Publications, 1981.)

Watson, Lawrence C. 1981. 'Dreaming as World View and Action in Guajiro Culture,' *Journal of Latin American Lore* 7(2):239–54

Watson, Lawrence C., and Maria-Barbara Watson-Franke. 1977. 'Spirits, Dreams, and the Resolution of Conflict Among Urban Guajiro Women,' *Ethos* **5**:388–407

Webb, Wilse B. 1975. *Sleep: The Gentle Tyrant* (Englewood Cliffs, N.J.: Prentice-Hall)

Weinstein, Edwin A., Roy A. Eck, and Olga G. Lyerly. 1969. 'Conversion Hysteria in Appalachia,' *Psychiatry* **32**:334–41

White, Robert. 1975. *The Interpretation of Dreams: The Oneirocritica by Artemidorus* (Park Ridge, N.J.: Noyes Press)

White, Timothy. 1983. *Catch a Fire: The Life of Bob Marley* (New York: Holt, Rinehart & Winston)

Whitten, Norman E. 1978. 'Ecological Imagery and Cultural Adaptability: The Canelos Quichua of Eastern Ecuador,' *American Anthropologist* **80**:836–59

1982. 'Towards a Conceptualization of Power in Amazonian Ecuador,' paper presented at the annual meeting of the American Ethnological Society, Lexington, Kentucky

Williams, F. E. 1936. 'Papuan Dream Interpretations,' *Mankind* **2**:29–39

Wittgenstein, Ludwig. 1953. *Philosophical Investigations*, trans. G. E. M. Anscombe (New York: Macmillan)

Wundt, Wilhelm. 1912. *Völkerpsychologie*, vol. 2 (Leipzig)

Zorrilla E., Javier. 1978. 'Sueño, mito y realidad en una comunidad ayacuchana,' *Debates* **2**:119–25

Index

Index

Index

Index

Index

SCHOOL OF AMERICAN RESEARCH ADVANCED SEMINAR SERIES

Published by the SAR Press

Chaco & Hohokam: Prehistoric Regional Systems in the American Southwest
P. L. CROWN & W. J. JUDGE, eds.

Recapturing Anthropology: Working in the Present
RICHARD G. FOX, ed.

War in the Tribal Zone: Expanding States and Indigenous Warfare
R. B. FERGUSON & N. L. WHITEHEAD, eds.

Published by Cambridge University Press

Dreaming: Anthropological and Psychological Interpretations
BARBARA TEDLOCK, ed.

The Anasazi in a Changing Environment
GEORGE J. GUMERMAN, ed.

Regional Perspectives on the Olmec
R. J. SHARER & D. C. GROVE, eds.

The Chemistry of Prehistoric Human Bone
T. DOUGLAS PRICE, ed.

The Emergence of Modern Humans: Biocultural Adaptations in the Later Pleistocene
ERIK TRINKAUS, ed.

The Anthropology of War
JONATHAN HAAS, ed.

The Evolution of Political Systems
STEADMAN UPHAM, ed.

Classic Maya Political History: Hieroglyphic and Archaeological Evidence
T. PATRICK CULBERT, ed.

Turko-Persia in Historical Perspective
ROBERT L. CANFIELD, ed.

Chiefdoms: Power, Economy, and Ideology
TIMOTHY EARLE, ed.

SCHOOL OF AMERICAN RESEARCH ADVANCED SEMINAR SERIES

Published by the University of New Mexico Press

Reconstructing Prehistoric Pueblo Societies
WILLIAM A. LONGACRE, ed.

New Perspectives on the Pueblos
ALFONSO ORTIZ, ed.

Structure and Process in Latin America
A. STRICKON & S. M. GREENFIELD, eds.

The Classic Maya Collapse
T. PATRICK CULBERT, ed.

Methods and Theories of Anthropological Genetics
M. H. CRAWFORD & P. L. WORKMAN, eds.

Sixteenth-Century Mexico: The Work of Sahagun
MUNRO S. EDMONSON, ed.

Ancient Civilization and Trade
J. A. SABLOFF & C. C. LAMBERG-KARLOVSKY, eds.

Photography in Archaeological Research
ELMER HARP, JR., ed.

Meaning in Anthropology
K. H. BASSO & H. A. SELBY, eds.

The Valley of Mexico: Studies in Pre-Hispanic Ecology and Society
ERIC R. WOLF, ed.

Demographic Anthropology: Quantitative Approaches
EZRA B. W. ZUBROW, ed.

The Origins of Maya Civilization
RICHARD E. W. ADAMS, ed.

Explanation of Prehistoric Change
JAMES N. HILL, ed.

Explorations in Ethnoarchaeology
RICHARD A. GOULD, ed.

Entrepreneurs in Cultural Context
S. M. GREENFIELD, A. STRICKON, & R. T. AUBEY, eds.

The Dying Community
A. GALLAHER, JR., & H. PADFIELD, eds.

Southwestern Indian Ritual Drama
CHARLOTTE J. FRISBIE, ed.

Lowland Maya Settlement Patterns
WENDY ASHMORE, ed.

Simulations in Archaeology
JEREMY A. SABLOFF, ed.

Chan Chan: Andean Desert City
M. E. MOSELEY & K. C. DAY, eds.

Shipwreck Anthropology
RICHARD A. GOULD, ed.

Elites: Ethnographic Issues
GEORGE E. MARCUS, ed.

The Archaeology of Lower Central America
F. W. LANGE & D. Z. STONE, eds.

Late Lowland Maya Civilization: Classic to Postclassic
J. A. SABLOFF & E. W. ANDREWS V, eds.

Participants in the advanced seminar
DREAMING: ANTHROPOLOGICAL AND PSYCHOLOGICAL INTERPRETATIONS.

Seated, left to right:

Douglass Price-Williams

Barbara Tedlock

William Merrill

John Homiak

Ellen B. Basso

Standing, left to right:

Michael F. Brown

Benjamin Kilborne

Bruce Mannheim

Waud Kracke

Gilbert Herdt